Property Management Kit For Dummies® 2nd Edition

D1033304

What to Do Before Showing a R...

✔ **Remove all the prior tenants' personal possessions and trash** after you have legal possession of the unit.

✔ **Check all plumbing (toilets, faucets, and pipes) for proper operation.** The plumbing should have the proper pressure and drain adequately. Make sure that nothing leaks. Change out old angle stops and install leak-resistant supply lines.

✔ **Test all appliances for proper operation.** Try out all the appliances and run the dishwasher through a full cycle. Verify that the oven's drip pan, broiler pan, and racks are there.

✔ **Examine all hardware.** Confirm that the locks have been changed or rekeyed and are operational. Pay attention to all latches and catches, doorknobs and pulls, door stops, and sliding doors.

✔ **Test all windows, insect screens, and window coverings.** They should be clean, unbroken, weatherproof, secure, and properly operational. All window locks should work as well.

✔ **Check all walls, ceilings, and baseboards.** The paint and/or wall coverings should provide proper coverage, without holes, cuts, scratches, nails, or bad seams. Look for signs of water intrusion and investigate and correct the cause of any such conditions.

✔ **Inspect all floor coverings.** They should be clean and in good condition. The flooring should be properly installed, with no bad seams.

✔ **Check bathrooms.** Thoroughly clean the toilet, tub, shower, sink, mirrors, and cabinets. Make sure the toilet paper holder and towel bars are clean. Put a paper sanitary ring around each toilet seat and a new roll of toilet paper in each bathroom. Look under sinks for moisture and address any noted problems.

✔ **Inspect all closets and storage areas.** Rods, closet dowels, hooks, shelves, lights, floors, and walls should be clean.

✔ **Check all counters, cabinets, doors, molding, thresholds, and metal strips.** They should be clean and fully operational, presenting no hazards.

✔ **Test each smoke detector and check all lighting and electrical outlets, including GFCIs and circuit breakers, for proper operation.**

✔ **Check all patios, balconies, and entryways.** They should be clean and physically sound. Railings should also be secure.

✔ **Test the heating and air conditioning for proper operation.** Be sure the thermostat, filters, vents, and registers are all in working order.

✔ **Check the rental unit's curb appeal, including the exterior landscaping, driveways, and walkways.** Keep them as neat and tidy as possible.

✔ **Perform a final walk-through of the entire rental unit for appearance and cleanliness.** Recheck the unit every few days it sits vacant.

For Dummies: Bestselling Book Series for Beginners

Property Management Kit For Dummies, 2nd Edition

How to Determine a Prospective Tenant's Rental Needs

One of the best ways to screen prospective tenants is to figure out what they need in a rental and gear your sales pitch accordingly. Here are some questions to ask over the phone:

- When will you need to move in?
- How many bedrooms do you need?
- How many people will be living in the rental?
- What size rental unit are you looking for?
- What would you feel comfortable with as a monthly rent?
- How long do you intend to live at this property?
- How much parking space do you require?

- Where are you living now?
- What, if anything, is wrong with your current rental property?
- Why are you looking to move?
- Where do you work?
- What do you do for a living?
- What types of pets do you have?
- When can you drive by the rental property?
- How can I reach you by phone?

How to Collect Rent Effectively

- **Have a written rent collection policy and go over it with each adult tenant prior to move-in.**
- **Institute a firm policy that rent is due on or before the first of the month.**
- **Always follow your rent collection policy, starting the first time the tenant's rent is late.**
- **Provide the tenant with electronic funds transfer or with stamped, preaddressed or business reply envelopes to make it simple for him or her to pay the rent on time.**
- **Refuse partial rent payments.** If you feel that you must accept a partial payment, have the tenant sign a partial rent payment agreement and personally serve new legal notices for nonpayment of rent.
- **Accept only one check for the entire rent if more than one tenant is living in a single rental unit.** This strategy helps you collect the rent more efficiently and reinforces the fact that each of your tenants is legally responsible for paying the rent.
- **Enforce and collect all charges for late and returned checks or dishonored electronic payments.**
- **Accept only cashier's checks or money orders if a tenant has two returned checks or dishonored electronic payments.**
- **Consider incentives to encourage prompt rental payments.** Be sure that all incentives are offered to all residents equally.
- **Promptly serve all legal notices to protect your legal options, even if you believe that your tenant will fulfill his or her promises.**

For Dummies: Bestselling Book Series for Beginners

Property Management Kit

FOR DUMMIES®

2ND EDITION

by Robert Griswold

Host of radio's *Real Estate Today! With Robert Griswold*

WILEY

Wiley Publishing, Inc.

Property Management Kit For Dummies®, 2nd Edition

Published by
Wiley Publishing, Inc.
111 River St.
Hoboken, NJ 07030-5774
www.wiley.com

Copyright © 2008 by Wiley Publishing, Inc., Indianapolis, Indiana

Published by Wiley Publishing, Inc., Indianapolis, Indiana

Published simultaneously in Canada

For general information on our other products and services, please contact our Customer Care Department within the U.S. at 877-762-2974, outside the U.S. at 317-572-3993, or fax 317-572-4002.

For technical support, please visit www.wiley.com/techsupport.

Wiley also publishes its books in a variety of electronic formats. Some content that appears in print may not be available in electronic books.

Library of Congress Control Number: 2008933076

ISBN: 978-0-470-29329-4

Manufactured in the United States of America

10 9 8 7 6 5 4 3 2

WILEY

About the Author

Robert S. Griswold is the coauthor of *Real Estate Investing For Dummies* with Eric Tyson. He has earned a bachelor's degree and two master's degrees in real estate and related fields from the University of Southern California's Marshall School of Business. His professional real estate management and investing credentials include the CRE (Counselor of Real Estate), the CPM (Certified Property Manager), the ARM (Accredited Residential Manager), the CCIM (Certified Commercial Investment Member), PCAM (Professional Community Association Manager), and the GRI (Graduate, Realtor Institute).

Robert is a hands-on property manager with more than 30 years of practical experience, having managed more than 800 properties representing more than 45,000 rental units. He owns and runs Griswold Real Estate Management, Inc., a property management firm with offices in southern California and southern Nevada.

Since 1995, Robert has been the Real Estate Expert for NBC San Diego, a network-owned and number-one-rated station. Every Saturday, he provides impromptu answers to viewers' real estate questions live on the air during *NBC News this Weekend*.

Once a week for 14 years, Robert hosted a live, call-in real estate news and information talk show called *Real Estate Today! with Robert Griswold,* heard throughout southern California on Clear Channel's AM 600 KOGO radio and around the world on the show's Web site at www.retodayradio.com. He has been twice named the #1 Radio or Television Real Estate Journalist in the Country by the National Association of Real Estate Editors in their Annual National Journalism competition. The first award was for *Real Estate Today! with Robert Griswold,* and the second was for his work for NBC News.

Robert is the lead columnist for the syndicated *Rental Roundtable* landlord-tenant Q & A column at www.rentalroundtable.com, which is also featured in the *San Diego Union-Tribune* and the *San Francisco Chronicle.* He also writes a nationally syndicated column, *Rental Forum,* at www.inman.com.

He's a nationally recognized real estate litigation expert, having been retained on more than 1,000 real estate legal matters — as well as serving more than 150 times as a court-appointed receiver, referee, or bankruptcy custodian.

Robert is a member of the National Faculty of IREM and a National Apartment Association (NAA) and California Department of Real Estate Certified Instructor. He's a licensed California and Nevada real estate Broker, a Realtor, and an active member of NAA and his local apartment association, the San Diego County Apartment Association. Since 2005, he has served as a Planning Commissioner in the City of San Diego.

In his spare time (?!), he enjoys travel (especially cruising!), watching his children excel in soccer, and participating in family activities with his wife, Carol, and their four teenagers, Sheri, Stephen, Kimberly, and Michael. Above all, he tries to retain his sense of humor and truly enjoy what he's doing!

Dedication

I dedicate this book to my father, Westcott Griswold, who's greatly admired by all who know him. I also want to thank my best friend and wife, Carol, for her 25+ years of love, support, patience, and persistence in attempting to bring the proper balance to my life. Of course, life's always exciting and has real meaning thanks to my four great teenagers — Sheri, Stephen, Kimberly, and Michael. I also want to express my appreciation to my mom, Carol, for her unconditional love and infinite encouragement. Most of all, I want to praise and thank God for the wonderful gifts and incredible opportunities He has given me.

Author's Acknowledgments

This book was made possible through the efforts of some very fine people at Wiley Publishing, Inc. Mark Butler initially believed in my concept for the first edition of *Property Management For Dummies*. Lindsay Lefevere was very supportive of my efforts to include a CD-ROM with forms for the second edition.

My Project Editor, Chad Sievers, made the rewrite fairly painless with some great suggestions, which have led to a phenomenal resource book for rental owners and property managers. My thanks also go to Copy Editor Jennifer Tucci for a masterful job. I'd also like to thank technical editor, Joe DeCarlo, who helped make sure that the information was accurate and that my advice hit the mark.

My interest in real estate can be traced back to my father and mentor, attorney Westcott Griswold, who advised me to excel in real estate, not law; and my friend and first real estate professor at USC, Dr. Rocky Tarantello. Thank you!

I was blessed to formally begin my real estate management career working with two of the most savvy, knowledgeable, and ethical men in real estate — thank you, Rod Stone and George Fermanian, for starting me on the right track. In my property management days, I've met many fine people, and two of the best are my friends property manager Wade Walker and attorney Steve Kellman. I also want to thank attorney Kathy Belville-Ilaqua for her review and sage advice on fair housing materials covered in the new edition.

I'll always be thankful to Carl Larsen, Homes Editor of the *San Diego Union-Tribune,* who started me in my writing career when he gave me a shot with the first *Rental Roundtable* column while his lovely wife, Sharon Larsen, assisted in creating my original book proposal.

My heartfelt appreciation also goes to the late syndicated columnist and newsletter author Bob Bruss, who offered encouragement and invaluable advice for my first two books and who reinforced the importance of sharing my personal experiences to illustrate my points.

Finally, I'd like to thank all of my NBC news viewers, *Rental Roundtable* and *Rental Forum* readers, and radio listeners who've educated me with their interesting and thought-provoking questions on literally every aspect of real estate management.

Publisher's Acknowledgments

We're proud of this book; please send us your comments through our Dummies online registration form located at www.dummies.com/register/.

Some of the people who helped bring this book to market include the following:

Acquisitions, Editorial, and Media Development

Project Editor: Chad R. Sievers
  (Previous Edition: Elizabeth Kuball)

Acquisitions Editor: Lindsay Lefevere

Copy Editor: Jennifer Tucci

Editorial Program Coordinator:
  Erin Calligan Mooney

Technical Editor: Joe DeCarlo

Media Development Producer: Josh Frank,
  Jenny Swisher

Editorial Manager: Michelle Hacker

Editorial Assistants: Joe Niesen,
  Jennette ElNaggar, David Lutton

Cover Photos: Ablestock.com

Cartoons: Rich Tennant (www.the5thwave.com)

Composition Services

Project Coordinator: Katie Key

Layout and Graphics: Reuben W. Davis,
  Stephanie D. Jumper, Christin Swinford,
  Christine Williams

Proofreaders: John Greenough, Penny L. Stuart

Indexer: Sherry Massey

Publishing and Editorial for Consumer Dummies

  Diane Graves Steele, Vice President and Publisher, Consumer Dummies

  Joyce Pepple, Acquisitions Director, Consumer Dummies

  Kristin A. Cocks, Product Development Director, Consumer Dummies

  Michael Spring, Vice President and Publisher, Travel

  Kelly Regan, Editorial Director, Travel

Publishing for Technology Dummies

  Andy Cummings, Vice President and Publisher, Dummies Technology/General User

Composition Services

  Gerry Fahey, Vice President of Production Services

  Debbie Stailey, Director of Composition Services

Contents at a Glance

Table of Contents

Introduction

Welcome to *Property Management Kit For Dummies,* 2nd Edition. You can discover many of life's lessons by doing some on-the-job trial and error. But property management shouldn't be one of them — the mistakes are too costly and the legal ramifications too severe. This book gives you proven strategies to make rental property ownership and management both profitable and pleasant.

About This Book

Many landlord-tenant relationships are strained, but they don't have to be that way. A rental property owner who knows how to properly manage his rental property and responds promptly to the legitimate concerns of his tenants will be rewarded with good people who stick around. The key is properly maintaining your rental property and constantly investing in upgrades and improvements. By doing this, you can be successful in meeting your long-term financial goals and realize that being a landlord is an excellent primary or secondary source of income.

This book is based on hands-on experience and lessons from my own real-life examples. I have an entirely different view from other property managers that your tenants are your customers, not your enemies, and as such, they should be treated with respect. Not everyone is cut out to be a property manager, and I want to make sure you understand not only the basics of the rental housing business but also some of the tricks that can make you glad you're a real estate investor.

Although this book is overflowing with useful advice and information, it's presented in a light, easy-to-access format. It explains how to wear many hats in the property management business: advertiser/promoter (in seeking tenants), host (in showing the property), handyman (in keeping up with and arranging for repairs), bookkeeper (in maintaining records), and even counselor (in dealing with tenants and their problems). Just as important, this book helps you maintain your sense of humor — and your sanity — as you deal with these challenges and more.

I wrote this book in essentially chronological order — from your first entry into the world of rental property ownership and your corresponding steps to prepare and promote your property to showing your rental and selecting the right tenants. As a result, reading the book cover to cover makes sense, but feel free to read the sections that are most relevant to you at any given time. Skip around and read about those areas that are giving you problems, and I'm confident that you'll find some new solutions to try.

To make your life easier, I've included many of the forms you need to be successful in managing your rental — whether you're just starting out with a single-family rental home or condo, you have a handful of rental units, or you possess a whole portfolio of rental properties. These forms are all on the included CD-ROM, so you can just print them right out, have your local legal counsel review them, and start putting them to use.

Conventions Used in This Book

To help you navigate this book, I use the following conventions:

- *Italics* highlight new, somewhat technical terms, such as *estoppel agreement,* and emphasize words when I'm making a point.
- **Boldface** text indicates key words in bulleted and numbered lists.
- `Monofont` highlights Web sites and e-mail addresses.

What You're Not to Read

I'd certainly love for you to read every single word I've written in this book, but I understand that you're a busy person. Face it: Managing rental property takes time, so you want to read just the essential info to help you find success. In that case, feel free to skip the following:

- **The sidebars:** These gray-shaded boxes are full of fun bits or humorous stories that are quite interesting (if I do say so myself), but not essential for you to understand just what you need to know.
- **Text with True Story icons:** These passages contain some of my real-life experiences to help keep you from making my mistakes.

Foolish Assumptions

In this book, I'm making some general assumptions about who you are:

✔ You're an unintentional property owner — someone who, through a series of circumstances, suddenly and unexpectedly came upon an opportunity to own property. Perhaps you inherited a house from a relative and, not wanting it to sit idle, you decided to rent it out. Or maybe you transferred to a job in another city and, because you've been unable to sell your home, you've been forced to rent the property to help cover the mortgage and operating expenses. Many property owners find themselves in the rental housing business almost by accident, so if you count yourself in this group, you're not alone.

✔ You're one of those people who has made a conscious decision to become a rental property owner. Perhaps, like many rental owners with a plan, you needed to buy a new, larger home and decided to keep your existing home as a rental property. Or maybe, while you were looking to own your own place, you found a great duplex and decided to live in one unit while renting out the other. In a world where people seem to have more and more demands on their time, many aspects of rental property ownership — like the capacity to supplement a retirement plan with additional sources of cash flow or the proven opportunity to build wealth — are very appealing. The key to achieving this success is finding a way to make money while still retaining control over your life.

Real estate offers one of the best opportunities to develop a steady stream of residual income that's being earned whether you're sleeping, participating in your favorite leisure activity, enjoying your retirement, or relaxing on vacation. Whatever the circumstances, the bottom line is the same: You hope to generate sufficient income from the property to cover the debt service, pay for all operating expenses, and possibly provide some cash flow along with tax benefits, appreciation, and equity buildup. The key to your success is knowing how to manage people and time. And this book has plenty to offer you on that front.

How This Book Is Organized

Property Management Kit For Dummies, 2nd Edition, is organized into six parts. The chapters within each part cover specific topic areas in more detail. So you can easily and quickly scan a topic of interest or troubleshoot the source of your latest headache! Each part addresses a major area of rental housing management. Following is a brief summary of what I cover:

Part 1: So You Want to Be a Landlord?

Managing rental property isn't everyone's cup of tea. The chapters in this part assist you in evaluating your skills and personality to see whether you have what it takes to manage rental units — or whether you should call in the property management cavalry. If a management company is the answer to your prayers, I show you how to select one, what to expect, and how much it'll cost in this part. Finally, the day of your escrow closing has arrived and the ink is dry, so flip here to find out what your immediate priorities are as you take over your new rental property.

Part II: Renting Your Property

The most important aspect of rental housing is keeping the unit occupied with paying tenants who don't destroy it or terrorize the neighbors. In this part, you figure out how to prepare the property for rent, set the rents and security deposits, develop a comprehensive (yet cost-effective) advertising campaign, and show your rental unit to prospective tenants. Because all tenants look great on paper, I also fill you in on some tricks and techniques for establishing good tenant selection criteria.

Part III: The Brass Tacks of Managing Rentals

This part takes you from moving in your new tenants to moving them out — and everything in between. You get some strategies for collecting and increasing rent, retaining tenants, and dealing with those few tenants who give you a headache whenever your paths cross. Minimizing vacancies and retaining tenants is the key to success as a rental owner. But when your tenants complain incessantly, decide to repaint in nontraditional colors, or stop paying the rent, the real challenge of managing rental housing begins. In this part, you discover techniques for dealing with these issues and more.

Part IV: Techniques and Tools for Managing the Property

Assembling the right team of professionals — from employees to contractors — is one of the main ways to find success as a landlord. Another way involves maintenance, which can be one of the largest controllable expenses most rental owners face. In this part, I also shed light on how to meet the minimum standards required for your rental property to be habitable and the pros and cons of different alternatives for handling maintenance.

Last but most certainly not least, because landlords and property managers are sued more than any other business entity, you definitely want to review the issues of crime, fire protection, environmental hazards, and the safety and security of your rentals — and I help you do that here, too.

Part V: Money, Money, Money!

Having the proper insurance for your rental properties and property management activities can be a complex topic, so in this part, I guide you through the ins and outs of insurance. Taxes are another inevitability of the rental property business, so here's where you can find basic info on property taxes, the way rental property income is taxed, and some of the tax advantages of owning rental property. With all that money going out for insurance and taxes, you also want to know just how much cash flow your rental empire is generating, so I provide you with some basics on rental accounting and recordkeeping.

Every seasoned rental owner should look for additional sources of income beyond rent, including the opportunities and pitfalls of lease options, which I cover in this part. The effect of government-subsidized housing programs continues to play an important role in many communities, so here you can find info on the advantages and disadvantages of working with public rental assistance programs. Niche rental markets — like those catering to students and pet owners — are also worthy of your consideration, and I let you know how you can use them to your advantage.

Part VI: The Part of Tens

Here, in a concise and lively set of condensed chapters, are the tips to make the difference between success and foreclosure. In this part, I address the benefits of owning rental properties and tips to rent your vacancy today. I also suggest you check out the CD for a bonus Part of Tens chapter on ten common management mistakes and how to avoid them.

Property management and rental housing laws are dynamic, with something new arising every day. So because I'm just that nice of a guy, I also offer an appendix to help you navigate them. Count on the invaluable resources in this appendix to keep you current and improve your management skills.

Icons Used in This Book

Scattered throughout the book are icons to guide you along your way and highlight some of the suggestions, solutions, and cautions of property management.

Keep your sights on the bull's-eye for important advice and critical insight into the best practices in property management.

Remember these important points of information, and you'll have great success as a rental property owner.

This icon highlights the landmines that both novice and experienced rental property owners need to avoid.

This icon points your page-turnin' fingers to the enclosed CD-ROM to review (and ideally use) the file or form being referenced.

Focus on this icon for real-life anecdotes from my many years of experience and mistakes. When you've managed more than 40,000 rental units in 30 years, you see some interesting situations. Now, I share them with you.

Where to Go from Here

Like any great resource book, you must read it! *Property Management Kit For Dummies,* 2nd Edition, is designed to be perfect for experienced or seasoned landlords, as well as rookies who still think all tenants are nice and prompt with rent payments.

Whether you're contemplating rental real estate, looking to fine-tune your proven landlord secrets, or facing total financial ruin at the hands of the Tenant from Hell, *Property Management Kit For Dummies,* 2nd Edition, offers chapter after chapter of solid rental property management advice, especially for the small rental property owner. It explains how to attract qualified prospects; select and screen tenants; maintain the rental rate; handle security deposits, rental contracts, broken water pipes, late rents, tenants who overstay (and don't pay), and more. Find the topic you want to know more about and start reading right there. ***Remember:*** Everything is manageable and workable — if you know what you're doing!

Property Management Kit for Dummies, 2nd Edition, helps you protect your investment and maintain your sense of humor, as well as your sanity, as you deal with one of the most unpredictable professions in life — property management. Consider this book your Property Management Bible, written just for you.

Part I

So You Want to Be a Landlord?

The 5th Wave — By Rich Tennant

© RICHTENNANT

"The paperwork for your mortgage seems to be in order. Now, if we can tap a vein for your signature we'll be all set."

In this part . . .

Managing rental property isn't for the faint of heart, but it can be very rewarding for the right person. The chapters in this part guide you through the process of figuring out whether you have what it takes to manage rental property or whether you're better off leaving it to a pro — someone you hire to do the dirty work for you. I also fill you in on what you need to know if you're taking over ownership of a rental property, including how to deal with the current tenants and inform them of your policies and procedures. This is the part for you if you're just starting to think about purchasing a rental property but aren't quite sure what that entails.

Chapter 1

Property Management 101

You probably already have some idea of what property management is about, because you've likely rented an apartment or house at some point in your life. Even if you haven't, I bet you've noticed the less-than-flattering portrayal of landlords on television shows such as *I Love Lucy* or *Three's Company*. Or perhaps you've heard horror stories from rental property managers you know about tenants who make their lives a living nightmare.

The movies have also been quite unkind to rental property owners and managers. I often feel it should be mandatory for all rental property owners and managers to watch *Pacific Heights*. This film tells the infamous story of a young couple who scrimped and saved every nickel they could to invest in a pricey Victorian-era subdivided house in the Pacific Heights neighborhood of San Francisco, only to have a con man destroy their dreams as he systematically breaks every rule in the book — including the breeding of roaches and physical destruction of the premises.

But don't be fooled into thinking that property management isn't important or rewarding. The key to long-term success and wealth building through real estate ownership lies in the foundation you acquire as a hands-on property manager. For instance, often you start out managing rental properties owned by someone else and gain a great deal of experience that you can use for your own portfolio.

There are many positive reasons for becoming a rental property owner or manager — and just as many ways of doing so. Perhaps you've saved up the down payment to purchase your first small rental unit and hope to see your investment grow over the years as a nice retirement nest egg or a supplement to your current source of income. Maybe you want to invest in a medium-sized apartment building and build some equity as well as rental income to supplement or replace your current source of income. Perhaps you've inherited Aunt Gertrude's run-down cottage and need to find a good tenant who'll care for it and pay the rent on time. Or maybe you've recently closed on your new primary residence only to find that selling your existing home isn't as easy as the real estate agent promised.

Whether you plan to become a full- or part-time property manager, you need to know what you're doing — legally and financially. This chapter serves as a jumping-off point to the rental property world. Here you can find useful, practical info, tips, and checklists suitable for novice or seasoned rental property managers. So get ready for some practical advice from the Tenant Trenches to help you handle situations when they arise!

Understanding What Property Management Really Is

Property managers provide consumers with a product known as shelter. In other words, as a property manager, you're supplying tenants with a place to live in exchange for the payment of rent. Although property management doesn't seem that complex, you can avoid the many mistakes unprepared property managers make by knowing what you're getting into.

The following sections give you a quick overview of the pros and cons of property management. Chapter 2 provides more in-depth analysis of these advantages and disadvantages to help you determine whether renting your property's the right choice for you.

Considering the pros

Property management can be a rewarding and fun venture. I can't imagine my life without some aspect of property management in it (why else would I have written this book, right?). Following are some of the reasons I get such a kick out of this business:

- **Variety:** Personally, I enjoy the variety of tasks and challenges found in property management. Sure, some aspects of it are repetitious. Rent's due every month after all. But for the most part, every day in property management is something new.

- **Interaction with different people:** If you're a people person, you'll find that property management is a great opportunity to meet all types of people. Not everyone you encounter will be someone you want to make your close friend, but you'll certainly have the chance to work with a smorgasbord of personalities.

✔ **Development of skills:** Property management requires diverse skills, because you must handle so many different tasks (like marketing, screening, and maintenance, just to name a few). But it also allows you to grow those skills beyond the basics through patience and passion, like by moving from advertising your rental unit in a basic way to analyzing ad campaigns for unrelated products and applying those concepts to rental housing.

✔ **Experience with real estate investment:** As you manage rental property, you obtain the necessary skills to become a successful real estate investor. Of course, some real estate investors succeed without ever being hands-on property managers because they hire others to handle the task for them. However, I believe every rental property owner should gain that real estate investment expertise by actively working as a property manager for several years.

Confronting the icky parts

You can't expect all aspects of property management to be fun. Just like your primary job, some days run smoothly; others are filled with problems. Here are a couple of the bad aspects to being a property manager:

✔ **Long hours:** Because you're dealing with housing, you can't guarantee when you're going to be needed. It may be 3 p.m. or 3 a.m. Like me, you can expect to be constantly on-call, even when you're on vacation, in order to deal with issues that only the rental owner or property manager can decide. Fortunately, you can minimize these inconveniences by planning carefully and hiring competent and reliable employees and vendors who can prevent many unexpected emergencies through good management and maintenance. However, owning and managing rental property remains a 24/7, year-round commitment.

✔ **Difficult tenants:** Despite the great people you meet, property management has its fill of difficult and challenging personalities, including people who're downright mean and unpleasant. As a rental property owner and manager, you have to be prepared for adversarial and confrontational relationships with others. Collecting the rent from a delinquent tenant, listening to questionable excuses, or demanding a contractor come back and do the job properly requires patience, persistence, and a fair but firm approach.

The good news is that these negatives can be found in many other careers or professions that don't offer the benefits and satisfaction you can get from property management. So in my opinion, the pros outweigh the cons.

Renters drive rental property management

The Census Bureau reports that more than one-third of the U.S. population, or 80 million people, are renters occupying 36 million rental units, including nearly 12 million single-family home rental properties.

Despite these impressive numbers, the individual property owner still dominates the rental housing industry. According to the National Multi-Housing Council, individuals own nearly 85 percent of the small rental properties with 2 to 4 units and nearly 60 percent of the residential income properties with 5 to 49 rental units. In comparison, one of the most popular ways for individuals to invest in real estate is through Real Estate Investment Trusts (REITs), which have exploded onto the market with the acquisition of billions of dollars of high-profile rental real estate assets. Yet, in spite of the significant publicity they've received in the real estate media, REITs actually own less than 10 percent of all residential rental housing units in the U.S.

Eyeing the Types of Real Estate Available

Before you run out and purchase a rental property, you first need to have a good idea of the different types you can own. Most real estate investors specialize in properties with specific uses. Investment properties fall into classifications such as residential, commercial, industrial, and retail.

For the purpose of this book, I focus only on residential real estate, because the majority of rental real estate is housing, and the basic concepts are easy to understand and master. (After you master the basic concepts of residential real estate, you may want to consider other types of property management.) The best practices I present here are applicable for these types of residential rental properties:

- **Single-family houses and condominiums or townhomes:** Most real estate investors start with a rental home, condo, or townhome, because these properties are the easiest ones for most novice landlords to gain experience on. They may be located in a community association property where all the common areas are the association's responsibility.

- **Duplexes and small multi-family or subdivided houses:** This category includes properties with 2 to 4 units but can be up to 15 units. Often these properties are the first choice for real estate investors who plan to live in one of the units or want to take the next step up from investing in a single-family rental home or condo.

- **Small multi-family apartment buildings:** These buildings usually have between 15 and 30 units and are best run with on-site management and regularly scheduled maintenance and contractor visits.

> ✔ **Medium to large multi-family apartment buildings:** These properties are larger buildings that can have 30 or more rental units in a single location with an on-site manager or maintenance staff. Owning one of these properties is the goal for many real estate investors who look forward to being able to hire a professional property manager and just check their bank account for their regular cash distributions.

No matter what type of residential real estate you're involved with, you need to understand the basics of property management. You must market or staff a property differently depending on its size and location, but many of the fundamentals are the same regardless.

Over the course of your tenure as a rental property manager, you're probably going to manage several different types of properties. That's just one of the challenging yet fulfilling aspects of the job. For example, you may start out managing single-family rental homes or condos and then see your investments or career progress to larger rental properties. Sometimes people in the rental housing business start out as on-site employees for large rental properties, learn the ropes, and later apply that knowledge to become the Donald Trump of rental houses in their area.

Owning and managing all types of rental property can be lucrative, and I suggest you jump in where you have your first opportunity, because no rules mandate your starting position.

Renting Your Property

One of the first and most important lessons I learned when I started in property management more than 30 years ago is that vacant real estate isn't a very good investment. You need to fill those vacancies and keep them filled with tenants who pay on time. Just try looking in the mirror and telling yourself that all the rent came in last month. I bet you can't do it without smiling!

Of course, renting your property and retaining your tenants doesn't just magically happen; it requires a plan and a lot of work. But you want to work smart and not just hard, so that's why I show you some of the best practices for preparing your rental units, setting your rents, attracting qualified prospects, and closing the sale.

In order to be a successful property manager, you need to follow certain steps. The following sections cover the highlights of what to do — from getting your property ready for tenants to getting prospects to sign on the dotted line. Chapter 4 expands on where it all begins: the acquisition of the rental property. Part II then helps you position your new rental property within the rental market and discover how to find good tenants.

Factors that influence real estate as an investment

Almost everyone has heard the old adage that the top three keys to success in real estate are location, location, location. This adage is more than just a cliché. Unlike a stock investment, real estate can't be easily liquidated and reinvested into another investment opportunity in a different geographic area. Real estate success is closely correlated to a property's location.

Real estate's also a very cyclical business that's subject to the Economics 101 concepts of supply and demand. During economic business expansions, the demand for real estate is strong, enabling owners to raise rents. With the higher rents, real estate developers can build new properties, which causes the supply of real estate to catch up with the demand and forces rent increases to slow or disappear. When the business economy begins to slow, the demand declines, and once again you have an abundance of rental real estate. This cycle typically repeats every seven to ten years but can go longer. One of the best reasons for investing in residential real estate is that it tends to be the most stable sector of the real estate market.

Thanks to very generous tax laws, for many years, real estate investors really didn't have to worry about the cash flow generated from their properties. An owner's ability to generate tax losses that could be offset against earned income, plus other creative tax strategies, outweighed the common sense goal of generating more income than expense. Positive cash flow was just an added benefit.

The bottom line: After you purchase your property, you can't effectively control or change its location. Nor can you really influence the overall business economy or real estate cycles.

Seem perplexing? Many late-night so-called investing gurus try to sell you their DVDs, but if you're looking for honest advice on the proper way to find, evaluate, and invest in residential real estate, then I suggest you read *Real Estate Investing For Dummies,* which I coauthored with Eric Tyson.

Preparing the property

Before you can rent your property, you have to make sure it's ready for a tenant to move in. However, you can't simply put a For Rent sign up and expect to rent to the first caller. You need to spend some time properly preparing the property. And by "some time" I mean a lot.

Relax! Tear up that application to those cable shows that completely renovate your fixer-upper for free because you *can* prepare your property yourself. Just remember to focus on the inside as well as the outside. Chapter 5 shows you the best way to determine what to upgrade and renovate in order to meet the needs of your target market of prospective renters. I also explain how to ensure that your property's *curb appeal,* or its exterior appearance, makes your potential new tenants want to see the inside of it and not keep driving by to the next property on their list.

During this stage, you really get to test your decorating skills on a budget, because you don't want to overimprove the property. But if you're too tight and try to get by with anything less than your best effort, be ready for the majority of those individuals showing interest in your rental unit to be the least-qualified prospective tenants.

To get the great tenants, you need to guarantee your rental property compares favorably to other properties in your area and makes that important positive first impression. This impression starts on the exterior with a neat and well-maintained appearance and continues with a clean and inviting interior with the features and amenities expected by prospective tenants in your area.

Properly preparing the rental unit also often requires the use of outside vendors or contractors. What you don't contract out — tasks like basic cleaning, maintenance, and painting — you need to do yourself. You also need to know how to perform a careful inspection to make sure the rental unit's ready to show. I give you details about how to accomplish all these tasks in Chapter 5.

Knowing how much to charge

Understanding what you can charge your tenants is far from arbitrary. Setting the rent in particular can be tricky — especially if you've just spent hours investing your time and sweat into renovating and scouring your rental unit to make it sparkle.

In such cases, overestimating the market value of your rental unit becomes very easy, because you have so much personally invested. But your prospects aren't likely to be impressed that you laid the tile. Instead, they'll quickly point out that the color of the carpet doesn't match their furniture, but if you lower the rent $300 per month, they'll consider taking the unit off your hands, almost as if they're doing you a favor. You may be able to structure some mutually beneficial rental concessions, but don't be a pushover.

Many rental property owners are simply too nice. Maybe you're someone who has trouble bargaining and holding out for the top fair value dollar, kind of like my mother-in-law, a sweet but overly generous woman — especially when it came to yard sales. My wife and I are glad no one ever offered Rita 50 cents for our car!

In addition to setting the rent, you need to make the following decisions before a tenant moves in:

✔ **The amount of the security deposit:** Setting security deposits is a function of not only market conditions but also limitations on the amount you can charge and whether that amount's fully refundable. These restrictions are determined by your state laws. Determining whether you want to pay your tenants interest on the deposits you hold is also subject to law, but certain advantages can warrant doing so even where not required — especially for long-term tenants.

The best way to make these decisions is to understand your local real estate market and conduct market surveys to see what others are doing. If everyone else has security deposits set at approximately half of a month's rent, requiring your new tenants to come up with a security deposit of two full months' rent upon move-in is difficult.

✔ **The type of rental contract:** Another important decision that has lasting consequences is deciding whether a lease or month-to-month rental agreement is best for your property. Such conclusions are often reached after conducting a market survey and understanding the pros and cons of each type of contract.

Check out Chapter 6 for more info on determining how much to charge, setting deposits, and figuring out what type of rental contract to use.

Arousing prospects' interest

A successful property manager needs to understand the role of marketing in creating demand and meeting the needs of local renters. Fortunately, your marketing and advertising possibilities have increased dramatically with the advent of the Internet and social media. You (or perhaps your teenage children) can develop a fantastic Web site with digital photos and floor plans. Just make sure you're following all the Fair Housing laws as you work to generate rental traffic.

In Chapter 7, I review the various electronic and nonelectronic options available for promoting your rental property and attracting prospective tenants.

Turning prospects' interest into property visits

The ways to attract potential tenants are endless, but the fundamentals of getting them to visit your rental property are centered around your ability to answer their questions on the phone. You need to understand how to qualify your prospects both for what you want in a stable, long-term resident and what they need in order to call your rental property their "home" for years.

Converting your e-mails or phone calls to actual property visits is the next essential step to creating maximum interest in your rental unit. Chapter 8 explains how to get prospective tenants to view your property.

The way in which you show your rental property to prospects is important. Avoid walking from room to room stating the obvious. Instead, point out certain benefits of your rental unit's unique or special features. Just don't oversell the product and talk fast like a late-night TV used car salesman. Ultimately, the best technique for showing your rental property is letting the property show itself, as I explain in Chapter 9.

The best result you can expect to achieve at the property-viewing stage is convincing the prospect to complete your rental application and put down a holding deposit. What the prospect can expect from you at this time is the receipt of any mandatory disclosures.

Picking your tenants and signing the deal

Property management isn't exactly the dating game, but you do want to gather information (while following all Fair Housing laws to the letter) and select a prospective tenant who meets or exceeds your minimum written rental qualification standards. Tenant selection's probably the one single step in the rental process that can make or break you as a property manager, and I devote a lot of detail to this important topic in Chapter 10.

What seems to be a fairly straightforward process can actually be tricky due to the various limitations on the questions you can ask and the information you can request from interested applicants. Follow the same procedure for everyone so as to comply with Fair Housing laws and determine how you're going to verify each prospect's rental application. Be sure to select your tenant of choice based on objective criteria and then properly communicate your decision to both the approved tenant and the unsuccessful applicants.

Getting Your Hands Dirty: Managing the Property

You never hear from your tenants, yet the check seems to come in the mail each month. Managing your rental unit seems easy — just like you pushed a button! But after a year of progressively busting out with pride at your exceptional property management skills, you decide to drive by the property . . . only to find that your retirement plans and financial nest egg are candidates for a remake of *Animal House!*

In the next several sections, I present the practical, in-the-trenches part of property management that can help you get familiar with every day-to-day eventuality related to the operational side of property management and the life cycle of a tenancy.

Moving tenants in and out

Coordinating the move-in of a new tenant is one of your most pleasant tasks, because this time is your best opportunity to ensure your tenant starts out on the right foot by explaining your rental rules and guidelines. Chapter 11 helps ensure your move-in process runs smoothly.

But all good things must come to an end. That end should start with you making sure that the move-out date is mutually agreed in writing and that the tenant understands your expectations, policies, and procedures via a tenant move-out information letter. I share more about how to make the move-out process as painless as possible for all involved in Chapter 15.

Collecting rent and keeping the good tenants

You can greatly improve your chances of making the rent collection process a positive experience by emphasizing your rent collection policy when your tenant first moves in and by asking all the who, what, where, and how questions of rent payments.

But no matter how carefully you screen your tenants and how thoroughly you explain your rent collection policy, sometimes the inevitable happens and your tenant's unable to pay the full rent when it's due. What do you do? Start by issuing reasonable but firm policies when the tenant moves in and enforcing your grace period and late-period policies. Then when your tenant doesn't pay the rent or doesn't live up to his or her responsibilities under the rental contract, you're prepared to take the appropriate legal action to regain possession of your rental property as quickly as possible. Chapter 12 provides more in-depth info to help you collect rent.

Turnover is your number one nemesis as a rental property owner. Although it's inevitable, your ability to renew your leases and provide incentives for your tenants to stay and pay can be significant in controlling your expenses and maximizing your rental income. That's why keeping your tenants, particularly your good tenants, is a smart move. After tenants have lived at your property for a while, you can quickly determine which ones are the better ones by asking yourself a few questions:

- ✔ Who pays the rent on time?
- ✔ Who quickly lets you know when the unit needs maintenance?
- ✔ Who takes care of the property, perhaps by cleaning up outside debris and planting flowers?

One of the best ways to ensure your good tenants stay with you is to develop a tenant-retention program where you offer them incentives. This action shows that you appreciate them. Chapter 13 offers more on the importance of developing a good landlord-tenant relationship from the perspective of your tenants. It also reveals your tenants' most important needs — good communication, timely maintenance, respect for their privacy, consistent policies, and a good value for their rental dollar.

Handling troublesome tenants

Despite your best tenant screening efforts, you're going to make the wrong decision at some point and allow a problem tenant to move in or have a good tenant who turns sour. But you can lessen the number of these incidents by getting to know some of the problems you may encounter and how to deal with them early on:

- **Late or missed rent payments:** The timely payment of rent is the lifeblood of real estate investing because you can't pay your mortgage or expenses without it. A written rent collection policy is a valuable tool to minimize these problems.

- **Loud tenants:** It only takes one boisterous tenant to disrupt the tranquility of the whole neighborhood. Developing and implementing rental policies and rules can avoid your problem tenant chasing the good tenants away.

Chapter 14 gives you some additional tools to effectively deal with these problem tenants. I also describe the best way to handle common tenant problems and the pros and cons of alternatives to an eviction. But because avoiding eviction doesn't always work, I make sure you have everything you need to know to go to court, present a winning case, and collect your judgment. Life's full of unexpected events, so I also include suggestions on how to cope with tenants who

- Fall into bankruptcy
- Refuse to leave
- Insist on leaving early or want someone else to take their place
- Have personal relationships that deteriorate during their tenancy
- Pass away at your property

Maintaining the property

Are you familiar with the saying, "To own is to maintain"? When you have only a few rental units or are just starting out, you often do much of the maintenance work on your units yourself. But as you acquire more properties or advance in your primary career, you need to explore the benefits and consequences of using employees. If you own a larger rental property, having an on-site employee who's responsible for its day-to-day management is absolutely mandatory.

To keep your rental property in tip-top shape, you also need to work with outside vendors and suppliers who are pros within their industry. Always keep in mind that you get what you pay for and that maintenance can be one of the largest expenses faced by most landlords. Part IV helps you navigate the nitty-gritty hands-on aspects of managing employees and contractors and maintaining your property.

Protecting your investment

Like many property managers, you probably consider your property an investment. If you continuously lose money, having the property isn't worth the hassle or the expense, right? Not to worry. Although you can't predict bad weather or crime, you can safeguard the value of your investment by

- ✔ **Being aware of environmental and natural hazards that can occur:** Minimize your risk or be prepared in case of crime or environmental hazards such as natural disasters, fire, carbon monoxide, or mold. Chapter 18 discusses what you need to know.

- ✔ **Buying the necessary insurance:** You can't avoid buying insurance, so I make sure you know enough to be dangerous when your insurance agent says you need coverage for snowstorms at your duplex in Phoenix. Chapter 19 covers the types of insurance you need to consider.

- ✔ **Paying your taxes:** Taxes aren't likely to be your favorite subject, but they're important. Property taxes are a reality of life almost everywhere; Chapter 19 makes sure you know how they're calculated and what you can do to minimize your tax payments by appealing your property's assessed value when market conditions decline.

- ✔ **Keeping detailed records:** You're going to be so successful as a rental owner and manager that I need to make sure you have good record-keeping and financial reporting so you can keep track of all the money you make. Chapter 20 reveals some simple ways to handle filing and features my analysis of several of the most popular accounting software packages offered for property management.

- ✔ **Increasing your cash flow:** Sometimes recouping all the costs for your rental property isn't easy, so you may need to find ways to get more cash in your hands. A wide assortment of options is waiting for you, including government-subsidized housing programs, special niche housing markets, and different lease options. Chapter 21 focuses on these ways to increase your cash flow from some of the traditional sources of non-rent revenue you may not have considered before.

Chapter 2

Do You Have What It Takes to Manage Your Own Rental Property?

Congratulations! Either you already own rental property, or you've made the decision to buy. Real estate is great whether you're looking for a steady, supplemental retirement income or a secure financial future. Most residential rental property owners want to become financially independent, and real estate is a proven investment strategy for achieving that goal.

But after you sign your name on the dotted line and officially enter the world of owning rental property, you face some tough decisions. One of the very first concerns is who handles the day-to-day management of your rental property. You have units to lease, rents to collect, tenant complaints to respond to, and a whole host of property management issues to deal with. So you need to determine whether you have what it takes to manage your own rental property or whether you should hire and oversee a professional property management firm. Owning investment real estate and managing rental units are two separate functions, and although nearly everyone can invest in real estate, the management of it takes time, special skills, and the right personality.

In this chapter, I start by highlighting the importance of relationships with people because property management is really people management. Next, I give you the lowdown on some of the advantages of owning rental property, and then I help you assess whether you have what it takes to manage your own property.

Understanding That Managing Rental Property Is a People Business

Some rental property owners find themselves managing their own properties without even knowing what management requires. Managing the physical aspects of your rental properties (the buildings and money) and keeping track of your income and expenses are fairly straightforward. However, many rental property owners' most difficult lesson is the management of people.

Rental management requires you to deal with many more people than you may think. In addition to your tenants, you interact with rental prospects, contractors, suppliers, neighbors, and government employees. People, not the property, create most rental management problems. An unpredictable aspect always exists in any relationship with people.

As with most businesses, the ability to work with people is one of the most important skills in being a successful property manager. If you enjoy interacting with people and can work with them and they can work with you, then you have a good start to becoming a prosperous property manager.

Identifying the Types of Real Estate Owners

Rental property management has been around for hundreds of years, since property owners first realized they could earn income on their land and buildings by renting them to tenants. These days, the title of landlord is no longer bestowed only on the landed gentry. There are as many different ways that people become property owners as there are types of rental properties. Although the nature of the business has changed over the centuries, today you can classify rental property owners in the two categories in this section. However, no matter what category you find yourself in, one thing is constant: The key to your success is management.

The inadvertent rental property owner

Many property owners find they're in the rental housing business almost by accident. Although solid reasons to invest and own rental real estate exist, many owners begin their real estate careers by fate or through circumstances beyond their control. Here are a few examples:

✔ You may have inherited a house from a relative and don't want it to sit idle.

✔ You may have transferred to a job in another city and can't sell your home, so you're forced to rent the property because you want it occupied and some income to help cover the mortgage and operating expenses.

✔ You're looking to own your own place and found a great duplex where you can live in one unit and rent out the other one.

Whatever the circumstances, the bottom line is the same. You, the owner, hope to generate sufficient income from the property to cover the debt service, all operating expenses, and possibly even provide some cash flow along with appreciation and equity buildup.

The long-term investment rental property owner

With the tremendous increase in the value of real estate over the past decade, many individuals have found that real estate investing is a key element of their diversified investment portfolio. And why not? Real estate is a cornerstone of the American dream. Many people strive for years to own their first home and then realize the tremendous investment opportunity offered by income-producing rental real estate.

In today's world, more and more demands are placed on your time, so many aspects of rental property ownership are very appealing. People want to supplement their current retirement plans with additional sources of cash flow, and real estate has a proven track record as one of the greatest wealth builders of all time. Most folks find that generating a stable income without having to punch a time clock or not being limited to earning an income only for time spent working for someone else is very appealing. Even most professionals, like lawyers and accountants, are constrained in their income to their billable hours. The more hours they work, the more money they usually make. Yet even lawyers and accountants are limited in the actual number of hours they can work, thus limiting their income potential.

The long-term investment category allows you to accumulate more wealth in your lifetime than you can with just one source of income. Real estate investments provide additional cash flow and significant asset value over time. So what are you waiting for? The time to begin your real estate ownership and management career is now. The sooner you start, the sooner you can achieve your personal and financial goals. The key is to find a way to make money while still retaining control over your life. Real estate offers one of the best opportunities to develop a steady stream of residual income that's being earned whether you're sleeping, enjoying your favorite leisure activity, or even retired or on vacation.

Recognizing the Advantages of Owning Rental Property

A great advantage to building wealth through real estate is the ability to use other people's money. Your initial purchase of the rental property is likely to be achieved with the help of financing from a lender. Then your tenants provide the monthly funds to assist you in making the debt service payments as well as the payments for ongoing operating expenses and capital improvements.

The wide availability and low cost of real estate financing make real estate investing a viable and realistic option for virtually everyone. Most people purchase real estate using leverage gained by borrowing from the seller or a lender. *Leverage* is when real estate is purchased with financing, and it usually consists of a cash down payment from the buyer along with a loan or other people's money. There are two types of leverage:

- ✔ **Positive leverage:** Positive leverage is where you're able to earn a return not only on your cash investment but also on the entire value of the real estate. The ability to control significant real estate assets with only a small cash investment is one of the best reasons to invest in real estate. For example, you may purchase a $100,000 rental home with $20,000 in cash and a bank loan for $80,000. If the home value doubles in the next decade and you sell this home for $200,000, you've turned your $20,000 cash investment into a $100,000 profit.

- ✔ **Negative leverage:** Real estate has enjoyed a long run of steady appreciation from the mid-90s through 2005, but you must remember that real estate doesn't always appreciate and can even decline. Negative leverage can wipe out your entire investment with just a 20 percent decline in the market value of your rental property. So if you buy a rental home for $200,000 with $40,000 in cash and $160,000 from your bank only to see the economy falter or the local real estate market sour, you may find that you have to sell your rental home for less than your acquisition price. If you sell the rental home for only $160,000 after the costs of sale, you may just have enough to pay off your bank, and your cash down payment of $40,000 simply evaporates. Negative leverage is unfortunately the experience of many investors and homeowners who've purchased real estate in the last few years using little or no cash down payments. The real estate market has stopped appreciating and has actually declined fairly significantly in most areas of the country, and many owners find that their mortgage balance exceeds the current value of their property.

Although you can actually purchase some rental properties without a down payment, remember that you get what you pay for. The rental properties that are the best performers in the long run are generally not available with creative financing.

Limited exceptions do exist where you can reposition a poorly performing property in an essentially good neighborhood. Although these opportunities exist in some areas of the country, they're only for the most experienced real estate investors and property managers with a high tolerance for risk. Don't invest in no-down-payment rental properties in a rental market outside of your own area or even a local area where you don't know the neighborhood extremely well. If you do, you'll likely be the next seller offering the property and may even be willing to pay someone to take it off your hands!

Rental real estate also offers you the opportunity to pay off your mortgage by using your tenant's money. If you've been prudent in purchasing a well-located rental property in a stable area, you should have enough income to pay all the operating expenses, utilities, maintenance, taxes, insurance, and your debt service. Each month your property becomes more valuable while your tenant is essentially paying all your expenses, including principal and interest payments on your loan.

Your lender and tenant aren't the only ones who can help you with the purchase of your rental investment property. Even the government is willing to offer its money to help your cash flow and encourage more investment in real estate. In calculating your income tax obligations each year, the government allows rental property owners to take a deduction or offset to income for depreciation. *Depreciation* isn't an actual out-of-pocket cash expense but an accounting concept that provides you with an allowance for expected wear and tear. Depreciation deductions basically reduce the taxable income from rental properties and give you more cash flow during your ownership. See Chapter 19 for an explanation of how depreciation can defer income taxes during ownership until you sell your rental property.

Over time, you may find that your rental income collections grow faster than your operating expenses for increased monthly cash flow. That's why many economists feel real estate is a superior investment, because historically real estate has been a very effective hedge against inflation. And after your tenants have finished paying your mortgage for you, you suddenly find that you have a *positive* cash flow — in other words, you're making a profit.

Eyeing the Unique Characteristics of a Good Manager

Good management equals good financial results. Having tenants who pay on time, stay for several years, and treat the property and their neighbors with respect is the key to profitable landlording. However, finding those individuals is easier said than done. One of the greatest deterrents to financial independence through real estate investments is the fear of management and dealing with tenants. That's why management is so important, but what exactly makes a good manager? The next several sections take a closer look at the many different aspects of managing your own rental properties.

Realizing that good management makes a difference

In order to have a firm grasp on managing your rental property, you need to understand what good management really is. *Good management* is having a well-maintained rental property that's occupied with a paying tenant on a long-term lease who treats the property like her own. As with many things in life, managing well is much easier said than done, but by doing your homework in advance and understanding what it takes to be a good manager, you can reduce those beginner's mistakes.

Who hasn't heard or even personally experienced horror stories about a greedy or downright unpleasant landlord who took advantage of his tenants? The image of rental property owners and managers as overbearing, stingy, and snoopy has become part of the culture. Of course, you've probably also heard about tenants who don't pay their rent, damage the rental property, and harass the neighbors and the owner. Virtually all these horror stories are true, but it isn't a coincidence or bad luck that they happen to the same rental property owners again and again.

Unfortunately, bad management can bring down a rental property investment. For example, owners have problems when they lose control of their rental properties. If you choose the wrong tenant or fail to address certain maintenance issues, your real estate investment may turn into a costly nightmare. A novice rental property owner can quickly find the property turning into a money pit.

Experience is a great teacher — if you can afford the lessons. In rental management, you can be financially devastated when you have a mortgage to pay and your new tenant gives you a rubber check for the security deposit and first month's rent. And to make matters even more challenging, you may find that your occupant has skipped town after trashing your rental unit.

Lucky for you, good property management skills can be mastered. Where can you start? Check out the following:

✔ **This book and accompanying CD:** *Property Management Kit For Dummies,* 2nd Edition, is a valuable resource that guides you right through the dangerous minefield of property management.

✔ **Professional organizations:** These types of organizations have qualified staff who can present educational offerings for property owners and managers. Two of the better organizations include

- The Institute of Real Estate Management (IREM) at www.irem.org

- The National Apartment Association (NAA) at www.naahq.org

Separating your personal style from sound management

The first encounter with owning real estate for many rental property owners is their own personal residences. Owning and maintaining your home is actually very good experience for many aspects of rental property management. For example, you may be very handy fixing that leaky faucet or painting cabinets. However, owning a home doesn't give you all the skills needed to become a successful rental property owner. The main difference you need to remember is that a rental property is an investment — nothing more, nothing less. Although in a perfect world you would find your rental property personally appealing, remember it's an income-producing investment.

At your home, you're in full and direct control of making sure there's enough money to pay the debt service on the property. And you take a very serious interest in making sure that little maintenance problems are addressed while they're low-cost items. As a homeowner, you also probably have experience at trying to live on a budget.

However, in rental property management you look for results that keep your tenants happy and your costs reasonable. Here're some examples:

✔ You need to have the ability to separate your own personal taste and style from the practical aspects of managing rental property.

✔ You don't live on your rental property, so make sure the furnishings and the condition of the property appeal to the broadest number of potential renters. You may love to decorate and really look forward to upgrading your '70s rental unit décor, including the ubiquitous old shag carpet and flowered Formica countertops.

✔ You also need to be very practical and think about the long-term implications of your management decisions. For example, you may prefer drapes for window coverings in your own home; however, vertical blinds are much more practical for a rental property. Although they may not be as luxurious as draperies, blinds are durable, last longer, and are much easier to clean.

Home business opportunity

Many people who manage their own rental properties value the aspect of being their own boss. They often run their business from a home office. Many people today are looking for an opportunity to work at home, and rental management can provide the second income with flexible hours.

You may also expand your real estate holdings to the point that you outgrow your home office or prefer to have a separate business location. Many rental properties offer the opportunity to live and have a small separate management office on-site.

Managing your time

For most rental property owners, managing their rental units is a part-time job. They handle tenant calls, collect the rent, show the units, and even perform most maintenance in the early evenings or on weekends. However, managing your time is an important part of managing your rental properties. Time management is really about evaluating how much time you have and then looking for ways to streamline your tasks so that you make the best use of your time.

Although it can be a part-time job, don't be fooled. Rental management takes a lot of time, patience, and hard work to be successful. At first, most people assume they're equipped to handle any and all property issues. They may even find they can manage one, two, or three units without any problems or time conflicts. They enjoy managing their rental properties and appreciate the cost savings. However, as their portfolio grows, the need to be very efficient in handling management activities becomes essential. The challenge of being a landlord is finding the time required for this second job.

The good news is that time required to be a landlord is in your control. If you master the proper skills of marketing, tenant screening, and tenant selection, you can greatly reduce the amount of time you spend managing rental property. (Check out Chapters 7 and 10 for more info.) You also have to work smart, or you may find that your time is better spent in other areas than management, because time is money.

Delegating management activities

As a landlord, you may look at all the tasks you have to do and get a bit over-whelmed. However, choosing to deal with some responsibilities yourself and delegating some of them to others can make your job much easier to handle. To manage your property to the best of your ability, you need to look at your own set of skills to determine which tasks you can do and which ones you need to delegate.

Throughout this book, I provide various ways that you may delegate certain management activities and responsibilities to your very own personal team of experts comprised of the following:

✔ **A property manager:** Ultimately, you can delegate all the management activities to a professional property manager. However, having a property manager doesn't mean you're totally off the hook. Depending on the arrangement with your property manager, you may still find yourself providing the oversight. (Check out Chapter 3 for more on using a property manager.)

✔ **A maintenance professional:** For many owners, a contractor can handle the maintenance of the rental property and grounds more efficiently and effectively. The skills required to be successful with managing your own rental properties are different than the skills needed to handle your own property maintenance. Most rental property owners find that using trusted and reasonably priced contractors is the best alternative. You may not have the requisite skills or equipment to do the work properly and quickly, or you may discover that you're only able to find time in the evenings or weekends. Painting a rental unit is faster if you have the right equipment and experience. Although doing your own painting may seem more cost-effective, any savings will quickly be lost if the rental unit sits vacant for additional time. The old saying that time is money is very true with rental housing. (Refer to Chapter 16 for how to find the right maintenance personnel.)

I once was hired by a client to manage a large 100-unit rental property with nearly 30 vacant rental units. The rental market was actually pretty good, and together we knew we could rent the units after they'd been painted and cleaned. The owner had always managed the property personally and used only in-house maintenance personnel for all work, including painting. Consequently, the owner wanted to have the in-house maintenance person paint two units per week, but that would take nearly four months until all the units were rent-ready. I was able to demonstrate that hiring an outside painting contractor and having the in-house maintenance focus just on the cleaning of the rental units would get all 30 units rent-ready in less than a month. Even though the outside painting contractor was an expense the owner didn't want to incur, it was the better way to go because we were able to rent the units quickly and more than cover the additional costs. Sometimes the cheapest way isn't the best way to approach a problem.

✔ **An accountant:** Many owners may not have the patience and discipline to keep accurate accounting records that are so important at tax time and prefer to have a bookkeeper take care of the recordkeeping. A bookkeeper can help you manage your records and bills. See Chapter 20 for more information on accounting.

✔ **A legal expert:** Some landlords may look forward to their day in court, but most find the experience unrewarding and problematic. Using a local landlord-tenant attorney is a good idea when you have problems involving legal issues that may end up in court.

✔ **A rental locator service:** Some owners use a rental locator service to provide prescreened rental applicants. Your level of delegation may very well depend on whether you own one or ten rental units.

Knowing that your style is unique

The most important fact to remember is that no one will ever manage your rental property like you will. Accept that fact and then determine whether you're cut out for property management. Remember, property management isn't just a question of style. Ultimately, it comes down to sound, responsible practices.

You're motivated more than anyone else to watch out for your real estate investments. Only you work through the night painting your rental unit for the new tenant move-in in the morning. Who else would spend a Hawaii vacation looking through the local newspaper classifieds for creative ad ideas?

Be honest with yourself. Know your strengths and your weaknesses as a property manager. You may find you're able to do the job but wind up with frazzled nerves and doubts. If you aren't truly excited and challenged by handling your own property management tasks, then you're not likely to have success in the long run. If you decide that you can't do it all yourself, then you may need to delegate (see the preceding section).

Being Honest with Yourself about Your Skills and Experience

One of the first steps in determining whether to completely self-manage your rental property or delegate some or all the duties is to analyze your own skills and experience. Many very successful property owners find they're better suited to deal-making, so they leave the day-to-day management for someone else. This decision is a personal one, but you can make it more easily by thinking about some of the specifics of managing property.

Property management requires basic skills, including marketing management, accounting, and people skills. You don't need a college degree or a lot of experience to get started, and you're sure to pick up all kinds of ideas about how to do things better along the way.

Examine your own personality. Are you a people person? Serving as a landlord is a labor of love; you must love people, you must love working with your hands, and you must love solving problems. Most of all, you must be able to do all this without getting much back in the way of appreciation.

Whether you're confident you have what it takes to be a good rental property manager or you're still not sure, take stock of yourself and your abilities by answering the following questions. Interview yourself as though you were a job applicant. Ask the tough questions. And, more important, answer honestly.

- ✔ Are you a people person who enjoys working with others?
- ✔ Are you able to keep your emotions in check and out of your business decisions?
- ✔ Are you a patient and reasonably tolerant person?
- ✔ Do you have the temperament to handle problems, respond to complaints, and service requests in a positive and rational manner?
- ✔ Are you well-organized in your daily routine?
- ✔ Do you have strong time-management skills?
- ✔ Are you computer literate?
- ✔ Are you meticulous with your paperwork?
- ✔ Do you have basic accounting skills?
- ✔ Do you have maintenance and repair abilities?
- ✔ Are you willing to work and take phone calls on evenings and weekends?
- ✔ Do you have sales skills?
- ✔ Are you a good negotiator?
- ✔ Are you willing to commit the time and effort required to determine the right rent for your rental unit?
- ✔ Are you familiar with or willing to find out about the laws affecting property management in your area?
- ✔ Are you able and willing to visit your rental property regularly?
- ✔ Are you willing to consistently and fairly enforce all property rules and rental policies?
- ✔ Are you interested in finding out more about property management?
- ✔ Are you willing to make the commitment to being your own property manager?

Ideally, you answered yes to each question. This assessment isn't scientific, of course, but it does raise some important issues, particularly the level of commitment that you need to succeed as a rental property manager.

You need to be fair, firm, and friendly to all rental prospects and tenants. Treat everyone impartially and remain patient and calm under stress. Be determined and unemotional in enforcing rent collection and your policies and rules. And maintain a positive attitude through it all. Not as simple as it looks, is it?

Even if you didn't answer with an enthusiastic "yes" to all the questions in this section, you may still make a good rental property manager if you're prepared to be flexible and learn from your property management experiences. The really good property managers graduated from the school of hard knocks.

If your assessment revealed that your skills may be better served doing something other than managing your own property, turn to Chapter 3 for some alternatives. Owning rental property can still be a great investment, even if you don't manage it yourself.

If you're impatient or easily manipulated, you aren't suited to being a property manager. Conveying a professional demeanor to your tenants is important. You want them to see you as someone who'll take responsibility for the condition of the unit. You must also insist that tenants live up to their part of the deal, pay their rent regularly, and refrain from causing unreasonable damage to your property.

Chapter 3

Managing Your Property Yourself or Hiring a Pro

The late-night TV real estate gurus can make real estate investing sound so simple. But just as important as buying the right property for the right price, the key to success in real estate is a well-managed property.

Initially, you may try to manage your rental property yourself, particularly if you have a single-family rental home or duplex. So in this chapter, I guide you through the pros and cons of managing your own property (as opposed to hiring a pro to do it for you). If you're like most owners, though, at some point you'll consider hiring a professional property management firm. So I also give you some tools for evaluating property management companies, from the services they offer to the fees they charge. I discuss the importance of experience, qualifications, and credentials. Also, I reveal some of the common tricks management companies use to generate additional income that aren't in your best interest.

Even if you ultimately decide that *you* are the best manager for your rental property, the more you know about how the professionals manage property, the better you'll be at management yourself.

Managing Your Rental Yourself

With your first rental, you probably do all the work yourself — painting, cleaning, making repairs, collecting rent, paying bills, and showing units. In this section, I let you know some of the advantages and disadvantages to doing it all yourself. Use this information as a way to help you decide whether you want to go it alone or whether hiring a pro is for you. If you decide the latter, check out the information later in this chapter about working with a professional management company. This is one of the most important decisions you make as a rental property owner, so take the time to look at all your options.

Recognizing the advantages of self-management

If you have the right traits for managing property (see Chapter 2 to help determine whether you do), and if you have the time and live close to your property, you should definitely do it yourself. Managing your own rental property has some distinct advantages. By keeping direct control of the management of your rental property, you can

- **Save on a monthly management fee.** If you purchase a single-family rental home or condo as an investment property, you most likely won't be able to generate enough money to pay for a professional property manager and make a profit — at least not right away.

- **Save on maintenance costs.** *You* decide who does the repair work or mows the lawn. Doing your own maintenance or yard work is usually a good idea; if you hire someone else to do it for you, the cost can devour your monthly cash flow in a hurry.

Develop a list of reliable, insured fix-it and landscape personnel who do good work and charge low rates. Even if you hire someone to manage your property for you, you're better off choosing the maintenance contractors yourself, rather than turning over the decision — and your money — to a professional property management firm.

Paying attention to the drawbacks

If you're just starting in the world of property management, you may be thinking of it as a part-time venture — something you'll do in addition to your day job. And if you want, you can keep it that way by limiting the number of properties you own to just a few. By managing your own property, you may

- **Damage your day job.** If you're a higher-income, full-time professional, rushing off on weekdays to handle some minor crisis at your rental unit is not only impractical, it can be downright damaging to your career. Most employers have little tolerance for a second job, particularly one that often has unpredictable and unscheduled demands.

> ✔ **Spend far too much time.** If you earn your living regularly from something other than managing your rental property, managing that property may not be worth your valuable time. Rental management can take up more time than anticipated — either because you've bought more rentals, or because you just didn't anticipate the time requirements. Remember, property management often requires working in the evenings and week-ends, when most prospective tenants want to see your vacant rental units, and tenants are home to allow access for repairs.

As a jobholder, look at your annual income and figure out approximately what you earn per hour. Do the same for the cash you're saving by managing your own property. Unless your management efforts produce significant cash savings compared to your job, you may be better off hiring a property manager for your rental units. The same guideline holds true even if you're an independent business owner or self-employed. Your schedule may be more flexible than the typical fixed workday of a 9-to-5 employee. But if you're earning $50 an hour as a consultant, devoting hours of your productive work time to managing rental units, which may amount to savings of only $25 an hour, may not make sense.

Managing your property from a distance

If you own rental property in another city or state, you may initially consider managing your unit from afar. As long as your tenants mail their rent checks and make only a few maintenance demands, this arrangement can work but it's a fragile one. One major problem, or a few minor ones, can turn the job of managing the rental property into a nightmare.

Many real estate investors are attracted to the prospects of higher returns by purchasing rental properties in out-of-state areas. But even with lower acquisition costs and supposedly decent rents, many of these investment opportunities are too thin to allow for hiring a local professional property manager. Consequently, long-distance property management becomes tempting. My strong advice is to think twice about handling your own rental property maintenance from hundreds of miles away. You need to be in the immediate area to routinely inspect and maintain a rental property, especially when a roof leak or broken pipe demands immediate attention.

I once had a client who hired me after having a very bad experience trying to manage his single-family home from another state. He'd been transferred more than 1,000 miles away by his company but wanted to rent his home as an investment. He found a nice family to rent to, and everything was fine for the first six months. Then one day he got an urgent call from his tenants, complaining that torrential rains caused the roof to leak, making the house uninhabitable. The owner, still out of state, asked his tenants to assist him in hiring someone to repair the roof. The work was botched, and he wound up flying back and forth twice to straighten out the mess before finally getting the roof fixed properly. This negative experience ended up costing thousands, easily wiping out whatever small profit he could've made.

Exploring Professional Management

Many rental property owners who are just starting out drift blindly into self-management by default, because they assume they can't afford a management company without having investigated the cost. Some simply don't want to give up part of their profit. "Why pay someone to manage my rental property when I can keep the money myself?" is a common refrain. Other owners would really prefer to hire a professional management company, but they've heard so many horror stories that they don't know whom to trust. Many of their concerns are real — some property managers mismanage properties and lack any semblance of ethics.

Luckily, you can avoid hiring the wrong management company by following my advice on how to choose a good property manager. The following sections touch on some important points for you to consider if you're contemplating using a professional management company.

Eyeing the pros and cons of using a pro

If you think that hiring a professional management company may be the right choice for you, take the time to study this option. Here're some pros of using management firms:

- They have the expertise and experience to manage rental property, plus knowledge about current laws affecting rental housing.

- They're able to remain fair, firm, and friendly with tenants.

- They have screening procedures and can typically screen tenants more objectively than you can yourself.

- They handle property management issues throughout the day and have staffing for after-hour emergencies.

- They have contacts and preferential pricing with many qualified, licensed, and insured suppliers and vendors who can quickly and efficiently get work done.

- They handle all bookkeeping, including rent collection.

- They have well-established rent collection policies and procedures to follow when tenants' rental payments are late.

✔ They have an online presence with Web sites that provide detailed information and photos of all their available rental properties.

✔ They handle all aspects of hiring employees so you don't have to process time sheets, calculate and submit payroll, generate paychecks, or oversee all the legal requirements that come from having employees.

✔ They can be excellent sources for purchasing additional properties, because they're often the first to know when their current clients want to sell.

Of course, management companies have disadvantages as well:

✔ Using a management company for small rental properties that you've recently acquired may not be cost-effective because the management fees can run up to 10 percent of your gross income.

✔ Some smaller management companies may not be technologically advanced and aren't able to offer online services such as rental applications to prospective tenants and ACH (Automated Clearing House) or electronic rent payments or maintenance requests to current tenants.

✔ Some management companies may have in-house maintenance that charges markups or surcharges on supplies and materials, as well as increased labor costs.

✔ They often won't have the same care, consideration, and concern you have for the rental property.

✔ They often charge extra to fill vacancies, or they may take longer to fill the spots if the property management firm has several other vacancies they're dealing with at the same time.

✔ Some management companies require the tenants to drive to their offices to apply for the rental, pay rent, or request maintenance, which can be a disadvantage if the management company isn't located close to the rental property.

✔ Management companies may not be as diligent in collecting delinquent rent, particularly if the management contract provides that they keep all late fees and other administrative charges.

✔ Some management companies may try to falsely impress you with low maintenance expenses when they're really not spending enough on repairs and maintenance needed to properly maintain the property.

✔ Management companies affiliated with "for sale" real estate brokerages may be more interested in a large real estate commission from a sale and may not provide the best property management services.

Even the best property managers need and seek the input of the property owner so they can formulate a property management plan that will achieve the owner's personal investment goals. A good property manager always remembers that the rental property belongs to the owner, not the property manager.

Understanding what a property manager does

A good management company may be able to operate your rental properties better and more efficiently than you can on your own. Its superior knowledge and experience can result in lower costs, higher rents, better residents, and a well-maintained property. A good management company more than pays for its costs, allowing you more time to take up additional properties or other pursuits. Of course, a poor management company can cut into your profits, not only with its fees but also with improper maintenance and poor-quality tenants who run your property into the ground. A bad property manager can leave you in worse shape than if you'd never hired one in the first place.

Professional property managers normally handle a wide range of duties. If you hire a full-service management company, you typically get the following services:

- ✔ Enforcement of the property's rules and regulations
- ✔ Performance of rental market surveys and rental cost setting
- ✔ Preparation, advertisement, and showing of the rental unit
- ✔ Preparation of regular accounting reports
- ✔ Property inspection
- ✔ Rent collection
- ✔ Repair and maintenance of the rental unit
- ✔ Response to tenant complaints
- ✔ Tenant screening and selection

More limited or a la carte management services are also available from some management companies. Maybe you just need help with the rental of your property and are willing to pay a leasing fee. Or perhaps you want a property manager who charges only a small fee to cover the basic service and not much more. Maybe you want someone to just handle your accounting. The bottom line: You can pay for just the items that tickle your taste buds instead of shelling out for the full-course menu.

Telling the good from the bad

Management companies typically accept responsibility for all operations of the property, including marketing, tenant selection, rent collection, maintenance, and accounting. The right property manager can make a big difference in the cash flow your rental unit generates, because he finds good replacement tenants quickly or makes sure that maintenance is done in a timely manner without breaking your budget. You need a property manager who's committed to helping you get the optimum results from your rentals. The following sections help identify what to think about when searching for a management company and what to ask potential managers so you can find the right fit.

Finding the right management company for you

When searching for a management company, you want to ensure you find one that suits you. Size alone isn't the determining factor in whether a professional property manager can deliver quality service. Some management companies specialize in large rental projects, whereas small operations may focus on managing individual home rentals and apartment complexes with only a few units. Don't assume that a big company managing mega-complexes will do the best job for your duplex or that a small company has the credentials, experience, and knowledge you need. Try to find property managers familiar with your kind of rental unit.

With a little research, you can find the right fit for your property. Keep the following in mind to help you locate the right company for you:

✔ **Check references, particularly the management company's other clients.** Make a few extra phone calls to check references and don't sign a management contract until you feel confident that the company you hire has a sound track record. Checking with the property management company's chosen referrals isn't enough. Ask for a list of all its clients and contact the ones with rental properties similar in size and type to your own. Make certain the rental owners you contact have been with the property management company long enough to have a meaningful opinion on the quality of the service and are truly unbiased.

✔ **Make sure the firm you hire manages property exclusively.** This guideline is particularly important when selecting a management company for a single-family home, condo, or very small rental property. Many traditional real estate sales offices (as opposed to property management firms) offer property management services; however, property management is often a *loss leader* (meaning it costs more for the real estate sales office to manage your property than they're charging you for that service, because they're hoping to get your business later on when you're ready to sell the property). Many property managers in real estate sales offices don't have the same credentials, experience, and expertise as employees of a property management firm. The skills required to represent clients in *selling* property are entirely different than the skills required to *manage* property. You can always hire a firm that sells only real estate when the time comes to dispose of your rental property.

✔ **Verify that the property manager and the management company have current licenses that are in good standing.** You can call or use the Internet to double-check. Most states require property managers to have a real estate license and/or a property manager's license. Simply holding a license doesn't ensure exceptional services, but it does show that the property manager is motivated enough to comply with state law.

✔ **Examine the property manager's credentials.** The Institute of Real Estate Management (IREM), an organization of professional property managers, provides professional designations, including the Certified Property Manager (CPM) and Accredited Residential Manager (ARM). A very select group of management firms have earned the Accredited Management Organization (AMO) designation. These designations signify excellence and dedication. See the included CD for more information, plus details on the National Apartment Association's designations.

✔ **Confirm that the property management company is properly insured.** The company should carry insurance for general liability, automobile liability, workers' compensation, and professional liability. The management company is your agent and will be collecting your rents and security deposits, so it should also have a fidelity bond to protect you in case an employee embezzles or mishandles your money. Look for a management company that has separate accounting for each property managed. Many property managers use a single master trust bank account for all properties. Although this is legal in most states, avoid this practice because, typically, the number one violation encountered during audits of property managers by state oversight agencies is related to shortages and other misuse of the master trust bank account.

In most management contracts, property management companies have the ability and right to perform emergency repairs without advance approval from the owner. Of course, this clause allows the property management company to take care of problems that occur unexpectedly. Most management contracts contain clauses that allow property managers to undertake repairs up to a specified dollar amount without the owner's advance approval. When you're in the early stages of working with a new management company, make sure you closely monitor its expenses. Even though it may have the legal right to use funds up to a certain amount, the company should always keep you informed as the owner. "No surprises" is one of my favorite sayings!

Repairs serve as a profit center for many management companies. They may offer very low property management fees knowing they'll make it up through markups on repairs — and often the repairs aren't even necessary. Look for a property management firm that doesn't mark up materials, supplies, or maintenance labor.

Knowing what to ask a prospective management company

The quality of your property management company directly affects the success of your real estate investments and your peace of mind. Visit the management company's office and spend time interviewing the specific property manager who'll have control of the hands-on management of your property. Here are some important questions to ask as you interview management firms:

- Can you provide a list of exactly what management services are provided, including dates I will receive reports, and a breakdown of management costs?

- Can you explain your methods of generating interest in my rental property and selecting tenants in compliance with all Fair Housing laws?

- Can I contact several of your current and former client references with rental properties that are similar in type, size, and location to mine?

- Is your firm an Accredited Management Organization (AMO) recognized by the Institute of Real Estate Management (IREM)?

- Do your staff members hold IREM's distinguished Certified Property Manager (CPM) designation or Accredited Residential Manager (ARM) designation?

- Is your firm an active member in good standing with a local affiliate of the National Apartment Association (NAA), and does it hold any NAA designations?

- Who will actually manage the day-to-day activities at my property? What are his qualifications, and does he exclusively manage real estate?

- Do you provide 24/7 on-call maintenance services with a live person answering the calls who also has e-mail capability?

- If maintenance is provided in-house or by an affiliated firm, do you only charge the actual cost of labor and materials without any surcharges, markups, administrative fees, or other such add-ons?

- Do you pass along any volume purchasing discounts fully and directly to clients for appliances, carpeting, and other items without any markups?

- Do all funds collected for applicant screening fees, tenant late charges, and other administrative charges go directly to the owner and not the manager?

- If allowed by law, are all employees given pre-employment screenings that include thorough background checking by an independent security consultant, plus drug and alcohol testing by a certified lab?

- Do you carry Errors and Omissions coverage of at least $500,000, plus general liability coverage of at least $2,000,000?

- Do you have a $500,000 Fidelity bond and a Forgery and Alterations policy of at least $25,000 for all employees?

 ✔ Are your legally required state and/or local licenses current and without any history of violations?

 ✔ Do you have separate bank trust accounts for each client rather than a single master trust bank account containing multiple owners' funds?

When you hire outside property managers, treat them as valued members of your management team — but be sure they know you're the team manager and understand your long-term goals. If you're looking for appreciation and preservation of your rental property's value, then make sure the management company keeps your rental property in great condition and looks for long-term stable tenants rather than just premium rent from short-term rentals. Of course, the manager should ask before spending significant amounts of your money, and he should keep you informed on a regular basis.

Compensating your property manager

Management companies are compensated in a variety of ways, and the type of fees and typical compensation vary widely throughout the country. Make sure you understand the compensation of your property manager, but never evaluate the management company based on the management fee alone.

How property management companies charge

The typical professional management fees for single-family homes or individual rental condominiums are 10 percent of the actual collected income with an additional fee earned each time the unit is rented. The rental fee can range from a flat fee of $250 to $500 or a percentage of the monthly rental rate, such as 50 percent. If the rental home or condo has a high rental value, then the management fee is often lower, in the 7 to 10 percent range.

When a property manager considers how much to charge you, she typically looks at the following pieces of information:

 ✔ **The amount of time required to manage the property:** An experienced property management company owner knows the average number of hours the property manager, the accounting staff, and other support personnel will spend each month on managing your property. She then calculates a management fee schedule that should generate the fees necessary to provide the proper management company resources to effectively manage your rental units. If you have larger rental properties, management fees don't typically include the services of any on-site manager, superintendent, or caretaker, who is paid separately.

 ✔ **The size, location, condition, and expected rental collections of the property:** Generally, the larger the rental property, the lower the management fee as a percentage of collected income. Fees vary by geographic area and by the income potential of the rental unit, with a higher-end rental property commanding a lower percentage management fee.

However, for certain properties that may be more difficult to manage, the management company may have higher management fees or additional charges for certain types of services or for a certain period of time. Management companies may also propose charging a minimum monthly management fee or a percentage fee (opting for whichever of the two is greater). For example, a property that's in very poor physical condition and needs extensive repairs and renovations requires a significant increase in the time spent by the property manager in bidding and supervising the improvements. This additional time is worthy of separate compensation to the property manager.

Try to find a company with a management fee that's a percentage of the collected income; this kind of fee is a strong motivator to the management company to ensure the rents are kept at market rate and actually collected on time. Never pay a management fee based on the potential income of a rental unit, only on actual collected income.

What to prepare for when considering compensation

Your management company's compensation can be affected by more than just the standard considerations mentioned in the preceding section. Knowing how to look beyond the basics can help you save money in the long run and make your investment in a management company more worthwhile.

Keep the following in mind when analyzing your property manager's compensation rate:

- **Set a specific deadline for filling vacancies.** Distressed rental properties often require extensive maintenance and repairs and typically have very low occupancy and require extensive marketing and leasing activities. The *lease-up* (filling all your vacant units) of this type of property is usually an extra cost item, because the property manager will spend much more time managing this property. As an owner, structuring the compensation so that the management company has an incentive to get the property leased-up as soon as possible is best.

- **Watch out for management fees that seem too low.** When this scenario occurs, it's a good indication that the property managers are spread too thin and may not properly manage your property. Poor management can result in unhappy tenants, which leads to higher turnover and longer periods of vacancy without rental income.

- **Understand that leasing fees are often justified and usually not negotiated.** The most time-intensive portion of property management is tenant turnover. When one tenant leaves, the property manager must make the unit rent-ready. Then she must show the property and screen the tenants. Leasing fees may vary, but you can usually expect either a flat fee of a few hundred dollars or a percentage of the rent, such as half of the monthly rental rate.

A friend of mine who's a mechanical engineer by profession was relocating to another state and wanted to retain his beautiful suburban home in case he was ever transferred back to the area. He inquired into the cost of hiring a professional management firm and was shocked by the wide variation in management fees quoted. So he began asking more questions of one prospective management company and learned that this particular property manager was already overseeing more than 170 other rental units and homes. My friend quickly calculated that this property manager would only be able to spend an average of one hour a month on the management of his rental home, including rent collection, accounting, tenant calls, property inspections, and all the other property management duties — for a management fee that was quoted at 10 percent, or over $150 per month. Be sure you know how many other rental properties will have a claim on your property manager's time before you sign up!

Making sense of management agreements

The management agreement is a pivotal document; it spells out the obligations of the property management company to you, the client. Be sure to study the fine print — it's tedious but necessary in order to avoid unpleasant surprises. Even the management agreements available through state and national real estate organizations can contain clauses that are clearly one-sided in favor of the management company.

For example, many management agreements call for the property manager to collect and keep all the income from applicant screening fees, late charges, or returned check charges. Of course, property managers justify this policy on the basis that they incur additional time and costs when handling such situations. But these fees should belong to you, because you want to give the property manager a financial incentive to fill your unit with a tenant who pays rent on time and cares for the property. A management fee based on actual rents collected is a better arrangement.

Read on to find out what other nuggets may be hidden in the fine print of your management agreement — and how to protect your investment:

- ✔ **The "no management fee charged when the unit is vacant between tenants" line:** Although this seems like an arrangement that saves you money, especially when rental revenues aren't coming in, the property manager can rush to fill the vacancy without properly screening tenants — and a destructive tenant can be worse than no tenant in the long run.

- ✔ **The "hold harmless" clause:** This clause protects the property manager from liability for his own errors in judgment or the mistakes of the workers the firm sends to your rental unit. One solution is to include a "reasonable care" provision so the property manager is motivated to be diligent in his management and avoid workers he knows have had problems in the past. Your agreement should also mention such obvious requirements as informing you of what's happening with your rental property.

✔ **The long-term management contract request:** Some property management companies request long-term management contracts that can't be cancelled or can only be cancelled for cause. Avoid signing any property management contract that can't be cancelled by either party with or without cause upon a 30-day written notice. A property management company that knows it's only as good as its most recent month's performance will stay motivated to treat your property with the time and attention needed to get top results.

✔ **The confusing language trick:** If the property manager won't agree to reasonable clarifications of the contract language or a complete list of the services provided for his fee, he may not go out of his way to help you later. Consider this refusal a warning sign and find a property management company willing to accept your reasonable terms.

✔ **The "I'll use my own agreement that suits my best interests" maneuver:** Many property managers use their own proprietary agreements written strictly in the best interests of the property management company. So be sure to have your attorney review this agreement very early in the discussions with your potential property manager.

Make sure all your concerns are addressed in the management agreement. You need to know exactly what weekly or monthly reporting the company provides, when your property expenses will be paid, and who's responsible for payment of critical items like mortgages, insurance, and property taxes. Leave nothing to chance.

I include some sample property management agreements on the accompanying CD. You can use them to better familiarize yourself with these contracts, or you can see which one (or even combine elements into a new agreement) is best suited to your rental properties and your personal situation. Ultimately, you can propose your property manager sign your agreement, but only after you have it reviewed by an attorney.

Being aware of the tax consequences

As a rental property owner, you're running a business and must file Schedule E with your federal tax return. The tax laws allow your rental housing business to deduct all operating expenses, including the costs of advertising, maintenance, payroll, insurance, property taxes, and management fees, whether paid to yourself or a property management firm. *Note:* Federal and state tax codes change from year to year, so discuss your personal tax situation with your accountant or tax preparer in advance.

Although your expenses are deductible, they erode your net income from your property. If your annual expenses are greater than rent revenues, you may find that you can use those losses to help ease the tax burden from your full-time job or other sources of income unrelated to your rental property. But a loss is a loss, and trying to keep your rental property in the black is still a good idea, even if you have to pay some taxes on the income.

The IRS's passive loss rule states that all real estate rental activities must be treated as passive with an exception that some taxpayers are allowed up to a $25,000 deduction. However, real estate investors who can be classified as real estate professionals are permitted to deduct all their rental real estate losses from their ordinary income, such as current employment income (wages, commissions), interest, short-term capital gains, and nonqualified dividends. See Chapter 19 for more information on whether you meet the stringent IRS requirements to qualify as a real estate professional.

Even though federal real estate taxation laws consider most real estate activities passive rather than active investments, definite tax advantages exist for those individuals who're actively involved in the management of their rental properties. The definition of *actively involved* allows you to hire a property management firm and still take advantage of the tax write-offs available for rental income property, as long as you're involved in setting the rents and policies for the property.

Chapter 4

Taking Over the Property

· ·

In This Chapter

▶ Understanding what to look for before the deal is final

▶ Helping existing tenants through the transition process

· ·

Somewhere during the process of thinking about investing in rental property, you may have considered acquiring a rental property already occupied with tenants. On the surface, in fact, this kind of opportunity looks like a positive, because you don't have to advertise and select tenants yourself — at least not right off the bat. But just how positive an experience you have taking over an occupied rental property depends on the quality of your tenants. Some real estate investors actually prefer to acquire vacant rental properties so they can renovate the units and select their own tenants.

In this chapter, I assume you've made your decision to purchase a rental property, and I focus on some of the important issues involved in taking over that property. Here you find out how to begin the all-important task of implementing your own policies and procedures with the existing tenants, who may be living under an entirely different set of rules. The proper procedures for taking over a rental property actually begin before you're legally the new owner. Ensuring your transition goes smoothly requires some know-how, and in this chapter I give you exactly that.

For more information on evaluating potential rental property acquisitions, proper due diligence steps, and property inspections, plus ideas on how to hold title to your rental properties, check out *Real Estate Investing For Dummies* by me and coauthor Eric Tyson (Wiley).

Knowing What to Get Upfront

If you're thinking about buying a rental property, you need to start by investigating all aspects of it and its current tenants, if any. After all, no one is going to represent your interests as well as you. During the *due diligence period,* which is when your *escrow* (an account for funds and documents held by a neutral third party in a real estate transfer until all the conditions have been met, per the written instructions of the seller and buyer) and purchase are pending, put on your Sherlock Holmes cap and ask lots of questions. Don't be shy. Talk to the tenants, the neighbors, the local government officials, and the property's contractors or suppliers to be sure you know what you're getting. When in this situation, remember my favorite motto: "No surprises."

Most sellers are honest and don't intentionally withhold information or fail to disclose important facts; however, the old adage "Buyer beware" rings particularly true in the purchase of rental real estate. Resolving questions and issues now through regular communication with your seller eliminates some very unpleasant and possibly contentious disagreements with your tenants in the future.

The due diligence period may be your best or only opportunity to seek adjustments if important issues have been misrepresented. When you sign your name on the dotted line, the deal's done. You can't go back and ask the seller where the tenant's security deposit is. So even though taking over your new rental property can be chaotic, don't fall into the trap of just verbally verifying the facts. Confirm all information in writing and begin setting up a detailed filing system for your new property.

In the following sections, I cover some items to make sure you have in writing *before* the deal is final. You can also check out the Property Takeover Checklist and Exterior Property Inspection forms on the accompanying CD.

A list of personal property included in the sale

Take an inventory of all the personal property included in the sale. This list may include appliances, equipment, and supplies owned by the seller. *Remember:* Don't assume anything is included in the sale unless you have it in writing and be sure to verify that all items indicated are actually at the property before you close the deal. One of the most significant disputes can arise if there's a misunderstanding about who owns the appliances in the rental unit. For example, if the seller says all the refrigerators belong to the rental property owner (as opposed to the tenants), you want to verify that in writing with each tenant. Otherwise, you run the risk of a serious dispute or loss in future years as tenants take appliances when they leave, claiming that fancy fridge belongs to them.

Be sure to record and maintain a list of all your appliances' serial numbers, because some ingenious tenants have been known to sell the new appliances in their rental unit and replace them with used appliances. Watch out for this tacky tactic when there's a change in ownership or management.

A copy of all tenant files

Make sure you have all the appropriate paperwork in the tenant files. These documents include rental applications, current and past rental contracts, move-in inspection checklists, full payment history and any rent increase documents, all legal notices, maintenance work orders, current contact information, and correspondence for each and every tenant.

A seller-verified rent roll and list of all tenant security deposits

A *rent roll* is a listing of all rental units with information on the tenants' names, move-in dates, current and market rents, and security deposits. Be sure you get a written seller statement that no undisclosed verbal agreements, concessions, or side agreements have been made with any tenant regarding rent or security deposits.

When acquiring an occupied rental property, be sure you follow state or local laws in properly handling the tenant's security deposit. (See the accompanying CD for more info on state laws concerning security deposits.) Most state laws require the seller and/or purchaser of a rental property to advise the tenants *in writing* of the status of their security deposit. These laws usually give the seller the right to either return the security deposit to the tenant or transfer the deposit to the new owner. Here's why you want the latter to happen:

- ✔ If the seller refunds the security deposits, you now have the challenge of collecting them from tenants already in possession of the rental units. Avoid this scenario by strongly urging the seller to give you a credit for the full amount of the security deposits on hand in escrow and have each tenant agree *in writing* to the amount of the security deposit transferred during the sale. Close the loop by sending each tenant a letter confirming his or her security deposit amount.

- ✔ If your state doesn't require you to hold the tenant security deposits in a separate bank account, your credit from the seller lowers the amount of funds required at the close of your escrow. Of course, you must be able to refund the remaining balances (after taking proper deductions) of any tenant security deposits when the individuals move out.

Without written proof to the contrary, some crafty or desperate tenants may later claim they had a verbal agreement with the former owner or manager for a monthly rent credit or discount for maintaining the grounds, or that they were promised new carpeting or another significant unit upgrade. If this scenario happens to you, offer to get the former owner or manager on the phone to verify the tenant's story. In my experience, when you offer to verify the story, the tenant typically begins to backpedal, and the truth comes out. But to avoid any surprises, obtain a written statement from each tenant indicating that no verbal agreements exist, and no promises have been made by the former owner.

A copy of all required governmental licenses and permits

Rental property owners in many areas are now required to have business licenses or permits. Contact the appropriate governmental office in writing and make sure it's properly notified of the change in ownership and/or billing address. Often these governmental entities have stiff penalties if you fail to indicate the change in ownership in a timely manner. The office eventually learns of the change, because it monitors the local recording of deeds and receives notification of changes in billing responsibility from local utility companies. Don't delay the inevitable. Make sure you have current copies of all state and local rental laws and ordinances affecting your rental property.

Check out Appendix B and the accompanying CD for resources for state landlord-tenant laws.

A copy of all the latest utility bills

Get copies of all account and payment information for every utility that provides services to the rental property. These utilities may include electricity, natural gas, water/sewer, trash collection, telephone, cable, and Internet access. Prior to the close of escrow, contact each of the utility companies and arrange for the transfer of utilities or change in the billing responsibility as of the estimated escrow closing date. If provided with sufficient advance notice, many utility companies are able to have the final meter reading and/or billing cutoff coincide with the close of escrow, which prevents the need to prorate any of the utility billings between the owners.

Let me reiterate: Verifying the accuracy of all utility bills is extremely important. One of my expert witness cases involved a water utility improperly charging a property owner for sewer charges related to a water meter used only for irrigation. (Some water utilities allow for "irrigation only" meters that are exempt from sewer charges because the water never enters the sewer system.) In this case, the utility company had been collecting sewer fees for many years until the discrepancy was brought to its attention. The property owner did receive lower billings in the future, but state law protected the municipal utility company from refunding any overcharges beyond the previous 12 months. The owner's thousands of dollars in overpayments were a rather expensive lesson.

Some consultants actually offer to review utility bills to ensure you're being charged the proper amounts based on the correct billing rates. These professionals are usually compensated on a contingency basis through a percentage of the savings they're able to achieve.

A copy of every service agreement or contract

Make sure you obtain copies of all the service agreements and/or contracts. These documents may include agreements made with maintenance landscapers, pest control services, boiler maintenance services, laundry leases, and other providers. Review all current contractors and service providers the current owner uses.

If you plan to terminate the services of a particular contractor or service provider, the seller may be willing to voluntarily send a written conditional notice of termination indicating that, should the property sell as planned, the provider's services will no longer be needed as of the close of escrow. You are then free to make your own plans for services and can even renegotiate with the current company for better terms. Of course, if you find the seller already had favorable pricing from the contractors or service providers, you may be able to negotiate the same terms.

A copy of the seller's current insurance policy

One of the most important steps you handle when taking over your new rental property is securing insurance coverage. You need to make sure you have the proper insurance policy in place at the time that you legally become the new owner. Although the seller's policy won't protect you in any way, request a copy of her policy or declaration of coverage, because this information can be very helpful to your insurance broker or agent when analyzing the property to determine the proper coverage you may need.

Always seek the advice of a professional insurance broker or agent when obtaining insurance coverage. Have your agent run a *loss history* on your new property to determine whether any losses have been claimed. You may find that the property has had significant claims in the past, which impacts your ability to find reasonably priced insurance coverage. The loss history can also show some of the problems that have occurred at the property, including several small instances that can indicate a larger problem, such as plumbing leaks.

A final walk-through can save you headaches

Before you close escrow, you want to take a final walk-through to make sure the property hasn't been damaged prior to closing. I was an expert witness in a case where the new buyers learned this lesson the hard way because they didn't visit the rental home before closing.

After the sale was complete, the new buyers excitedly went to see their new rental property, which had sat vacant for nearly a week during escrow. They were shocked to find the rental home completely flooded and severely contaminated with mold. The buyer sued the seller, claiming that someone had intentionally or inadvertently left the water supply line valve to the refrigerator ice maker open, allowing

water to cover the entire first floor. The buyers were unable to prove that the damage occurred while the property was still owned by the seller, so the seller's insurance company denied the claim.

Ultimately the buyers' insurance company agreed to pay for some of the damage, but not before the buyers went through more than two years of expensive and emotionally draining litigation and lost a lot of money because the property sat vacant the entire time. Everything could've been avoided if the buyers had simply inspected the property just before the close of escrow and stopped the sale until the damage had been addressed.

Although you may trust your insurance broker or agent implicitly, don't allow your escrow to close until you have written documentation confirming that your insurance coverage is in force. Even though it may seem improbable, many times a property suffers a catastrophic loss or liability claim a mere matter of hours after it changes hands, and the new owner's insurance coverage isn't yet in place.

When you receive the current insurance information, take steps to verify the accuracy of all records. If certain representations about the types and amounts of coverage are made verbally but not given in writing, then you need to protect yourself by sending written documentation to the seller and all brokers and agents to confirm any information you've received. This step can be important in preventing future disputes about the representations made by the seller or any of the brokers or agents.

Working with the Current Tenants during the Transition

If you're like most rental property owners and you're acquiring property that's already occupied, the tenants are probably well aware of the pending ownership change. Tenants are typically full of apprehension when their rental unit is changing ownership, not because they think you'll be an unreasonable landlord, but because of the uncertainty of change. So be sure to begin your relationship with your tenants on a positive note. In the following sections, I guide you through the transition process step by step.

Meeting with the tenants in person

When you first acquire your new rental property, contact your tenants in person and reassure them that you intend to treat them with respect and have a cordial yet businesslike relationship. Deal with your tenants' questions honestly and directly. The most common concerns are usually the potential for a rent increase, the status of their security deposit, the proper maintenance or condition of their rental unit, and the continuation of certain policies, such as allowing pets. If you're not honest with the tenants, you'll lose credibility if you later decide to implement changes that you didn't acknowledge up front.

Provide your tenants with a letter of introduction during this brief in-person meeting. This letter provides your contact information, plus explains your rent collection policies, the status of tenants' security deposits, and the proper procedures for requesting maintenance and repairs.

Be sure to request an opportunity to perform a property walk through with each tenant. Let the tenant know whether you'll be implementing your own standard lease or rental agreement form as well.

Inspecting the rental unit

Although you most likely had a brief chance to view the interior of the rental unit during the due diligence period before escrow closed, walking through again with the tenant now that you're the owner can be helpful. However, know your state laws. In most states, tenants don't have to let you enter their rental units unless you have a legal reason and have given proper advance notice. If you set a voluntary appointment, the tenant knows you're coming and can prepare.

Don't just knock on the door and expect to walk through your tenant's rental unit. But if you're already at the rental property delivering your letter of introduction, you can schedule a mutually convenient time to meet. Some tenants will be glad to meet with you right then, but don't necessarily count on that. Giving your tenants time to think about any issues they'd like to discuss is beneficial for you both.

The former owner of the rental property may have had a policy of documenting the condition of the rental unit at the time the tenant took possession of it. If so, you may want to compare the noted condition on the Move-In/Move-Out Inspection Checklist (see Chapter 11) when you actually walk through the rental unit. If proper documentation of the move-in condition wasn't made, consider preparing such information during your walk-through. This information allows you to establish some sort of baseline for the unit's condition to use upon the tenant's move-out, which then helps you determine the proper amount of the security deposit to return to him.

Using a new lease or rental agreement

Another first step to take as the new owner of a rental property is to begin converting your existing tenants to your own lease or rental agreement. If you have a single-family rental or a small rental property, implementing your own rental agreement as soon as legally allowed is relatively easy. However, with larger rental properties, you may want to gradually transition to a new contract upon tenant turnover.

Your tenants already have one of the following:

- A valid written lease
- An expired written lease that has become a month-to-month rental agreement
- A written month-to-month rental agreement
- A written rental agreement for some period of time less than a month
- A verbal agreement

Although you may want to make some changes in the terms or policies, when you acquire an occupied rental property, your legal and business relationship is already established by whatever agreement the tenants had with the former owner. Wait until the expiration of the contract to change the terms — or provide the tenant with proper legal notice of any proposed changes.

Consider the potential impact of making significant changes in the rental rates or policies immediately after you acquire the rental property. For example, although you may have strong feelings against allowing pets on your rental property, your tenants may have pets already. Although you legally have the right to implement your no-pet policy upon lease renewal or upon giving proper legal notice, you're almost guaranteed a vacant rental unit if you do so. Impose your policies over a reasonable time frame, but be sure you're aware of the potential financial consequences in the short run.

The sooner you begin to convert your new property to your rental contracts, the better. Establish uniform policies at all your rental units so the terms and policies are consistent for all your tenants. This action is extremely important to avoid possible Fair Housing violations, as discussed in Chapter 10.

The tenant information the seller provided you during escrow may be outdated. One quick way to update your records is to have the tenants voluntarily complete your rental application form. In many states, you may not have a strong legal argument for requiring existing tenants to provide this information; however, many tenants will understand your reasoning and not mind. Other tenants may be reluctant to complete an entirely new rental application. Even if you receive initial resistance, seek this updated information prior to renewing any lease. You need to be able to properly determine the financial qualifications of your tenants, particularly if you anticipate future rent increases.

Evaluating the current rent

When you acquire a rental property, part of your research is to establish its fair market rental value. If a tenant's current rent is below market value, one of your toughest decisions as the new owner of a rental property is how to handle rent increases.

As the new owner, you often have much higher mortgage payments and typically higher expenses to make necessary repairs and upgrades to the property than the last owner did. Some tenants get very upset and antagonistic about any rent increase, however, and you won't be able to appease them.

Fortunately, the majority of tenants just expect to be treated fairly and honestly. They understand you may have higher expenses and will reluctantly accept a rent increase as long as two basic conditions are met:

- ✔ **You don't raise the rent beyond the current market rent for a comparable rental unit in the area.** Give tenants documented information on comparable rentals in your area to show them you're not asking for an unreasonable rent.

- ✔ **You're willing to make basic repairs to the rental unit.** Don't ask tenants to shell out extra cash without proving you're committed to maintaining and even improving the property.

Seek cost-effective improvements or upgrades that enhance the rental unit. Most tenants just want to be sure they're receiving some of the benefit of paying higher rent. And if you're asking for more rent, be willing to reinvest a portion of the rent increase into improving the rental property. Clean the carpet, repaint the interior of the rental unit, or send in a maintenance person for a few hours to repair the miscellaneous items that need attention. Of course, if you have a very good and stable tenant, you may want to consider more significant upgrades to the rental unit. Replacing the carpet, installing a new appliance or countertops, or adding a ceiling fan and microwave oven may be an incentive for your golden tenant to sign a new lease at a higher rental rate.

Although tempting, be wary of making significant renovation or repairs to the rental property before the close of escrow. If the sale of the property doesn't go through as planned, you may have spent considerable sums to upgrade the seller's property without any recourse.

Buying unoccupied rental property

The takeover procedure for an unoccupied rental property or one that has vacant rental units isn't much different than the procedure for taking over an occupied property. Many times you may actually prefer to have the property vacant so you can quickly implement a plan to upgrade and get the property rent-ready as soon as possible. If you want an occupied rental property vacant upon the change of ownership, make the vacancy of the rental unit a condition for the close of escrow. *Remember:* After you own the rental property, every day the rental unit sits vacant is lost income you can never recoup, so you want to work diligently during the escrow time frame to make as much progress as possible.

Begin your marketing and advertising of the rental property to coincide with the close of escrow and completion of the rental unit renovation. Time is of the essence if you want to minimize any lost rent.

Part II
Renting Your Property

The 5th Wave   By Rich Tennant

"I'm well aware that I ask a lot from my rental applicants, Mr. Harvey. However, sarcasm is rarely required."

In this part . . .

The chapters in this part guide you through the process of actually renting your property — everything from getting your rental unit ready to setting the rent and advertising. I also give you some great tips for showing your property to prospective tenants and fill you in on the importance of good tenant screening policies. So if you have a vacancy on your hands — or you will soon — read on.

Chapter 5

Getting Your Rental Property Ready for Prospective Tenants

In This Chapter

▶ Knowing how to get the most from your property through internal and external improvements

▶ Developing a system for being rent-ready

▶ Making sure safety is a priority

▶ Working with a professional to prep your unit for rental

ou may think of preparing your rental property as one of the most basic property management functions, but actually doing so is critical to your overall success. Because vacant rental units don't generate rental income, you need to fill your vacancies with good, stable, rent-paying tenants as quickly as possible. But how? By making sure the interior, exterior, and grounds of your vacant rental units are clean and in rent-ready condition when you show them to prospective tenants.

In this chapter, I help you figure out whether you need to upgrade your rental unit before a new tenant moves in. And I fill you in on the proper methods of preparing the rental unit so you can get the kind of tenant you want in as little time as possible.

Coming Up with a Plan to Handle Vacancies

The first step in getting good tenants is to develop a plan to get each vacant unit in top condition. Ideally, your vacating tenant will be cooperative and allow you access to the rental unit so you can determine what items need to be cleaned, repaired, replaced, or even upgraded. As you walk through the unit, take lots of notes on its condition and what needs attention in order to get it ready to rent again. Your notes are the foundation for a detailed plan to help you attract several qualified rental prospects who want to lease the unit at the rate you're seeking. The next few sections can help you put that plan into place.

Not everyone appreciates or values the same features in a rental unit as you. This is a rental property and, just as the old saying states, "Beauty is in the eye of the beholder." The features and amenities that appeal to you may not be worth the extra investment from the perspective of your target tenant market. For example, although you prefer expensive travertine floor tiles in your own home, you may soon find that more durable flooring products can tolerate the heavier wear and tear of rental units much better. Although cleanliness has universal appeal, some features such as ceiling fans and microwaves will appeal more to some prospective tenants than others.

Considering renovations and upgrades

Almost every rental unit has the potential for renovation or upgrades, giving you the opportunity to create real value in your units. When you have a dated rental unit, you have to decide whether to renovate it and increase the rent or leave it be and settle for the same old rent. Be sure to evaluate the cost of the renovation or upgrade versus the rent increase you can get out of a particular improvement *before* you start renovating. You need to be sure you'll get your money back from your investment. The following sections help you figure out how much to renovate, what features prospective renters like to see, and what you need to do to stay within the law.

Not convinced renovating is worth thinking about? You may think you're saving time and money by allowing a new tenant to lease a rental unit that hasn't been properly prepared. After all, if Bob doesn't mind that the unit isn't rent-ready, why should you? Unfortunately, this strategy isn't as problem-free as it seems on the surface. In fact, it's a big mistake. Why? Because the kind of tenant you attract with a rental unit that hasn't been properly prepared is someone who has lower standards and may even be desperate. New tenants who accept a dirty and poorly maintained rental unit surely won't make any extra effort to leave the property in good condition when they depart.

Determining whether to renovate: What's your return?

When you're considering making renovations and upgrades, you need to understand what they can and can't do for you. Many times renovations and property upgrades result in increased net income and higher property value. However, sometimes the renovations may not justify the investment.

To consider the *payback* of a proposed improvement, calculate the total installed cost of the upgrade and divide your answer by the monthly increase in rental income. For example, if you modernize your rental property and install a dishwasher for $400 and consequently increase your monthly rent by $25, the payback is 16 months. Whether 16 months is an acceptable payback and worth the initial investment of $400 is determined by each owner. Just remember that you're not only increasing your monthly gross income but also identifying your increased property value as a result of higher net income, a value that makes your rental property worth more to a buyer when you look to sell your rental property.

Every real estate investor has different expectations, but generally any payback of less than 24 months is good, especially when you look at the increase in property value that accompanies increased net income. See *Real Estate Investing For Dummies* by me and coauthor Eric Tyson (Wiley) for more discussion of ways to increase the value of your rental property.

Eyeing what prospective renters want

Some tenants value certain improvements more than others. So the main question is: What features and improvements do most prospective renters want (which in turn can give you more money in terms of a higher rent)? You can't come up with an exact answer to what amount of increased rent a particular upgrade will generate. For example, a new granite countertop in the kitchen or new light fixtures in the dining room or bathroom have a different impact on each prospective tenant; some are willing to pay more for those amenities, and others aren't.

Feeling a bit confused about what direction to take to figure out the features prospective renters want? Never fear! The following tips can guide you:

- ✔ **Keep in mind what features and strengths your prospective renters will find in competitive rental units.** Look for outmoded or outdated features in your own unit. Perhaps most of your competition offers dishwashers, but you don't have one in your unit. You may want to install a dishwasher so that you remain competitive. Or maybe your unit has a very old dining room light fixture that you can easily replace with a modern light fixture or ceiling fan with a light kit. Another simple upgrade is to replace your old electrical switches and outlets for a more modern look. New hardware on the kitchen cabinets is also a low-cost upgrade. Pay particular attention to those items that are quick, easy, and inexpensive to replace, but can really improve the overall look of your rental unit.

- ✔ **When upgrading or replacing your current appliances, standardize the brand and model wherever possible.** This advice is particularly true for certain appliances that have modular components that can be easily replaced to give the appliances a new look and extended life. Stoves, ranges, ovens, refrigerators, and washers and dryers fit into this category. When other appliances such as microwaves, dishwashers, and garbage disposals fail, it's simply more cost-effective to replace the units. So for this latter category of appliances, you want to take advantage of appliance vendors who have certain models on closeout or special pricing. Bonus: Tenants generally don't pay that much attention to the brand of the garbage disposal, so you may as well take advantage of any specials. Buying a discontinued brand or model of a stove, however, may save you money up front but cost you much more in the long run, when you're unable to find replacement parts.

If you have an older rental property, renovating may be more difficult due to some of the hazardous materials used in your unit's original construction. Hazardous materials like asbestos or lead-based paint aren't cheap to remove. Often, you're better off just leaving the materials in place as long as they haven't been disturbed. Consult with hazardous materials removal experts before determining the extent of the renovation and the proper methods to ensure that all hazardous materials are safely maintained. Also, check with your local building code enforcement or health department for requirements regarding the proper handling and disposal of hazardous materials.

Obtaining the appropriate permits

When you're considering renovations or upgrades to your rental unit, make sure you get the appropriate building permits or licenses as required in your area. You don't need to be a code expert, but having a general understanding of both local housing codes and state housing laws is important. Evaluate your property and ensure that the planned work will meet current building codes. Every state and many local municipalities have building codes that dictate the minimum standards to which all buildings must comply. Often, they have housing, fire, and health and safety codes as well. Reviewing rental housing industry publications can alert you to significant changes in these codes.

If inspectors find that your rental property isn't in compliance with the proper codes, then you may receive violation notices and potentially expensive fines. Building codes are regularly updated and changed, and typically, properties aren't required to meet the new code requirements unless the properties are renovated, and new building permits are obtained. Be sure you or your contractors are aware of the code requirements and incorporate the necessary code-compliance measures in your renovations to ensure the safety of your tenants and to protect yourself from violations and fines.

Paying attention to the exterior and common areas

You want to make sure your rental prospects' first impression of your rental property is a positive one. If the property's exterior and grounds don't look nice, your prospect won't even bother to see the interior — where you've just installed new appliances and high-quality carpeting.

A poor first impression of your rental unit's exterior is hard to reverse — regardless of how great the inside may look. That's why you want to make a great first impression. In order to do so, you need to think about *curb appeal,* or how your property looks to a prospective tenant when she first visits.

To attract tenants who'll treat your property properly and stay for years, keep the following suggestions in mind:

- ✓ **Start at the street and carefully critique your property as if you were entering a contest for the best-looking property in your area.** First impressions are critical, and one of the key areas seen by all prospective tenants is the front entry. Make sure the entryway is clean, well-kept, and well-lit. Clean the front door or apply a new coat of paint or stain. Buy a new welcome mat. Remove or replace a broken screen door or mailbox. Also, check the driveways and walkways and make sure they're as neat and tidy as possible.

- ✓ **Be sure your grounds and exterior areas are sparkling clean and the landscaping is well-maintained.** Believe it or not, you can renovate your grounds inexpensively by picking up trash and junk, removing weeds, properly watering the grass, and using the right fertilizer. A nice green lawn, healthy shrubs, and shade trees enhance any rental property. Savvy rental property owners know that landscaping is one of the most cost-effective ways to significantly upgrade a unit.

- ✓ **Check all patios, balconies, and entryways.** They should be clean, and the railings should be secure.

- ✓ **Make sure the building structure is presentable and inviting.** Although major architectural changes are often cost-prohibitive, you can do a lot with a little paint, landscaping, and cleanup. The good news is that these items generally don't cost much compared to the positive benefits you gain. Some specific exterior improvements to consider are ground-level or hanging planters, brass house numbers, awnings, or freshly painted fence or house trim. See *Flipping Houses For Dummies* by Ralph R. Roberts and Joe Kraynak (Wiley) for examples of exterior and landscaping renovations that can completely change a property's curb appeal and even reposition tired rental properties.

Making sure the interior is up to snuff

The most qualified, stable renters always have choices, no matter how good or bad the rental market. You're in competition for these excellent tenants, and you need to make sure your rental unit stands out from the rest. A prospective tenant's positive first impression of your rental property's exterior soon disappears if its interior isn't just as sharp and well-maintained.

Curb appeal in a community association

If you own a rental unit in a community interest development (CID), commonly referred to as a community association or homeowners' association (HOA), the responsibility for the maintenance and repair of the common areas typically falls to the association. Contact the association or its property manager to advise someone of any common area concerns you have. The association has a vested interest in ensuring the proper maintenance of the premises, as well as maintaining a sense of desirability for owners and tenants, but it may require some persuasion to take action.

Community associations are nonprofit entities run by volunteer boards of directors who are often reluctant to assess their owners and spend money to upgrade or modernize aging properties. Rarely do you find an association with plentiful reserves and well-maintained property unless it has strong leaders willing to make beneficial upgrades a priority. So you may need to get involved as a member of the association and use your expertise to demonstrate to the other owners (many may be owner-occupants) that proper maintenance can actually reduce long-term operating costs as well as maintain higher property values, which is a concern to all owners.

Don't show your rental unit until it's completely rent-ready. Prospective tenants often have a hard time seeing a unit's potential. If you show them a dirty rental unit, they'll *always* think of it that way. Although you may lose a couple of potential showing days by taking time to prepare the unit, you benefit in the long run by signing a more conscientious tenant. Trust me when I say that tenants who are more careful in the selection of their new rental home are planning to stay longer, and this is exactly the type of tenant you want.

When preparing a rental unit for a new tenant, don't overlook or forget a single item. I recommend using an inspection checklist (like the Interior Unit Inspection Checklist included on the CD) to guide you through the process and assist you with final inspection. Here's a list of what to go over in preparation for your new tenant:

- ✔ **When you have legal possession, remove any personal possessions and trash left behind by the previous tenant.** Be sure that you follow any state or local laws providing the former tenant an opportunity to reclaim any abandoned personal property.

- ✔ **Check all plumbing (toilets, faucets, and pipes) for proper operation.** Make sure nothing leaks, the plumbing has the proper pressure, and everything drains adequately.

- ✔ **Test all appliances for proper operation.** Run the dishwasher through a full cycle. Be sure the oven's drip pan, broiler pan, and racks are included.

✔ **Try out all hardware.** Rekey or change the locks and make sure they're operational. Pay attention to all latches and catches, doorknobs and pulls, doorstops, and sliding doors.

✔ **Check all windows, window or insect screens, and window coverings.** Verify that they're clean, unbroken, secure, and properly operational. Test all window locks to be sure they work as well.

Window treatments can make your rental property look great. After all, what's not to like? You control the appearance of your rental property from the street, and your tenant receives attractive and functional window coverings. The various window treatments are now very affordable and can really make a difference, so be sure to explore all your options and find out what's most desirable in your local area. Choose window coverings that appeal to your prospective tenants and are easy to maintain. I recommend vertical blinds or drapes, because they're much easier to maintain and clean than miniblinds.

✔ **Inspect all walls, ceilings, and baseboards.** Confirm that the paint and/or wall coverings provide proper coverage, without holes, cuts, scratches, nail pops, or bad seams.

✔ **Examine all floor coverings.** Make sure floors are clean and in good condition. All flooring should be properly installed, without bad seams.

✔ **Check all bathrooms.** Thoroughly clean the toilet, tub, shower, sink, mirrors, and cabinets. Check the toilet paper holder and towel bars to be sure they're clean. Put a paper sanitary ring around each toilet seat and a new roll of toilet paper in each bathroom.

✔ **Look over all closets and storage areas.** Clean rods, closet dowels, hooks, shelves, lights, floors, and walls.

✔ **Examine all counters, cabinets, doors, moldings, thresholds, and metal strips.** Verify that they're clean, fully operational, and present no hazards.

✔ **Test smoke detectors, lighting, and electrical outlets, including all ground fault circuit interrupters (GFCI, also referred to as GFI) and circuit breakers, for proper operation.** Make sure all electrical components work at move-in; it's then the tenant's responsibility to notify you of any problems during the tenancy.

✔ **Check the fireplace.** If your unit has a fireplace, clean out ashes and debris. Have the chimney flue inspected periodically based on the amount of usage.

✔ **Inspect the heating and air conditioning unit(s) for proper operation.** Be sure the thermostat, filters, vents, and registers are all in working order. Contact a professional if necessary.

> ✔ **Perform a final walk-through of the entire rental unit for appearance and cleanliness.** Be sure to recheck the unit every few days because dust can settle quickly in a vacant unit. I've also seen an unpleasant surprise in the form of dead pests or insects that took their time expiring from recent pest control efforts. Nothing stops a good conversation with a great prospective tenant faster than stumbling upon a dead bug!

Preparing Your Rental Unit the Right Way

One of the best ways to maximize your rental income is to develop a system to improve your efficiency by completing your rent-ready process in minimum time. But you may be so overwhelmed by the amount of work you need to get done in the amount of time you have that you don't stop to consider the order you should do it in. I recommend you stick to the following order to maximize your time and efficiency:

1. General cleaning

2. Maintenance, including repairs and upgrades

3. Painting

4. Final cleaning

5. Carpet or floor covering cleaning

General cleaning

As soon as the old tenants move out, clean the vacant rental unit. During this initial cleaning, you should

> ✔ **Remove all trash left behind by the former tenants, including anything remaining in drawers, cabinets, and closets.**
>
> ✔ **Wipe down countertops and shelves.**
>
> ✔ **Sweep or vacuum the floors.**
>
> ✔ **Wash the windows, window coverings, and doors.**
>
> ✔ **Clean out the storage areas, including the attic, basement, or garage, as applicable.**

If you can't gain access before the tenants vacate, now's the time to walk through the unit and come up with your plan for getting it ready to rent again.

Forget second chances when it comes to showing a rental

Early in my property management career, I learned a valuable lesson about the importance of cleanliness and first impressions. I'd just arrived at a rental property for a management inspection and was speaking to the on-site manager when a prospective tenant entered the rental office and asked to see a vacant unit. She was a local college student out apartment hunting with her mother. I told my manager to go ahead and show the unit, and explained I'd just follow along if they didn't mind.

Together we left the rental office. The property grounds were very well-maintained, and the on-site manager did a great job getting to know the prospect's needs and determining the right unit to show. With the manager's help, the prospective tenant and her mother decided on seeing an upstairs unit, away from the street.

Everything was going great . . . until we got to the actual unit. A dirty, cobweb-filled entryway led us to an interior (that hadn't been tidied in at least a week!) where we could see a large tree branch hanging precariously over the balcony rail. Before seeing the unit, the prospective tenant and her mother had been very positive, even discussing how soon she could get approved and move in. Afterward, they stopped asking questions, barely answered any, and became very noncommittal.

Learn from my mistake: Remember that the cleanliness of the rental unit is paramount and *never* show a rental unit without having gone through it yourself just prior to the showing.

Maintenance and repairs

Maintaining and inspecting everything in your rental property while it's vacant is important. Properly completing this inspection doesn't mean you need to be a certified repair technician; just be able to ensure that the interior unit systems are operational for the standard day-to-day usage you expect from your new tenants. If you aren't certain what to look for or if anything seems awry, then be sure to contact a repair professional who's qualified for the building system that needs inspecting.

The majority of the items requiring maintenance in your vacant unit are minor, such as sticking closet doors, loose door knobs and towel bars, and burnt-out light bulbs. But be sure to carefully and regularly evaluate the current condition of all systems and equipment, including plumbing, electrical, appliances, and heating, ventilating, and air conditioning (HVAC). Keep the following in mind:

✔ **Carefully inspect all plumbing fixtures.** Look for leaky faucets, clogged aerators, or running toilets. Test the angle stops or shutoff valves for all toilets, washers, dishwashers, and faucets, including under each sink, and look for signs of leakage. Even small leaks can be a major problem if not detected and repaired quickly.

✔ **Inspect and test the electrical components of the rental unit.** Make sure the circuit breakers or fuses are all in place and are operating properly. Replace burnt-out light bulbs and check light switches and outlets. If possible, verify that the cable or satellite television and telephone lines are working, too.

✔ **Inspect each of the appliances and make sure that they're operating properly.** Stoves and ovens contain modular parts, and you can replace the burner drip pans and control knobs very easily, because replacement parts are readily available for most major appliances. Run the dishwasher through a cycle and look carefully for any signs of leaks around the gasket or underneath near the pump housing.

✔ **Conserve energy by turning off the water heater, furnace, and air conditioning units at the breaker and setting the refrigerator/freezer to low.** Your turnover work should also include the cleaning or replacement of all filters. This simple, low-cost item greatly improves the energy-efficiency and lowers the wear on the equipment. Keep records indicating the date the filters were changed and be sure to remind your tenants when they should be changed again.

Tenants are becoming increasingly aware of the importance of conservation and energy-efficiency when selecting their homes. If you install water-saving fixtures, pilot-less ignition gas stoves and water heaters or tankless water heaters, weatherproofing, insulated windows and doors, and energy-efficient appliances, you'll have a competitive advantage in the rental marketplace. Be sure to emphasize your "green" efforts in promoting your rental property.

✔ **Check the pool/spa.** If your property has a pool or spa, have a professional evaluate its condition and provide a written report documenting the findings, including the state of the equipment and the water quality. This evaluation establishes a baseline that can often head off any tenant complaints down the road.

✔ **Perform maintenance that will minimize the likelihood of pests.** Caulk all cracks around the windows, foundations, drains, and pipes that may afford entry into the rental unit. Almost every rental property will have the need for pest control at some point in time. An occasional cockroach or ants in search of water or food are commonplace, and there are consumer products available to handle these limited situations. However, use professional exterminators to treat more significant problems and talk to your exterminator about establishing a regular schedule for follow-ups to be sure your rental unit is free of pests.

Painting

The next step in getting your vacant rental unit ready is painting. The keys to success here are preparation and knowing what to paint when. Follow these steps to turn your unit into a rental work of art:

1. **Select and purchase the paint you want to use.**

   Remember, standardized colors are best, so you can easily and affordably touch up your rental unit instead of having to completely repaint it. One coat of a high-quality flat white latex paint is usually sufficient, so use this standard to help determine the quantity you need to buy. *Note:* You may require more gallons if you're changing the paint color to a much lighter shade than the current version. Try and use the same brand paint because colors can vary by brand.

   Plan to use a semi-gloss paint in kitchens and baths for easy cleanup and resistance to moisture. Although this type of paint may cost more, you save in the long run because purchasing higher-quality paint means you don't have to repaint the entire unit when it inevitably turns over.

2. **Take everything off the surfaces you're painting.**

   Remove all nails, screws, picture anchors, and other similar items. Detach all door hardware and electrical coverplates, too.

3. **Strip all dirt from the painting surfaces.**

   Make sure the walls in particular have been cleaned of any dirt. Treat grease, crayons, water stains, and other blemishes with products designed for that specific purpose.

4. **Check that walls are properly patched.**

   You may also need to do some scraping and sanding to ensure your new coat of paint adheres properly.

5. **Start painting.**

   Paint the unit in its entirety (yes, I mean walls, doors, door and window frames, baseboards, closets and closet dowels, and ceilings), unless you've recently painted the whole unit and only need to touch up one or two walls. Lucky you!

   If you have acoustic ceilings, be aware that these present special problems, particularly if they contain asbestos. Always consult with a professional painter or licensed acoustic contactor before attempting to patch or paint an acoustic ceiling and note that spraying paint is better than using a roller.

Don't paint damaged surfaces and/or those surfaces showing signs of moisture without determining the source of the problem and correcting it. Wet or moisture-damaged drywall indicates either plumbing leaks or water intrusion into the interior of the property. The sooner you identify the culprit and make the necessary repairs, the better.

6. **Replace everything you removed from your painting surfaces, after the paint has dried.**

   Reinstall all the switch plates and outlet covers, replacing any that are damaged or covered with paint.

7. **Clean up any lingering mess.**

   Remove any paint that has strayed or splattered onto the floor, windows, countertops, cabinets, appliances, and woodwork. Don't allow sinks or bathtubs to be used for paint cleanup.

Final cleaning

Cleanliness sells. And the only people you want as renters are the ones who only accept dirt in their home as a temporary condition. For many rental property owners, the thought of cleaning up after someone else is too much to bear. Luckily, many local cleaning services do a great job for a very reasonable price. *Remember:* You don't have to do everything yourself.

However, if you decide to clean the unit yourself, keep the following pointers in mind:

✔ **Pay particular attention to the kitchens and baths.** A dirty or grimy kitchen or bathroom can be a real turnoff to potential tenants. Be sure you clean and re-grout the tile, completely caulk around all countertops and bathroom fixtures, and clean the single dirtiest spot in most rental properties — the shower door track. For a final touch, install a new toilet seat and place a paper sanitary ring around the toilet to indicate it's been professionally sanitized.

✔ **Focus on smell.** If a rental unit doesn't smell clean, it won't matter how diligently you've cleaned it. Rental property owners often overlook the importance of the sense of smell. Consequently, you can have a real advantage over the competition for an amazingly small investment by recognizing this underappreciated sense's value. Here're a few ideas:

   • Use a pine oil or lemon disinfectant and cleanser to neutralize any bad odors from prior tenants.

   • Place baking soda in the refrigerator and drains, plus grind a lemon in the garbage disposal, to suppress any bad odors.

- Put a cinnamon stick in a shallow pan of water, and place it in the oven on low heat.

- Go to your favorite big box discount store to find many affordably priced liquid potpourris available in a variety of scents.

- Avoid certain fragrances that may be offensive to your prospective tenants.

In a short time, your rental unit will be filled with pleasant scents that remind your prospective tenants of Mom and apple pie. Why? Because this is a time when you want to go with something with a mass appeal rather than your personal favorite scent — essence of yak.

Carpet or floor covering cleaning

Cleaning the carpet or floor covering is the last step in preparing your rental unit for new tenants. Most floor coverings, such as linoleum or sheet vinyl, can be cleaned during the final cleaning stage; however, carpet cleaning should be handled only by outside contractors with professional truck-mounted steam cleaning equipment. The cost of professional carpet cleaning is very competitive, and you can't achieve the same results with the non-truck-mounted equipment that's readily available for rent at your local grocery or hardware store.

Unless they're obviously damaged, thoroughly clean your floor coverings before deciding to make replacements. The best choice in floor covering material is determined by your tenant profile, your prospective tenants' expectations, and your competition in the area. Linoleum or sheet vinyl is very competitively priced, and the range of materials available is impressive. The most common problem with sheet vinyl is that any damage requires complete replacement. Some rental owners avoid sheet vinyl and prefer individual floor tiles that can be replaced as needed; however, these tiles quickly trap dirt at the seams and can look unsightly. Be sure to select neutral colors and basic patterns.

If the carpets are too dated, severely worn, or badly stained and damaged, replace them. Carpeting is a decorator item, and care should be taken to select colors and styles designed for use in rental property. I recommend selecting a standard carpet style in a couple of basic colors for all your rental properties. Although sculptured carpet works well for some units, a nonsculptured carpet with short *knap,* or fibers, available in one or two neutral colors has the broadest appeal. If you own a lot of rental units and have proper storage space available, purchasing your standard carpet by the roll can offer significant savings. The extra carpeting can be used to patch or even replace a full room if needed; however, be aware that each roll of even the same carpet style and color can be different, because the manufacturer's dye lot may vary slightly each time the carpet is produced.

Many rental property owners make the mistake of purchasing a higher grade of carpeting and trying to save money on the carpet pad. But the carpet pad can make all the difference in the world. Consider using a higher grade of rebond padding with a medium-grade carpet for competitively priced, yet excellent, results.

Inspecting Safety Items

Although tenants need to take an active role in and have the ultimate responsibility for their own safety, you need to check all safety items upon unit turnover. The most basic items found in virtually every rental unit include door locks, window locks, and smoke detectors. Be sure these items are in place and working before the new tenant takes occupancy. See Chapter 18 for tips on how to ensure your tenants are protected.

Focus your safety inspections on the following items:

- **A small fire extinguisher:** Even if not required by code, I recommend each rental unit should have one. Although there's always the potential liability that the tenant won't use the fire extinguisher properly, most lifesaving professionals advise it's worth having because quickly using a fire extinguisher can keep a fire from spreading. Of course, the tenant should first ensure someone is immediately contacting 911 or the appropriate agency before attempting to put out the fire.

- **Adequate locking mechanisms:** Many local and state building codes have specific requirements concerning the types and specifications of door lock sets. Recent trends in legislation are requiring that all windows that open and are accessible from the ground have proper window locks. Window or insect screens should be in place and in good condition. The primary purpose of window screens is to keep the elements and insects out; however, screens can also have some value as a crime deterrent.

- **Smoke detectors:** They're very inexpensive and extremely important to your tenants' safety. Check with your local fire department for its code requirements, because some departments expect smoke detectors to be electrically hard-wired, and others may still allow battery-operated units. Contact your local fire safety or building officials for the latest info on fire and safety codes. Many of the rules have changed in recent years, particularly regarding the number and locations of required smoke detectors. Consider complying with any recommendations, even if the action isn't required in existing rental units.

Make sure your records clearly indicate that you tested the smoke detectors and found them to be operating properly before your new tenant moved in. Afterward, the tenant must not disconnect or disable them in any way. The tenant is also responsible for replacing the batteries and regularly testing the smoke detector and alerting you in writing if they don't operate properly.

✔ **Other important items:** Your rental unit preparation work should also include testing of the ground-fault circuit interrupters (GFCI or GFI) in kitchens and baths, plus any other safety items, such as carbon monoxide detectors and radon detectors, if you have them.

At some rental properties, your tenants may be tempted to use portions of the roof area for personal activities like sunbathing, hanging clothes, watching fireworks, or hosting parties (just to name a few). Allowing tenants' roof access is never a good idea, because roofs are only designed to shelter the rental unit from natural elements, not to handle foot traffic. If you let tenants up on your roof, you risk potential premature damage to it and exposure to significant liability if someone gets injured.

Be sure the house number or address is clearly marked on the exterior of your rental unit with at least 6" alphanumeric characters so it's easy to locate the property from the street. This simple measure can be a huge help to lifesaving personnel in an emergency.

Using Outside Contractors

Determining how to handle the required turnover work in vacant rental units is one of the toughest decisions rental property owners have to make. Owners of large apartment buildings have maintenance personnel on staff and many contractors ready to assist them as needed. They routinely handle vacant units and just need to schedule the work. But owners of small rental properties are typically on their own to either handle the work personally or locate contractors to quickly prepare the vacant units.

Even if you're inclined to do your own turnover preparation work, understand that certain maintenance functions requiring specialized or licensed training are best handled by outside contractors. For example, it would be unwise for you to act as an exterminator or a contractor dealing with environmental hazards, or to attempt to recharge the coolant in an air-conditioning unit. Specific regulations are in place, and unique knowledge is required in these areas.

Your skill level, time constraints, and opportunity cost may help determine whether you do some chores yourself or hire a pro. For example, cleaning, painting, and light maintenance may be items you feel qualified to handle, can complete promptly, and believe won't cause you to forgo significant income in other areas. When in doubt, let others do what they do best while you focus on what *you* do best: managing your rental property investment.

Every day your rental unit sits vacant costs you rental income you can never recover. If you decide to paint your own rental unit, it may take you six days working in the evenings and on weekends to completely paint a single-family rental home. If the rental market is strong and the daily rental rate is $50 per day, you're actually losing money you could've had if you'd hired professional painters for one day's work at $300.

Regardless of how much work you choose to handle yourself, you need to have a list of competent and competitively priced service companies and suppliers on hand for those times when you need a quick response. Your local affiliate of the National Apartment Association (NAA) or Institute of Real Estate Management (IREM) can often provide names of service companies. Carefully check references and the status of any bonds or licenses with the appropriate governmental agency and ensure the company has the proper insurance in place prior to commencing any work on your property. (Flip to Chapter 16 for more on the ins and outs of working with contractors.) If services exceed $600 in a calendar year and the vendor isn't a corporation or LLC, you need to file Form 1099 with the IRS.

Chapter 6

Rent, Security Deposits, and Rental Contracts: The Big Three of Property Management

*B*efore you can begin to advertise and show your rental unit, you need to set your asking rent, determine the appropriate security deposit, and have a rental contract ready to go. Not sure where to start? Don't worry.

This chapter gives you some tips on figuring out what to ask for rent and determining an appropriate security deposit. It also guides you through the advantages and disadvantages of leases and month-to-month rental agreements and gives you recommendations on how to get the benefits of each.

Setting the Rent

Setting the rent is an important decision because your net income from your rental property is determined by the amount of rent you charge. Although you may be tempted to pull numbers out of the air, resist that urge. If your rent is too high, you'll have difficulty renting your vacant unit. If it's too low, you'll have plenty of prospective tenants, but not enough money to cover your costs and generate a return on your investment. Finding the optimum price takes time and effort, which is why it's one of the most critical steps in being a successful rental property owner.

You can use two common methods for determining how much rent to charge for your rental property — return on investment and market analysis. This section takes a closer look at these two options and helps you figure out which method is best for you.

Knowing how much money you need to break even is important for evaluating the potential return on your real estate investment. But the reality is that the amount you need or want to collect in rent is subject to market conditions, the desirability of your rental property, and your abilities as a rental property owner.

If you currently own a rental property, you probably already know how much rental income is necessary to cover your mortgage and other basic operating expenses. If you're looking to buy a rental property, determine your minimum income needs *before* the deal is final. If you purchase a rental property that already has tenants on a long-term lease, you don't need to address the issue of rent immediately because the tenants' rent is set through the end of their lease. If they're not on a lease or have a lease that's expired, then they're most likely on a month-to-month rental agreement — which only requires you to give sufficient written notice of a rent increase. (For more information on working with existing tenants, see Chapter 4).

Whichever category you're in, you need to determine market rents so you can calculate the appropriate rent when it comes time to renew a lease or consider increasing rents to market level.

Examining the return on your investment

The first step in determining your rent based on the return on your investment is to calculate your costs of owning and operating the rental property. Estimate costs for your mortgage, taxes, insurance, maintenance, leasing, management, and profit on invested funds.

For example, if your annual expenses per rental unit are $12,000 for your mortgage and tax payments and $7,000 for other annual operating expenses, plus you want a 10 percent ($5,000) annual return on your original cash investment of $50,000, you need to generate a total rent of $24,000 per year, or $2,000 per month. (Of course, this simple calculation doesn't account for increasing equity or other tax advantages of real estate, but it's a place to start.)

Although you may have calculated that you need $2,000 per month to achieve your estimated break-even point (including your 10 percent profit), if the rental market has determined that comparable units are readily available for $1,750, you may not be able to fully achieve your financial goals at this time. With most real estate investments, the initial returns may not match your original projections. Yet in the long run, rents often increase at a greater rate than your expenses, thereby improving the return on your investment.

To avoid surprises, use a conservative budget that anticipates rental income at $50 to $100 per month below the full market rent for a comparable rental unit, plus provides for a vacancy allowance of one full month each year. In my experience, some tenants don't fulfill their lease obligations, leaving you with a vacancy even if you had a 12-month lease, so be conservative in your expectations.

For example, if you feel that the comparable monthly rent for your rental property is $1,600, estimate your projected rental income based on a conservative asking rent of $1,500 per month. Then anticipate receiving this amount for 11 months rather than 12. After allowing for one month of vacancy, your gross rental income projection falls from $18,000 annually to $16,500.

Many new rental property owners make a major mistake by overestimating the potential income from their rental property. They develop unrealistic operating budgets or projections by using above-market rents, not allowing for rental discounts, and anticipating virtually no vacancy or bad debt. When reality strikes, they're faced with negative cash flow and the possibility of losing their rental property. Avoid this situation by playing it safe and staying conservative with your estimated income.

Setting the rent is particularly critical if you own single-family or condo rental units and other small rental properties because the rent loss from an extended vacancy or one bad tenant can seriously jeopardize your entire investment. If you're among this group of rental property owners, be conservative in setting your rents, cautious in screening tenants, and aggressive in keeping your rental properties in excellent condition to attract good, long-term tenants who pay on time.

Conducting a market analysis of rents in your area

You can determine the amount of rent to charge by calculating a desired return on your investment and setting the rent accordingly (see the preceding section), but typically the best way to set your rent is to conduct a market survey of comparable rental properties in your area. Why? The answer's simple: Most rental markets have a finite limit to what prospective renters want to pay for a comparable rental unit, and tenants don't care how much you paid for the unit or how much you continue to spend in operating costs.

Following are two schools of thought about performing a rent survey to determine the proper asking rent for your units:

✔ **Pose as a prospective renter, and ask all the typical questions a prospect may ask.** The owner or manager will give you only the information that a prospective tenant needs about the property.

✔ **Be honest and tell the owner you're a rental property owner doing market analysis.** This is the method I recommend, particularly if you have a small rental property. Most rental owners will cooperate and share the information you need. They may even be willing to give you additional important information you can't get otherwise, such as the length of time their rental units have been vacant, the number and types of phone calls they've received to date, the actual occupancy rate for the properties, and the feedback from their own research into rental rates and vacancies in the local rental market. This behavior is especially true if they've recently rented their properties and are no longer competing with you for prospective tenants.

Keep in mind that the owners of competing large apartment communities probably won't provide you with any information about their current occupancy. This number is important, however, because it can provide a good indication of overall demand for rental units in the market. Over the years, I've discovered some creative ways to determine actual vacancy levels:

- Talk with the mail carrier who delivers to the complex because he or she can tell you whether it's completely full or relatively vacant.

- Ask a common vendor, such as a carpet-cleaning firm or exterminator, that services your property and the large apartment complex for the inside information you need.

- Drive through the property at night to see how many parking spaces are being used.

In order to determine the market rents in your area, do your homework and locate comparable rental properties. *Comparable properties* are those properties that your tenants are most likely to have also considered when looking for a rental unit. They may be located right in the neighborhood or all the way across town. For example, many of your rental prospects may work at the hospital located six blocks west of your property. But your rental prospects are just as likely to choose a rental within six blocks of the hospital in another direction. So your comparable properties can be 12 blocks away. Don't assume your comparable properties are solely in your own neighborhood.

When you've determined which rental units are comparable, finding out the current market rent is easy. Begin by checking the For Rent signs in your area and calling for the asking rent and other details. The local or regional newspaper usually has ads listing the units for rent in the area along with some details and a phone number to call for more information. Although calling about ads gives you some good general information, you need to see the rental properties in person to truly determine whether they're comparable to yours.

Be careful to distinguish between the asking rents quoted on signs or by phone. Many landlords (especially those with single-family homes or condominium rental units) can be negotiated down from the asking rent pretty easily. Most owners of individual rental units can't afford vacancies for more than a couple of weeks and quickly lower the rent if qualified prospects show interest in their rental properties, so you need to base your decisions on signed leases, not asking prices.

Remember, rental rates can vary greatly from neighborhood to neighborhood and even from street to street, because many factors affect rents, including the following:

- ✔ Landscaping
- ✔ Property features, such as location, age, and size
- ✔ Reputation of the neighborhood or rental property
- ✔ Traffic noise
- ✔ Views

As a result, determining the proper asking rent isn't scientific. Setting your rent a little too high at first is better than setting it too low, because you can always reduce your asking rent slightly if you encounter too much resistance. Of course, be honest and make downward adjustments for aspects of your rental property that aren't as competitive or desirable as those of the comparable properties in your area.

When estimating the proper market rent for your unit, be careful not to make adjustments based strictly on your own personal preferences. The rental value of a particular property is subjective and can vary dramatically from one person to another. For example, you may prefer upstairs units and believe they should be priced higher than comparable downstairs units. Although many prospective renters may agree with you, just as many prospects may similarly value a downstairs unit because they may not want to climb stairs.

The accompanying CD has a Market Survey form you can use to compare and contrast your rental property with other comparable properties and assist you in determining the appropriate rental rate.

The following sections break down some additional items to think about when conducting your market analysis.

Considering rental concessions in determining your rent

When you contact other rental property owners or managers to determine an *effective rent,* the actual net rent after all concessions and discounts, for your property, be prepared to receive a rent quote but don't expect to hear about rental concessions. A *Rental concession* is basically a discount given to entice a prospective tenant to sign a rental contract. Landlords tend to give concessions in softer real estate markets where the demand for apartments has slowed, so identifying potential concessions is important in your comparison because you need to know what the net or actual collected rent is. If you don't, you may overprice your rental units.

To find out the actual effective rents, with concessions included, I recommend you contact rental property owners or managers after they've rented their units and concluded marketing efforts. Now that their properties are occupied, they're more likely to cooperate and give you accurate, complete information regarding their agreed-upon terms.

Calculate the effective rental rate by dividing the total rent by the length of the rental period. *Note:* The total rent may be affected by various rental concessions. For example, say a competitive property in your area recently rented at $1,200 per month on a one-year lease, but the first month's rent was waived. Then the effective rent is $1,100 per month. Divide the total rent of $13,200 by the 12 months of the lease. The effective rental rate is thus $1,100 per month.

Without knowing about the rental concession, you may mistakenly think the comparable unit rented at $1,200 per month. As a result, you may set your asking rent too high or be hesitant to offer your own rental concessions to stay competitive with what you think is a higher price. Just remember that every day your rental unit sits vacant because your rental rate is higher than the competition's is money lost.

Deciding whether to market your rental property using gross rents or net rents

After completing your analysis of your local rental market and taking into consideration any concessions, you need to set your final asking price. You can do so by formulating a marketing strategy to ensure you get the best price for your rental property.

Here are your options:

- ✔ Quote a higher gross asking rent, which is similar to the "suggested retail price" that stores use, and then offer rental concessions to attract the attention of your prospective target market.

- ✔ Go with a lower effective asking rent that is the net of the rental concessions prevalent in the market.

If you like to negotiate and can sell the special offer, the gross rent method is for you. Inevitably, some prospective tenants are attracted to rental properties offering specials; at least that's the impression I get when some prospects call about a rental property and the first words out of their mouths are, "What's your special?" Be sure to watch out for tenants who are just looking for the special discount off the rent up front, because they likely aren't the long-term quality tenants you want (and need) to be a successful rental property owner.

Have you ever heard about the great bargains available on cruise vacations booked at the last minute? Well, the concepts of inventory management and lost revenue also apply to the rental housing industry. Units that sit vacant for too long are usually overpriced, and each day that passes with your rental property vacant is more lost rent you can never collect. Either re-evaluate your asking rent or concessions or see what you can do to make your rental unit superior to the competition to secure those long-term tenants.

Not into wheeling and dealing? Perhaps you prefer telling your prospective renters that unlike all the other landlords offering gimmicks and special deals, you're all about cutting the hype and offering them the best net monthly rental rate. In my experience, many tenants find a lower, straightforward rental rate quote more attractive, especially if they plan on staying for a long time.

Regardless of which marketing strategy you take, avoid the temptation to set your rent based on the number of occupants your rental unit can hold. Some landlords have a policy that the base rental rate is for a certain number of tenants; they then charge more for each additional tenant in the unit. This practice is sometimes called *per head* rent. However, the Department of Housing and Urban Development considers such policies violations of the Fair Housing Act. The only exception is if you can show a legitimate *business necessity,* or verifiable increased cost to maintain your rental property, such as higher water or sewage bills. If you think you can prove a business necessity, check with your landlord-tenant legal expert before setting rents. Otherwise, take my advice and avoid these turbulent waters.

Ultimately, your marketing strategy is often influenced by what's most commonly done in your local rental market, but don't be afraid to incorporate your personal style.

Dealing with potential rent control issues

Most areas of the country don't impose limits on the rental rate you set for your property. Rent control is currently only found in Washington, D.C. and a handful of states: California, Maryland, New Jersey, and New York. If you own a rent controlled property, you need to obtain a current copy of the ordinance and fully understand the implications of local rent control when setting your asking rent. You also need to know how you can implement future rent increases because rent control limitations may influence your initial asking rents.

If you're limited to only nominal future rent increases, be very patient to make sure you get the maximum rent possible for a new incoming tenant, because this base rent will be a factor in your rental income for the entire duration of the tenancy. In other words, if you lower your rent by $100 to quickly rent your property, you may be negatively affecting your income stream for many years.

Coming Up with a Fair Security Deposit

As an owner of rental property, you need to make sure the security deposit you collect adequately protects you from tenant damage or default. The *security deposit* serves as the protection you need before turning your real estate asset (the rental unit) over to a tenant. It needs to be large enough to motivate the tenant to return the rental property in good condition, plus serve as an accessible resource to cover the tenant's unpaid rent or reimburse the costs to repair any damage. If your security deposit's set too high, many qualified tenants may not be able to afford the move-in costs for your rental property, resulting in fewer applicants.

State laws typically limit the amount of the security deposit you can collect and regulate its return, along with any lawful deductions. If you collect the first month's rent upon move-in, this money is *not* considered part of the security deposit. Some states specifically allow certain small rental owners to be exempt from these rules. See the CD for more information on state laws about security deposits.

The next several sections help you determine the right amount for your security deposit.

Figuring what you can legally charge

Many states limit the amount you can collect as a deposit to the equivalent of one or two months' rent. The limit varies in each state depending on certain factors, such as whether the rental is furnished, whether the tenant is on a lease or a month-to-month rental agreement, whether the tenant has pets or waterbeds, or whether the tenant is a senior citizen.

In most rental markets, the security deposits are well below the maximum allowed by law. While staying within the legal limits, I recommend you collect as large of a security deposit as the market can bear.

Security deposits are more than just money you hold for protection against unpaid rent or damage caused by your tenant. Although the actual cash amount may be relatively small compared to the overall value of your rental property, the security deposit is a psychological tool that's often your best insurance policy for getting your rental unit back in decent condition.

When trying to determine how much to charge for your security deposit, make sure you avoid the following potential costly mistakes:

  ✔ **Don't lower the security deposit or waive a security deposit payment.** If the funds required to move in are too high, collect a reasonable portion of the deposit prior to move-in and allow the tenant, in writing, to pay the balance of the security deposit in installments. This type of written agreement usually indicates that any funds paid by the tenant are first applied to the security deposit and then applied to the rent. Don't allow the tenant to miss or delay payment of any subsequent security deposit installments. Take legal action immediately if the tenant misses making any security deposit payments or fails to pay the rent in full.

For single-family homes, I strongly advise getting as large of a security deposit as possible. Aside from the inherent increased value of the rental home itself, you likely have tremendous value in the grounds, landscaping, and pool or spa (if applicable) — meaning much more of your valued property can be damaged by tenants. Rental homeowners also tend to inspect or visit their property less frequently, and it takes only a few weeks of inadequate watering or shoddy landscaping maintenance to find you've suffered significant damage. See Chapter 17 for advice on ways to convince tenants that landscaping or pool/spa maintenance are best left to professional contractors.

✔ **Don't completely eliminate security deposits.** Property owners in *soft* or low-demand rental markets often offer free rent or "no security deposit" move-in specials. Prospective renters attracted by such offers typically aren't the types to become long-term stable tenants who treat your property with respect and care about peaceful, harmonious living with their neighbors.

Although staying competitive is important, I recommend avoiding free rent or "no deposit" specials whenever possible. Offer to pay the prospective tenant's security deposit instead. You still receive the first month's rent when your tenant moves in, and he can potentially receive a security deposit refund if the property is in good condition at move-out. Essentially a form of free rent (because you're crediting the tenant, not receiving money), this move reduces the total funds your incoming tenant must pay. Unlike a risky move-in special, you're offering the concession at the *end* of the lease, not the beginning. As a result, you're less likely to attract tenants who move from landlord to landlord in search of up-front freebies. You also have a better shot at creating a strong psychological and practical motivation for the tenant to fulfill the terms of his lease. Why? Because that security deposit cash comes in handy for covering the costs of moving to a new residence . . . after several good years at your property, of course.

Keeping security deposits separate from your other funds

Security deposits are liabilities from an accounting point of view because these funds legally belong to the tenant. You hold them in trust as protection in case the tenant damages the property or defaults in paying rent.

Because the funds don't belong to you, several states require security deposits to be held in a separate bank trust account instead of being mixed in with other funds from your rental properties or personal resources. Some states even insist you provide your tenant with a written notice indicating the location of this bank trust account at the beginning of the tenancy.

Keeping the security deposits separate from the rest of your funds means they're readily available whenever a tenant moves out and is potentially entitled to the return of some or all of her money. Doing so, even if not required in your area, can be a great way to avoid cash flow problems. Say a tenant fulfills all contractual obligations before move-out and deserves a security deposit refund. If you commingled her deposit with your personal funds, you may find your current cash availability can't cover a large security deposit refund within the short time frame required by law in most areas. This situation can lead to legal action by the tenant and additional penalties and interest. The lesson? Always make sure you have available funds to cover the potential refund of security deposits.

Avoiding nonrefundable deposits

A *nonrefundable security deposit,* which is allowed in some states, is a portion of the deposit that you, the property owner, retain no matter what's allowed by state law. A nonrefundable security deposit may sound like a good idea, but it may also send a message to the tenant that he has to pay for the costs of preparing the rental property for the next tenant. My 30 years of experience with tenants leads me to question the benefits of nonrefundable security deposits in most instances because the incentive is gone for tenants to keep and maintain the property in the best condition.

In fact, I recommend avoiding nonrefundable fees in general in favor of seeking a higher, fully refundable security deposit so you have funds to cover damage repairs and cleaning, if necessary. It's a good day as a rental owner or property manager if your tenant vacates and leaves the rental property in good condition, so I prefer to have the entire security deposit be refundable.

Approximately a dozen states have specific laws permitting rental property owners to have nonrefundable security deposits or fees. These fees cover the costs of services such as cleaning, repainting, or redecorating. Some states have very specific limitations on these nonrefundable deposits or fees and don't allow charging for any excessive costs incurred. On the other hand, several states don't have laws specifically prohibiting nonrefundable deposits and leave such decisions to the mutual agreement of the property owner and the tenant.

Regardless of where you live, not using nonrefundable deposits allows you to avoid potentially time-consuming disputes with your tenants, such as what happens if the $150 nonrefundable cleaning deposit is insufficient to cover the $250 costs for cleaning a filthy rental property.

Paying interest on security deposits

Several states have laws requiring rental property owners to pay interest on a tenant's security deposit. You can find some basic information about security deposit interest on the CD, but check with your local affiliate of the National Apartment Association for the exact requirements in your area because the laws differ dramatically from state to state.

The method of calculating interest varies greatly, with some states providing a formula tied to the Federal Reserve Board rates or flat percentage amounts. Most states require interest payments to be made annually and at termination of the tenancy.

No laws prevent you from voluntarily paying interest on deposits, and some owners offer to pay interest as a competitive advantage or an inducement to collect a larger security deposit. If you're able to get a much larger deposit, I recommend paying interest on it. The additional peace of mind is worth the relatively small amount you'll pay in interest.

Last month's rent

Until recently, many rental property owners collected the first month's rent, the last month's rent, and a security deposit from new tenants, a method that has some disadvantages. I strongly recommend you collect the first month's rent, plus a security deposit equal to or greater than one month's rent, because collecting the "last month's rent" can create unnecessary problems.

If the rental rate increases during the tenancy and you've already collected a lesser amount as the "last month's rent," upon move-out, the tenant (and often the court) will likely take the position that the "last month's rent" has already been paid in full, even though the rental rate has increased. When giving rent increases, many owners fail to also require the tenant to increase the amount held as the "last month's rent." Plus,

in some states, the designation of "last month's rent" limits your use of these funds to only that specific use. Thus, even if the rental unit is extensively damaged and the security deposit is fully exhausted, the "last month's rent" can't be used to cover those damages.

Set your security deposit to an amount that's different than the monthly rental rate to minimize your tenant's chance to claim he thought the security deposit would cover his last month's rent. Ideally, you can collect a security deposit that's higher than the monthly rental rate. But even if you collect a deposit that is $25 to $50 less than the monthly rent, you effectively eliminate any tenant attempt to claim the deposit was for the last month's rent.

Increasing deposits

If you have a long-term tenant and your rents have increased significantly over time, you may want to consider increasing your security deposit amount. This move is legal as long as you comply with the normal requirements for any change in the terms of the rental agreement.

For example, if you have a fixed-term lease in effect, you must wait until the lease expires or rolls over to a month-to-month rental agreement before requiring an increase in the security deposit. If you have a month-to-month rental agreement, then you can increase the security deposit the same way you raise the rent, typically by giving the tenant a written notice 30 days in advance. Either way, remember that you're subject to the maximum security deposit amounts as set by state law, if any.

The accompanying CD has information on some of the basic state requirements for security deposits such as interest, if any; the maximum amounts you can request; and the time limits to return deposits, plus links to all state landlord-tenant laws for other legal issues.

Choosing the Type of Rental Contract You Want

Another important decision you need to make before you begin advertising and showing your rental is whether you want to use a lease or a month-to-month rental agreement. The *rental contract,* whether a lease or a month-to-month rental agreement, is the primary document that specifies the terms and conditions of the agreement binding the property owner and the tenant. It's a contract between the owner of the rental property and the tenant for the possession and use of the rental property in exchange for the payment of rent. The following sections give you the lowdown on the two types of agreements.

Contemplating a lease

A lease is a fixed-term contract that obligates you and the tenant for a set period of time, and some owners like the commitment required from the tenant. The most common lease terms are for 6 months, 9 months, or 12 months, and the majority of leases are written to automatically convert to a month-to-month rental agreement after the expiration of the initial term. However, some leases are for fixed terms, and the owner and tenant must agree to sign a new lease for the tenant to stay.

A lease is advantageous for tenants because it locks the rent in place for the term of the lease, and it's potentially advantageous for you because you can theoretically count on having a tenant for a set period of time.

Rental property owners generally charge a lower rental rate for leases than for month-to-month rental agreements, because tenants on a lease aren't associated with as high a risk of turnover as individuals on short-term agreements. Yet in 15 years of writing a nationally syndicated landlord-tenant Q & A column, I've received hundreds of inquiries from tenants seeking suggestions for a compelling story or legal argument to break their long-term leases. Whether they just wanted the lower up-front cost offered by a lease or their personal needs changed, all of them wanted out of their long-term commitments. So be cautious and don't offer more than a $10 per month discount for long-term leases, unless your local market conditions warrant a higher amount.

With a lease, you can't increase the rent or change other terms of the tenancy until the lease expires. Also, you can't terminate or end the tenancy before the lease expires, unless the tenant doesn't pay his rent or violates another term of the lease. Should you wind up in court, you'll have the burden of proof, meaning you're the one who has to prove the tenant didn't live up to his part of the contract.

Although the lease legally binds both you and your tenant, the current landlord-tenant laws in virtually every state favor tenants. A tenant can walk away from a lease without difficulty, and in most states, the owner has the duty of mitigating or minimizing the potential damages. This legal mumbo jumbo means you must make a reasonable effort to re-rent the premises and can only charge for the rent incurred until the new tenant begins paying rent.

Eyeing a periodic rental agreement

Some owners prefer the flexibility offered by a month-to-month rental agreement over the rigidity of a lease. A *month-to-month rental agreement* is commonly used by rental property owners. It's essentially a 30-day lease that automatically renews each month, unless the owner or tenant gives the other proper written notice (usually 30 days) to terminate the tenancy. Month-to-month rental agreements give you much more freedom than leases, because you can increase the rent or change other terms of the tenancy on 30 days' notice. They can also be easily modified for short-term rentals by converting the rent payment period from monthly to weekly or biweekly.

Of course, month-to-month rental agreements have their downsides:

⮕ Your tenants may be concerned about the possibility of changing rental rates or policies.

✔ Your tenants may worry about having to relocate on short notice, leaving you to wonder whether you're likely to have a tenant locked in for a certain lease term.

✔ Your tenants may not like moving and want to stay somewhere long-term.

Although the month-to-month rental agreement does allow your tenants the right to move at any time merely by giving a 30-day written notice, the reality is that most tenants don't like to move and will often stay long-term. The majority of tenants only move because of a job transfer or another significant reason, or because the rental owner doesn't properly maintain the property.

The wide variations in laws regarding notice requirements for changing or terminating month-to-month rental agreements clearly illustrate the importance of knowing your state and local landlord-tenant laws. Some states don't have any statutory requirements for giving notice; others mandate a time frame such as 10 or 15 days. The majority of states require 30 days' notice, but four states (California, Delaware, Georgia, and Hawaii) currently require property owners or managers to give more than a 30-day written notice when changing agreement terms or terminating a month-to-month tenancy. For example, in California, property owners with tenancies greater than one year must provide a 60-day termination notice, whereas the tenant only needs to provide 30 days' notice. Rent increases in California can also be subject to either 30 or 60 days' notice, depending on the amount and timing of the increase in conjunction with previous increases. Check out the accompanying CD for more information on state landlord-tenant laws and acquaint yourself with the laws in your particular area.

Get familiar with and respect the types of agreements typically offered in your local rental market. If competing properties are all offered on month-to-month rental agreements, you may find it difficult to attract plenty of well-qualified rental applicants if you're insisting on a 12-month lease.

Getting your contract in writing

No matter which method you use, never allow a tenant to take possession of your rental property without fully executing your written rental contract. Some tenants refuse to sign documents so they can claim they had a verbal agreement that's much different than the one you had in mind.

The CD contains both a standard Lease Agreement and a Month-to-Month Rental Agreement. Be sure to have an attorney specializing in landlord-tenant law review these documents and all other forms in this book or on the CD before using them in your area. In some states, special language must be included in the leases and rental agreements. For example, Florida has required language about radon, and many states have required information that must be given to tenants concerning access to a sexual offender or child molester database.

Standard lease forms are great, but they don't allow you to add your own clauses. However, you can modify the terms of your rental agreement fairly easily with the Addendum to Lease or Rental Agreement shown in Figure 6-1 and included on the CD. Perhaps you want to add the requirement that the tenant acknowledges receipt of the rules and regulations of the community or homeowners' association and is responsible for any fines or assessments resulting from his or her breach of the rules. This condition can be easily incorporated into the lease by using the Addendum. *Remember:* Be careful about adding additional clauses or language to your lease or rental agreement without seeking the advice of an attorney.

Although oral rental agreements of up to one year are binding, make sure all your leases or rental agreements are in writing, because so many issues surrounding those agreements involve monetary considerations. Memories fade and disputes can arise that are usually resolved in the tenant's favor should legal action be required and proof to the contrary can't be found in writing. Courts expect the property owner or manager to operate his or her rental housing business in a professional manner and to have clear documentation at all times.

Addendum to Lease or Rental Agreement

This Addendum to the lease or rental agreement entered into this _____ day of _____, 20 ____ between _____ (Tenant) and _____ (Owner) for the premises located at: _____ (Rental unit).

This Addendum shall be and is incorporated into the Lease or Rental Agreement dated the ____ day of _____, 20 ____ between Tenant and Owner.

Tenant and Owner agree to the following changes and/or additions to the Lease or Rental Agreement:

_____
_____
_____
_____
_____
_____
_____
_____

This Addendum to be effective as of _____, 20 ____.

Dated: _____   Dated: _____

OWNER: TENANT(S):
Property Name:_____

By_____   _____
    Owner or Agent for Owner

                                                              _____

                                                              _____

Figure 6-1: Addendum to Lease or Rental Agreement.

Oral agreements create the potential for charges of discriminatory treatment. Always put all terms and conditions in writing, even if you intend to have only a short-term agreement, or you know the tenant personally. Oral agreements often can't be substantiated and aren't always enforceable.

Seeking the best of a lease and a rental agreement

In my experience, the number one reason tenants insist on a lease is that the rent's locked in for a minimum period of time. But in most instances, especially in rental markets where rent increases aren't likely, owners want the flexibility and latitude afforded by the month-to-month rental agreement. If the tenant doesn't abide by the terms of the lease, she can simply terminate the rental agreement without having to prove the breach in a court of law.

Despite this discrepancy in desires, it's possible to achieve both goals. I strongly recommend using a month-to-month rental agreement in conjunction with a Rental Rate Guarantee Certificate (found on the accompanying CD). This method affords your tenant the benefits of a stable rental rate for a minimum period of time *without* restricting your ability to change other rules or even ask the tenant to leave in 30 days if problems arise.

If your local market conditions dictate a longer fixed rent term than what's indicated on this certificate, you can make an even more significant impression on a great prospective tenant by using a black marker or felt pen to clearly cross out "six months" and fill in a longer term. Be sure to print this certificate onto specialty paper to give it a valuable look.

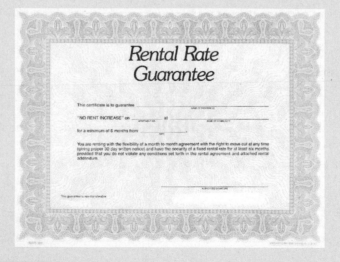

Chapter 7

FOR RENT: Generating Interest in Your Rental

. . . .

In This Chapter

▶ Planning your marketing strategy

▶ Figuring out the role advertising plays

▶ Making sure you don't violate any Fair Housing laws in your marketing efforts

▶ Finding the advertising tactics that best meet your needs

. . . .

More than almost any other single item, locating and renting to good-quality tenants makes your experience as a property manager enjoyable and profitable. But finding a good tenant can be a long process if you don't know how to do it. So in this chapter, I take you through the process from beginning to end — from creating a marketing plan (which helps you narrow your focus and set goals) to writing solid print ads to using the incredible resources of the Web to broaden your reach for prospective tenants. Start here if you just found out one of your units will be vacant in a month or if you've already had a vacancy for twice that long. It's never too late to start advertising effectively, and in this chapter, I give you all the tools you need to do exactly that.

Developing a Marketing Plan

A *marketing plan* can be anything from a formal written outline of your marketing strategies to some general marketing ideas you keep in mind as you try to find renters for your property. If you own only one or two properties, or if you own 20 or 30 rental units in multiple locations, you may not think you need a marketing plan. Developing one may seem like an unnecessary use of your time and energy. But the basic concepts of a marketing plan are important for *all* rental property owners, regardless of the number of rental units you own.

The key to success in owning and managing rental properties is to keep your rental units full with long-term paying tenants who treat your rental property and their neighbors respectfully. But first you need to determine the best way to attract and retain these highly desirable tenants. The following sections help you develop a marketing plan to do just that.

A good marketing plan consists of strategies for attracting prospective tenants and retaining your current tenants. Keeping your current tenants is so vital to your long-term success as a rental property owner that I devote Chapter 13 to figuring out how to make it happen.

Determining your target market

One of the first steps in developing a basic marketing plan is to determine the *target market* for your rental property. The target market consists of rental prospects who are most likely to decide that your rental unit meets their needs. Your target market can be relatively broad or fairly narrow, depending on the location, size, and features of your rental property. If you have multiple rental properties, you may find that each property has a different target market or that the target markets overlap.

The likelihood of finding responsible renters is often a numbers game. The more prospective renters you're able to attract, the greater your opportunity to carefully evaluate their qualifications and select the most qualified applicant.

In order to identify your target market, make sure you carefully evaluate your rental unit by looking at the following features that make it unique:

- **Location:** What are some of the benefits of your property's location? Is it located near employment, medical services, shopping, schools, or other important neighborhood or regional facilities? Paying attention to your property's location may provide you with a target market that includes employees of certain companies or people who need to live near certain local facilities.

- **Size:** Larger units tend to be more attractive to families or roommates, whereas studio units are more suitable to single renters or couples.

- **Amenities:** A property that allows pets and has a large yard typically appeals to pet owners and/or renters with children. If your rental property has storage space or a garage, some hobbyists may be particularly interested in what you have to offer.

When you compare the attributes of your rental property to the needs of all prospective renters in your rental market, you'll probably discover that certain renters may find your rental unit meets their needs more than others. You can use this knowledge to target specific audiences, but your rental efforts must never discourage, limit, or exclude *any* prospective renter from having an equal opportunity to qualify and rent from you.

If you don't attract and retain tenants, you can rest assured your competition will. You're competing with other owners and property managers for the best tenants, even if you only have a few rental units. In most rental markets, prospective tenants have many options, and the most responsible tenants are very selective, because the rental unit they choose will be their home sweet home.

Thinking about what your renters stand to gain from your property

After you've established who your most likely rental prospects are, you need to shift your focus to incorporating and implementing the concept of a target market into your rental marketing plans. This time is when I usually think of the WIFM concept. *WIFM* stands for *what's in it for me,* and this theory represents the thought processes of virtually all consumers (including your potential tenants) when evaluating a purchase decision. (I discovered this important idea at the national faculty training sessions of the Institute of Real Estate Management.) The WIFM concept reminds you that, in general, people are most interested in the benefits they personally receive in any given relationship or business transaction.

When it comes to marketing and advertising your rental property, the important concept of WIFM can help you see the rental decision process through the eyes of your prospective tenants, making your goal of finding long-term, stable tenants more attainable. Unfortunately, rental property owners and managers are human, and they often fail to critically evaluate the advantages and disadvantages of the product they're selling — their rental housing unit. As a rental property owner or manager, you have a competitive advantage if you understand the opportunities and challenges presented by your particular rental property and the specific rental unit that's available. You can also beat out the competition if you find ways to improve your property's weaknesses or narrow your marketing focus to those specific types of tenants who'll be attracted to your rental property.

Understanding the Importance of Good Advertising

Tenants rarely come looking for you. Your local newspaper may have a column for "Housing Wanted" (if so, lucky you!), or one of your current tenants may contact you inquiring on behalf of a friend who's looking for a rental unit. These scenarios are the exception, not the rule. The majority of your tenants come from the efforts you make to locate qualified rental prospects.

Advertising is how you let people know you have a vacant rental property available. If people don't know you have vacant units, then they can't rent them. When advertising is done well, the money you spend on it is extremely worthwhile. But when it's done poorly, advertising can be another black hole for your precious resources. Advertising is more of an art than a science at times, because what works for one particular rental property may not work for another. The next few sections give you the lowdown on the role of advertising in renting your property and what you can do to get your property rented.

Review the information from your marketing plan about the most marketable features and attributes of your rental property and present it to rental prospects in your advertising.

Eyeing the different approaches

Advertising for rental properties is no different than advertising for large superstar corporations with market research firms. The key to success in any type of advertising is determining how you can reach your target audience. In the case of rental property advertising, you want to reach that very small, select group of qualified renters who'll be interested in your rental property when it's available to rent.

Although you can creatively and effectively advertise your rental property in many different ways, two of the fundamental differences between the advertising methods at your disposal are the precision with which you reach your target audience and the ultimate cost involved.

Consider these two different approaches:

- ✔ **Rifle approach:** This type of advertising is very specific and targets a narrow group of prospective renters. The best rifle approaches to advertising are word-of-mouth referrals and "For Rent" property signage. But if you rely solely on these approaches to find tenants, you may end up with vacant properties much longer than you want.

- ✔ **Shotgun approach:** This type of advertising blankets the market with information to renters and nonrenters, qualified and unqualified alike. Although their circulation numbers have been declining, many of the major daily newspapers in most metropolitan markets can still deliver impressive readership numbers — especially on weekends. However, they can't tell you how many of those readers are actually reading the rental property ads or looking for an apartment on the specific day your ad runs.

Looking at your property through your prospective tenants' eyes

I once had a rental property located near a major university. The property had several vacancies in the 2-bedroom/1-bath units. Because I was wary of renting to large numbers of undergraduate students interested in only short-term leases for the school year, my marketing plan was to attract university faculty or graduate students whom I thought would have a roommate and be perfect for the 2-bedroom units on a year-round basis. Although many prospective tenants looked at the units, my actual rentals were very slow and the 2-bedroom vacancies remained unacceptable. Clearly, I was trying to define and force the rental market and prospective renters to adapt to my perception of their needs.

When it became obvious that my rental efforts weren't having much success, I began carefully reviewing the comments of prospective tenants. I found that my target faculty and graduate students preferred to live alone on a long-term lease so they could have a quiet place to work or study without roommates. With this new view of my prospective tenants' needs, I quickly realized I could market my 2-bedroom/1-bath units to my target market with a new approach.

Armed with this knowledge, I revised my marketing efforts by changing my advertising in the college newspaper to read, "1 bedroom plus den." This move led to an increased interest in the property as well as a greater occupancy percentage and more long-term leases. Just by changing the way the units were advertised, I found that I was able to reach my original target market of faculty and graduate students who wanted to live off campus.

Remember: While observing all Fair Housing laws, look at your rental property from the perspective of the most likely tenants. Then promote and accentuate the features of your rental property that are of greatest interest to that market. But always be careful not to discourage prospective tenants from renting your property.

Many methods of advertising your rental property fall into the shotgun category; very few methods fall into the rifle category. Regardless of which method you choose, remember that advertising is, for the most part, a numbers game. Reach enough readers and you're bound to find a few who're looking for a rental property like yours on a given day. In an ideal world, you pay only for the ability to reach that limited number of qualified renters in your area who're looking for a rental property just like yours and who want it the day it's ready to rent. Of course, this ideal isn't reality, but it gives you a goal to strive for when you evaluate the different ways you can advertise.

Knowing which approach gives you the most bang for your buck

Creating interest in your rental property used to be as simple as putting up a sign or placing an ad in the local newspaper. Although the methods of informing potential renters in your area about your rental property may still include these tried-and-true techniques, the success and broad reach of the Internet means you have many other excellent options to consider. The target market for your rental property has a lot to do with which method of advertising works best for your particular rental unit.

One of the best ways to determine your rental property's most desirable features for your target market is to use the *what's in it for me* (WIFM) concept and ask your current renters what they like about where they live. You may also figure out from talking with the qualified *rental traffic* (all the people who look at your property, not just those who agree to rent) what they find of interest in your rental property. The key is remembering your rental property has different features that appeal to different prospective renters. Over a period of time, you can determine certain common factors that most prospective tenants desire. Incorporate these selling points into your marketing and advertising efforts.

One size rarely fits all. When it comes to advertising a rental property, you need to employ a combination of both the shotgun and the rifle approach (described in the preceding section) to be successful. Clearly, both methods have advantages. Referrals and property signs often give you good exposure to renters in your local area, whereas newspaper and Internet ads have the ability to let people relocating to your area know about your rental property as well. Check out Table 7-1 for the pros and cons of various advertising tactics.

Table 7-1   Pros and Cons of Different Advertising Tactics

Approach	*Pros*	*Cons*
Community bulletin boards	Inexpensive	Narrow market
Direct mailings	Inexpensive	Low response rate
Flyers	Allow more details	Limited distribution
Internet	Ease of use; decreasing cost	Uncertain effectiveness for smaller properties
Local employers	Qualified prospects	Narrow market
Newspaper	Broad reach	Potentially expensive
Property signs	Very effective; inexpensive	Narrow market
Rental publications	Widely used by prospects	Expensive for small properties
Word-of-mouth	High credibility; inexpensive	Narrow market

Getting your property to rent itself

Before you spend money on advertising, take another look at your property with a critical eye or ask someone you know to critique it. You probably have a relative or friend with a sharp eye for finding little details that aren't quite right. So put these individuals to work helping you identify and correct those nagging items that detract from your rental unit. Even the best advertising campaign in the world can't overcome a poor physical appearance. Making sure your property looks good on the outside as well as the inside significantly improves your chances of finding just the right tenants.

The best advertisement for your rental unit is its curb appeal or exterior appearance. *Curb appeal* is the impression created when a prospective renter first sees the building from the street. The importance of a good first impression is well documented in business and clearly applies in rental housing, too. A property that has well-kept grounds with green grass, trimmed shrubs, beautiful flowers, and fresh paint is much more appealing to your prospects than a property that looks as though it's seen better days.

Curb appeal can be positive or negative. Positive curb appeal can be generated by having litter-free grounds, well-manicured landscaping and lawns, well-maintained building surfaces, a clearly identifiable address, and clean windows. Any property amenities (such as a swimming pool and parking lots) should also be clean and well maintained.

Properties with negative curb appeal can be rented, but finding a tenant often takes much longer. You may have fewer qualified prospects to choose from, or you may have to lower the rent. Because time is money in the rental housing business, the lost revenue caused by poor or negative curb appeal is often much greater than the cost to repair or replace deficient items. Besides, a well-maintained and sharp-looking property often attracts the type of tenant who treats your rental property with care and respect — and pays a higher rent.

Keep in mind that poor curb appeal is the direct result of poor management. There's no excuse for poor curb appeal, and no one benefits from it. You can never regain your lost revenue, and your property value ultimately declines.

Being Aware of Fair Housing Laws

Whether you're the owner of a single rental unit or a small- to medium-size multiple unit rental property, you're subject to Fair Housing laws whenever you advertise. These laws prohibit advertising that indicates any preference, limitation, or discrimination based upon race, color, ethnicity, religion, sex, familial status, or physical or mental disability. Consequently, any discrimination in rental housing advertising is illegal and can result in very severe penalties.

The 1988 Federal Fair Housing Amendments Act also states that rental property owners and managers can't

- Target certain groups by advertising in select media only
- Imply a preferred type of tenant through the use of discriminatory language, locations, logos, or models in advertising
- Refuse to show, negotiate for, or rent housing
- Refuse to supply rental information or accept applications
- Make housing unavailable
- Determine discriminatory applicant qualification or selection criteria
- Set different rental rates, terms, conditions, or privileges for the rental of a dwelling
- Direct people to certain parts of a community, building, or floor
- Provide different housing services, facilities, or maintenance
- Enforce restrictions or different provisions in rental contracts
- Falsely deny that housing is available for inspection or rental
- Persuade owners to rent or deny anyone access to or membership in a facility or service related to the rental of housing
- Post discriminatory notices or statements, or evict a tenant on the basis of protected class

Following Fair Housing regulations begins with advertising to all qualified prospects, continues throughout the screening and tenant selection process, and remains a key issue during the entire tenancy. If you plan to be in the rental housing business, make sure all your advertising, tenant screening, and selection, plus your management and maintenance policies, reflect both the intent and the letter of the law. Also, be aware that Fair Housing laws are constantly being redefined and expanded. Ignorance of the current law isn't an acceptable excuse if your policies and procedures are challenged.

Whenever you have the space available in your rental advertising, be sure to include the Equal Housing Opportunity logo. This logo may not be an option in certain ads, such as newspaper classifieds, but it should be included in all other advertising, like flyers, brochures, community bulletin boards, direct mailings, and Web ads. You can download the logo for free at HUD's Web site. Just go to www.hud.gov, type **Equal Housing Opportunity logo** into the Search bar in the upper right corner, and navigate to the logo homepage. Then download to your heart's content!

If you have any questions about discriminatory housing practices, contact the Department of Housing and Urban Development's Office of Fair Housing and Equal Opportunity, which oversees the creation and enforcement of federal Fair Housing laws. Find it online at www.hud.gov/offices/fheo or call 800-669-9777. (If you're hearing impaired, call the TTY line at 800-927-9275.)

All rental property owners must comply with federal (and often state and local) Fair Housing laws. Know the laws for your area and make sure you don't violate them, even inadvertently. Check with local landlord-tenant legal experts, your local apartment association, or the National Apartment Association (NAA) for more information about Fair Housing laws in your area. To contact the National Apartment Association, write to 4300 Wilson Boulevard, Suite 400, Alexandria, VA 22203, or call 703-518-6141. You can also visit the NAA online at www.naahq.org. Find the location of the NAA's Affiliated State or Local Association in your area by checking out the CD or by visiting the NAA Web site.

Analyzing Your Advertising Options

When it comes to advertising, you need to think like a tenant. Most rental property owners have been renters at some point in time. You may have personal experience as a renter looking for the right place to live. Perhaps you found the search frustrating, or maybe you developed a successful system for finding quality rental properties at a fair price. Your experience as a renter can be helpful as you place your ads.

Many rental property owners may remember that, when they began looking for their own rental years ago, they either drove around the area or sought out advertising specific to a particular geographic location. Although most prospective renters nowadays still practice these methods of researching their rental area of interest, many tenants have realized the advantages of online rental shopping. These renters ultimately go out to see each rental property that meets their needs — but not before narrowing their search to just a few properties via the Internet.

Most renters dislike moving to an unfamiliar area. Although moving is enough of a disruption in your daily routine, adapting to a completely different neighborhood is even worse. Thus, the majority of renters relocate within the same geographic area, unless they're faced with a major change in employment, school, or another significant factor that requires a distant relocation.

The following sections outline the different ways you can reach your prospective tenants, from word-of-mouth to the Internet. Use more than one form of advertising and find your new tenant even quicker.

Talking the talk: Word-of-mouth referrals

Often the best source of new tenants is a referral from one of your rental property's neighbors, one of your other tenants, or possibly even the tenant who just vacated your unit. Many times, referrals also come from coworkers or friends. Word-of-mouth is often your most effective and least expensive method of finding new tenants, especially if people like your rental property or where it's located.

In the long run, your best source for new tenant leads is other satisfied tenants. So keep your current tenants content and treat your departing tenants properly with timely accounting and return of any remaining security deposit balance. Tenants talk, and bad news travels faster than good news.

Many of your tenants or other people who own or rent in the area may have a family member or friend looking to relocate. Creating a sense of community in which your tenants have friends in the immediate area can lead to longer tenancies and lower tenant turnover. This combination translates directly into improved cash flow for you.

If your tenants or neighbors give you referrals, you may consider rewarding them or thanking them in a couple of different ways. Regardless of the kind of reward you give to referring tenants, the key is to make them feel appreciated for the referral. Here are some ways to reward your referring tenants:

- ✔ **Referral fee:** Typically, referral fees are $50 to $200 in cash or rent credit, and are only paid after the new tenant has paid the full security deposit and the first month's rent and has actually taken occupancy. In a soft rental market, where the supply of vacant apartments exceeds the demand, some owners and property managers may even offer referral fees of up to 50 percent of the first month's rent. The market conditions in your area dictate the appropriate level of referral fee for your rental property. You can also offer a higher amount for multiple referrals.

  Some property managers or owners give half of the referral fee upfront and the other half after the new tenant has lived in the unit for a specified number of months, in order to ensure the tenant plans to stay a while. In my experience, however, the referral fee is more effective if the full amount is paid immediately upon the new tenant taking occupancy. Although on some occasions the referred tenant doesn't stay for more than a month, this situation is usually nothing that the referring tenant can control, so he shouldn't be penalized.

As with all policies, be sure to offer your referral fees consistently and equally to all tenants to avoid any Fair Housing concerns.

✔ **Improvements or upgrades to the tenant's rental unit:** When cash or a rent credit is inappropriate (like in states where a real estate license is required for referrals), you can offer enhancements to the rental unit, such as installing a new ceiling fan, hanging new wallpaper, cleaning the carpet, or repainting the unit. Certain types of improvements may have a long life and stay with the rental unit after the current tenant leaves, making your rental unit more marketable and justifying a higher rental rate to a future tenant.

The psychological impact of giving an immediate reward for a referral can be very motivating. You can also adjust the amount of the referral fee for certain rental units that may be more difficult to rent or for certain times of the year when you have more trouble renting vacancies. For example, if you normally offer a $100 referral fee, you may want to consider offering a $200 fee for any referral given between Thanksgiving and the middle of January, because this time of year is often very slow for rental traffic. (No one likes to move during the holidays or in inclement weather!)

Have any rental applicant referred by word-of-mouth go through the same tenant application and thorough background check as any other applicant. Any deviation in your normal application and tenant selection process can support later allegations that you favor certain incoming tenants. Always screen every referral carefully, but be particularly careful if the referring tenant has a poor payment history or has created other problems. Just as a referral from an excellent tenant often leads to another excellent tenant, a referral from a problem tenant often leads to another problem tenant.

Showcasing your site: Property signs

A property sign is the first step in most rental property advertising programs, because it's one of the most economical ways to promote your vacancies. The use of a simple "For Rent" sign can be very effective and can generate great results for minimal cost. In certain areas with limited availability of rental units, a sign on the property is all you need to generate multiple qualified rental applicants. In the following sections, I explain how to determine if property signs are an appropriate tactic in your area and, if so, how to make them work for you.

Weighing the weight of a sign on your marketing efforts

An advantage of the property sign is that callers already know the area and have seen your building's exterior. Consequently, the attractiveness and aesthetic qualities or curb appeal of a rental property are essential. The rental property must look good from the street or else rental prospects won't even bother to stop and see the property's interior.

A disadvantage of signs is that they announce to the world that you have a vacant rental unit. In some areas, this proclamation can lead to vandalism or the unwanted use of your property for parties or criminal activity. For this reason, many rental property owners post rental signs while the unit is still occupied by the outgoing tenant and then remove the signs when the unit's empty. Depending on your tenant and her level of cooperation, you may also want to indicate on the sign that the current tenant shouldn't be disturbed.

Often the current tenant is very cooperative and glad to show the rental unit. But be sure to consider whether the current tenant is your best representative. Obviously, if she's leaving under difficult circumstances or her housekeeping or demeanor isn't the best, then you may be better off waiting and showing the rental unit after the tenant has vacated.

Making your signage stand out from the competition

If you choose to put up a property sign, do so as soon as you find out you have an upcoming vacancy, unless your property's curb appeal is poor or signs aren't allowed. Be sure to use rental signs that are in perfect condition, with large, crisp lettering that's easy to read. The condition of the sign reflects the image of your rental property — whether good or bad. A well-maintained sign provides a good first impression. A faded, worn out, or tacky sign is worse than no sign at all. Consider the following when developing and placing your signage:

- ✔ **Visibility:** Make sure your signage is clearly visible from the street and the lettering is large enough to read. Ideally, a two-sided sign should be placed perpendicular to the street so passing vehicles can view it more easily.

  Drive by your property from both directions at the usual speed of traffic and make sure your sign can be seen and understood easily. The main objective of property signs is to get the driver's attention with the words "For Rent," or a similar basic message. You want the driver to pull over and write down the details and the phone number.

- ✔ **Content:** Don't get carried away or put so much info on the sign that it can't easily be read from the street. Include the phone number and date of availability in a very clear spot. You can also add the number of bedrooms and bathrooms, as well as any special features. Clearly indicate your rental rate on the sign, because you need to make sure prospective tenants know what to expect. Including the rental rate can even pre-screen tenants who aren't financially qualified.

  On the other hand, when the exterior of the property doesn't do justice to the actual rental unit, you're better off *not* including the rental rate on your property sign. Because you're usually not there to show the rental unit at the time the prospective tenant sees the sign, she may think the rent is either too high or too low and immediately decide not to call. The value of some rental units can't be appreciated until a prospect has seen the unit's interior.

✔ **Location:** Place your signage in a prominent location. Property signs don't work as well if your rental unit isn't on a busy street or if your sign isn't easily noticeable from a main road. Property signs on dead-end streets or cul-de-sacs are still worthwhile, but don't expect the kind of response you'd get if your sign were on a major thoroughfare or arterial roadway.

If your property is on a side street that's relatively close to a major road, you may be able to obtain the cooperation of the owner of a nearby property with a high-visibility location, unless such signage placement is prohibited by local law. Approach the owner about the possibility of placing a rental sign for your property on his land — either on a temporary basis only when you have vacancies or on a more formal ongoing basis (with a formal contract drafted by an attorney, outlining rights and terms and a financial incentive for the owner). Typically, you can expect to pay the landowner $25 to $100 per month to put your sign on his property, depending on the size and location of the sign.

Any off-site rental sign should clearly indicate the location of your rental property. Make sure the property where you place your sign is comparable to your rental property in terms of curb appeal. A property that's vastly superior to yours can actually deter potential renters. Naturally, a property that has poor curb appeal discourages prospective renters from any further inquiry into your rental property, even if your property is in much better condition. As with all signs, first impressions are very important and leave a lasting image in the minds of your prospective renters.

Broadening your horizons: The Internet

The Internet is available to almost everyone, making this medium an exceptional source of prospective tenants for owners of medium to larger rental properties. But even for owners of small rental properties, the Internet can be a useful tool to augment the more conventional advertising methods discussed throughout this chapter. The next two sections break down how to make Web-based advertising work for you.

Where to advertise online

In the past, major online resources didn't cater to the small rental property owner. Now, many online advertisers have seen the success of Craig's List, a Web site that features free advertising in many major metro areas (unless you're a broker, then you have to pay), and have realized the significant number of potential advertisers they're missing. Prospective tenants want the option to search specifically for the larger, professionally managed apartment communities, as well as rental homes and condos or small rental properties, so most online rental property advertisers have expanded their listings to include all types.

The opportunities to promote your rental vacancy online have exploded over the past several years to boast a number of choices both locally and nationally. Although this list is dynamic with new firms and mergers among competitors, here are some of the more popular and successful online advertising venues:

- ✓ *Apartamentos Para Rentar:* www.pararentar.com
- ✓ *Apartment Guide:* www.apartmentguide.com
- ✓ *Apartments.com:* www.apartments.com
- ✓ *Craig's List:* www.craigslist.org
- ✓ *For Rent:* www.forrent.com
- ✓ *Rent.com:* www.rent.com
- ✓ *RentalHomesPlus:* www.rentalhomesplus.com

The Internet also allows you to establish your own Web page. You can post your marketing pieces on your site and refer potential tenants to the Web page address right in your advertising. That way, prospective renters can go to your site and gain additional information at their convenience. Moreover, when a prospective renter calls, you also have the option of referring him to the Web page for more information.

What to include in an online ad

The online rental info you can offer is unlimited. Of course, you need to make sure you get the basics out there before trying anything flashy:

- ✓ **General geographic location of the unit:** Prospects want to know whether your property is near the places they frequent the most or whether it's in a safe part of town. In many cities, the name of your neighborhood makes an immediate impression on your prospect, which can be good or bad for you depending upon the reputation of the particular neighborhood. So if the address may give a negative impression, leave it out.

- ✓ **Number of bedrooms and bathrooms:** This number is often a major determining factor for many renters. Always let prospects know what to expect from your property.

- ✓ **Major features or amenities:** Inquiring minds want to know what makes your rental property better than all the others in the area.

✔ **Monthly rent:** Listing your monthly rent in your ad lets prospective renters know your requirements right upfront. Most prospective renters are scanning through rental ads trying to eliminate the ones that aren't worth calling about. Generally, any ad that doesn't give the prospect enough information to determine his level of interest is immediately disqualified.

✔ **Telephone number and e-mail address where you can be reached:** If prospective tenants don't know how to reach you, then you definitely won't receive any inquiries about your unit.

✔ **Who pays for the utilities:** This bit of info can be a key factor for renters on tight budgets.

✔ **Whether the unit is furnished:** Some renters may not want to hassle with providing their own furniture; others may not want to use a recliner or dresser that's been around the block a few times.

✔ **Address of the property:** Include the address unless the rental unit doesn't have excellent curb appeal.

With a digital camera, you can place photos of your rental property online. If you have a wide-angle digital camera, you can even put interior photos online, which is very helpful if the property is currently occupied and you can't or don't want to bother the current tenant by showing the place. You can also provide floor plans and detailed directions.

If you're really computer savvy or know someone who is, you can provide a narrative soundtrack that augments your online info, or you can just include some music. Keep in mind though that music can be annoying to many Web site viewers. The last thing you want to do is run potential tenants off with your favorite Barry Manilow song, so either choose something more generic or give your prospects a muting option.

Reading all about it: Newspapers

Until recently, the most commonly used medium for advertising rental properties was newspaper classified ads. The Internet has since taken over as the best source for prospective tenants in many metropolitan areas, but local newspaper ads can still be very effective if you follow these basic advertising rules:

✔ Attract the reader's attention.

✔ Keep the reader's interest.

✔ Generate a desire to find out more about your property.

✔ Convince the reader to contact you for more information.

Important considerations when using newspaper advertising include where to advertise, the size of your newspaper ad, what to include in the ad, and the schedule on which your ad should run. I cover each of these issues in the following sections.

Which newspaper should you advertise in?

In most metropolitan areas, you have several newspapers to choose from for advertising your rental unit's availability. Typically, you have one major regional newspaper and one or more neighborhood newspapers as well. Local or neighborhood newspapers are often more reasonably priced and can reach the renters already in the area. Some local or neighborhood newspapers even offer free ads. So do you advertise in the local weekly throwaway or the regional major daily? Unfortunately, there's no right answer to this question. You really need to try each newspaper and see which one works best for a particular rental property.

The key to effective advertising isn't the overall number of calls you receive, but the number of dollars per qualified renter you spend on advertising. Effective advertising in most major metropolitan areas typically costs $20 to $50 per qualified prospect. So if your Sunday newspaper ad costs $100, you want to receive inquiries from two to five qualified prospects every time the ad runs. Of course, you can expect to receive additional inquiries from unqualified prospects, but you can measure the effectiveness of your ad by noting how *few* unqualified prospects call in response to it.

Many of the larger newspapers have online editions or relationships with Internet firms that specialize in advertising rental properties. For example, the *Chicago Tribune* partners with Apartments.com so it can offer you a print ad in its local newspaper and an online ad that can generate calls from around the nation.

How big should your newspaper ad be?

Newspapers typically offer two different types of rental housing ads: display and classified. Display ads are much more effective and visually eye-catching; they're also significantly more expensive and beyond the needs and budgets of most small-time rental property owners. Usually, only the owners or managers of large apartment buildings in your area use display ads on a regular basis.

Owners or property management companies with multiple properties in a certain geographic area also use display ads, because they're able to combine several of their rental properties into one large display ad, making the ad more cost-effective. If you're a small rental property owner, unless you have multiple properties with vacancies in the same general geographic area, use the classified rental housing advertising section of your newspaper.

Wondering how to make a less flashy classified ad stand out to prospective tenants? The trick is to develop a classified rental ad that's efficient but doesn't place a higher priority on low cost while sacrificing the ability to attract and keep a prospective renter's attention. Your rental ad needs to be easily readable. One of the best ways to achieve readability in an ad is through the use of *white space*. White space is the blank space that makes your ad stand out from the others, many of which are so crammed with information that readers instinctively skip them.

Consider yourself lucky if a prospective renter spends more than just a few seconds looking at your rental ad. If you can't attract and keep his attention in those brief seconds, he'll move on to the next ad. So when it comes to writing your ad, you want to provide as much information as possible, while also keeping the ad readable. But know that the overall size of the ad needs to be kept to a minimum, or you risk a major shock to your advertising budget.

Most renters actually prefer to rent from small-time rental property owners, which is why classified ads can be very effective. Classified ads need to be directed to a specific target market and should stress the particular advantages of a rental property from the tenant's point of view.

What should you include in your newspaper ad?

Effective newspaper ads (like the ones shown in Figure 7-1) provide the basic facts (see the earlier section on what to include in an Internet ad for more on these), plus a *hook,* which is a call to action that helps your rental ad stand out from the rest. The hook can be monetary, or it can be an improvement to the rental property — basically anything that makes your ad grab the prospect's attention. Offering a tenant the opportunity to select new tile floor covering in the kitchen or entryway or providing a ceiling fan as an extra bonus are both excellent hooks.

Even in tight rental markets, providing an incentive for the prospect to immediately call on your ad is smart. For example, you can offer to waive the fee for the tenant's credit report if the prospective renter calls the day the ad runs. The credit report typically costs you less than $20, but this kind of offer makes your ad much more interesting to most cost-conscious renters.

Figure 7-1:
Good newspaper ads like these can help you find the right tenant quickly.

#1 Rated Schools!

Hidden Valley executive home. 4 bedrooms, 3 baths, 2250 sq. ft., 3-car garage pool/spa, fenced yard, lush landscaping, a/c, washer/dryer, f/p, gardener incl, pets welcome. $1,995/mo. Avail. 7/1. 423 Sycamore Lane. 555-1212

Cherry Hills Close to Everything

Lg. 1 & 2 BR townhouse apts, on bus route. Walk to schools, stores, medical center. Tennis, pool, spa, no pets. Owner-paid utilities. Furnished units avail. From $575. Maple Grove Apts. 575 Watson Rd. Mention ad for free credit check. Daily 9-6. Call (800) 555-1212

Although leaving out some information saves you money in the cost of a classified ad, don't forget that incomplete information either leads to qualified prospects skipping over your ad or to many unqualified prospects calling and asking you every question under the sun.

Be careful with abbreviations in newspaper ads. Although abbreviating some words can stretch your advertising dollar without cutting into your message, the use of abbreviations often discourages tenants from reading your ad. If your ad can't be understood, it won't generate the phone calls you want. And if your ad doesn't generate phone calls, you've wasted your time and money. I recommend using basic abbreviations only if most rental property advertisers in your area commonly use them.

How often or on which days should your newspaper ad run?

Although the Saturday or Sunday editions of many major metro papers have the most rental ads, running your ad on these days can be quite expensive. Newspapers often have specials that encourage you to run your ad for longer periods of time, which gives you more exposure.

Be sure to change your ad weekly, at least. Tenants often skim ads for several weeks when they're beginning to look for a new rental unit. If they see the same ad for more than a week, they may assume your rental unit is undesirable. This advice is also true if you have many rental properties and run the same ad each week. Potential tenants may incorrectly think it's for the same unit every time.

To address or not to address

Opinions tend to differ about including a rental property's address in a newspaper ad, but I generally recommend including it. This information gives prospects the exact location of your property and helps them independently determine whether it's one they're interested in renting. The only situations in which you shouldn't indicate the address in the newspaper ad are when the curb appeal isn't up to your high standards or when the exterior appearance of the rental unit is deceptive and gives the impression that the unit is small or undesirable in light of the asking rent.

If you include directions with your address, make sure they're correct and easily under-standable. Ask someone who's not familiar with your rental property or the area to proof-read your ad to make sure the landmarks, cross streets, or directions provided make sense. If rental prospects can't find your property, you can safely assume they're not going to be interested in renting it. Although a more direct route to your rental property that goes past the local landfill may exist, have your prospects take the next freeway off-ramp and backtrack some-what to your property to avoid any unpleasant areas of town. This first impression can be very important. The advertising and presentation of your rental property is marketing, and when it's done properly, it'll make your job as a rental property owner much easier.

Some newspapers offer discounts if you run the same ad for consecutive days, but doing so can be expensive. Instead, run a larger ad on the primary rental housing advertising day and then run a reference ad the rest of the week to lower your overall cost. For example, if the Sunday edition of your local newspaper is the primary day for rental housing ads, place a large ad on that day. Then on Monday through Saturday, run a small, two-line ad that simply states, "Kensington — 2bd/2ba available soon. See last Sunday's ad."

When your ad first appears, be sure to check the newspaper yourself to confirm it's listed in the proper classification and is worded exactly the way you wrote it. Newspaper ad reps are very skilled at taking down complicated ads with abbreviations, but mistakes can and do occur. There's nothing worse than not receiving any phone calls because your ad was placed in the wrong classification or because the phone number was listed incorrectly.

Checking your ad for accuracy may be relatively simple if you regularly subscribe to the newspaper. However, if you don't subscribe to it, be sure to have your newspaper ad rep send you a *tear sheet,* a sample of the page on which your ad ran. If the newspaper makes a mistake in your ad, be sure to notify it at once and ask for a corrected ad to run at no charge.

Some newspapers offer special ads for guaranteed results. For example, if your rental property doesn't rent after your ad has run for a week, a paper may give you up to an additional week of ads for free. Check with your newspaper sales rep for planned special sections featuring rental housing articles and news features. These special sections are written with the renters in mind and can increase your ad visibility to prospective tenants.

If your rental unit is located near a military installation, be sure to run an ad in a military newspaper. The military also has housing referral offices at many bases, and all branches require transferees to register with the housing referral office. Contact this office with your information.

Papering the neighborhood: Flyers

Distributing and posting flyers informs the neighbors that you have a rental unit available, which can be helpful to them because they may know someone who wants to live close by. You can use flyers to direct people to more information (including maps and additional photographs) on a Web site. See the earlier section, "Broadening your horizons: The Internet," for the scoop on using the Net to advertise your property.

Flyers allow you a lot more space in which to describe your rental unit. You can go into detail and list many of the features that aren't cost-effective to list in a newspaper ad.

The cost to reproduce flyers is very nominal and can run about $5 for 500 black-and-white flyers on white paper stock. For an extra $5, consider printing your black-and-white flyer on colored paper. If you really want to stand out, you'll need to pay about $25 for 500 color flyers. The extra money is well worth it. Although keeping your costs low is always important for rental property owners, remember that you may be losing $20 to $40 each day your rental property sits vacant — and that's money you never get back again! So if you have a rental property that looks great with a four-color flyer, spend the extra $20 and generate those important rental leads today!

In the following sections, I explain how to create and distribute flyers for the maximum positive impact on your rental property.

Making high-tech flyers

With the wide availability of word processing programs, making great-looking rental flyers that contain all the pertinent info, plus a photo and a map, is very easy. Although the widely used word processing programs have everything you need to make basic flyers, I highly recommend you invest in basic desktop publishing software. Several great desktop publishing programs are available, but three of the easiest to use are *Microsoft Publisher, PrintMaster Gold,* and *Broderbund's PrintShop.* These programs have templates that simplify the process and provide you with the graphics and additional features to make your flyer look sharp.

Another invaluable tool for all rental property owners is a digital camera, which helps you prepare advertising that works! A high-quality photo can easily separate your rental property flyer from the others that may be circulating at any given time. Check out Figure 7-2 for a great example of a flyer that effectively uses photos to draw attention to a property.

Some people think a handwritten flyer actually has greater appeal and implies that the owner is a nonprofessional who has a rental unit at a below-market rental rate. This reasoning may be true, but I believe having a sharp, easy-to-read, typeset flyer with a high-quality photo and detailed map provides superior results.

Although your goal is to rent your property quickly, the reality is that you'll be marketing your rental unit over a couple of weeks. This guideline is particularly true if you're able to start your marketing during the current tenant's notice period. One of the problems with flyers (just like political placards) is that it's difficult to know which ones are current and which ones are stale. I recommend putting a date on your flyers and keeping them fresh. You should also consider having a series of flyers with a different look, each promoting a different open house. Include the monthly rent on your flyers so prospects can immediately determine whether your rental property is in their price range.

Executive Home for Rent

The top-rated Horizon school district and plenty of room! 4-bedroom, 3-bath executive home with over 2,250 square feet of living space and a 3-car garage. Master bedroom suite has over 500 square feet and large walk-in closet. Other bedrooms are oversized with large closets. Plus, a large home office with shelves. Large fenced backyard is perfect for children and pets. Pets are welcome! Separate fenced pool and spa. Lush, mature landscaping, air conditioning, full-size washer and dryer included. Fireplace in family room, formal dining room with bay window, upgraded appliances. Side-by-side refrigerator, double oven, range top, dishwasher, disposal, trash compactor, shutters, intercom, and CD stereo system throughout home, built-in bookcases and lots of storage. Available on 7/1. 423 Sycamore. $1,995 per month. First month's rent plus $2,000 security deposit will move you in!

Call 555-1212 today and mention this flyer for a free credit check.

Figure 7-2:
Flyers are a great way to attract attention to your property.

Distributing flyers

The key to success when it comes to flyers is distribution. Either pass out your flyers personally or consider hiring a reliable individual to distribute them door-to-door in the area where your rental unit is located. You can also have the flyers distributed to locations that current and prospective renters are likely to visit.

Make sure your flyers are never placed into the official U.S. mail receptacle, because doing so is illegal. If you're considering direct mail distribution, contact a firm that specializes in direct mail services.

Although it's often suggested that renters look for a new rental in the last two weeks of the month, I've noticed that in most areas you can always find renters on the market throughout the entire month. Begin distributing your flyers as soon as possible. Each week, distribute the latest version with the current info and dates so that they're fresh.

Flyers can be targeted to a specific geographic area and can be very effective in reaching good rental prospects. You can distribute flyers to local employers who often have housing referral offices or employee bulletin boards, or you can post them in the housing referral offices at local military installations and universities. Be sure to receive permission before posting your flyers or else they'll quickly disappear, and you'll have created enemies instead of allies who can help you fill your vacancies! Flyers, like all forms of advertising, are only as good as their distribution, so be sure to distribute them in the high-traffic areas where renters are most likely to see them.

Focusing on rental publications

Most major metropolitan areas have one or more rental publications that offer display advertising of rental properties. Following are two widely circulated rental pubs (both of which also have a presence on the Web):

- *For Rent* offers biweekly, full-color rental advertising for most major cities with 61 publications covering more than 190 markets. It offers $1/4$-, $1/2$-, and full-page ads, which are generally listed by geographic area. *For Rent* has a handy index that allows prospective tenants to search for certain features. This pub promotes the fact that its biweekly format allows owners and property managers to change ad content more often. *For Rent* also offers a Spanish language publication called *Apartamentos Para Rentar* in many areas of the country.

- *Apartment Guide* is available monthly with more than 90 editions for the major metropolitan areas in 39 states. Its page format is smaller than *For Rent,* and it says that its size is an advantage, because it's easier for rental prospects to carry and use. *Apartment Guide* offers full-color $1/2$- and full-page ads, and it categorizes the ads in sections that relate to certain geographic segments of a metro area.

Rental publications are primarily designed for the larger rental housing communities and are a cornerstone of these communities' marketing programs. Most rental publications offer smaller display ads designed for medium-size rental properties. However, unless your rental property has several vacancies at the same time, using a rental publication may not be cost-effective.

Strategic distribution equals success in all advertising. Rental publications demonstrate this truth clearly as they battle for positioning on the shelves of major grocery stores and convenience store chains. They race to get the best locations for their curbside racks and make sure that all the major employers and military bases have a good supply of their latest issues. In most major metropolitan areas, rental publications are a dominant source of rental traffic.

If you're thinking about advertising in a rental publication, take the time to determine which one has the best distribution in your area for your target market. For example, you may have determined that the local hospital and medical services facilities just a few blocks from your rental property are potentially a great source for rental prospects. If you find that only one rental publication is distributed on-site to employees, start evaluating it to see whether it can offer you advertising that meets your needs and is within your budget.

Creating chat: Community bulletin boards

Community bulletin boards can be very effective advertising avenues in certain small areas or college towns. Often the local self-serve laundries, pharmacies, hospitals, or grocery stores have bulletin boards where you can post information at no cost. You may find that you're limited to a 3-x-5 card, but you can tailor your posting to the people who'll be most interested in and attracted to your rental property. Post several identical cards so that interested prospects can simply take a card with them. This tactic also allows you to use the back side for more information, including a detailed map and directions to your rental property.

If your rental property has unique features, like a garage or large backyard, you may have some additional promotional opportunities. Carefully evaluate your rental property and determine its unique aspects and the specific target market most interested in these specific elements. For example, a rental property with a large yard appeals to renters with pets, so a listing on the bulletin boards found at the local pet store may reach that specific target market. Likewise, a rental property with a garage appeals to patrons of an auto supply or hardware store.

As with any ad in which the property address is clearly stated, a disadvantage to this advertising technique is that you may be promoting your possibly vacant rental unit to some people who may be more interested in having a party or stealing your appliances than renting the unit. One way to minimize this problem is to post on community bulletin boards while the unit is still occupied and clearly state that the rental property will be available at a future date. You should also consider indicating that the current tenant shouldn't be disturbed.

Going where the jobs are: Local employers

The local employers in your area are a great source for rental prospects. Employees of these companies most likely have stable jobs and are looking for long-term rentals. Many companies have employee assistance or housing referral offices that work with their employees to help them find reasonably priced housing. Most rental properties located in metropolitan areas are located near at least one major employer. As a sharp rental property owner, you may have already determined that the employees of certain major firms are part of your target rental market.

Likewise, the major firms in your area have a vested interest in their employees being able to find good-quality and affordable rental housing in close proximity to their location. Progressive employers are always looking for inexpensive ways to assist their employees and improve morale. To capitalize on this desire, you can offer all employees of companies that participate in your corporate referral program an incentive to rent at your property. This incentive can mean waiving the application fee, allowing the security deposit to be paid over the first 90 days, or even discounting the monthly rent.

Meandering through other tactics to try

If the other marketing tactics listed in this chapter don't appeal to you, you may find success through property brochures, direct mailings, leasing agencies, or broker referrals. Although most owners of small- to medium-size rental properties don't find these services advantageous, you may want to consider the following as part of your marketing plan:

- **Property brochure:** A property brochure isn't necessary for most small rental property owners. However, if you have a rental property with more than ten units, you should seriously consider developing a basic one. The benefit of a rental brochure is that the prospective tenant can take the information with her and easily share it with a coapplicant. I recommend a simple tri-fold brochure that can be printed on both sides of 8½-x-11-inch paper. With a basic word processing or desktop publishing program, you can easily create a customized brochure for your rental property. It should include a floor plan and an area map that highlights the key places for employment, shopping, schools, and transportation.

- **Direct mailings:** The key to success with direct mailing is to have a good flyer or brochure combined with a mailing list that reaches your target market. If you've already developed your flyer or brochure, using this same marketing piece in a direct mail advertising campaign is a natural next step. Of course, like all advertising, direct mail is only effective and cost efficient if you can get your specific marketing piece into the hands of a prospective renter for your rental property when he's looking for a place to rent. Use an outside direct mail firm for the most time- and cost-efficient handling of direct mail.

- **Leasing agencies:** *Leasing agencies,* or rental locator firms, often have working relationships with major corporations and relocation services and have excellent tenants looking for high-end rentals, usually in major metropolitan areas. Some offer their services for no charge to the renter and are compensated by the property manager when the prospect signs a rental contract. Other leasing agencies charge tenants for their service and are only compensated when they find a rental unit that meets the renter's needs.

  Tenants relocating to an area typically don't have the time to search for a rental property and want the leasing agency to handle matters for them. They also aren't often candidates for purchasing a home, because they're only staying for a specific assignment or because they want to rent in the area before making a purchase decision. You often encounter a trade-off with these renters: They're usually very well qualified, but they're not as likely to rent long-term. But the reality is that not all tenants stay for a long period of time anyway, and if you know that a certain tenant will only be with you for a set period (such as a one-year lease) you can adjust the rental rate to reflect this rental term.

✔ **Broker referrals:** Besides selling real estate, many real estate agents are also in the business of referring renters to property managers. Many of the calls real estate agents receive are from individuals relocating from other areas who contact an agent inquiring about a future home purchase. Although they may have long-range plans to purchase, they often rent while they become familiar with the area.

Real estate agents don't mind referring renters to an owner or property manager, because they know that today's renter may likely be tomorrow's home purchaser. Real estate agents are also very interested in referral fees from owners or property managers. Although the referral fee may be a small amount of money compared to the potential commission the real estate agent can earn on a sales transaction, agents are willing to be patient and accept a small reward in the short run, knowing that the big money will be earned down the road.

Check the laws in your state, because some states prohibit the payment of commissions to anyone other than real estate licensees.

Chapter 8

Handling Prospects When They Come A'Calling

In virtually all instances, the landlord-tenant relationship begins with the initial rental inquiry. This inquiry can be a traditional phone call or an electronic communication, such as an e-mail. If you successfully master the proper handling and prequalifying of rental prospects and become skilled at selling prospects on your rental property, you'll find owning and managing rental property to be a profitable and pleasant experience.

Armed with the info in this chapter — and some practice — you can become adept at quickly screening prospects and convincing the qualified ones that you have the rental unit they want. In this chapter, I explain the importance of preparing for communication with prospects, using the phone and electronic media as effective marketing tools, and handling prospects all the way from the first contact to the rental showing.

Understanding Why First Impressions Are Important

Most everyone knows the old adage that you only get one chance to make a first impression. That's sage advice for most businesses, but it's especially true when people are looking to make such an important decision as which rental property will be their next home.

As a rental property owner and manager, it's easy to see that the correlation between successfully attracting and securing long-term tenancies with qualified tenants can be influenced by that first impression. Your rental property isn't the only one on the market, and your rental prospects have many options, so remember that you're competing for the best renters with everyone in your area who has a vacant rental property. You need to make a positive impression to stand out from your competition.

Do you ever go to a restaurant and feel like everything is so chaotic that you're never going to get the best service or meal? You probably leave and don't even give the restaurant a chance to surprise you with a good experience. This behavior is human nature, and the same concepts are true in rental housing. Everyone's looking for the piece of mind and reassurance that they're making the right decision about something very important — where to live.

Being organized and professional from your very first contact through the entire rental process instills confidence in your prospective tenants that you have the ability to meet their housing needs. A professional attitude and presentation also let them know that if problems occur with the rental property, you're likely to address their concerns promptly.

The way you advertise or promote your rental property is part of making the first impression in rental housing, but the chief impression-making factor is that very first time you have contact on the phone or in person with prospective tenants. One way to make a positive first impression is to be organized and professional, and using technology helps you achieve this state by being easy to reach and responsive to rental inquiries. Nothing turns off rental prospects faster than an inability to get in touch with you. Even the most diligent prospects only call once or twice before giving up and moving on to other rental properties. Of course, if you answer prospects' calls promptly on your cellphone but are distracted because you're at the grocery store or your child's soccer game, don't expect to secure a rental property showing.

You also need to be prepared with all the information necessary to present your rental property in the best light to your prospects and to answer their questions. Remember each of your contacts with every rental prospect by taking good notes on tracking forms so that you can recall which features prospects like most about your rental property, as well as any concerns they express. People like to feel important and that they're really being listened to. Being able to recall prior conversations or correspondence can be a powerful tool in ultimately closing the sale and securing a rental contract.

After your prospects are willing to make a commitment and apply for your rental property, you need to have your rental application and rental contract, with all addendums, ready for their review. A disorganized rental property owner doesn't get a second chance. Being prepared allows you to focus your energies on evaluating each rental prospect to find the most qualified applicant who'll be your next long-term tenant.

Making the Most of Technology

The goal of advertising your rental property is to reach the pool of qualified prospective renters who're currently looking for a new rental property and inform them that you have one that may be desirable to them. When your advertising and promotion generate interest in your rental unit, expect a ringing telephone or a flooded e-mail inbox. Many of the online advertising options explained in Chapter 7 allow prospective renters to immediately contact you via e-mail, or even submit their rental applications electronically. This e-submission is a great feature for rental prospects from out of town, but it most certainly doesn't replace the benefits of the traditional telephone.

If your rental prospects can't reach you, they immediately lose any potential interest in you and your rental property. So you need to make sure you can be easily reached by prospective tenants — and current tenants — at all times.

Advances in telecommunications technology have made rental housing management much more efficient today than it was even just a few years ago. However, with so many options, you need to know how to use communications technology effectively and efficiently. In the following sections, I cover the basics of doing just that. Later in this chapter, I share more specific information on using the telephone in particular — because the telephone is still your main link to your prospective tenants.

Using your phone to your advantage

The telephone is traditionally your primary way of staying in touch with prospective tenants. Although the recent trend toward electronic communication, especially for an initial inquiry in response to an online ad, has made keeping in contact with prospective tenants much easier, the telephone is still your main communications tool.

Because of the limitations and misunderstandings that can occur with short, cryptic e-mail messages, the telephone will forever have an important role. Its direct, instantaneous form of two-way communication still offers the best means of communicating when a prospect is considering your rental property. Prospective tenants have many questions that can't be simply answered via e-mail. Likewise, you want to be able to ask them important questions to make sure they meet your rental criteria.

Using the telephone isn't just about putting your phone number in your classified ad or on your rental sign. Today's telephone comes with all kinds of special features that can help you manage your property more effectively. I cover these features in the following sections.

The telephone's importance in property management

Some property management books recommend never placing your phone number in your rental ads. Instead, they suggest you market your rental property strictly by advertising and by holding open houses where interested tenants can all view the property at the same time. The concept of an open house is very good, but not until you've prequalified the rental prospects.

In my experience, omitting your phone number from your ads eliminates a large number of qualified rental prospects who don't have the time for or interest in racing all over town to attend open houses at rental properties that may not even meet their needs. Your most qualified rental prospects are often people who value their time very highly. Consequently, the Internet and e-mail can be useful for your prospects by helping them solidify their interests in your property. But that's where the usefulness of electronic communication ends. Ultimately, your prospects need the type of specific information they can only receive through a phone call.

You may think that you're able to conserve some of your *own* time by not accepting phone calls, but you'll have a different opinion after your first three-hour open house where only a couple of unqualified rental prospects show up. Or, even worse, you may not get any prospects at all. Now *that* is a counterproductive afternoon!

Spend the necessary time talking with your prospects. Don't just take the quick and easy route offered by electronic communication. E-mail plays a prominent role in communications during a tenancy, but the telephone is your primary business tool when dealing with prospective tenants.

Call forwarding

If you're advertising a property for rent and the only contact number you provide is your home number, for example, but you work outside of the home all day, you won't be available to take the incoming calls you need. If this is the case, you may want to consider using a cellphone where you *can* be reached during the day, or where you can at least be immediately notified of incoming calls.

If you don't want to list your work phone number in your advertisements, you can still use your personal cellphone, your home phone (if you have one!), a separate rental property phone line you've established, or a pager by enabling the *call forwarding* feature available through most phone companies. With call forwarding, you simply set up your phone to forward all calls to another phone number — basically any number where you can be reached. And you can turn the call forwarding off when you return home.

Caller ID

Another great phone feature you can use to increase your time management efficiency and lower your costs is caller ID. When you pay for caller ID through your telephone company, your phone displays the phone number of the party placing the incoming call. Caller ID is a great way to get the return phone number of your prospective renters in case they neglect to leave their contact information for you. But remember that when you call your prospective tenants, they likely also have caller ID, so be sure to call from a phone number you don't mind revealing to them. If you don't have a number like that, you can enable the feature that blocks your phone number from being displayed.

Why do you need to have the telephone number of a prospective renter? Having a prospective renter's number allows you to call her back and follow up with more information or get an update on her rental status. You can also use her number to reconfirm an appointment to see the rental property. And later, during the applicant screening process, you can use the phone number as a cross-check when she submits her rental application to be sure she's giving you the correct information.

Voice mail

As a rental property manager, you should have a voice mail system or an answering machine that can handle calls 24 hours a day. The outgoing voice mail or answering machine message should provide callers with your digital pager number or your cell number in case of emergencies. (This info is important for current tenants, and it lets prospective tenants know you'll be there for them if they need you.) You can also record detailed info about the rental property for your prospective tenants; this tactic helps tenants prescreen themselves. They won't waste their time — and yours — if the property you describe is out of their price range.

Most renters spend quite a bit of time browsing online and looking through various rental housing publications. They typically make many phone calls before beginning the process of physically looking at a rental property. As a result, you want to make the information-gathering process as smooth and efficient for your prospective renters as possible because you're competing for the top qualified prospects.

Renters are interested in knowing certain basic information up front, allowing them to narrow their choices. Many renters may not even be aware of this fact, but subconsciously they're often looking for any excuse to eliminate your rental property from their list. To keep their attention, you need to develop an information system for your rental property that makes renters feel relaxed, comfortable, and interested in actually seeing your property.

In addition to your name, include on your voice mail system or answering machine recording the following information about your rental:

- ✔ Location, including directions
- ✔ Number of bedrooms and square footage
- ✔ Rental rate and security deposit requirements

- Qualifying information, such as minimum income and whether pets, excluding service animals, are accepted
- Property features and benefits

Provide callers with a Web site address, if you have one. On the site, you can include photos, plus the preceding information, and allow prospective tenants to prequalify if they're interested in learning more about your rental property or seeing it in person.

As with all forms of communication, if your rental prospects leave messages, you need to be able to return their calls promptly, or you can expect to lose them to your competitor. The most qualified renters are the ones who get snapped up first, and these are the tenants you really want. Don't let them get away!

Knowing which devices you need

In addition to the telephone, standard equipment for many rental property owners includes the following:

- **Cellphone:** A cellphone is virtually mandatory for rental property owners. It's an invaluable way to instantly keep in touch with your current tenants, as well as prospects responding to your ads or signs.
- **Personal digital assistant (PDA):** When you're planning appointments with contractors or prospective tenants, you can immediately record your schedule on your PDA, which is a small, hand-held computer. With many PDAs, you can download and synchronize your mobile database with your main PC back at your home or office.
- **Digital pager:** A digital pager allows callers to leave either a voice message or an alphanumeric message entered through the caller's telephone or typed into a computer keyboard.

Preparing for Rental Inquiry Phone Calls

Whether you were ever a Boy Scout or not, you're probably familiar with the Boy Scout motto, "Be prepared." This motto applies to the management of rental properties in many ways, but one of the most important is being prepared when the telephone rings. If you handle rental inquiry calls properly, you not only make your life much easier but you also get the tenants you want. In the following sections, I discuss the importance of preparation and the steps necessary to make sure you're ready when the phone rings.

Working vacation

I enjoy traveling and need to stay in touch with my property management office, so I always like to have the latest high-tech communication devices. Throughout the more than 30 years I've been in property management, I've seen a tremendous evolution in technology — from the large brick that was my first cellphone in the late '80s to the latest-generation BlackBerry I now use. Today's PDA combines e-mail, cellphone, contact database, calendar, and Internet all in one — something unheard of in the early days of cellphones.

The ability to be contacted anytime, anywhere has its pros and cons, but I feel this increasing communication technology allows me to travel more than in the past and still be available as necessary to properly manage my rental properties and interact with my tenants, vendors, and staff. Now I can travel to most parts of the globe and still receive e-mail messages and phone calls on my trusty PDA. Of course, this accessibility can lead to unpleasant surprises

on your bill when you receive a nonemergency call from your tenant that was billed at $8 per minute. Be sure to check with your communications provider about roaming charges before traveling and find out the most effective way to communicate from your anticipated travel destination.

An alternative to having your own PDA is making use of Internet cafés or the expanding number of locations offering wireless Internet access. With these sites, you can find inexpensive Internet connections virtually anywhere in the world and access Web-based e-mail through a number of services (such as Google Gmail, Microsoft Hotmail, and Yahoo! Mail).

Trust me when I say that the advances in technology are extremely important for efficiency in owning and managing your rental property, and allowing you the opportunity to find some rest and relaxation. Isn't technology at work a wonderful thing?

Even though it may not be the first information your prospects receive about your rental property with so much now found online, the rental inquiry phone call is a critical step that marks the beginning of the rental process. The purpose of this call is to get to the next step: showing the rental unit. Master the art of the rental inquiry phone call, and most of the time you can set appointments with only qualified rental prospects. And that's the name of the game in property management!

Having the basic tools ready

Advertising costs you a lot of time and money, so you don't want to begin looking around for a pen, some paper, and your notes about the rental property when the phone starts ringing. You also don't want to take phone calls on your PDA or cellphone if you're not in a position to devote the proper attention to the caller. Rental prospects can tell the difference between the prepared rental property owner and the one who doesn't seem to have a clue. They also form an impression of how you're likely to handle any problems they may encounter with the rental unit in the future. Most sharp renters (and those are the ones you want) are looking for a professional, businesslike rental property owner, so that's what you need to be.

The benefits of a professional phone technique are one of the main reasons I recommend having a separate business location for the management of your rental properties. This location doesn't have to be a separate office in a commercial setting; it can simply be the corner of your bedroom or an office at home. Consider having a separate phone line as well. A separate phone line allows you to quickly distinguish between personal phone calls and rental business phone calls. It also helps you treat each kind of call accordingly.

You can find many great resources on the proper use of the telephone in business, and the very first advice these resources typically offer is how to answer the phone and what to say. But when it comes to the management and leasing of rental properties, I believe that success with the telephone begins with being prepared to use it *before* your first rental inquiry call. In the next few sections, I cover some basic tools to have on hand before your first call comes in.

Telephone Prospect Card

A *Telephone Prospect Card,* like the one shown in Figure 8-1 and available on the CD, can assist you in gathering information from your rental prospect such as his name and telephone number, how he heard about your rental unit, and his particular needs in terms of move-in date, size, and other requirements. This information can help determine whether your rental property meets the needs and wants of your prospect.

You can also use the Telephone Prospect Card whether you show your rental property to a prospective tenant or need to follow up on qualified rental prospects. Finally, you can use it to track the rental advertising source, which allows you to make sure you continue using only the advertising media that pay off.

One of the primary reasons to track your rental calls is so you can clearly see the results generated by your advertising. The number of generated phone calls isn't the most important factor in determining which advertising medium is the best for your rental property. The key factor is the number of *qualified* rental prospects. In an ideal situation, getting just a few calls from very qualified prospects is much better than getting a number of rental inquiries from unqualified prospects (which is just a waste of your valuable time).

Telephone Prospect Card

Name _____ Date of initial call _____ Time _____
Current address _____ City _____ Daytime Phone _____
Rental location (s) discussed _____ Cell Phone _____
How did you learn about our rental? _____ Email _____
When will you need to move in? _____ How many bedrooms do you need? _____
How many people will be living in the rental? _____ What size rental are you looking for?

_____
What would you feel comfortable with as a monthly rent? _____
What do you do for a living? _____ Do you work? ___ Where? _____
Where are you living now? _____ How much parking space do you require? _____
What is wrong, if anything, with your current rental property? _____
Why are you looking to move at this time? _____
What types and sizes of pets do you have? _____
When can you drive by the rental property? _____ Mentioned Equal Opportunity Housing? ____
What other rental properties have you seen/plan to see? _____
Notes

_____
_____
_____

Follow-up

Rental location(s) shown _____ Date shown _____ Quoted rent/deposit
_____
What did prospect like best about the rental unit? _____
Objections, if any? _____
Most important features and amenities to prospect _____
Rental application completed? _____ Holding deposit? _____ Date to follow-up _____

Figure 8-1:
Telephone
Prospect
Card.

Property Knowledge Sheet

One of the best ways to answer your rental prospect's questions is to prepare a *Property Knowledge Sheet* for each rental property location. This document (check out Figure 8-2 and the CD for an example) contains all the basic information about your rental property, such as the size and type of the unit and the unit number if it's in a multi-unit property. Additionally, it should include the unit's age, type of construction, and other important details.

A thorough Property Knowledge Sheet also contains important information about the local neighborhood and general area. Just like the Chamber of Commerce or Visitor's Information Bureau, you want to be able to answer questions about your locale. Rental prospects are very interested in knowing about employment centers, transportation, local schools, childcare, places of worship, shopping, and medical facilities. You can really make a positive impression on your rental prospect if you can tell him where the nearest dry cleaner or Thai restaurant is located.

You want to have all this vital info from your Property Knowledge Sheet at your fingertips so that you can be ready to answer your rental prospect's questions. The more you know about your property and the surrounding area, the more easily you can find some important reasons for your rental prospect to select your unit over the competition's.

Property Knowledge Sheet

Property Information

Rental address _____Unit # _____ City _____ Zip code _____
Office hours (if any) _____ Square footage of unit(s) _____
Unit mix—Studios _____ 1 Bedroom _____ 2 Bedroom/1 Bath _____ 2Bedroom/2 Bath _____Other _____
Rent—Studios _____ 1 Bedroom _____ 2 Bedroom/1 Bath _____ 2Bedroom/2 Bath _____ Other _____
Application fee _____ Security deposit _____ Concessions _____
Age of rental _____ Type of construction _____ Parking _____
Recreational facilities _____ Laundry _____ Pets _____
Storage _____ Utilities (who pays?) _____AC/Heat _____
Appliances _____ Floor coverings _____
Special features/comments _____
_____
_____

Community Information

School district _____ Grade school _____ Jr. high _____
High school _____ Jr. college _____College _____
Trade school _____ Pre-school (s) _____
Childcare _____ Places of worship _____
Police station _____ Fire station _____ Ambulance _____
Electric _____ Natural gas _____ Telephone _____ Cable _____
Water _____ Sewer _____ Library _____ Post office _____
Hospital _____ Pharmacy _____ Vet _____
Other medical facilities _____
Nearby employment centers _____
Transportation _____
Groceries _____Other shopping _____
Local services _____
Restaurants _____
Comments _____

Rental Market Information

Rental competitors/rental rates/concessions _____
_____
_____
Our competitive advantages _____
_____
Our disadvantages _____
_____

Figure 8-2:
Property
Knowledge
Sheet.

This document can definitely give you the edge over your competition. Particularly with the advent of the Internet, many rental prospects know more about the area and the other rental options than you may know without doing your research. Because you often find yourself competing with large multi-family rental properties, you need to be prepared to answer important questions about both your rental property and the surrounding area. Often immediately knowing a detail, such as whether your prospect can find a certain childcare center locally, can make the difference between success and failure.

The time you spend answering all the rental prospect's questions can provide you with useful information. Be sure to take good notes about the source of your rental traffic and any important comments made by each prospect. Then you can improve your results by incorporating this feedback into your future advertising for that same rental property.

For example, maybe prospective renters indicated that they had trouble finding the property. This is a common problem and one that successful rental property owners know is a serious challenge to success. If your prospective renters can't find the property, it's unlikely they'll rent from you. *Remember:* You're competing with a lot of other rental property owners, and the best-qualified renters don't need to make extraordinary efforts to find a good-quality rental property.

Comparison Chart

You may find that you have a vacancy in a *soft rental market,* when the rental market has a lot of rental units available for prospective tenants. Using a *Comparison Chart* can be very helpful in this kind of market, especially if your rental property has distinct advantages over others nearby. A Comparison Chart is really a marketing strategy commonly used by the owners and managers of large rental properties, but the concepts of it are very helpful for the owners of small- to medium-size rental properties too.

A Comparison Chart can

✔ **Provide very useful information to prospective renters who may not be aware that they're comparing apples to oranges when looking at various rental properties:** Comparison Charts are particularly useful to rental property owners who may have a competitive advantage that's not readily apparent to uninformed prospects. For example, your rent may be slightly higher than the rent charged by your competition, but you may pay for the utilities, whereas tenants at your competition's apartments have to pay for their own utilities. This scenario is becoming a more likely example with the advent of many larger properties installing submetering for utilities, as discussed in Chapter 17.

✔ **Level the playing field and allow you to inform your prospective tenants of the actual costs of your rental housing (and the competition's housing):** Another potential advantage of your property may be that your rental property has reserved parking, but the competition requires its tenants to scramble for parking spaces on the street. Or maybe your rental units have much more square footage than the competition. Many older properties are more aesthetically pleasing, with mature landscaping and beautiful shade trees. These are all factors that may not be readily apparent to prospective renters, and they can give you the upper hand over the competition.

Check out Figure 8-3 for an example of a Comparison Chart highlighting four properties. In looking at the chart, prospective tenants can see that although Sunshine Apartments has the lowest rent, when you add in the $75 monthly utilities, its tenants are paying $25 more per month than they'd pay at Maple Grove, and they don't get the reserved parking, on-site maintenance, lush landscaping, or free credit check. In this situation, Maple Grove Apartments is the obvious better deal for tenants, even though the monthly rent is higher. Madison Avenue Apartments and Camelot Townhomes, however, when the utilities are taken into consideration, both level out at $700 per month. But Madison Avenue Apartments has better landscaping and Camelot Townhomes has reserved parking. In this situation, tenants would need to decide which of these perks is more important. The key point: By providing an honest Comparison Chart, you're saving your prospective tenants legwork and highlighting the advantages of your apartment over others. The CD has a blank template you can use when making your own comparisons.

Comparison Chart

Property	Rent	Owner Paid Water and Heating	Tenant Paid Water and Heating (with estimated costs)	Reserved Parking	Onsite Maintenance	Lush Landscaping	Free Credit Check
Sunshine Apartments	$600	No	Yes ($75/month)	No	No	No	No
Madison Avenue Apartments	$625	No	Yes ($75/month)	No	No	Yes	No
Maple Grove Apartments	$650	Yes	No	Yes	Yes	Yes	Yes
Camelot Townhomes	$700	Yes	No	Yes	No	No	No

Figure 8-3: Use a Comparison Chart to highlight your property's competitive advantages.

Answering the phone

As your key marketing tool, when your rental phone line rings, you need to stop what you're doing. Take a deep breath and even close your eyes briefly so you can be focused on the call. Be sure to answer the telephone no later than the third ring; rental prospects generally have a list of calls they plan to make, so they're rarely patient. If you don't answer in the first few rings, they'll begin dialing the next phone number on their list and probably won't take the time to call you again.

Because positive first impressions are always very important, remember that the goal of your initial contact is to project a friendly, helpful, and professional image. These two pointers can help:

✔ **Have a smile on your face and speak clearly.** This is one phone technique that really does make a difference. Your positive attitude and enthusiasm can make a very important first impression. Even if you're not in the best of spirits at the moment the phone rings, don't sound rushed or hurried. You don't want your rental prospects to feel that they're imposing upon you.

   If you sound disorganized and hesitant on the phone, the prospects will likely feel that you're incompetent and not the type of rental property owner whom they can trust and count on if they have a problem or need a repair. However, if you come across in your initial contact with the rental prospects as polite, knowledgeable, organized, and confident, they'll respect your skills as a rental management professional. Prospects will see that you treat the rental of your property as a business, not a casual hobby.

✔ **Control your atmosphere to maintain a professional image.** If you run your rental management business from your home and your rental prospect calls and hears children screaming in the background or other distracting noises, you'll be making a very unprofessional impression. Controlling your environment can be especially challenging with the advent of cellphones, which are great for improving your availability, but often you may not be in a location where it's conducive or safe (if you're driving) to take phone calls. In these situations, let the call go to voice mail and call the prospect back at your earliest convenience.

As with any business, you may find that a rental inquiry call comes in when you're right in the middle of another situation that can't wait. Or you may think that if you're not prepared, it may actually be better to let your voice mail system or answering machine take a message. I suggest you still answer the call right away and give your caller the choice to be placed on hold, or let her know you can call her right back if she prefers. The majority of rental prospects aren't willing to leave a message, and you lose an opportunity to speak with them personally as a result. Asking the caller if she can call back in a few minutes is a very risky strategy and one that I don't recommend, because the odds of her calling back are remote. Remember that the majority of calls made by rental prospects to small rental property owners require leaving a phone message, and you can really stand out by answering your calls personally.

If you're fortunate enough to have an exciting and chaotic home life, then you need to take steps to make sure your rental inquiry calls can be distinguished from general household calls. For a nominal charge, many local phone service providers offer a call waiting service that gives you two phone lines for one phone number. You can also have two separate lines or a service with distinctive ring tones so you can distinguish your personal calls from your rental business calls. If other members of your household pick up the phone during your conversation, you can easily get distracted, so let the people in your household know how to tell the difference between regular calls and business calls.

Providing and obtaining the basic info

Rental inquiry calls are different from most of the calls you normally make in business. I often find that both parties are simultaneously trying to eliminate the other as a prospect and trying to get as much information without giving out any information of their own. But this approach isn't the best because you're trying to make a telephone presentation of your rental property. Instead, you need to have a give-and-take approach whereby you share the basic information that prospects need while making an initial assessment of their qualifications.

The beginning of many rental inquiry phone calls follows a standard pattern. Being aware of this pattern and knowing where your parts fit in can help you successfully make a professional and positive impression in the first few minutes. Here's how to handle the start of a basic rental inquiry call:

1. **Let the caller inquire about your rental unit and whether it's still available.**

   The caller also typically asks about the size of the unit and the rental rate. Always answer his questions directly.

2. **Greet the caller by name to develop a rapport.**

   People generally like to be called by their names. If the caller hasn't already volunteered this information, you may want to mention your first name again and ask for his name. If he gives you his name, be sure to ask his permission for you to call him by his first name. Often a prospect provides his last name only. In this case, show respect by using an appropriate title when you call him by his surname.

3. **Ask the prospect for a return phone number.**

   If you have caller ID, verify that you have the best telephone number to reach him.

After you get past the initial formalities, begin prompting the caller for the information you both need. For example, you need to know when the rental prospect is looking to move in, how many people (and the number, type, and size of pets, if applicable) will be residing in the rental, and what he's comfortable with as a monthly rent.

An easy way to remember the basic questions you need to ask are to remember the six *w*'s — who, what, where, when, why, and how (yes, I realize that's technically five *w*'s and one *h,* but you get the point). Remember to use your notes and provide the prospect with immediate feedback so that he knows you're interested in his call and are really trying to determine whether your rental unit meets his needs.

Following are some examples of questions you can use to help determine your prospect's requirements:

- When will you need to move in?
- How many bedrooms do you need?
- How many people will be living in the rental?
- What size rental are you looking for?
- What would you feel comfortable with as a monthly rent?
- How long do you intend to live at this property?
- How much parking space do you require?
- Where are you living now?
- What's wrong, if anything, with your current rental property?
- Why are you looking to move at this time?
- Where do you work?
- What do you do for a living?
- What's your gross monthly income?
- What types of pets do you have?
- When can you drive by the rental property?
- How can I reach you by phone?

This basic initial give-and-take of questions and answers quickly determines whether the rental inquiry conversation is worth continuing. The prospect is looking for the opportunity to eliminate your rental property if you don't have what he needs at the time that he needs it. Likewise, if it appears that your rental property may be a good fit, you still need to explore whether the rental prospect is qualified and meets your screening requirements.

Take notes on this Q & A so you can summarize each prospect's needs and wants during the initial phone conversation. Bring these notes to rental showings so that you know what aspects of your rental property are of greatest interest to each renter. Plus, people really appreciate the fact that you care enough to write down what they're looking for instead of just trying to sell them what you have to offer.

Selling the prospect on your property

A key element to success in selling a rental prospect on your rental property is your ability to build rapport with the prospect on the phone. As you answer her initial questions, take the opportunity to highlight some of the desirable or unique aspects of your rental. For example, if the prospective renter asks about the number and size of the bedrooms, you can reply, "The house has four bedrooms, each with a separate closet. The master bedroom is very large at 15 feet by 12 feet. Will this accommodate your needs?" Or maybe you can say, "The backyard is completely fenced and is very large. Do you have any pets?"

Your goal is to turn the features of your property into benefits for the prospective tenant. You need to do this by painting a picture of the property in her mind. For example, if your rental property has a swimming pool, you can talk about how nice it is to come home at the end of the day and enjoy a refreshing swim or a favorite beverage.

The entire goal of the rental inquiry call is to get the qualified prospect to see your rental property. You can't — and shouldn't — sign a rental contract on the phone!

As the rental property owner, you definitely want to tell your story about what a great rental property you have. Then, when you've grabbed the prospect's interest and determined that your rental unit meets her needs, you want to begin evaluating her qualifications in light of your requirements and needs. If you fail to hook the prospect, you never get to the next step. Of course, you want to be sure to prescreen the prospective tenant during this initial phone call so that you invest your valuable time only with qualified rental prospects.

Prequalifying the prospect over the phone

After you pass a prospective tenant's basic needs requirements, begin asking your own qualifying questions. You need to confirm when the prospect is looking to move, the size of the rental he requires, and his financial qualifications. Both you and the rental prospect need this basic information, and together you go through this ceremonial dance with the goal being to advance to the next stage — the showing of the rental unit.

But how do you know what to ask or what to watch for when prequalifying prospects? Read on for some guidance to help you find the best tenants for your rental property.

Holding a balanced conversation

Think of a rental inquiry call as a tennis match, with each side taking a turn presenting questions and gathering the answers needed to make a decision. Ultimately, both parties must agree that the rental unit may meet the needs of the rental prospect, and the rental prospect may meet the owner's established tenant screening criteria. This is the first step toward achieving your main objective of the call — getting a commitment from the prospect to make an appointment to see your rental unit in person.

Using open-ended questions and a pleasant manner, obtain basic information from the tenant to determine whether he meets your rental requirements. You should also determine whether you're speaking with the actual decision-maker, or whether this prospect is really gathering information for someone else. Although you always prefer to deal with the primary decision-maker from the initial contact on, you need to be skillful in prequalifying all the prospects without alienating your immediate contact, because the immediate contact is likely to have considerable influence on the decision as well.

The answers to your basic questions determine whether you need to go on to the next step. For example, if currently you have only a studio apartment available, there may be no need to show this particular rental unit if the prospect says six applicants are planning to live in it. However, some Fair Housing advocates may claim you're discriminating on the basis of familial status or national origin if you don't show a studio apartment to applicants with six people proposed to live in the unit.

Your goal during the rental inquiry call is to give the caller enough information about your rental property that he can determine whether he has enough genuine interest in the property to make it worth his time to actually see it in person. Likewise, you want to obtain enough information about the rental prospect and his coapplicants to prequalify them for your rental property. Matchmaking is a two-way street.

Naturally, not every rental property is a match for every rental prospect. Your goal isn't to convince *all* the callers that they must see your rental property in person. Showing a rental unit to an uninterested or unqualified rental prospect is one of the most frustrating experiences in a rental management career. Showing property to qualified and interested prospects, however, is one of the most important factors in successful time management for rental property owners and managers.

Eyeing the qualities of desirable (and not-so-desirable) tenants

You can begin the process of prequalifying your rental prospect over the phone instead of having to wait until you meet him when he tours the rental property or completes a rental application. By chatting with a prospective tenant during the very first phone call, you're starting the all-important screening process right then and there.

Determining you're on the phone with a qualified rental prospect is easy if you know what to look for. Of course, you need to verify this information before making a commitment to rent your property, but if you can say, "Yes" to each of these statements, chances are you have a qualified prospect:

- ✔ You have a rental of the appropriate type and size available when the prospect needs it.

- ✔ The prospect meets your minimum qualifying standards for income, credit history, and employment history.

- ✔ The prospect has enough cash to pay the entire first month's rent and the full security deposit.

- ✔ At least one of the prospects is of legal age to sign the rental contract.

- ✔ The proposed number of occupants is appropriate for the particular rental unit.

- ✔ The prospect has an acceptable rental history and is vacating current living accommodations legally.

- ✔ The prospect is willing to live within your property guidelines, such as no pets or no smoking allowed in the rental unit.

When trying to identify qualified prospects, you also want to watch out for less desirable prospects who don't meet your rental criteria. During the rental inquiry call, make sure you're not dealing with a *professional tenant,* someone who jumps from rental to rental frequently. Even during your first call, certain red flags may indicate you're dealing with someone who's trouble. A potential sign is a rental prospect who asks very few questions about the property and the area but is very interested in things like your move-in special or whether you can lower the rent or allow the security deposit to be paid over the first three months.

If a prospect seems interested in moving in too quickly, watch out. Although you may think that finding someone who wants to move in right away is great for cutting your rent loss, this eagerness may be an indication that the person has something to hide or is just looking for his next landlord victim. Maybe his current landlord just served him with eviction papers for nonpayment, and he needs to leave before he's physically removed. It can take up to two or three months for eviction actions to become a matter of public record, so your prospective tenant's credit report may turn up clean initially even if he's had recent problems. Be wary of subtle hints of trouble as early as the first phone call.

Handling phone objections

If you've done your homework, you're well prepared and know the answers to questions about the rental unit and the surrounding area. Being prepared for rental inquiries includes anticipating reasonable objections and providing honest answers to your prospect tenant. Your goal isn't to convince the unqualified prospect who truly isn't a good match for your property to waste everyone's valuable time and come see the rental unit when it obviously won't work. Instead, your goal is to anticipate some of the more common objections and have info ready that allows you and the prospect to determine whether the mutual interest is high enough to warrant going to the next step — showing the unit.

I once managed a rental property with a centralized location, but it was also right under the flight path of a major airport. The ideal location near major employment and recreational centers made our property very desirable, but the proximity to the airport was quite obvious, and it was well-known that many rental properties in the area had significant problems with noise. Logically, almost all our rental prospects who visited the property raised this concern, but even many of the callers brought up the noise because they were familiar with the area. What they didn't know was that when the property was built, the architects had designed the rental units with special double-pane soundproof windows and extra insulation so that interior noise wasn't a problem. Knowing the perception of rental properties in the area, we incorporated the soundproofing features right up front in our phone rental presentation.

You may hear the complaint or concern that your older, 20-unit rental property doesn't have individual washers and dryers in every unit, as found in competitive properties in your area. Instead, your property features a centralized laundry room with new washers and dryers and a large folding table for tenants' convenience. Anticipating that some prospects are looking for individual washers and dryers and will raise an objection when you don't have this feature means you're prepared. You know that the competitors also have smaller units with less storage, because the washer/dryer takes up important closet and storage space. You also know that your competitor's tenants have to pay for the water, whereas you pay for the water usage at your property. These are important facts that you can politely mention to the prospect over the phone. When showing the rental unit to a prospect, you can provide her with the Comparison Chart covered earlier in this chapter.

Converting phone calls to rental showings

If your initial phone conversation goes well, the prospect will want to tour your rental property. You've already invested a lot of time and energy into the rental inquiry call, so this is the moment of truth when you find out whether your prospect is really interested in your rental. Maybe he's just gathering information for a future move, or maybe he's checking out similar rental properties to determine if the rent increase he just received from his current landlord is justified.

You've answered a lot of questions, taken careful notes highlighting the prospect's needs and wants, and built up a rapport. You wouldn't have invested this much time in a prospect unless you felt that your rental met his needs and that he was very likely to pass your tenant screening criteria. So now isn't the time to become passive and tell him to call you back if he's interested. Nor is it the time to sheepishly suggest, "Stop by the open house this weekend, if you're in the neighborhood."

You need to be assertive and come right out and ask him to visit your rental property so you can personally show him your rental unit. If the prospect shows any signs of hesitating, you need to directly ask him if something's wrong. Your prospective tenant may then admit that he's just filed bankruptcy or that he plans to use your rental property for an iguana farm. Asking questions is one of your best tools; be sure to do it.

The rental prospect may indicate that he's interested in the rental property based on your conversation, but he wants to drive by it before actually making an appointment for a rental showing. This caveat is fine and can be another useful tool in maximizing your efficiency as a rental property owner. Two scenarios can happen if the prospect wants to do a drive-by before scheduling a rental showing:

- He calls back and asks for an appointment, or asks for the time of your next open house, and you can rest assured he'll show up.
- He drives by the property and finds that it's not suitable for him.

In both cases, allowing the prospect drive-by is a positive step. In the former case, the prospect isn't presold on the area and curb appeal of your rental property alone; in the latter, the prospect doesn't waste your time scheduling a personal tour.

Many rental management advisors suggest you improve your efficiency by allowing prospective tenants to tour your rental property on their own. These advisors suggest giving prospects the combination to a lockbox at the rental property or allowing them to drop by and pick up a key. These advisors usually recommend that you ask for a $25 cash deposit or that you hold a prospect's driver's license as an incentive to return the key. Be extremely careful in this kind of situation, because you may find that a prospective tenant has stripped the appliances or severely damaged the property while inside. Or worse, a prospect may decide your rental property's perfect and just move right in!

Many prospects make a rental showing appointment only to drive by the property a few minutes before the actual appointment and then skip the appointment if they don't like what they see. Another common scenario is one in which the prospect has already decided that your rental isn't going to be his next home, no matter how great the interior and how competitively you price the rental. But he feels guilty and doesn't want to skip out on you, so he shows up for the appointment and goes through the motions of looking at everything for close to an hour. Just imagine how many hours are wasted because your prospect may have taken the opportunity to gauge the neighborhood and curb appeal of the rental property before meeting for a scheduled rental showing.

Planning Ahead for Open Houses and Walk-Throughs

One of the most time-consuming aspects of owning and managing rental property is the time spent filling vacancies. And the biggest time trap for most owners who don't have a system already in place is the rental showing. If you were to schedule a separate appointment with every interested rental prospect, you'd be making trips back and forth to the property constantly. Unless you live or work very close to your rental property, you can quickly find that you're spending hours showing the rental to one prospect after another. That's why having a strategy for showing your rental — whether you plan to have an open house or set up individual appointments — is the best way to go. The next few sections can help you formulate that strategy.

Holding an open house

Because your time is valuable and you have many qualified prospects interested in seeing your rental property, you may want to consider holding an *open house*. An open house allows you to efficiently show the rental property to several interested rental prospects within a couple of hours. A successful landlord doesn't make a dozen trips to show property to a dozen different rental prospects. Open houses are also beneficial because having multiple prospects viewing the property can create a sense of urgency and competition, which often generates multiple applicants for your rental property.

One of the other benefits to holding an open house is that many rental prospects feel more comfortable touring a rental property with other prospects around. These folks may be concerned about meeting someone they don't know in a vacant rental property. And you, too, should be very concerned about your own personal safety for the same reasons. Holding an open house can eliminate, or at least reduce, any safety concerns you — and your prospects — may have.

Creating a sense of urgency

When you ask your prospect to come out and see your rental property, you may get a non-committal response or an excuse that she can't make it no matter how many different appointment times you offer over the next week. Of course, the most popular excuse you can expect to hear is that she's just begun calling, and your rental ad is the first one she called on. This statement may be true, so you need to be polite and patient. But if you're truly her first call, then it's likely she called you first for a reason — your advertising made your rental sound like her best option. So patience can be a virtue, as long as you're not *too* patient.

Be honest, but don't hesitate to let the prospect know you already have or will soon be receiving many more rental inquiry calls. Let her know that it's your intent to sign a rental contract with the most qualified rental prospect but that you also process the rental applications in the order in which they're received. So if you have two or more qualified applicants, you may lean toward the first qualified rental prospect who submitted an application. This knowledge creates a sense of urgency for the caller.

If you anticipate receiving interest in your rental property from multiple callers, set up one or two open houses so you can show the rental property to several interested prospects in just a couple of hours instead of making multiple trips. In tight rental markets, this method often creates a competitive or even auction-like environment, in which one prospect doesn't want to lose out to another. There's nothing like a little competition to instill a call to action in potential renters!

Select a time for your open house that's convenient for you and most working people (preferably during daylight hours). For example, an open house on Saturday from 11 a.m. to 2 p.m. usually gives rental prospects a good opportunity to see your rental property at a convenient time for them, while saving you from having to make multiple trips. In the summer months, a weekday afternoon from 4 p.m. to 7 p.m. may be a good option. Combining a weekday afternoon open house with one on the weekend can also be very effective. That way, virtually all prospects can fit the rental showing into their busy schedules.

An open house promoted strictly in a newspaper ad isn't a good idea, because you may end up with many unqualified renters walking through your property. But an open house where you invite all qualified prospects whom you've spoken with in response to your ad is a good way to efficiently lease your rental and create that sense of urgency and competition among prospective tenants.

Scheduling individual appointments

If you're in a depressed rental market or find that you need to fill a vacancy during the holidays, you may not be able to generate enough interest from prospects to schedule an open house for multiple renters. In this case, you need to be prepared to show your rental unit in the evenings and on weekends, because that's often when prospects are available. Of course, you can still try to consolidate your appointments to a certain time frame, but don't push this scheduling too far. Asking prospects to conform to your calendar may turn them off.

If you have to schedule individual appointments to show your property, be sure you have the phone numbers for your prospects. Almost everyone has a cellphone these days, so call each person to verify the rental showing before making a special trip to the property. By calling, you're also reassuring the prospect that you'll be there and won't be delayed.

Crime is a concern in virtually all parts of the U.S. Making an appointment to show a stranger your rental property can be an opportunity for someone criminally inclined. Be alert and take reasonable steps to protect yourself. If you ever have an uneasy feeling about a prospective tenant, decline the rental showing rather than risk personal injury. Limit your rental showings to daylight hours and bring someone with you, if at all possible. If you'd prefer, tell your rental prospect to meet you outside, right in front of the property or at another public location, and require a picture ID before showing the unit. You can then use your cellphone to call a family member or friend and tell that person the name and driver's license number of your rental prospect. If you want, have someone call you on your cellphone to check in throughout the showing. Of course, if you ever feel uncomfortable, be polite yet firm, end the rental tour, and leave immediately. Don't ever put yourself in a dangerous situation!

Providing directions to the property

When you have a commitment from the rental prospect to come to the property for an open house or rental showing, make sure you can provide clear and easy-to-follow directions from anywhere in your area. Many Internet sites can provide your prospect with personalized directions from her location to your rental property. Because many of your prospects likely have Internet access, the need to provide directions to your property may not seem to be a priority.

However, giving directions may not be quite as simple and unimportant as you may think. Often the online directions don't offer the most scenic or time-efficient path to your rental property. You always want to offer your own directions, or at least suggest a route that approaches your rental property from a certain direction.

Carefully consider the best route for your rental prospect. Take into consideration the traffic conditions she faces at the time of the open house or appointment. Think about which route presents the neighborhood in the best light. You want the route to be direct, but don't hesitate to have the prospective tenant come in from a different direction if doing so provides her with important information, such as the great shopping, schools, or other benefits of the area near your rental property.

Chapter 9

Strutting Your Property's Stuff: Making Your Property Stick Out

. . . .

In This Chapter

▶ Making a good first impression on prospective tenants

▶ Signing up high-quality tenants for your rental property

▶ Knowing how to give tenants the scoop on the environment and safety of your property

. . . .

To successfully rent your property, you need to show prospective renters why yours is better than all the others on the market. After you take the steps to prepare your property (see Chapter 5) and market it (check out Chapter 7), it's time to let prospective renters see what you have — and entice them to sign on the dotted line in the process.

In this chapter, I cover the proper way to show a rental unit, handle objections (which are really a sign of interest by your prospective tenants), and close the deal. I also make sure you're aware of important governmentally required disclosures that all rental property owners or managers must share with their tenants.

Showing Your Rental Unit

When your rental prospects arrive, you want to make a good first impression before you even open the door to your rental unit. Be sure to greet your prospects with a smile and introduce yourself. Ask for their names and shake their hands. Refer to the notes you made on the telephone prospect card during your initial phone conversation to let them know you remember speaking with them (flip back to Chapter 8 for tips on how to conduct this conversation). This thoughtfulness gives prospective tenants a good feeling that you're not just going through the standard rental spiel.

Listen to any questions or concerns that may have come up since you spoke on the phone. Ask your prospective tenants whether they found your directions accurate and easy to use. Also, ask whether they have any other needs that they're looking for in a rental property that haven't already been discussed.

Don't just let your prospects wander through the rental unit by themselves. (Of course, this general rule is particularly true if you're showing an occupied rental unit.) Listen carefully to your prospects and anyone accompanying them as you informally guide the party through the rental unit. Pay close attention to the features your prospective tenants indicate are of particular interest or any comments they make during the walk-through. But be careful not to come across as too pushy or overselling because this behavior turns off a lot of qualified prospects who dislike pressure-selling techniques. For more information on preparing your rental for walk-throughs, see Chapter 5.

No matter whether you're showing a vacant rental or an occupied rental, the next two sections focus on what you need to do to get your property rented.

Showing a vacant rental

If you're showing a vacant rental, act more like a tour consultant than a tour guide during the unit tour. Don't be too controlling; instead, let the prospects view the rental in the manner that suits them. Some prospects go right to a certain room, which gives you a clue about the importance they place on that aspect of the property. Of course, if the prospects hesitate or are reluctant to tour on their own, you can casually guide them through the rental property yourself.

There are as many different ways to show a rental unit as there are rental property owners. Remember the information provided by each prospect and customize the tour by beginning with the feature or room you feel has the most interest for him. Don't head straight to *your* favorite feature. When in doubt, start with the kitchen, then transition to the living areas and the bedrooms.

Keep the following pointers in mind when showing a vacant rental:

> ✔ **Encourage your rental prospects to see the entire rental property.** Don't overlook any garage or storage areas and the exterior grounds or yard, if applicable. You want to be sure prospective tenants have an opportunity to observe the conditions of all portions of the rental property and ask any questions. Doing so minimizes future claims that you discriminated against a prospect by selectively showing your rental property.

✔ **Listen and observe the body language and facial expressions of your prospects while they walk through the property.** When you begin showing the interior of your rental, avoid making obvious statements such as, "This is the living room" or, "Here's the bathroom!" You don't need to oversell if your prospective tenants seem pleased, but you should feel free to point out the benefits of your rental property. (Take in prospects' reactions and comments; then chime in with something along the lines of, "It sounds like this neutral-colored carpet will go great with your living room furniture" or, "The view of the sunsets from the kitchen is so relaxing.")

✔ **Have a tape measure with you.** Vacant rental units look smaller than occupied ones, so a tape measure can assist your prospects in immediately determining that their bedroom set will fit in the master suite. If your prospects express concerns that their furniture won't fit in your rental, consider this strategy: Set up a partially or fully furnished model rental unit to demonstrate what furniture will fit inside. Although this tactic may not be feasible for most single-family home or condominium rental units, it can work quite well for medium to larger apartment properties that regularly have vacant units or have a market for furnished rentals. Smaller rental properties can use a *vignette,* which is a rental unit that has been decorated with towels, books, and knickknacks to give the unit personality. Sometimes you can even close the sale by offering to give new renters these small items.

If you're holding an open house, you can quickly find yourself dealing with multiple prospects who all seem to have better timing than a synchronized swimming team. Do your best to courteously greet and speak with each prospect individually. At the very least, cover the basic information and get the first prospects started on the property tour before beginning to work with the next prospects. Be sure to communicate clearly that you'll answer all questions and treat all prospects openly and fairly to avoid any allegations of favoritism or discrimination.

Showing an occupied rental

If you're showing an occupied rental unit, be sure to consider the inherent advantages and disadvantages. On the plus side, your current tenant can be a real asset if she's friendly and cooperative and takes care of the property, because prospective tenants may want to ask her questions about her living experience at your property. But not all tenants take the same level of care with your rental property or want to help you re-rent it when they're getting ready to move.

Always keep these tips in mind when showing an occupied rental unit:

- **Consider your current tenant's attitude.** If she's being evicted, isn't leaving on good terms, or has an antagonistic attitude for any reason, don't show the rental unit until the property is vacated. Your tenant's cooperation will be required, but you may be able to complete your rent-ready preparation work and any rental unit upgrades at this time as well. This strategy also works if your current tenant hasn't taken good care of your property's grounds or landscaping, or if her furnishings may be objectionable to some prospective tenants.

- **Know your local laws regarding showing occupied units.** In most states, if the tenant is at the end of her lease or has given a notice to vacate, the rental property owner is specifically allowed to enter the rental property in order to show the unit to a prospective tenant. Of course, you must comply with state laws, which require you to give your current tenant advance written notice of entry prior to showing the unit. She may agree to waive the notice requirement, but make sure you have this agreement in writing.

- **Work with your tenant to coordinate scheduling.** Do your best to cooperate with the current tenant when scheduling mutually convenient times to show the rental. Be sure to respect her privacy and avoid excessive intrusions into her life. To ensure the cooperation of your tenant, you may even want to offer her a small bonus after she vacates, as a part of her security deposit disposition.

- **Try to get copies of recent utility bills from your current tenant.** Having current bills on hand is helpful if your prospective renters have any questions about utility costs. Prices for electricity, natural gas, water and sewer, and trash service are becoming significant items in the budgets of many renters. You don't want your new tenant to be financially unable to handle the typical monthly utility costs of your unit, because this difficulty may impact her ability to pay your rent. If your rental property has "green" or energy-efficient features or appliances, you may be able to use low utility costs as a marketing tool.

Although the current tenant may legally be required to allow you and your prospects to enter the rental unit for a showing, she doesn't have to make any effort to ensure the property is clean and neat. Nor is she required to help you in your efforts to impress the prospect. Keep this fact in mind when deciding whether you want to show your rental unit while it's still occupied.

Taking the First Steps to Get the Renter Interested

Although some rental units may rent themselves, the reality is your success as a property manager may be directly enhanced if you become skilled in properly presenting the best features of your rental unit. You should use the meeting with your prospective tenant to evaluate whether the rental unit will be a good fit for the tenant.

This section walks you through the steps of prequalifying your tenant, handling objections, and closing the sale with a completed rental application. I also cover the advantages of priority waiting lists and holding deposits.

Prequalifying your prospect during the rental showing

While you're touring the rental, prequalify the prospective tenant for your unit by verifying the information he provided during your initial phone conversation. Refer to your notes and confirm his desired move-in date and employment, the number of occupants, the rental rate, and other important information. Also, make sure the prospective tenant is aware of your rental policies and any limitations on pets or other important issues.

You don't want to be abrupt or refuse to let the rental applicant begin looking at the property until he answers numerous questions. However, verifying the basics upfront can save a lot of time if there's a misunderstanding or if the prospect's needs have changed.

If you don't take the time to review the information a prospect provided to you on the phone, as well as your rental terms and expectations, you may find some the prospect glossed over certain problems or indicated your rental policies were just fine when really they weren't. Of course, this individual's strategy is to wait until you think you've successfully rented the unit and are just about to sign on the proverbial dotted line when he springs the truth on you. Maybe his dying aunt has suddenly asked him to care for her 200-pound Doberman or his paycheck was delayed and he can only pay your security deposit in installments. You don't need these surprises, so confirm all the basics sooner rather than later!

Resolving your prospect's objections

Almost every rental prospect expresses some concerns or reservations about some physical aspects of the rental property, the area, your rental rate, or other terms. No rental property exactly meets the needs of each prospective tenant, so don't be caught off guard when you inevitably run into objections.

Objections come in many forms. Some are a test to see whether you'll lower the rent or make some improvements to the rental property. Others are sincere issues that are generally more tangible and specific in nature.

If you've been listening carefully to the prospect and taking notes, then you can anticipate and handle some objections before she even brings them up. In many instances, objections can actually present an opportunity to reassure your prospect that your rental property meets her needs.

If the prospect raises a question and you don't know the answer, make a note and promise to get back to her as soon as possible. Avoid the temptation to give an immediate answer that may not be right. Why? Because some rental prospects ask questions they already know the answers to just to test your sincerity. Most objections can be overcome if you discuss them openly with the prospective tenant and provide honest feedback. Giving the prospect a response and attempting to answer positively is important.

Convincing your prospect

After you qualify the prospect, you need to convince him that you have the best rental unit available. Renters want more than just a place to live. They want to feel they can communicate with you if a problem arises. They also appreciate when someone shows an interest in their lives. And by showing an interest, you're clearly setting yourself apart from other property managers. I believe prospects accept rental units that aren't exactly what they're looking for if they have positive feelings about the rental property owners or managers.

I realized how important the property manager can be to renters when I transferred a popular manager from one property to another very early in my property management career. Ginny had been our on-site manager at a 300-unit rental property for nearly five years before we gave her a promotion to a 400-unit rental community a few miles away. I was shocked when more than 50 of Ginny's current residents decided to give notice and move with her to the larger property (despite the higher rents and hotter summers at that location).

I've never seen a rental unit that can rent itself; *you* need to make the difference. No matter how closely your rental unit meets the stated needs and wants of your prospects, they often hesitate and doubt their own judgment. You don't need to be pushy, but you should be prepared to actively convince prospective tenants that your rental property is right for them.

The best way to avoid problem tenants who pay late, damage your property, or disrupt the neighbors is not to rent to them in the first place. Screening your next tenant begins with the very first phone call. Tell the prospect you'll run his credit report and call his references. Don't waste your time convincing prospects who don't seem to fit your criteria for a high-quality tenant.

Inviting your prospect to sign on

When you've convinced your prospect that your unit is the right one for her, it's time to close the sale. This is one area where many rental property owners and managers suddenly get cold feet. They can do a great job handling the initial telephone inquiry, preparing and showing the rental property, and even resolving objections, but when it comes down to asking the prospect to commit — they become shy and freeze.

Your goal is to receive a rental commitment from the prospect by having her complete your rental application and pay any pre-move-in screening fee, her first month's rent, and a full security deposit on the spot. Of course, you still need to thoroughly screen the prospect and confirm she meets your rental criteria before asking her to sign a rental contract.

If despite your best efforts, the prospect is still undecided, make sure she gives you a holding deposit. Remind her that you may make a deal with the very next prospect, and she'll be out of luck. Of course, if you have a lot of demand for your rental units, you should develop a priority waiting list, which is covered later in this chapter.

Having your prospect complete a rental application

You need to offer every interested prospect the opportunity to complete a written rental application for two important reasons:

- ✔ **You want to have all the information so you can begin the screening process and select the best tenant for your rental property by using objective criteria and your rental requirements.** The rental application is the key document you use to verify information and conduct your entire tenant screening procedure. I cover tenant screening in more detail in Chapter 10.

- ✔ **You want to avoid having prospects accuse you of discriminating against them by not permitting them to fill out the rental application.** Don't prejudge an applicant. The prospect may have already volunteered enough information about his financial situation and tenant history that you believe it would be a waste of time and effort for him to complete an application. Even in such a situation, always be sure to offer your rental application to every rental prospect of legal contracting age.

Figure 9-1 shows you the first page of a standard rental application. Check out the accompanying CD for a full Rental Application you can use.

RENTAL APPLICATION AND APPLICATION FEE RECEIPT

GRISWOLD REAL ESTATE MANAGEMENT

VERIFIED BY

NAME _____ First ___ Last ___ Middle ___ CO-APPLICANT _____ First ___ Last ___ Middle

PRESENT ADDRESS _____ Street ___ City ___ State ___ Zip Code

TELEPHONE(___) ___ DATE OF BIRTH ___ CO-APPLICANT DATE OF BIRTH

SOCIAL SECURITY NO. ___ DRIVERS LIC.# ___
CO-APPLICANT ___ CO-APPLICANT
SOCIAL SECURITY NO. ___ DRIVERS LIC. NO# ___

NAMES AND AGES OF ALL PERSONS TO RESIDE IN APARTMENT ___

EMPLOYMENT HISTORY (Last Five Years) · USE REVERSE SIDE IF NECESSARY

PRESENT EMPLOYER ___ SUPERVISOR'S NAME ___ TELEPHONE (___)

ADDRESS ___ Street ___ City ___ State ___ Zip Code

GROSS SALARY ___ JOB TITLE ___ DATE EMPLOYED ___

FORMER EMPLOYER ___ TELEPHONE (___)

ADDRESS ___ Street ___ City ___ State ___ Zip Code

GROSS SALARY ___ JOB TITLE ___ PERIOD EMPLOYED From ___ To ___

CO-APPLICANT'S
EMPLOYER ___ SUPERVISOR'S NAME ___ TELEPHONE (___)

ADDRESS ___ Street ___ City ___ State ___ Zip Code

GROSS SALARY ___ JOB TITLE ___ DATE EMPLOYED ___

OTHER INCOME ___

AUTOMOBILE Year ___ Make ___ Color ___ License ___ Year ___ Make ___ Color ___ License ___

HOW MANY PETS DO YOU HAVE? ___ WHAT TYPE? ___ DO YOU HAVE A WATERBED? ___

Have you or any proposed occupant listed above ever:
been convicted or pled guilty to a misdemeanor involving violence, sexual misconduct, or honesty? ___
been convicted or pled guilty to any felony? ___; been evicted or asked to move out? ___
broken a lease or rental agreement? ___; declared bankruptcy? ___; been sued for nonpayment? ___
been sued for damage to rental property? ___; had a recorded lien, garnishment or judgment? ___
If yes to any of the above, please indicate year, location and details: ___

Figure 9-1:
Rental
Application.

Have several rental applications and pens available at the property. Although you want to make sure you offer an application to every prospect, you don't just want to hand them out and let the prospects leave without making commitments.

Here are some important guidelines to remember when having prospects complete rental applications:

✔ **Every prospective tenant who is currently 18 years of age or older should completely fill out a written application.** This rule applies whether the applicants are married, are related in some other way, or are unrelated roommates.

✔ **Before accepting the rental application, carefully review the entire form to make sure each prospect has clearly and legibly provided all requested information.** Pay particular attention to all names and addresses, employment information, Social Security numbers, driver's license numbers, and emergency contacts. Any blanks should be marked with an "N/A" if not applicable so that you can tell those items weren't inadvertently overlooked.

✔ **Each prospective tenant must sign the rental application authorizing you to perform your pre-move-in screening, verify the provided information, and run a credit report.** You can't legally obtain and review a consumer credit report without an applicant's permission.

✔ **All prospective tenants need to show you a current driver's license or other similar photo identification so that you can confirm that they're providing you with their correct names and current addresses.** Identity theft is a growing concern; make sure you know exactly who you're renting to.

You may be asked by the prospect — or you may decide on your own — to go over the rental application with him and assist him in providing the information. If you do so, be very careful to ask only questions that are part of the rental application. Avoid asking questions that may directly or indirectly discriminate. Don't ask the rental applicant about his birthplace, religion, marital status, children, or a physical or mental condition. You *can* ask him if he has ever been convicted of a crime and whether he is at least 18-years-old.

Holding your prospect's deposit

Some rental prospects are willing to make firm commitments, but they either won't or can't give you the full security deposits and first month's rent. Maybe they just don't have the funds at the time, or maybe they want to reserve your rental while looking for a better property. In these situations, you may want to ask for a holding deposit to allow you to take the rental unit off the market for a limited period of time while you obtain a credit report or verify other information on the rental application.

Don't allow the prospective tenant to reserve your rental property with a small holding deposit for more than a couple of days. Two days gives you more than enough time to screen the prospect; any additional time the rental unit is off the market often translates into rent you never see. After you approve the rental prospect, try to have her sign the rental contract. If the prospect still insists she needs additional time, have her agree to pay the daily rental rate or refund her holding deposit and continue your search for more interested prospects.

By taking the rental unit off the market, you're forgoing the ability to rent it to someone else. If the prospective tenant fails to rent your property for any reason, you've potentially lost revenue while the unit has been vacant and reserved. On the other hand, rental prospects don't want to pay rent while you're running them through your tenant screening process. The solution is to use a written Holding Deposit Agreement and receipt, like the one shown in Figure 9-2 (also available on the CD), which outlines the understanding between you and the prospective tenant.

Holding Deposit Agreement and Receipt

On the date below, _____ (Owner) received $ _____ from

_____ (Applicant) as a Holding Deposit for the premises located at:

_____ (Rental unit) on the terms and conditions set forth herein.

1. Rent of $ _____ per month shall be payable in advance on the first of each month. The tenancy will begin on the _____ day of _____, 20____, but subject to any present tenant vacating or the unavailability of the rental unit.
2. Of the total funds hereby received by Owner, the sum of $ _____ is an Application Fee that the Applicant understands and agrees is nonrefundable. The Application Fee represents the estimated costs incurred by the Owner in obtaining and verifying the credit information, employment and references of the Applicant and similar tenant screening functions.
3. Of the total funds hereby received by Owner, the sum of $ _____ represents a Holding Deposit.
4. The Applicant has paid the Application Fee and Holding Deposit to the Owner in the form of cash, cashier's check, money order or personal check. Owner is free to deposit all funds received herein and shall maintain this Holding Deposit in liquid funds subject to review by Owner or its agents of the Applicant's rental application.
5. Applicant shall be entitled to a full refund of the Holding Deposit within _____ days if the Owner determines that:
   a) The Owner does not approve the Applicant's rental application; and/or
   b) The premises are not available on the agreed date
6. Upon notification by the Owner to the Applicant that their rental application has been accepted, the Applicant agrees to execute all lease or rental agreement and related documents and pay any balance still due for the first month's rent and full security deposit. Applicant understands that once their rental application has been approved, the rental unit is being taken off the rental market and reserved for the Applicant and any or all other potential Applicants will be turned away.
7. If after acceptance of the Applicant's rental application, the Applicant fails to comply, the Owner may immediately deduct from the amount received the sum of $ _____ per day (daily rate) for each day the rental unit is vacant from the date the Applicant's tenancy was to begin through the date the rental unit is rerented to another tenant, but not in any event to exceed 30 days. It is agreed that the daily rate is calculated as an amount equal to 1/30th of the above monthly rental rate. In addition, the Owner shall be entitled to retain reasonable administrative fees and advertising expenses associated with remarketing the rental unit. The Applicant agrees that the daily rate plus the actual incurred administrative expenses and advertising costs are reasonable and liquidated damages since the actual damages would be difficult or impossible to ascertain.
8. The Owner, within _____ days after the rental unit is rerented, shall return to Applicant, to the Applicant's address shown below, any remaining balance of the Holding Deposit and shall include an itemization of the Owner's damages.
9. If any legal action or proceeding is brought by either party to enforce any part of this agreement, the prevailing party shall recover, in addition to all other relief, reasonable attorneys fees and costs. By signing below, both the Owner and Applicant acknowledge and accept all terms contained herein.

_____   _____
Applicant's Signature   Applicant's Signature

_____   _____
Applicant's Name (print)   Applicant's Name (print)

_____   _____

_____   _____
Applicant's Address   Applicant's Address

_____   _____
Date   Owner/Agent

Figure 9-2:
Holding
Deposit
Agreement.

If you use a holding deposit, you must have a written agreement or else you're very likely to encounter a misunderstanding or even legal action. State laws regarding holding deposits vary, yet they're almost uniformly vague and can easily lead to disputes.

Developing priority waiting lists

If you have several qualified rental prospects interested in your rental unit, you'll only be able to rent to one of them. Use the tenant selection criteria covered in Chapter 10 to select the most-qualified prospect.

If you have other qualified prospective tenants, you may have other rental units at the same property, or in close proximity, that would interest them. If those other units aren't available right at the moment, you may be able to offer your prospects a spot on your *priority waiting list,* which is just a way for you to keep track of qualified tenants for whom you simply don't yet have available rentals instead of turning them away. Being in this situation is a dream come true for many rental property owners or managers.

If potential tenants express a desire to rent your property at a future date, and you know other rentals are available in the area, the prospects may be interested because your rents are lower than market value. (Otherwise, they'd simply find another comparable rental somewhere else instead of waiting.) If you have a long waiting list, make sure it's because your rental property is desirable — not because you're charging too little in rent.

Some prospective tenants are simply looking for a great rental property several months in advance. Although you can't hold your rental property vacant and off the market until these folks are ready to rent, you can lock them in for one of your rental units that may be coming available at the time they're prepared to move. This situation is especially typical for prospects relocating from out of town and making a trip to look for a rental a few weeks or months before they officially move. You may be able to pre-rent your rental units even before they become vacant (and that's a great position for any property manager to be in).

When you create a priority waiting list, don't just write the prospective tenants' names on a piece of paper, because this approach gives you no commitment, and the chances of those prospects returning to rent from you are slim. Prospective tenants' levels of commitment increase if you prequalify them, take partially refundable deposits, and give them written confirmations that they're on your priority waiting list. You may even want to offer to lock in a rental rate if they rent from you within a certain number of months.

Inform your prospective tenants they're on the waiting list. Also, if you own multiple rental units, be sure to let your prospects know you can't guarantee that a certain property or rental unit will be available when they're ready to move in, because you can't control when your current tenants will vacate.

Give prospective tenants the right to cancel and let them know that the portion of their deposits not used for the tenant screening process are fully refundable at any time.

As with all rental policies, you need to apply your priority waiting list policy uniformly to all prospects. So if you have a priority waiting list, be sure to let all prospective tenants know about it and don't restrict anyone from being added to the list. Otherwise, you can be accused of discrimination.

Handling Mandatory Disclosures and Environmental Issues

One of the major challenges to being a successful rental property owner is keeping abreast of the constantly evolving health and safety requirements in your state that affect rental properties. In addition to providing your tenants with a clean and habitable rental property, you need to take precautions to ensure the rental is a safe and healthy environment.

Although failing to meet required state and federal disclosures leads to definite legal implications and substantial liability, most rental property owners genuinely don't want to see their tenants get sick or injured. In the following sections, I cover some of the most common issues facing rental property owners today.

New federal, state, and local legislation is constantly under consideration, and rental property owners must stay current with all requirements or face serious consequences. Check the CD for links to state landlord-tenant laws to find out about any state disclosure requirements.

Lead-based paint

As a rental property owner, you need to be aware of the dangers of lead and the federally required disclosures regarding it. More than 40 states now have lead hazard reduction laws in place, some of which require testing and careful maintenance, in addition to the federal disclosure requirements.

Although lead-based paint isn't a hazard when in good condition, it can be a serious problem (particularly for young children) when it cracks, peels, or turns to chalk due to age. Lead has been banned from paint since 1978, but even to this day, older rental housing units may contain paint manufactured before that time. You can't tell whether paint contains lead just by looking at it; a special lead test is the only way to verify the existence of lead.

Lead-based paint isn't easy to remove. If your rental property has lead-based paint, hire a licensed contractor to address concerns about lead.

Unfortunately, removing lead can be quite expensive. Often the best solution is to manage the lead in place rather than completely remove it, because the removal processes of sanding and scraping can release large amounts of lead dust.

If you have any concerns about lead hazards, review the extensive resources available from the Environmental Protection Agency (EPA) and the National Lead Information Center (NLIC) by visiting www.epa.gov/lead or by calling 800-424-LEAD (800-424-5323).

Most rental property owners use a Lead-Based Paint Disclosure Form (see Figure 9-3) to ensure they have complied with the Residential Lead-Based Paint Hazard Reduction Act of 1992 (see the nearby sidebar for more info). Pull this form from the CD, print it online at www.epa.gov/lead/pubs/lesr_eng.pdf, or contact the NLIC at 800-424-5323 for a copy.

The Residential Lead-Based Paint Hazard Reduction Act also requires you to provide tenants with an information pamphlet by the EPA entitled "Protect Your Family From Lead In Your Home." You can get this pamphlet online at www.epa.gov/lead/pubs/leadpdfe.pdf in both English and Spanish. You can receive clarification on the law from the NLIC by calling 800-424-5323. California and Massachusetts are currently the only states with their own pamphlets on lead-based paint hazards that the EPA has authorized for distribution in lieu of the EPA pamphlet.

Whichever pamphlet you provide your tenants, be sure you comply with the federal law and keep a copy of the disclosure form signed and dated by the tenants. This written record of compliance with the disclosure requirements must be kept on hand and readily available for review in case of an investigation or audit for a minimum of three years. Remember that you only need to make the required disclosure once, even if a tenant renews an existing lease.

Rental property owners or managers who fail to follow the federal regulations for lead-based paint can face significant fines. To enforce these regulations, the federal Housing and Urban Development (HUD) agency and the EPA are working together to investigate complaints from prospective tenants and/or current tenants who believe they may have been exposed to lead-based paint. If a tenant doesn't receive the required EPA or approved state information pamphlet or the disclosure statement, the owner or property manager may be subject to

- ✔ A notice of noncompliance
- ✔ A civil penalty of up to $11,000 per violation for willful and continuing noncompliance
- ✔ An order to pay the injured tenant up to three times his or her actual damages
- ✔ A criminal fine of up to $11,000 per violation

Disclosure of Information on Lead-Based Paint and/or Lead-Based Paint Hazards

Lead Warning Statement

Housing built before 1978 may contain lead-based paint. Lead from paint, paint chips, and dust can pose health hazards if not managed properly. Lead exposure is especially harmful to young children and pregnant women. Before renting pre-1978 housing, lessors must disclose the presence of known lead-based paint and/or lead-based paint hazards in the dwelling. Lessees must also receive a federally approved pamphlet on lead poisoning prevention.

Lessor's Disclosure

(a) Presence of lead-based paint and/or lead-based paint hazards (check (i) or (ii) below):

(i) _____ Known lead-based paint and/or lead-based paint hazards are present in the housing (explain).

_____

_____

(ii) _____ Lessor has no knowledge of lead-based paint and/or lead-based paint hazards in the housing.

(b) Records and reports available to the lessor (check (i) or (ii) below):

(i) _____ Lessor has provided the lessee with all available records and reports pertaining to lead-based paint and/or lead-based paint hazards in the housing (list documents below).

_____

_____

(ii) _____ Lessor has no reports or records pertaining to lead-based paint and/or lead-based paint hazards in the housing.

Lessee's Acknowledgment (initial)

(c) _____ Lessee has received copies of all information listed above.

(d) _____ Lessee has received the pamphlet *Protect Your Family from Lead in Your Home.*

Agent's Acknowledgment (initial)

(e) _____ Agent has informed the lessor of the lessor's obligations under 42 U.S.C. 4852(d) and is aware of his/her responsibility to ensure compliance.

Certification of Accuracy

The following parties have reviewed the information above and certify, to the best of their knowledge, that the information they have provided is true and accurate.

Lessor	Date	Lessor	Date
Lessee	Date	Lessee	Date
Agent	Date	Agent	Date

Figure 9-3: As a property owner, you're required by law to give a lead-based paint disclosure form like this one to any tenants or prospects if your property was built before January 1, 1978.

Courtesy of U.S. Environmental Protection Agency

Recently, the EPA and HUD began aggressively enforcing these regulations and levied significant and well-publicized fines against rental property owners and managers who haven't complied with the law. Government testers have been known to pose as prospective tenants, and federal agents have scoured leasing and maintenance records looking for evidence that property owners or managers knew or should have known about the existence of lead-based paint hazards on their property. This is *not* an area where you want to tempt fate. Make sure you comply with this law and keep the required documentation on file in an easily retrievable location for at least three years.

Painting a clearer picture of lead-based paints

The federal Residential Lead-Based Paint Hazard Reduction Act of 1992 covers all dwellings built before 1978 and requires rental housing owners or their property managers to notify tenants that the rental property may have lead-based paint. Testing for lead-based paint or removal isn't currently required under federal law. However, you must disclose any known presence of lead-based paint or hazards and provide all tenants with copies of any available records or reports pertaining to the presence of lead-based paint and/or hazards.

In addition to all housing constructed after January 1, 1978, some limited rental property exemptions from federal lead-based paint disclosure regulations do exist. Exempt properties include the following:

✔ Housing for the elderly or persons with disabilities (unless children under the age of 6 are living there)

✔ Short-term rentals of 100 days or less

✔ Certain university housing, such as dormitory housing or rentals in sorority or fraternity houses

✔ Zero bedroom units, such as studios, lofts, or efficiencies

✔ Housing that has been inspected and certified as "lead-free" by a state-accredited lead inspector

Be sure to contact the EPA or your state health and environmental agency for specific information. If you're advised that your property is exempt, be sure to receive written verification before ceasing to follow the federal requirements.

In pre-1978 properties, lead is usually found on:

✔ Doors, door jambs and frames, railings, and banisters

✔ Exterior painted surfaces

✔ Interior trim

✔ Windowsills and horizontal painted surfaces

Asbestos

Asbestos has received a lot of media coverage over the last 20 years. You may remember the federal government's concerns about asbestos in schools and the major efforts to remove asbestos-containing materials from those facilities. Currently, federal rules only require you to investigate or remove asbestos in rental housing when you're doing renovations that may disturb the asbestos, or when you demolish any portion of the housing. Check with your local and state officials for any disclosure requirements they may require. Some jurisdictions insist asbestos materials be disclosed to tenants, along with a warning not to disturb them.

Asbestos is a mineral fiber that historically was added to a variety of products to strengthen them and provide heat insulation and fire resistance. In most products, asbestos is blended with a binding material so that as long as it remains intact, fibers aren't released into the air, and no health risk occurs. Asbestos fibers are microscopic and can be positively identified only with a special type of microscope.

The concern in most rental properties is that asbestos-containing materials may be disturbed, causing them to release microscopic fibers, which can be inhaled into the lungs. For example, many older apartments have popcorn or acoustic ceilings containing asbestos, which can be disturbed by installing a ceiling light or fan. The asbestos fibers don't self-destruct but remain in the air for a long time, increasing the risk of disease. Some asbestos materials are *friable,* meaning they crumble into small particles or fibers. Asbestos-containing materials can also crumble easily if mishandled. Even if the asbestos-containing material was originally intact, asbestos can be released into the air if the material is sawed, scraped, sanded into a powder, or subjected to some mechanical processes.

A common cause of the release of asbestos in rental housing is inappropriate or unsafe handling of asbestos-containing materials during remodeling or renovation of the property. If you plan to do any renovations that may disturb asbestos or plan to demolish your building, federal law requires a comprehensive survey before the work begins. Any asbestos found during the survey must then be handled appropriately. To be valid, the survey must be conducted by trained asbestos personnel.

Products containing asbestos aren't usually labeled. Asbestos was commonly used until 1981. Now, it's estimated that more than 3,000 products still in use today contain asbestos. These products, which can be found in many rental properties, include acoustic ceilings, vinyl flooring and tile backings, flooring *mastic* (a type of adhesive), building insulation, wall and ceiling panels, carpet padding, roofing materials, pipe and duct insulation, patching and spackling compounds, and furnaces. Do *not* assume that a property built or remodeled after 1981 doesn't contain asbestos products.

According to the American Lung Association, if you have asbestos-containing substances in your rental property, do the following:

- ✔ **If the substance is in good condition and the asbestos won't be disturbed, leave it alone.** Be sure to warn the tenants not to disturb these materials and have them notify you immediately if these materials are damaged in any way.

- ✔ **If the material is damaged and can release fibers in the air, you should have it repaired or removed.** Always seek the advice of a professional environmental firm to evaluate and recommend the best course of action concerning asbestos.

  - Repair usually involves either sealing or covering asbestos material. Sealing is also commonly referred to as *encapsulation* and involves coating materials so that the asbestos can't be released. Encapsulation is only effective for undamaged asbestos-containing

> material. If materials are soft, crumbly, or otherwise damaged, sealing isn't appropriate, and the substances should be removed by a qualified professional.
>
> - Removing asbestos-containing materials is an expensive and hazardous process to be completed only by trained personnel using special tools and techniques, and should be a last resort. A licensed contractor who specializes in removing asbestos-containing materials should be used, because improper removal can very easily increase the health risks to the workers, yourself, and your future tenants. Also, unauthorized removal of asbestos can be illegal. Punishment can include hundreds of thousands of dollars in fines or prison.

Asbestos is a very dangerous material if disturbed or in poor condition. Don't attempt to test for asbestos on your own. Hire a professional environmental testing firm, because the act of breaking open potentially asbestos-containing material to obtain test samples may release asbestos into the air and create a very dangerous situation.

Radon

Radon, a radioactive gas, is a known cancer-causing agent that the EPA cites as the second leading cause of lung cancer in the United States and claims 20,000 lives annually. Found in soil and rock in all parts of the U.S., radon is formed as a byproduct of the natural decay of the radioactive materials radium and uranium. Radon gas is invisible; it has no odor or taste. Its presence in the interior of buildings has been found to cause lung cancer. However, most radon found in buildings poses no direct threat to human life, because the range of concentration is generally below the minimum safe level.

Although currently no federal requirements exist regarding disclosure or even testing for radon gas, it's a potentially serious health issue and one that's receiving more attention. Be aware of radon levels in your rental units and check with local authorities for more information about the prevalence and appropriate precautions that should be taken to avoid radon exposure. (Florida and New Jersey have been particularly aggressive in addressing the radon problem.) Be sure to check with your local authorities for any specific disclosure requirements.

Although radon may be found in all types of homes and buildings throughout the U.S., it's more likely to occur in the lower levels of tightly-sealed, energy-efficient buildings where insulation limits the flow of air from the inside to the outside and ventilation is poor.

The lowdown on asbestos

The federal Occupational Safety and Health Administration (OSHA) has developed regulations that apply to any building constructed prior to 1981. These pre-1981 buildings are presumed to have asbestos unless the owner tests the property and verifies that asbestos or asbestos-containing materials aren't present.

Exposure to asbestos can lead to an increased risk of lung cancer; *mesothelioma,* a cancer of the lining of the chest and the abdominal cavity; and *asbestosis,* a condition in which the lungs become scarred with fibrous tissue.

No known safe exposure level to asbestos exists. However, when the asbestos is intact and can't become airborne, exposure to it isn't a problem. Smokers who inhale exposed asbestos fibers have a greater risk of developing lung cancer than nonsmokers. Although most people who get asbestosis have usually been exposed to high levels of asbestos for a long time, even a short but significant exposure can cause harm. The symptoms of asbestos-related diseases don't usually appear until about 20 to 30 years after the first exposure to asbestos.

Testing for radon

The only way to know whether your rental property has radon at unhealthy levels is to conduct short-term and/or long-term radon testing. Fortunately, radon tests are inexpensive and easy to use. The quickest way to test for radon is with a short-term test, which remains in your home anywhere from 2 to 90 days, depending on the device. Long-term tests remain in your home for more than 90 days. Because radon levels tend to vary from day to day and season to season, a long-term test is more likely to tell you your home's year-round average radon level than a short-term test.

You have two choices when testing for radon:

- ✔ **Do it yourself.** The do-it-yourself radon test kits are available in hardware stores, and some laboratories provide kits through mail order. Make sure you get one that meets EPA standards or your state's requirements — the test kit usually says so on the package. The price of a simple short-term radon test kit starts at about $10 (or about $20 for a long-term kit) and includes the cost of having a laboratory analyze the test. Discounted radon test kits are available from the National Safety Council by calling 800-767-7236.

- ✔ **Hire a professional.** For information on the detection and removal of radon, you can contact the EPA National Radon Hotline by calling 800-767-7236 or by visiting the EPA Web site at www.epa.gov/radon. This Web site has contacts for state agencies that regulate radon, plus information on finding a qualified radon reduction provider.

If your tests reveal radon in one particular unit of an apartment building, have all the other units tested immediately and notify all other tenants in the building of the problem promptly. Remember that even if your radon test shows low radon levels in one unit, there may be high levels in other parts of the building.

Repairing a radon problem

Fixing a radon problem usually involves repairs to the building. Therefore, you as the building owner, not your tenant, are responsible for having this work done. If your rental property has high radon levels, you can take steps to see that the problem is fixed by installing equipment, such as fans, blowers, and ducts, to reduce radon gas levels. The EPA advises that radon reduction costs between $800 and $2,500 for a single-family home with an average cost of $1,200. For a larger rental property, the costs depend on the size and other characteristics of the building.

Radon reduction work generally requires a trained professional. To find out which radon reduction system is right for a building and how much those repairs will cost, consult a professional radon contractor. The EPA and many states have programs set up to train or certify radon professionals. Look online for your state radon office, because it can provide a list of individuals who have completed state or federal programs. It can also provide a list of EPA-approved radon *mitigators,* or reduction specialists, in your state.

Sexual offenders

Virtually every state has a version of *Megan's Law,* legislation which requires certain convicted sexual offenders to register with local law enforcement. The local law enforcement then maintains a database on the whereabouts of the registered sex offenders, and it often makes this information available to the public.

Megan's Law is named after 7-year-old Megan Nicole Kanka of Hamilton Township, New Jersey, who was raped and murdered in the summer of 1994 by a convicted child molester who was living in her neighborhood without her parents' knowledge. Less than 90 days after Megan's abduction, New Jersey passed Megan's Law, which required making information about the presence of convicted sex offenders in local neighborhoods available to the public.

In 1996, a federal version of this crime prevention law was passed, requiring the Federal Bureau of Investigation (FBI) to keep a national database of all persons convicted of sexual offenses against minors and violent sexual offenses against anyone. Prison officials are required to inform convicted sex offenders of their legal obligation to register with state law enforcement authorities. The state agencies are required to inform local law enforcement and the FBI as to the registered addresses for each convicted sex offender.

Local law enforcement authorities are then permitted to release the collected information as necessary to protect the public, but active community notification isn't mandatory.

Unfortunately, states aren't very consistent in their efforts to maintain and make this database available. The federal law allows each state to decide how to use and distribute the database information. The three options are:

- **Widespread notification with easy access:** This option allows notification to the public, including methods such as posting the names and addresses on the Internet or on a CD-ROM.

- **Selective notification with limited access:** This alternative allows notification only to those groups most at risk, such as schools and daycare centers.

- **Restricted notification with narrow access:** This option allows access only for a particular name or address.

Although registration is mandatory, often the addresses provided aren't verified, or the convicted sex offender may move and fail to reregister at his new address. Also, the accuracy of this database can vary widely based on the age of the information.

Some states require property owners or managers to provide a disclosure statement to each tenant advising her of the availability of the Megan's Law database. Whether you're required by state law to give your tenant a Megan's Law disclosure, if you're ever asked by a prospective renter about Megan's Law, be sure to refer her to local law enforcement authorities and make a written and dated note of the conversation for your files. For specific information on the requirements of Megan's Law in your state, call your local law enforcement agency, contact the Parents for Megan's Law (PFML) hotline at 888-ASK-PFML (888-275-7365), or check www.parentsformeganslaw.com.

Chapter 10

Eenie, Meenie, Miney, Mo: Selecting Your Tenants

In This Chapter

▶ Recognizing the value of proper tenant screening and written criteria for your process

▶ Confirming your applicants' information

▶ Informing applicants of the outcome

▶ Knowing the laws surrounding Fair Housing

*W*hen you own rental property, one of your most important tasks is screening and selecting tenants. Because the process of screening tenants is time-consuming, you need to have a system in place for doing it efficiently. Here I help you navigate these unfamiliar waters with ease.

Basically, with tenant selection and screening, you develop and use objective, written tenant selection criteria, consistently screen all rental applicants against these minimum criteria, and select the most qualified tenant based on your review.

With a system, tenant screening really isn't that difficult; it just requires assertiveness, diligence, and patience. Even after you've been managing your rental properties for many years, you still won't be able to just look at a rental application and know whether the applicant is qualified. You have to check the prospect's references, credit history, employment, income sources or assets, job stability, and tenant history. And you can't cut corners. Selecting a bad tenant is much worse than having a vacant rental unit. So choose your tenants wisely and profit in the long run.

Another critical part of choosing your tenants is making sure you handle the selection process without bias, abiding by all Fair Housing regulations. This concept can be a murky issue, but it's an important one you need to pay attention to no matter what your situation so that you're not slapped with a discrimination lawsuit.

Understanding the Importance of Screening

If you're like many rental property owners, you may be thinking, "Screening? Isn't that just a waste of time? After all, I trust my gut instinct when I meet people. I know which ones are good and which are just trouble." Although it does take time to verify all the information on your prospective tenant's rental application, it's time well spent. Relying on your instincts is very inaccurate, arbitrary, and, above all, illegal.

In order to increase your chances of finding a long-term, stable tenant and avoid charges of discrimination, your tenant selection criteria and screening process should be clear, systematic, and objective. Put this process in writing to ensure it's applied consistently and fairly to *all* rental applicants.

Establishing solid tenant selection criteria and performing a thorough tenant screening process doesn't guarantee a good tenant, but it does significantly improve your odds of finding one.

Setting up a systematic screening process is particularly critical if you only own a single rental or a small, multi-unit rental property. *Professional tenants* (people who go from property to property damaging the units or not paying rent) are experienced and shrewd. They know that the large, professionally managed rental properties have detailed and thorough screening procedures that attempt to verify every single item on their rental applications. If certain items don't check out, the professional property manager doesn't just trust her feelings on the prospective tenant. Professional tenants know that small rental property owners are easier targets, because the novice property owner is more likely to bend the rules than the professional.

Sometimes the mere mention of the tenant screening process is enough to make the rental prospect fidget and shift into the classic "I'm just looking" mode. Don't rush a prospect or allow one to hurry you through the tenant screening and selection process. The wrong decision can be financially devastating, particularly if you have just a couple of rental units with monthly debt payments.

Establishing Tenant Selection Criteria

Tenant selection criteria are written standards that you use to evaluate each prospect's qualifications as a tenant. Determine your exact minimum qualifications and adhere to them. Of course, your written criteria can't be discriminatory or violate any federal, state, or local Fair Housing laws.

These criteria can help you treat all rental applicants fairly to avoid claims of discrimination. Making the effort to develop written guidelines can also be useful as an objective evaluation technique to minimize the chance that you may be swayed by a charming prospect and find yourself lowering your standards and allowing a not-so-desirable tenant to occupy your valuable rental property.

The following sections break down the importance of tenant selection criteria and how you can develop your own.

Why having criteria is important

Giving all prospective tenants an overview of your rental screening procedure and requirements upfront lets them know exactly what you're looking for in a qualified rental applicant. Because these criteria are the minimum standards you accept, prospective tenants thus know why their rental application may be rejected.

Developing your own tenant selection criteria has several benefits:

- ✔ **Rental applicants know you're aware of and comply with all Fair Housing laws.** You want to make sure your tenants know they'll be evaluated objectively and fairly and that you promote equal opportunities in housing.

- ✔ **Rental applicants understand that rental activity and the preparation for it are dynamic processes.** Certain units may or may not be available even within the same day for legitimate business reasons. Outlining this policy and maintaining good records can minimize accusations of discrimination.

- ✔ **Rental applicants are aware that you abide by the reasonable occupancy limits suggested by most federal and state standards, while being conscious of the unit's limitations.** With the high cost of housing in many areas, some tenants are looking to occupy a smaller rental unit; you need to make sure that your property can handle the intended number of occupants while complying with standards.

- ✔ **Rental applicants know what to expect from your process of evaluating rental applications.** They know that all applications are thoroughly verified, that the process takes one or two days, and that you charge an application fee to cover some of your costs for the screening process.

- ✔ **Rental applicants realize that everyone applying for your unit is evaluated consistently and fairly.** They can review your requirements and evaluate their own qualifications to see whether applying is even worth their time.

More than 90 percent of your rental applicants are going to be good tenants who pay their rent on time, take good care of their homes, and treat you and their neighbors with respect. You just need to carefully guard against those few bad apples, so don't hesitate to deny prospects who can't meet your standards.

How to create your criteria

In order to establish your tenant selection criteria, review what you're looking for in a tenant. Your notion of the ideal tenant may be different from someone else's, but here are five important traits to look for:

- Someone who'll be financially responsible and always pay his rent on time.
- Someone who'll respect and treat the property as if it were her own.
- Someone who'll be a good neighbor and not cause problems.
- Someone who'll be stable and likely to renew his lease.
- Someone who'll leave the premises in a condition the same as or better than she found it.

In order to have the best results in selecting your tenants and ensure your rental prospects understand your tenant selection criteria, develop a *Statement of Rental Policy,* which is a formal, written statement explaining your screening criteria.

The accompanying CD has a sample Statement of Rental Policy that you can develop for your rental property and provide to each and every rental applicant over the age of 18. Your policy standards may be more or less stringent depending on your rental market and experience. But no matter what, you need to be sure that your standards comply with all state and local laws. I strongly advise that you have a local attorney who specializes in landlord-tenant law review your Statement of Rental Policy in advance.

Your Statement of Rental Policy should be given to each and every applicant with the rental application. If you have a multi-unit rental property with an office, clearly post the policy where all applicants can see it. If you don't have an office, insert the policy in an acrylic or similar holder, and place it in clear view on the rental unit's kitchen counter or another area where all prospects can see it as they walk through.

You aren't required to provide your rental prospects with copies of your written tenant selection criteria. Although you must offer all prospects rental applications and process each one received, you can benefit when prospects make their own decisions not to apply for your rental based on the criteria you've set up. The key is to follow these criteria without exception and have the information available if you're challenged.

Some rental property owners feel more comfortable discussing the tenant selection criteria right from the first rental inquiry call (which I cover in Chapter 8), whereas others wait and distribute copies only to those individuals who actually apply. You need to decide which policy works best for you and then apply it consistently.

Always be very thorough when you perform tenant screening and use the same process with all rental applicants. You run the risk of being charged with illegal discrimination if you deviate from your written standards for certain applicants. Many legally acceptable reasons to deny a rental application exist, but be sure that your requirements are clearly understood and followed just to be safe.

The fact that you carefully prescreen all prospects is a positive factor not only for you but also for your rental applicants, your current tenants, and your neighbors. In fact, you have a responsibility to your current tenants to weed out the unqualified prospects with a track record of disrupting the neighbors everywhere they go. Good rental prospects appreciate the fact that their neighbors had to meet your high standards, too.

Verifying Rental Applications

Bad tenants don't walk around with the word *deadbeat* printed on their foreheads. The tenant screening process requires you to be a detective, and all good detectives verify each fact and take thorough notes. You want to ensure that the rental prospect meets your minimum standards as outlined in your Statement of Rental Policy (see the preceding section).

I recommend that you use a Rental Application Verification Form, like the one available on the CD, to collect and review the necessary information that allows you to properly evaluate your rental applicant's qualifications. The following sections explain what info from the rental application you need to confirm before allowing a tenant to move in.

Keep copies of all rental applications, the corresponding Rental Application Verification Forms, credit reports, and all other documentation for both accepted *and* rejected applicants for at least four years. That way if anyone ever claims you discriminated against him or her, your best defense will be your own records, which clearly indicate that you had legal rental criteria, and you applied them consistently.

Confirming identity

The very first step you should take in verifying a rental application is to personally meet each prospective adult tenant. Require each prospective adult tenant to show you a current government-issued photo ID so that you can confirm each applicant is providing you with the correct name and current address. Advise your rental applicant that if his application is approved, you'll need a photocopy of his ID to be kept in his tenant file. Initial the rental application to record that you did indeed verify this information.

Inquire about any discrepancies between the application and the ID provided. Even if the explanation seems reasonable, be sure to write down the new information. Maybe an old address appears on the photo ID, which you can check out further through a credit reporting agency.

Having a photocopy of the ID for each adult tenant can be very important if a dispute concerning the tenant's identity arises in the future. In these situations, you need to be able to clearly show that you positively identified the tenant upon move-in.

Going over occupancy guidelines

Take a look at the rental application information provided by the tenant concerning the number of persons planning to occupy your rental property to ensure that the anticipated use is within your established occupancy guidelines.

One of a property manager's major concerns is excessive wear and tear of the rental unit. Clearly, the greater the number of occupants in a rental unit, the greater the possibility for wear and tear. Unfortunately, questions about occupancy have no simple answers, and the laws and regulations concerning occupancy standards aren't universally accepted. For example, the Department of Housing and Urban Development (HUD) guidelines state that property managers can limit occupancy to two individuals per bedroom. However, state and local restrictions must be followed as well. And in California, for example, the Department of Fair Employment and Housing has formulated the *2 + 1 occupancy standard guideline,* which states that a property manager must allow two individuals per bedroom, plus an additional occupant for the unit. In other words, three individuals may occupy a one-bedroom rental unit, and five individuals a two-bedroom rental unit, and so on.

Contact your local or state housing agency for information on its occupancy regulations. You must always apply the most generous occupancy standard.

In addition to occupancy standards, you also have to consider maximum occupancy limits. These restrictions are usually set by state and local health and safety boards, or building codes based on the square footage or size of the rental unit and its number of bedrooms and bathrooms. The maximum occupancy permitted under these code sections is often as high as seven persons in a one-bedroom rental unit. The occupancy of your rental unit should stay closer to the minimum rather than the maximum.

Unless you have a more generous state or local requirement, I recommend using the 2 + 1 minimum occupancy guideline. Although federal and most state and local occupancy standards allow a more restrictive policy, the burden of proof is on the rental property owner. If you feel you have a legitimate basis, meaning a supportable, nondiscriminatory business reason, for having a more restrictive occupancy standard, hire a consultant and have him or her make an independent evaluation and recommendation.

Some rental property owners illegally use the occupancy standard as a subtle tool to limit the number of rental applicants with children. HUD and state and local Fair Housing agencies receive a large volume of calls concerning familial status discrimination. In some areas, these complaints outnumber claims on the basis of all other protected classes combined.

Investigating rental history

You also want to confirm the applicant's rental history. To do so, contact her current landlord and go through the questions on the rental history portion of the Rental Application Verification Form. When you first contact the prior landlord, you may want to listen to his initial reaction and let him tell you about the applicant. Some landlords welcome the opportunity to tell you all about your rental applicant, so listen carefully.

Some rental applicants may provide you with letters of reference from their prior landlords, or even copies of their credit reports. This behavior often occurs in many competitive rental markets where only the prepared tenants have a chance to get a quality rental property. Although the more information you have, the better the decision you can usually make, be very careful to evaluate the authenticity of any documents provided by your prospects. Accept these papers but always perform your complete tenant screening process to independently verify all information.

Current or prior landlords may not be entirely forthcoming with answers to many of your questions. Most likely, they're concerned that they'll have some liability if they provide any negative or subjective information. If the information you receive on your applicant from the current landlord is primarily negative, you may not need to check with any other prior landlords. However, be wary that the current landlord may not be entirely honest; he may be upset with the tenant for leaving his property, or he may not say anything bad about a problem tenant so that he can get the tenant out of his property and into yours.

When a current or prior landlord isn't overly cooperative, try to gain his confidence by providing him with some information about yourself and your rental property. If you're still unable to build rapport, try to get him to at least answer the most important question of all: "Would you rent to this applicant again?" He can simply give you a "yes" or a "no" without any details. Of course, silence can also tell you everything you need to know.

Another useful screening tool is to request that each prospective tenant provide copies of his or her water and utility bills for the past year. Doing so verifies prior addresses and gives you an idea whether the applicant pays bills on time. (A rental prospect who can't pay utility bills in a timely manner is very likely to have trouble paying your rent.) You may also want to inquire with local law enforcement to see whether its records show any complaints at a tenant's prior address.

Validating employment and income

Although credit reporting agencies may provide information on your rental applicant's employment or other sources of income, they typically don't have all the information you need to properly evaluate this extremely important rental qualification criterion.

Independently verify the information and phone number the applicant puts on her application if you have any doubts about their authenticity. You may have reason for concern if an employer is a major corporation, and the telephone isn't answered in a typical and customary business manner, for example. You also need to be careful that you confirm the sensitive compensation and stability of employment questions only with an appropriate employer representative.

Occasionally, you may find that an employer doesn't verify any information over the phone. So be prepared to send letters requesting the pertinent information, and include a self-addressed, stamped envelope. Be sure to tell your rental prospect that you may have a delay in providing him with the results of your tenant screening process.

Your rental applicant should provide you with proof of his employment or other sources of income. This proof may be in the form of recent pay stubs, bank account statements, and other proof of income or assets. No matter how strong the information is, verify it directly with the employer or the other source of income.

Always require written verification of all sources of income that a rental applicant is using to meet your income qualification requirements. If you can't verify the income, you don't have to include it in your calculations to determine whether the applicant meets your minimum income requirements. Keep the following points in mind as you verify income:

✔ **When you have a rental applicant who relies on sales, commission income, or bonuses, make sure you review at least six consecutive months of pay stubs.** Of course, the best policy is to require all applicants with any income other than salary to provide copies of their signed tax returns for the last two years. Although you must be careful to determine that it's an authentic document, I have yet to find a rental prospect who overstates annual income on a tax return.

✔ **Pay close attention to applicants who seem to actually be overqualified or anxious to be approved and take possession of your rental unit.** Remember the old saying, "If it sounds too good to be true, it probably is." This adage definitely applies in the world of rental property, so keep it in mind at all times.

✔ **Be particularly careful of rental applicants who seem to have plenty of cash to pay your security deposit and first month's rent, but who don't have verifiable sources of income that seem consistent with their spending patterns.** The applicant may be involved in illegal activity, and you may need to evict him later at considerable expense and loss of income. Rental property owners can even lose their properties under certain circumstances if they fail to take action to eliminate the source of illegal activity on their property.

Several states and local jurisdictions have laws prohibiting a rental property owner from denying an applicant because he receives public assistance. California has gone further to include source of income as a state protected class, which means you can't have a requirement that the applicant must be employed, but simply that he has legal and verifiable income or financial resources to meet your stated requirements.

If you're in an area where source of income is a protected class, you may find you're violating Fair Housing laws if you have policies that favor employees of certain companies, or you favor specific types of employment — some property owners offer discounts to teachers, police, firefighters, and similar occupations. Traditionally, the source of income protection was to guard against discrimination of individuals who receive governmental assistance, but it's been expanded to include limitations on landlords who want to offer favorable terms to certain individuals based on their employment.

Reviewing credit history

You can and should check out an applicant's credit history by obtaining a *credit report*. This document shows all current and previous credit cards and loans with rating information on the timeliness of payments when due, plus all public record entries such as bankruptcy and judgment. Through a credit report, you can figure out whether an applicant has been late or delinquent in paying her rent or other living expenses.

If it looks too good to be true, it probably is!

I once managed a large rental property in a major city. I regularly visited the property and performed an inspection of both the physical aspects and the rental office procedures. One area of ongoing examination was the new rental application, which I reviewed to ensure it was being properly completed by each prospect and that the tenant screening process was being applied uniformly.

During one of my visits, I reviewed a rental application for a one-bedroom apartment that was in the process of being screened. The on-site manager spoke very highly of this younger person who had just graduated from high school, was looking for his first apartment, and listed an income of $750 per week. The manager then told me how, with more than

$3,000 per month in income, this applicant was financially qualified.

Having been in rental management for many years, I was curious about the weekly income, so I took a look at the rental application and noticed that the individual listed the local sports facility as his employer. Sure enough, upon subsequent inquiry of the employer and then the prospect, it became apparent that the applicant did indeed earn $750 per week. The problem was that he earned this amount only during the six months of the professional baseball season and only in the two weeks per month that the local team played games in town. This situation is a reminder of the importance of thoroughly inquiring into and verifying all claimed income or assets.

What to look for in a credit history

Following is a list of what to consider when reviewing a credit history:

- ✔ **A pattern of financial responsibility:** You want your prospective tenant to have a history of prudent or conservative spending. Avoid rental applicants who seem to be using excessive credit and are living beyond their means. If they move into your rental property and experience even a temporary loss of income due to illness or a job situation, you may be the one with an unexpected income loss as a result!

- ✔ **An accurate address:** You want to be able to verify prior living situations, so carefully compare the addresses contained on the credit report to the information provided on the rental application. If you spot an inconsistency, ask the rental prospect for an explanation. Maybe she was temporarily staying with a family member or simply forgot about one of her residences. Of course, be sure to contact prior landlords and ask all the questions on the Rental Application Verification Form just to make sure the applicant didn't neglect to tell you about that residence for a reason.

✔ **A false Social Security number:** You want to make sure you're reviewing the credit report of your actual applicant. People with poor credit or tenant histories have been known to steal the identity of others, particularly their own children, by using someone else's Social Security number. One way to prevent this problem is to make sure your credit reporting service provides a Social Security number search. (Check out the nearby sidebar for more info.)

Information obtained in credit reports must be kept strictly confidential and can't be given to any third parties. In some states, the rental applicant is entitled to a copy of his or her credit report upon request, and federal law allows anyone denied credit on the basis of a credit report to obtain a free copy of it.

Where to get your applicant's credit history

A credit report contains valuable information that can assist you in determining whether your rental applicant meets your resident selection criteria. However, the federal Fair Credit Reporting Act (FCRA) has very complicated restrictions on the proper use of this sensitive information that can be used improperly. In order to get a consumer credit history, you need to contact a tenant screening service in your area. You can find many companies that work specifically with the rental housing industry by going through your local National Apartment Association (NAA) affiliate or your local Institute of Real Estate Management (IREM) chapter.

The info you'll receive from the tenant screening service is based on the databases and records of the three dominant consumer reporting agencies (CRAs), which are

✔ **Equifax:** www.equifax.com

✔ **Experian:** www.experian.com

✔ **TransUnion:** www.transunion.com

With the wide choice of tenant screening services available, you may have a hard time deciding exactly what you need. I recommend you use a service that offers the following:

✔ A retail or consumer credit report

✔ An eviction search or tenant history

✔ An automated cross-check of addresses

✔ A Social Security number or Individual Taxpayer Identification Number search

✔ An employment or income and prior landlord reference verification

✔ A criminal records search

Asking for a Social Security number or not?

Problem: Some rental property owners or managers require applicants to provide a Social Security number (SSN). However, such a policy may risk a Fair Housing complaint, because only U.S. citizens or immigrants authorized to work in the United States can obtain an SSN. Many people (like those with student visas) simply don't qualify for one. Also, with the increased concern about identity theft and privacy rights, some of your rental prospects who *do* have an SSN may not feel comfortable providing it on your rental application.

Solution: An alternative to the standard SSN can be an Individual Taxpayer Identification Number (ITIN), which is issued upon request by the IRS to anyone earning income while living in the U.S. Credit reporting bureaus can use the ITIN the same way they use the SSN to provide you with information on your applicant's credit history.

Problem: Another concern with the SSN is that some credit reporting bureaus have been providing rental owners and property managers with eviction information that may be inaccurate or misleading. The credit bureaus' databases often include information about every eviction filed against an applicant, regardless of whether the matter was ultimately resolved in the tenant's favor. Being confronted with an erroneous eviction filing can be very disconcerting for falsely accused rental applicants.

Solution: If your applicant has an eviction filing on her credit report, you need to inquire further and see whether it was filed in error, dismissed, or resolved in her favor. In the meantime, know that most credit reporting bureaus are making efforts to ensure their individual databases reflect actual court judgments and not just filings.

The Internet is quickly changing the tenant screening procedures for many rental property owners. Consumer credit reports, tenant history, and criminal records search services are now available from your computer in a matter of seconds. This instant access often allows you to approve your rental applicant in minutes or hours, which can be a strong competitive advantage.

Many tenant screening firms are entering this electronic market locally and nationally, and all offer very impressive services designed to save you time and help you fill your vacancies faster. Using technology can improve the efficiency of your information collection for tenant screening and provide you with more details to make a better decision. However, don't rely strictly on computers and forget to personally contact past landlords, verify the applicant's income and employment, or consider your own dealings with your prospective tenant. Rental property ownership and management is still, and always will be, a people business.

What charges are involved

The cost of a tenant screening credit report varies widely. On an individual basis, tenant screening can run between $30 and $50. When you start adding an investigative or criminal records search in multiple areas, this expense can go much higher. Establish the specific level of screening services you want and then be consistent to avoid discrimination claims.

If you join a tenant screening service, you can get discounts of 50 percent or more on each credit report. Some companies offer memberships with minimum monthly fees. But only owners of multiple rental properties who run at least one tenant screening per month really benefit from membership. If you run fewer than a dozen tenant screenings annually, you'll usually find it cheaper to just pay a higher fee per report.

If you own just a few rental units, you may find that joining your local apartment association is a better deal than paying $30 to $50 per tenant screening. Not only do you have easy access to reasonably priced tenant screening services and consumer credit reports through your local apartment association but as a member you can take advantage of its education, publications, and forms. (The accompanying CD contains a complete list of all NAA affiliates and info on their educational programs and designations.)

Charging an applicant for tenant screening or a consumer credit report if you don't actually run one is illegal. If you receive a large number of rental applications, review them in the order they're received, one at a time. If the first applicant fails to qualify, begin processing the next application. Check your state laws to make sure you don't exceed any legal maximum charges and be sure to return any unused credit check fees to those individuals for whom you don't run the credit check. Try to keep your tenant screening fees as low as possible and set them based on the fees paid to a tenant screening company, the value of your time or salary expended, and any indirect expenses (like phone calls) for checking rental history. Of course, always be aware of your state or local laws regarding tenant charges.

Checking criminal history

Rental property owners' liability is increasing all the time. One area of particular concern is criminal acts committed by tenants. In most states, rental property owners have no legal duty to ask about or investigate the criminal backgrounds of applicants or current tenants.

Since the events of September 11, 2001, federal, state, and local law enforcement have made great efforts to standardize reporting of criminal activity. However, in many areas of the country, only a county-level criminal records search is possible. Additionally, many states only indicate felony conviction records and don't list convictions for misdemeanors involving violence, sexual misconduct, or dishonesty.

What's in a name?

I've served as an expert witness in many interesting litigation matters concerning real estate. One of my more memorable assignments was to consult with the Legal Aid Society of Alameda County, based in Oakland, California. It had received complaints from several people who claimed they were being repeatedly denied rental housing even though they had excellent jobs and perfect credit.

After a brief investigation, it became obvious that the problem was a particular Bay Area tenant screening service that wasn't accurately identifying rental applicants. When a rental applicant with a fairly common name was run through its database, the company provided the rental property owner with negative information on evictions and poor credit patterns. Unfortunately, because its information wasn't carefully screened and verified, the data wasn't applicable to the actual rental applicant. Some very responsible and qualified applicants were turned down simply because they had the same name as an individual with a very poor credit report.

The lesson? Always verify an applicant's name, Social Security number or Individual Taxpayer Identification Number, and several former addresses to ensure you're using the correct information in your screening efforts. Compare the Social Security card (if available) with information showing the approximate date and general geographic location of its issuance. You know you have a problem if your applicant is over the age of 40 and was born and raised along the East coast, yet the credit reporting agency indicates that the Social Security card was originally issued in Arizona in the last few years.

When reviewing a rental applicant's criminal history, you need to consider convictions only and not simply arrests. Because the U.S. legal system is based on the idea that someone is innocent until proven guilty, only those applicants who have criminal convictions should be denied. However, it's not really that simple. The federal Fair Housing Amendments Act considers past drug addiction a disability, and prior drug-use felony convictions alone may not be sufficient grounds to deny an applicant. (Fortunately, current drug use or the sale, manufacturing, or distribution of illegal substances isn't protected under Fair Housing laws.) Some states also limit the ability to deny housing to registered sex offenders. Always seek legal advice if you have any questions about the findings of a criminal records search.

With many tenants moving from area to area, performing a thorough criminal records search in every location the applicant may have lived can be cost prohibitive. Many rental property owners only request a criminal records search if the rental applicant indicates that he's been convicted of (or pled guilty or no contest to) a felony or a misdemeanor involving violence, sexual misconduct, or dishonesty. Be diligent in looking for any indications that may provide a clue to possible criminal activity, such as gaps in rental history while the prospect was incarcerated.

Consistency is the key to all tenant screening activity, including your efforts to minimize the chances of renting to someone who may present a direct threat to the health or safety of others. You need to establish a policy of either inquiring about past criminal history or running a criminal records search on *all* rental applicants to ensure that your rental screening process is applied uniformly.

Talking with all personal references

Although you may expect that all a prospect's personal references share only glowing comments about how lucky you'd be to have the applicant as your new tenant, investing the time to call all of a prospect's references is important for several reasons.

First, you occasionally find someone who tells you that the rental applicant is her best friend but she never loans him money or lets him borrow her car. Plus, if you call the given references and find that the contacts are bogus, you can use this information as part of your overall screening of the applicant.

Dealing with guarantors

If your rental prospect doesn't meet the criteria outlined in your Statement of Rental Policy, you may consider approving her application if she provides a cosigner or *guarantor*. The guarantor needs to sign a Guarantee of Lease or Rental Agreement form (shown in Figure 10-1, and also on the CD); however, a guarantor must be financially qualified and screened, or the guarantee is worthless.

Signing a separate Guarantee of Lease or Rental Agreement is better than asking the cosigner to simply sign the rental contract, because doing so avoids any confusion about whether the cosigner lives in the rental unit if you need to regain physical possession with an eviction action.

Require your guarantor to complete a rental application, pay the application fee, and go through a verification of income screening. This process is similar to your procedure for the applicant except you don't need to verify rental or criminal history. Keep in mind that the guarantor won't actually be living at the rental unit and thus will have his own housing costs. So in order to ensure that the guarantor can meet all his own obligations and cover your tenant's rent in case of a default, you need to account for the guarantor's cost of housing before comparing it to your income requirements.

Guarantee of Lease or Rental Agreement

On the date below, in consideration of the execution of the Lease or Rental Agreement, dated _____, 20 _____,

for the premises located at: _____ (Rental unit) by and between

_____ (Tenant)

_____ (Owner) and

_____ (Guarantor);

for valuable consideration, receipt of which is hereby acknowledged, the Guarantor does hereby guarantee unconditionally to Owner, Owner's agent, and/or including Owner's successor and assigns, the prompt payment by Tenant of any unpaid rent, property damage and cleaning and repair costs or any other sums which become due pursuant to said lease or rental agreement, a copy of which is attached hereto, including any and all court costs or attorney's fees incurred in enforcing the lease or rental agreement.

If Tenant assigns or subleases the Rental unit, Guarantor shall remain liable under the terms of this Agreement for the performance of the assignee or sublessee, unless Owner relieves Guarantor by express written termination of this Agreement.

In the event of the breach of any terms of the Lease or Rental Agreement by the Tenant, Guarantor shall be liable for any damages, financial or physical, caused by Tenant, including any and all legal fees incurred in enforcing the Lease or Rental Agreement. Owner or Owner's agent may immediately enforce this Guarantee upon any default by Tenant and an action against Guarantor may be brought at any time without first seeking recourse against the Tenant.

The insolvency of Tenant or nonpayment of any sums due from Tenant may be deemed a default giving rise to action by Owner against Guarantor. This Guarantee does not confer a right to possession of the Rental unit by Guarantor, and Owner is not required to serve Guarantor with any legal notices, including any demand for payment of rent, prior to Owner proceeding against Guarantor for Guarantor's obligation under this Guarantee.

Unless released in writing by Owner, Guarantor shall remain obligated by the terms of this Guarantee for the entire period of the tenancy as provided by the Lease or Rental Agreement and for any extensions pursuant thereto. In the event Tenant and Owner modify the terms of said Lease or Rental Agreement, with or without the knowledge or consent of Guarantor, Guarantor waives any and all rights to be released from the provisions of this Guarantee and Guarantor shall remain obligated by said additional modifications and terms of the Lease or Rental Agreement. Guarantor hereby consents and agrees in advance to any changes, modifications, additions, or deletions of the Lease or Rental Agreement made and agreed to by Owner and Tenant during the entire period of the tenancy.

If any legal action or proceeding is brought by either party to enforce any part of this agreement, the prevailing party shall recover, in addition to all other relief, reasonable attorney's fees and costs. By signing below, Owner, Tenant and Guarantor acknowledge and accept all terms contained herein.

_____   _____   _____
Tenant's Signature   Guarantor's Signature   Owner's Signature

_____   _____   _____
Tenant's Name (print)   Guarantor's Name (print)   Owner's Name (print)

_____   _____   _____
Tenant's Address   Guarantor's Address   Owner's Address

_____   _____   _____
Date   Date   Date

_____   _____   _____
Daytime phone number   Daytime phone number   Daytime phone number

Figure 10-1:
Guarantee
of Lease
or Rental
Agreement.

For example, if the proposed guarantor has a gross monthly income of $4,000 with a $1,000 mortgage payment, he has an adjusted gross income of $3,000. Assuming you have an income standard that requires the tenant to earn three times the monthly rent (and assuming the guarantor meets all your other screening criteria), this person can be the guarantor for your prospect as long as the rent doesn't exceed $1,000 per month.

Although a guarantor can be very important and can give you extra resources in the event of a rent default by your tenant, out-of-state guarantors aren't as valuable as in-state ones. Enforcing the rental contract guarantee against an out-of-state party can be very difficult, or even financially unfeasible.

Making your final decision

Selecting your tenant is one of the most important decisions you make as a rental property owner, because choosing your tenant has a significant positive or negative impact on your success. Ideally, you've already established written tenant screening criteria and a system for evaluating the qualifications of your rental applicants; if you haven't, flip back to the previous sections in this chapter.

Although you need to carefully follow Fair Housing guidelines, never compromise your tenant screening criteria or allow yourself to be intimidated into accepting an unqualified rental applicant. HUD and state Fair Housing agencies have consistently ruled that rejecting an applicant who doesn't meet your objective tenant screening criteria isn't discrimination, even if the applicant belongs to a legally protected class.

Some Fair Housing advocates recommend that you have a policy of considering the applications in the order they're received and accepting the first prospective tenant who meets your rental criteria. I feel that as long as you're consistent in your tenant selection methods that you should select the tenant who's best qualified. However, you need to be prepared for other qualified applicants who may feel they weren't treated properly. Clearly document your business reasons for selecting a certain applicant. Legitimate business reasons can include the following everything from higher income, more assets, much better references, superior credit report, and willingness to sign a longer term lease.

If you use the first qualified applicant method, be sure to note on the application the date and time it was submitted, as well as the date and time it was approved, and that the rental unit is no longer available. This information can be helpful if qualified applicants from protected classes claim you discriminated by accepting an application submitted after theirs or allege that you refused to show available units by claiming they were rented.

Some tenant screening services offer *risk scoring* of your rental applicant based on scoring models that they claim are designed to objectively predict an applicant's likelihood of fulfilling lease obligations. If you use one of these services, make sure you can meet the disclosure requirements of the federal Fair Credit Reporting Act (FCRA). Only use a tenant screening service that's willing to provide your denied applicants with a written, detailed notice of denial to rent that meets all FCRA requirements.

Notifying the Applicant of Your Decision

Rental property owners are legally allowed to choose among rental applicants as long as their decisions comply with all Fair Housing laws and are based on legitimate business criteria (see the preceding section for an idea of legitimate business reasons). Regardless of whether you accept or reject a rental applicant, be sure to notify him promptly after you make your decision.

If you approve the applicant, contact him and arrange for a meeting and a walk-through of the rental unit prior to the move-in date. Don't notify the other qualified applicants that you've rented the property until all legal documents have been signed and all funds due upon move-in have been collected in full.

One of the most difficult tasks you face as a rental property owner is informing a rental applicant that you've denied his application. You obviously want to avoid an argument over the rejection, but even more importantly, you want to avoid a Fair Housing complaint based on the applicant's misunderstanding about the reasons for the denial.

If you deny an applicant, notify him in writing. If you notify the denied applicant by phone only, you may have difficulty giving all the required details and disclosures. A written notice of denial to rent avoids a situation in which the applicant may unintentionally (or sometimes intentionally) form the opinion that you're denying his application in a discriminatory manner and file a complaint with the Department of Housing and Urban Development (HUD) or a state or local Fair Housing agency.

Using a Notice of Denial to Rent form (see Figure 10–2, also available on the CD) to tell the applicant in writing of your decision is an excellent idea. This form helps you document the various and valid legal reasons for your rejection of the applicant. This simple checklist also allows you to provide the applicant with the information required by the FCRA. If you reject an applicant based on his credit report, FCRA requires you to notify the applicant of his rights. You should provide the denied applicant with a letter containing the mandatory disclosures so that you have proof you complied with the law. (You must also provide this information even if you've approved the applicant but have required him to pay a higher security deposit or higher rent, or have a cosigner — see "Dealing with guarantors" earlier in this chapter for more on cosigners.) Your rejection letter should include:

NOTICE OF DENIAL TO RENT

To:
_____

All Applicants (full name) listed on application
Thank you for applying to rent at:
_____

We have carefully and thoroughly reviewed your rental application. We are hereby informing you of certain information required by the Federal Fair Credit Reporting Act. Based on the information currently in our files, your application has been denied for the following reason(s):

I. Rental History
__ Could not be verified   __ Unpaid or delinquent rent reported   __ Property damage reported
__ Disruptive behavior reported   __ Prior eviction reported   __ Other
_____

II. Employment and Income
__ Employment could not be verified __ Local employment could not be verified
__ Irregular or temporary employment   __ Income could not be verified
__ Insufficient income   __ Other _____

III. Credit History
__ Could not be verified   __ Unsatisfactory payment history   __ Collection activity
__ Bankruptcy filing   __ Liens, garnishments, or judgments __ Other
_____

IV. Criminal History
__ Conviction for (or pled guilty or no contest to) any felony, or a misdemeanor involving violence, sexual misconduct or honesty

V. Personal Reference
__ Could not be verified   __ Lack of non-related references   __ Negative reference
__ Other _____

VI. Application
__ Application unsigned   __ Application incomplete __ False information provided
__ Rental unit rented to prior qualified candidate   __ Other
_____

When a credit report is used in making this decision, Section 615(a) of the Fair Credit Reporting Act requires us to tell you where we obtained that report. The credit reporting agency that provided information to us was:
Name
_____

Address
_____

Telephone
_____

This agency only provided information about you and your credit history and was not involved in any way in making the decision to reject your rental application, nor can they explain why the decision was made. Pursuant to the Fair Credit Reporting Act, if you believe the information they provided is inaccurate or incomplete, you may call the credit reporting agency at the number listed above or communicate by mail.

You have the right to obtain a free copy of your consumer report from the credit reporting agency indicated above if your request is made within 60 days of the date of this notice. If you dispute any of the information in your report, you have the right to submit a consumer statement of up to 100 words into your report explaining your position on the item in dispute. The credit reporting agencies offer assistance in preparing your consumer statement.

If information was received from a person or company other than a credit reporting agency, then you have the right to make a written request to us within 60 days of receiving this notice for a disclosure of the nature of this information.

You may have additional rights under the credit reporting or consumer protection laws of your state or local municipality. For further information contact your state Attorney General or consumer affairs office.

_____   _____
Owner or Agent for Owner   Date

Figure 10-2:
Notice of
Denial to
Rent Form.

✔ The names, addresses, and phone numbers of all credit reporting agencies that provided you with information.

✔ A notice that the credit reporting agency only provides information about credit history, takes no part in the decision process, and can't give reasons for the rejection.

✔ A notice that the applicant has the right to obtain a free copy of the credit report from the credit agency if he requests it within 60 days of your rejection.

✔ A notice informing the applicant that he has the right to dispute the accuracy of the information on the report. He can also demand a reinvestigation or provide the credit reporting agency with a statement describing his position.

✔ A notice that if information was received from a person or company other than a credit reporting agency, the applicant has the right to make a written request within 60 days of receiving this notice for a disclosure of the nature of this information.

Keep a copy of all rejection letters for at least four years.

Avoiding Housing Discrimination Complaints

If you're in the rental housing business for long, you'll hear about a shocking settlement or award against a rental property owner for violating a Fair Housing law. Many of these awards or settlements can exceed $100,000. In a recent ten-year period, Fair Housing discrimination cases investigated by HUD alone resulted in awards of more than $42 million.

You may even have read about the facts of certain Fair Housing cases and thought to yourself that the defendants deserved to lose and that a discrimination case will never happen to you. That's probably true — if you're an educated owner and you know and abide by all federal, state, and local Fair Housing laws. The problem arises when rental property owners are unaware that their policies or practices are discriminatory. For example, you may think that you're just being a courteous and caring landlord by only showing rental applicants with children your available rental units located on the ground floor. But not giving applicants without children the same treatment you give others is a form of discrimination — even if that wasn't your intent.

Federal and state laws prohibit discrimination against certain protected classes in rental housing. These laws impact your tenant screening and selection process, and I cover the issues surrounding these laws in the following sections.

The ins and outs of Fair Housing

Discrimination is a major issue for rental property owners, and it has serious legal consequences for the uninformed. If you don't know the law, you may be guilty of various forms of discrimination and not even realize it until you've been charged.

Our legal system acknowledges two types of Fair Housing discrimination:

- **Treating members of protected classes differently from the way you treat others who aren't members of that protected class:** For example, say you have two applicants with similar financial histories, tenant histories, and other screening criteria, but charge one applicant who's a member of a certain protected class a larger security deposit. You may be subject to a Fair Housing discrimination inquiry or complaint on the basis of different treatment.

- **Treating all prospects equally, but having a disparate impact because of an individual's minority status:** If your occupancy standard policy is two persons per bedroom, you may be accused of familial status discrimination based on *disparate impact,* which is when a policy is the same for all applicants, but it has a much different effect on certain applicants and essentially creates an additional barrier to rental housing for families. Although you've set an occupancy standard policy that's applied equally to all tenants, your restrictive policy discourages applicants with children. This scenario is an example of disparate impact.

The federal Fair Housing Act prohibits discrimination on the basis of race, color, religion, ethnicity, sex, age, familial status, and physical or mental disability. Several states and many major cities have laws to protect individuals affected by other issues that aren't specifically protected under federal Fair Housing laws. Examples include occupation, educational status, medical status, sexual orientation, source of income, and physical body size.

Although several states still have laws prohibiting unmarried couples from living together, the majority of states have very broad Fair Housing laws forbidding all arbitrary discrimination on the basis of an individual's personal characteristics or traits. Always be sure to fully understand the Fair Housing requirements and limitations that apply to your rental property.

When renting your property, keep some of these specific pointers in mind:

- **Be careful not to inadvertently favor one sex as renters.** For example, some rental property owners may have the perception that male tenants aren't as clean or quiet as female tenants. Conversely, some owners with rental properties in rough areas may believe that male tenants are less susceptible to being victims of crime. As a result, these owners may attempt to restrict female tenants to upper-level rental units. Don't allow any stereotypes or assumptions to enter into your tenant selection criteria.

- **Consider adding Fair Housing posters in another language if you have a rental unit in an area where a significant portion of the local population doesn't speak English.** HUD offers free Fair Housing posters in many different languages so that you can easily find one that's most applicable to your locale.

✔ **Pay attention to age-related issues.** Although the federal Fair Housing Act doesn't specifically state that age is a protected category, many states and localities have laws that directly address the issue of age. Typically, you can deny rental applicants who're less than 18 years of age unless they are currently or were previously legally married, an active-duty member of the military, or emancipated by court order. In these cases, you must treat them just like any other adult rental applicant.

Following are three main exemptions to the *federal* Fair Housing laws:

✔ An owner-occupied rental property with four or fewer units.

✔ Single-family housing rented without the use of discriminatory advertising or without using an agent to facilitate or handle the leasing.

✔ Housing reserved exclusively for seniors that's intended for and solely occupied by persons 62 years of age or older (which includes spouses and adult children but excludes caregivers and on-site employees). Also HUD-certified seniors properties where 80 percent or more of the households are occupied by at least one person who's 55-years-old. In both cases, the exemption is only against claims of age discrimination.

Many states, and even local governments, have passed their own legislation that may apply to your rental property and affect the above exemptions. Don't count on an exemption and be sure to abide by all Fair Housing laws that may be applicable to your property, even if you think you're exempt. Abiding by all Fair Housing laws not only eliminates any potential complaints, but it's also simply the right thing to do.

Steering and chilling

Steering means to guide, or attempt to guide, a rental applicant toward living where you think she should live based on race, color, religion, ethnicity, sex, familial status, physical or mental disability, or another protected class. Steering is an illegal act that deprives persons of their right to choose to rent where they want. HUD has clearly indicated that not showing or renting certain units to minorities is one form of steering. Another form according to HUD is the "assigning of any person to a particular section or floor of a building" based on any of the protected classes listed previously.

Rental property owners often have only good intentions when they suggest that a rental prospect with children see only rental units near the playground. However, the failure to offer such an applicant an opportunity to see *all* available rental units is steering — and a violation of Fair Housing laws.

Steering can be subtle or very direct. Some examples of steering include

- ✔ Limiting families or persons with disabilities to ground floor units

- ✔ Offering families or minorities only units near the playground or by the laundry room or elevator, because noise makes these units less desirable

- ✔ Relegating families to certain buildings or sections of a building, or having separate family and adult buildings

A similar concept is known as *chilling,* which is making comments or establishing rules designed to discourage certain applicants from renting. Some examples of chilling include

- ✔ Pointing out property hazards to applicants with children that you don't point out to all applicants

- ✔ Showing only undesirable units in the hope that the applicant doesn't rent

- ✔ Questioning disabled or elderly applicants about their disabilities or whether they can care for themselves or should live alone

- ✔ Telling certain applicants something negative about the property that isn't true

Be very careful not to make any suggestions or comments that can be misinterpreted as steering or chilling. All rental applicants should receive the same information on the area, the property, and the full range of rental units available so that they can decide for themselves which units they want to see.

Children

Federal and state legislation has virtually eliminated "adult only" housing except for certain HUD-certified seniors properties. I always recommend that rental property owners openly accept renters with children. Families tend to be more stable, and they're looking for a safe, crime-free, and drug-free environment in which to raise their children. Along with responsible pet owners, who also have difficulty finding suitable rental properties, families with children can be excellent, long-term renters. And typically the longer your tenants stay, the better your cash flow.

Some rental property owners are concerned about renting to families with children because the property has hazards that may be dangerous for children. For example, the property may not have any safe areas for children to play. Although you may truly only have the children's best interests in mind, the parents have the right to decide whether the property is safe for their children. Of course, you do need to take steps to make your property as safe as possible by posting speed limit signs in your driveway or including restrictions on recreational use of driveways and parking areas.

Be careful not to discourage applicants with policies and guidelines for the conduct of children unless these rules are *safety-related*. For example, don't institute a policy against children riding bicycles on the property. Instead, you can have a policy that says *no one* is allowed to ride bicycles on the property. (This way, the policy doesn't discriminate against children; it's uniformly applied to all.) Avoid using any terms that are obviously directed at children, such as "minors," "toys," "tricycles," "diapers," "playing," and the like. Make sure all your policies are age-neutral except for certain health and safety issues. For example, some states have specific laws requiring rental owners to have policies that, in order to use swimming pools or spas, children under 14 must be accompanied by an adult.

Charging rental applicants with children higher rents or higher security deposits than applicants without children is illegal, as is offering different rental terms, such as shorter leases, fewer unit amenities, or different payment options. The property's facilities must also be fully available for all tenants, regardless of age, unless a clear safety issue is involved.

Reasonable accommodations

The federal Fair Housing Act requires property owners to make reasonable accommodations for tenants with physical or mental disabilities so that they're able to enjoy the rental property on an equal basis with tenants who don't have disabilities. The cost of these accommodations may involve a reasonable expenditure by the landlord, or the tenant may offer to make the accommodations at his expense. Requests for reasonable accommodations are valid if made verbally, but you should ask the tenant to make the request in writing. If that's not feasible, you can put the request in writing and have the tenant verify the information and sign or initial it.

The Fair Housing regulations state:

> "It shall be unlawful for any person to refuse to make reasonable accommodations in rules, policies, practices, or services, when such accommodations may be necessary to afford a handicapped person equal opportunity to use and enjoy a dwelling unit, including public and common areas."

Rental property owners are required to make reasonable adjustments to their rules, procedures, or services upon request. Landlords must refrain from assuming someone has a disability or inquiring if someone does. Each request for a reasonable accommodation must be considered seriously.

Examples of reasonable accommodations that you may be required to offer include

✔ Providing a parking space that's wider and closer to the rental unit of a wheelchair-bound tenant

✔ Arranging to read all management communications to a tenant with poor vision

✔ Allowing a tenant who receives income from a government agency to pay on a biweekly rather than monthly basis

Reasonable modifications

Federal law also provides that rental property owners are required to allow a tenant with disabilities the right to modify her living space at her own expense (except in project-based, HUD-subsidized housing, in which the landlord may be obligated to pay for reasonable modifications — see Chapter 21 for more on HUD-subsidized housing). The modifications can only be to the extent necessary to allow the resident an equal opportunity to use and enjoy the premises. If the modifications will make the unit unacceptable to the next tenant, the landlord may require that the current tenant agree to return the rental unit to its original condition upon vacating the property. The rental property owner can also require the tenant to pay the funds necessary to perform the needed restoration into an interest-bearing escrow account.

Reasonable modifications that tenants may request to make at their expense include

✔ Ramps at the rental unit entry

✔ Lower light switches and the removal of doors or widening of doorways to allow for wheelchair access

✔ Grab bars or call buttons in bathrooms

✔ Lower kitchen cabinets and the removal of base cabinet doors

✔ Service animals allowed in the pool area even though you don't permit other animals there

✔ Roll-in showers

The modifications must be reasonable. You can require the tenant to obtain your prior approval and ensure that the modification will be made in a work-manlike manner, including any necessary government approvals or permits. You can also require the tenant to provide verification that she fits the defini-tion of a disabled person and that a disability-related need exists for the modi-fication if the disability and the need aren't apparent. But you can't ask about the specific disability of the tenant that necessitates these changes.

Companion or service animals

If you have a "no pets" policy, keep in mind that Fair Housing law requires rental property owners to make "necessary and reasonable accommodation." One specific common accommodation is not having any limitations or not discouraging occupancy by tenants who need a *support animal.* Companion or service animals that assist tenants with daily life activities aren't pets; they're exempt animals and must be allowed in all rental properties, regard-less of any "no pet" policies. Fair Housing laws also prohibit you from requiring an animal or pet deposit, or increasing the tenant's security deposit because he has a support animal. Further, you can't make any rules limiting the types or breeds of animals (for example, allowing German shepherds only) or an unreasonable size restriction. You can, however, establish rea-sonable rules of conduct for the animals and should note that the tenant is still responsible for any damages done by the animal.

Some tenants seek the accommodation of a companion animal based on their need for comfort or companionship, and federal law requires owners and managers to grant the request if the tenant's claim is true and reason-able. The best method of determining reasonability is to obtain verification from the tenant's healthcare provider or other professional such as a medical doctor, therapist, or social worker. To avoid claims of discrimination or favoritism, set a consistent policy of requesting official verification before allowing any companion animals. Of course, like all potential housing discrimination issues, failing to consider a tenant request can lead to serious legal consequences.

Determining what's reasonable in the eyes of Fair Housing officials is always murky, so look at each request individually to make a proper decision. For example, a tenant in a one-bedroom apartment who requests to keep two large dogs as companion animals is being unreasonable, but the same request from a tenant in a large, single-family home with a yard is most likely a reasonable request. If you're uncertain as to whether a particular request is reasonable, seek direction from local Fair Housing agencies or legal counsel whenever possible. Ask these representatives to provide you with their written opinion or send you a letter outlining their verbal directive; be sure to keep copies of this documentation in your rental files.

Americans with Disabilities Act

Discrimination against people with disabilities in residential housing is covered in the federal Fair Housing Act. However, in July 1990, Congress passed the Americans with Disabilities Act (ADA) which has far-reaching impact on most commercial and retail real estate. The ADA has limited requirements for many rental property owners, because it applies only to the public areas and not the private or common areas of residential properties.

Under the ADA, all areas of a property to which the public is invited must be accessible by individuals with disabilities. For example, a rental property with an on-site office (and other public amenities, like a clubhouse, rental unit models, or a pool and spa area) must be accessible to persons with disabilities. The removal of existing physical barriers at the rental property owner's expense is required whenever it's "readily achievable and technically feasible." The ADA also establishes parking requirements if the residential property provides public parking, such as prospective resident spaces.

Often you'll be able to simply restripe your parking areas to provide the required parking but be careful, because many local municipalities have very specific parking requirements for multi-unit rental properties. You want to make sure before you make any changes that your new parking layout meets the minimum parking requirements for your property zoning. Check with your local building and code enforcement office for details.

The ADA applies to all residential properties, even those built prior to the passage of the law. Owners of residential properties occupied prior to March 13, 1991, are required to remove barriers to accessibility, but they aren't required to make changes that may cause undue hardship. Owners of properties occupied after March 13, 1991, must comply with ADA and should be in compliance with the federal Fair Housing Act, too. Professional complainants seek out ADA violations in both residential and commercial rental properties, so know what you're responsible for accommodating.

If you have a rental property with public areas, you may want to consider using the services of a qualified contractor, architect, or engineer with specific ADA knowledge to conduct a physical assessment and evaluation of your property and make compliance recommendations. You should also consult your rental housing legal advisor if you have any questions about ADA compliance. For more information on ADA requirements for residential rental property owners, visit the federal Department of Justice ADA Web site at www.usdoj.gov/crt/ada/adahom1.htm.

If your prospective tenant has a physical or mental disability that substantially limits one or more major life activities, or has a record of having such a disability, you must allow him to make reasonable modifications to your rental property, including common areas, if necessary for him to use the rental housing. Conditions qualifying as *physical* or *mental disabilities* are evolving, but this term can include mobility, hearing, and visual impairments; chronic mental illness; chronic alcoholism; AIDS or AIDS-related illness; or mental retardation. Many state and local laws are expanding the definition of their protected categories, so be sure to check with legal counsel if you ever have any questions regarding the rights of your tenants under federal or state Fair Housing laws.

Sexual harassment

Sexual harassment, in the world of property management, occurs when you refuse to rent to a person who rejects your sexual advances, or when you make life difficult for or harass a tenant who resists your unwanted advances. Most rental property owners understand the concern and find such behavior unconscionable. Yet this problem often arises when rental property owners hire someone to assist them with the leasing, rent collection, or maintenance requirements at their properties. If the vendor or contractor commits sexual harassment, the rental property owner is accountable because the offender is the employee or agent of the owner.

Make sure you have a clear written policy against sexual harassment, provide an open-minded procedure for investigating complaints, and conduct thorough and unbiased investigations that lead to quick corrective action, if necessary.

Part III
The Brass Tacks of Managing Rentals

The 5th Wave   By Rich Tennant

©RICHTENNANT

"Well, you've just gone over the line in breaking the no pets, no smokers clause in the rental agreement, Mr. Crawford."

In this part . . .

Managing rental property involves a lot more than just managing the property itself. Working with tenants — from orienting a tenant to your rules prior to move-in to having the paperwork in order when a tenant moves out — is what you'll spend a huge chunk of your time doing. So the chapters in this part take you through that relationship step by step. I show you how to help tenants at move-in and move-out times, how to increase the rent without losing your tenants, and how to retain the good tenants and deal with the bad ones. Chances are you can find the answer to any question you may have about your tenants in this part.

Chapter 11

Moving In the Tenants

After selecting your new tenants, you still have to complete one very important step to ensure you establish a good landlord-tenant relationship: moving in the tenants. In order to guarantee the tenants' move-in process goes smoothly, you need to hold a tenant orientation and rental property inspection meeting, which allows you the opportunity to present the rental property and your ownership and management skills in the best possible light. You also need to make sure your new tenants understand and agree to the policies and rules you've established for the rental property.

If you're organized and prepared, you'll be able to quickly and efficiently handle the necessary administrative steps to get the tenants into their new rental unit. Tenants are very excited and motivated to begin moving in to their new home, and you want this process to be smooth and pleasant for everyone.

In this chapter, I outline the important steps to start your landlord-tenant relationship off on the right foot, including scheduling the move-in date and the tenant orientation meeting, conducting the preoccupancy inspection and documenting the unit's conditions, providing important policies to tenants in a written format, and using creative ideas to welcome your tenants on move-in day.

Establishing the Move-In Date

When you inform your prospective tenant that his rental application has been approved, you need to determine a mutually agreeable move-in date. You and the tenant may have discussed this date during your initial telephone conversation or when you showed the rental property, but be sure to raise the issue again to guarantee you're in agreement of the date.

After new tenants have been approved, some suddenly stall on setting the move-in date. They may stall because they're still obligated under a lease or 30-day notice at another rental property and don't want to double pay. Unless you're willing to suffer additional rent loss that you can never recover, insist that the tenant begin paying rent to you on the originally scheduled move-in date. The time for your new tenant to negotiate the move-in date was *before* you approved him.

In some situations, your rental unit may not be available at your mutually agreed move-in date. Perhaps the prior tenants didn't vacate when they said they would, perhaps the rental unit was in much worse condition than you anticipated, or perhaps you just weren't able to complete the required prep work in time. If a delay in having the rental unit available as promised appears inevitable, communicate with your new tenant immediately. Often, a new tenant can adjust his move-in date as long as you give him reasonable notice. If he can't adjust his move-in date, communicate with him and try to work out other possible arrangements.

Sometimes new tenants ask whether they can move just a few items into the rental unit before your preoccupancy conference. Don't allow it! You create a landlord-tenant relationship simply by letting the new tenants have access to the rental unit without you present or by allowing them to store even a few items in the unit. If you have to cancel the rental for any reason, you then need to go through a formal legal eviction that can take several weeks.

Although the rental property should be in rent-ready condition before being shown to rental prospects, it can quickly get dirty or dusty if there's any delay between showing the property and moving in the new tenants. So before meeting with your tenant prior to move-in (covered in the following section), make one last visit to the rental unit and go through your rent-ready inspection checklist (flip to "Having the tenant sign an inspection checklist" later in this chapter for the scoop on this item) again just to make sure you don't encounter surprises when move-in day arrives.

Moving is very stressful for most people, and if your new tenant has a bad move-in experience, this feeling can last for months, or even stay in his mind throughout the tenancy. Many aspects of the tenant's move are beyond your control. Although you can't guarantee your new tenant a simple and painless move, you can take steps to ensure you're organized and ready to handle any complaints or concerns about his new home. If at all possible, arrange to be on the premises during his move-in so you can answer any questions.

Meeting with a Tenant Prior to Move-In

After you and your tenant have decided on a move-in date, you need to meet to deal with some of the technicalities, like walking through the property, signing paperwork, and handing over the keys. Getting together to do this is a very important step, and you need to do it before your new tenant actually moves in and takes possession of the rental unit.

Schedule a meeting with the tenant either for the day of the scheduled move-in or within just a few days before the move-in date. At this meeting, you review your property policies and rules, review and sign all the paperwork, collect the move-in funds, conduct a thorough property inspection with your new tenant, and complete the Move-In/Move-Out Inspection Checklist (which I explain later in this chapter).

The following sections walk you through each step of the move-in process.

Covering the rules with your new tenant

When you meet with your new tenant, start by giving her a copy of your house rules (see Figure 11-1 for an example of this kind of document). Give her a chance to read over the rules and ask questions, providing clarification as necessary. Then ask for her signature, which indicates she has received and understands the rules and agrees to abide by them.

The phrase *rules and regulations* tends to sound rather imposing to most tenants. So I recommend using the phrase *policies and rules,* or simply *house rules,* whenever possible. Some rental housing owners and managers use the phrase *policies and guidelines,* but I feel that you need to make it very clear that these are legally enforceable rules, not optional guidelines. Your policies and rules are separate from the rental contract, which is drafted by an attorney using lots of formal and hard-to-understand terminology. The rules you draft should be more informal and conversational in tone than your rental contract. Be sure to use clear language that's neither harsh nor demeaning.

Many owners and managers of single-family or small rental properties don't worry about detailed rules and regulations, because they think the rental contract covers it all. But setting up some basic rules that can easily be changed as necessary upon proper written notice to the tenants is a good idea. This tactic shows that you and your tenants are on the same page and gives you flexibility in managing your property.

Policies and Rules

We are proud of this property and we hope that your living experience here will be pleasant and comfortable. The support and cooperation of you, as our tenant, is necessary for us to maintain our high standards.

This is your personal copy of our Policies and Rules. Please read it carefully as it is an integral part of your rental agreement. When you sign your rental agreement, you agree to abide by the policies and rules for this rental property, and they are considered legally binding provisions of your rental agreement. If you have any questions, please contact us and we will be glad to help.

This document is an addendum and is part of the Lease or Rental Agreement, dated _____, by and between _____, Owner, and _____Tenant, for the premises located at: _____.

New policies and rules or amendments to this document may be adopted by Owner upon giving 30 days written notice to tenant.

Guests: Tenant is responsible for their own proper conduct and that of all guests, including the responsibility for understanding and observing all policies and rules.

Noise: Although the Premises are well constructed, they are not completely soundproof and reasonable consideration for neighbors is important. Either inside or outside of the Premises, no tenant or their guest shall use, or allow to be used, any sound-emitting device at a sound level that may annoy, disturb, or otherwise interfere with the rights, comforts, or conveniences of other tenants or neighbors. Particular care must be taken between the hours of 9:00 p.m. and 9:00 a.m.

Parking: No vehicle belonging to a Tenant shall be parked in such a manner as to impede passage in the street or to prevent access to the property. Tenant shall only use assigned and designated parking spaces. Tenant shall ensure that all posted handicap, fire zones, or other no-parking areas remain clear of vehicles at all times. Vehicles parked in unauthorized areas or in another tenants designated parking space may be towed away at the vehicle owners expense. Vehicles may not be backed in, and repairs and maintenance of any sort are not allowed on the premises. All vehicles must be currently registered and in operative condition. No trucks, commercial vehicles, recreational vehicles, motorcycles, bicycles, boats, or trailers are allowed anywhere on the Premises without advance written approval of the Owner. All vehicles must be parked properly between the lines of the parking space. Tenant shall ensure that their guests abide by all of these parking policies and rules.

Patios/Balconies and Entry Areas: Patios/balconies and entry areas are restricted to patio-type furniture and are to be kept clean and orderly. No barbecues or similar cooking devices may be used on the Premises without advance written approval. No items may be hung from the Premises at anytime, and all entryways and walkways must be kept free from items that could be a hazard. Owner reserves the right to require that items that detract from the appearance of the Premises be removed immediately upon request. No unauthorized storage is allowed at any time.

Wall Hangings: Pictures may be hung on a thin nail. Mirrors, wall units, hanging wall or light fixtures, etc. need special attention and professional installation. Please contact the Owner for approval in advance as damage to the Premises will be the responsibility of the Tenant.

Trash: Tenant is responsible for keeping the inside and outside of the Premises clean, sanitary, and free from objectionable odors at all times. Tenant shall ensure that all trash, papers, cigarette butts, and similar items are sealed in trash bags and placed in appropriate receptacles. No trash or other materials shall be allowed to accumulate so as to cause a hazard or be in violation of any health, fire, or safety ordinance or regulation.

Figure 11-1:
House
Rules.

When establishing and having your new tenant review your rules, keep the following points in mind to reduce the chances of any future headaches:

- ✔ **Make sure your tenant actually reads and follows your rules but try not to be too overbearing.** Review your rules with several of your friends and colleagues to find better ways to say the same thing. Be clear, direct, and firm, yet not condescending. And watch out for something called the *no index.* The no index happens when many of your rules are too blunt and negative, such as "No cash," "No glass in the pool area," "No storage on your balcony," or "No riding bikes on the grounds." Although each of these rules is reasonable and important for the safe and efficient operation of your rental property, you can say the same thing in a much more positive way. For example, instead of saying, "No riding bikes on the grounds," you can say, "Please walk your bikes in the common area." Or instead of saying, "No cash," you can say, "We gladly accept your checks or money orders." Phrasing the rules in a more positive tone and minimizing the no index makes the rules — and you — seem friendlier to your tenant.

- ✔ **Verify that your house rules are reasonable and enforceable.** They must not discriminate against anyone in a protected class. The term *protected class* refers to the federal antidiscrimination laws that "protect classes" of people because of race, gender, ethnicity, religion, and so on.

- ✔ **Be particularly careful to review your house rules to avoid any reference to children, unless the reference is related to certain health and safety issues.** For example, you can have a rule that states, "Persons under 14 must be accompanied by an adult while using the spa," because legitimate safety concerns exist regarding unattended children in spas. But a rule that says, "Children aren't allowed to leave bicycles in the common area" is inappropriate, because it singles out children and implies that adults can leave bikes in the common area if they want. A better way to handle this issue is to use wording that isn't age-specific, such as "No one is allowed to leave bicycles in the common area." With this verbiage, the rule applies to everyone and doesn't discriminate based on age.

- ✔ **Regularly review and make improvements in your house rules based on situations you've encountered.** But remember that you're not running a prison camp, and you don't want to alienate a tenant by harassing him or her with rules or controlling his or her day-to-day life.

As you revise your house rules, indicate the latest revision date in the lower left corner of the document so that your tenants know which rules are the most current. When you distribute this revised document, be sure to remind your tenants that these house rules supersede any prior versions. Get signatures from all your tenants, indicating they've received them and will comply.

TIP

And then there was light. . . .

Tenants usually aren't very anxious to begin paying for utilities, so you need to be sure your procedures clearly state that your new tenant must immediately contact the utility companies and put the utilities that are his responsibility in his name. Most rental property owners have the utilities revert to their name when the rental unit becomes vacant for unit turnover and rental showings. So if your new tenant doesn't change the utility billing information, you may end up paying for some of his utility bills. One way to make sure your new tenant handles this matter promptly is to confirm he's dealt with the utilities prior to releasing the mailbox key to him.

An even better way to avoid paying for the tenant's utilities is to have a policy as part of your tenant orientation meeting that you provide the contact information for all utilities. Then require your new tenant to contact all utility companies and establish the bills in his name while in your presence.

With the high cost of utilities, you need to be certain you and your tenants are on the same page regarding who is financially responsible for the rental unit's utility charges. In many states, rental property owners are required to disclose whether tenants are financially responsible for payment of any utility services outside of their rental unit. For example, exterior common area lighting may be connected to a rental unit or a common area natural gas barbeque may be connected to a tenant's gas meter. Besides disclosing this fact, many states require rental property owners to give tenants an appropriate rent credit for the common area utilities they help pay. Check the laws in your area and be sure to disclose this kind of information if you're so required.

Reviewing and signing documents

Tenants and property owners alike are usually aware of all the legal paperwork involved in renting a home. And although sifting through all that legalese isn't fun for anyone, doing so is important. Rental property owners and tenants each have specific legal rights and responsibilities that are outlined in these documents, and being aware of what you're agreeing to — and being sure your tenants know what they're agreeing to — is crucial.

In the next several sections, I outline the documents you need to go over with your new tenant and have him or her sign.

Rental contract

Be sure your tenant understands that when he signs your lease or month-to-month rental agreement, he's entering into a business contract that has significant rights and responsibilities for both parties. Before your tenant signs the rental contract, carefully and methodically review each clause.

Certain clauses in the rental contract are so important that you should have the tenant specifically initial them to indicate he's read these points and understands his rights and responsibilities in relation to them. For example, the tenant should initial the clause concerning the need for him to obtain his own renter's insurance policy to protect his property and cover him for liability claims (see Chapter 19 for more on educating your tenants about renter's insurance).

Have your new tenant initial that he's received the keys for the rental property and acknowledged that you had the locks rekeyed or changed since the last tenant vacated. Make sure the tenant reviews and signs any other rental contract addenda before letting him take possession of the unit.

Getting a tenant to sign your required legal documents can be very difficult after he has the keys and is in possession of the rental property. Even if the tenant fails to sign the rental contract, an oral landlord-tenant relationship is established when you give him the keys to the unit — and when you're relying on oral agreements, you and the tenant are likely to disagree on the terms. Regaining possession of your rental unit can be a long and expensive process, so be sure that every adult occupant signs all documents prior to handing over the keys.

Environmental disclosure forms

If you haven't already done so, be sure to give your new tenant copies of the required environmental disclosure form and the EPA pamphlet for lead-based paint and lead-based paint hazards, which are also required under federal law. (Turn to Chapter 9 for more info on disclosure of these hazards.)

Mold addendum

Mold is a common term for a variety of fungus types found virtually everywhere in our environment — both indoors and outdoors. Blaming elevated mold levels for alleged health problems caused by exposure to certain mold spores, which are often called *toxic mold,* is a fairly recent phenomenon. Such claims are very controversial, and currently, no federal regulations exist regarding permissible exposure limits or building tolerance standards for mold.

Mold can occur anywhere under the right conditions as long as it can find sufficient humidity or moisture and a food source, such as drywall or other common building materials. Mold can be prevented, but doing so requires the cooperation of both rental owners or managers and their tenants.

To minimize the possibility of mold concerns at your rental property, provide your tenant with a Mold Notification Addendum (shown in Figure 11-2; also on the CD) to inform and educate her on how she can help prevent mold growth through the proper daily lifestyle and housekeeping measures. This addendum indicates that you've inspected the condition of the property and deemed it free of damp or wet building materials upon tenant move-in. This document also verifies that no known issues of water intrusion, visible mold, or mildew exist. Be sure your tenant carefully reviews the addendum and signs her acknowledgment; give your tenant a copy for her records.

MOLD NOTIFICATION ADDENDUM

Page_____
of Agreement

This document is an Addendum and is part of the Rental/Lease Agreement, dated _____ between

_____ (Owner/Agent) and

_____ (Resident) for the

premises located at _____ , Unit # (if applicable) _____
(Street Address)

_____ , CA _____ .
(City) *(Zip)*

It is our goal to maintain the highest quality living environment for our Residents. The Owner/Agent has inspected the unit prior to lease and knows of no damp or wet building materials and knows of no mold or mildew contamination. Resident is hereby notified that mold, however, can grow if the premises are not properly maintained or ventilated. If moisture is allowed to accumulate in the unit, it can cause mildew and mold to grow. It is important that Residents regularly allow air to circulate in the apartment. It is also important that Residents keep the interior of the unit clean and that they promptly notify the Owner/Agent of any leaks, moisture problems, and/or mold growth.

Resident agrees to maintain the premises in a manner that prevents the occurrence of an infestation of mold or mildew in the premises. Resident agrees to uphold this responsibility in part by complying with the following list of responsibilities:

1. Resident agrees to keep the unit free of dirt and debris that can harbor mold.

2. Resident agrees to immediately report to the Owner/Agent any water intrusion, such as plumbing leaks, drips, or "sweating" pipes.

3. Resident agrees to notify owner of overflows from bathroom, kitchen, or unit laundry facilities, especially in cases where the overflow may have permeated walls or cabinets.

4. Resident agrees to report to the Owner/Agent any significant mold growth on surfaces inside the premises.

5. Resident agrees to allow the owner/agent to enter the unit to inspect and make necessary repairs.

6. Resident agrees to use bathroom fans while showering or bathing and to report to the Owner/Agent any non-working fan.

7. Resident agrees to use exhaust fans whenever cooking, dishwashing, or cleaning.

8. Resident agrees to use all reasonable care to close all windows and other openings in the premises to prevent outdoor water from penetrating into the interior unit.

9. Resident agrees to clean and dry any visible moisture on windows, walls, and other surfaces, including personal property, as soon as reasonably possible. (Note: Mold can grow on damp surfaces within 24 to 48 hours.)

10. Resident agrees to notify the Owner/Agent of any problems with the air conditioning or heating systems that are discovered by the Resident.

11. Resident agrees to indemnify and hold harmless the Owner/Agent from any actions, claims, losses, damages, and expenses, including, but not limited to, attorneys' fees that the Owner/Agent may sustain or incur as a result of the negligence of the Resident or any guest or other person living in, occupying, or using the premises.

The undersigned Resident(s) acknowledge(s) having read and understood the foregoing.

Date	Resident	Date	Resident
Date	Resident	Date	Resident
Date	Owner/Agent		

California Apartment Association Approved Form
www.caanet.org
Form 2.7 – *Revised 1/07* - ©*2007 – All Rights Reserved*
Page 1 of 1

Figure 11-2:
A Mold
Notification
Addendum.

Source: California Apartment Association™

Because the tenant has day-to-day control over the rental unit, you can't possibly know about mold problems as soon as they develop or know about all the conditions in the unit that can lead to mold. Emphasize to your tenants the importance of avoiding conditions that increase the chances of mold growth and instruct them to immediately notify you of any suspected problems.

The importance of smoke detectors

I once managed a great 70-unit apartment building that looked like it was pulled straight from a Gene Autry movie set. It had a very Western motif, which featured wood everywhere — covered wooden walkways, completely enclosed wooden carports, and wood decks. This property was a termite's dream! But it was also a significant fire risk. And that's exactly what one crazed friend of an evicted tenant must have thought when, in the middle of the night, he doused one of the apartments with gasoline and lit a match.

The intense fire spread quickly. Luckily, the on-site manager was walking back into the property from a movie and saw the fire soon after it started. He immediately alerted all the tenants in the adjoining units before calling the fire department. The property manager truly saved the tenants' lives. One tenant had taken her smoke detector down because of false alarms from cooking, and another tenant admitted that his smoke detector didn't go off in the fire because he'd taken the batteries out just a few days before when his radio needed batteries!

It's amazing no one died. This event will always be a vivid reminder to me that smoke detectors can save lives, but the only way they can do so is if they're properly maintained.

Smoke detector agreement

Inform your new tenant of the importance of smoke detectors. You may even want to create a separate Smoke Detector Agreement, like the one shown in Figure 11-3 (also on the CD). This document helps you be certain your tenant fully understands the importance of this vital safety equipment and realizes that he must take an active role in ensuring the smoke detectors remain in place, operate properly, and have electrical or battery power in order to protect him in case of smoke or fire.

Pythons and piglets and goats, oh my!

In managing rental properties over the years, I've seen just about every type of pet you can imagine. I once took over management of a small rental property where the owner allowed the tenants to have pets. I wasn't too concerned until it became obvious that the prior management company didn't have any limitations. I soon found out that we had everything from the usual dogs and cats to a large Burmese python and a pot-bellied pig. One tenant even had two goats on his patio. Strictly define exactly which animals are acceptable at your rental property — or you may be in for a big surprise.

Smoke Detector Agreement

This document is an addendum and is part of the Lease or Rental Agreement, dated
_____,

by and between _____,"Owner/Agent",

and _____ "Tenant",

for the premises located at: _____.

In consideration of their mutual promises, Owner/Agent and Tenant agree as follows:

1. The premise(s) is (are) equipped with a smoke detection device(s).

2. Each Tenant acknowledges the smoke detector(s) was (were) tested and its operation explained by management in the presence of the Tenant(s) at the time of initial occupancy and the detector(s) in the unit was (were) working properly at that time.

3. Each Tenant shall perform the manufacturer's recommended test to determine if the smoke detector(s) is (are) operating properly at least twice a month.

4. Initial here ONLY if the smoke detector(s) is (are) BATTERY OPERATED: _____

By initialing as provided, each Tenant understands that said smoke detector(s) and alarm is a battery-operated unit and it shall be each Tenant's responsibility to:

a.   Ensure that the battery is in operating condition at all times;

b.   Replace the battery as needed (unless otherwise provided by law); and

c.   If, after replacing the battery, the smoke detector(s) do not work, inform the Owner or authorized Agent immediately in writing.

5. Tenant(s) must inform the Owner or authorized Agent immediately in writing of any defect, malfunction or failure of any detectors.

6. In accordance with the law, Tenant shall allow Owner or Agent access to the premises for the purpose verifying that all required smoke detectors are in place and operating properly or to conduct maintenance service, repair or replacement as needed.

_____   _____   _____   _____
  Date   Owner/Agent   Date   Tenant

Figure 11-3:
Smoke
Detector
Agreement.

Many tragic instances have occurred in rental properties where fires broke out after tenants had completely removed or disabled the smoke detectors because they were annoyed with false alarms triggered by smoking or cooking. Some tenants fail to regularly test the smoke alarms or replace the batteries as needed. All tenants need to understand that you can only address conditions brought to your attention, so they must be actively involved in ongoing inspections of the rental unit to ensure their own safety.

Animal agreement

Marketing your rental property to tenants with pets can be very profitable, because you usually have lower turnover and higher rents. If your new tenant has pets, you need to have her complete and sign an Animal Agreement, (figure 11-4 also, available on the CD). The Animal Agreement outlines your house rules regarding your tenant's animals or pets.

This document is an addendum and is part of the Lease or Rental Agreement, dated _____,

by and between _____ ,"Owner/Agent",

and _____ "Tenant",

for the premises located at: _____.

In consideration of their mutual promises, Owner/Agent and Tenant agree as follows:

1. The Lease/Rental Agreement provides that without Owner/Agent's prior written consent, no animals whatsoever shall be allowed in or about the premises. Tenant shall not keep or feed stray animals in their rental unit or anywhere on the grounds. Tenant may not allow an animal to be in his rental unit or on the premises even temporarily. Tenant must advise his guests of this policy prohibiting animals or secure advance approval from the Owner/Agent.

2. Tenant desires to keep the following described animal (see attached photo), herein after referred to as "Pet", and represents it is a domesticated dog, cat, bird, fish, or _____. Said Pet is: Breed: _____; Size (Current and adult Height/Weight):_____; Color _____. Tenant represents to Owner/Agent that said Pet is not vicious, and has not bitten, attacked, harmed, or menaced anyone in the past.

3. Tenant agrees to comply with all applicable ordinances, regulations and laws governing pets. If the Pet is a cat, it must be neutered and veterinary proof is required. Tenant must provide and maintain an appropriate litter box and not dispose of litter in the toilets. If the Pet is a bird, it shall not be let out of the cage. If the Pet is fish, the water container shall not exceed _____ gallons and will be placed in a safe location in the rental unit. Pet shall not be fed directly on carpet or any floor covering in the rental unit. Tenant shall prevent any fleas or other infestation of the rental unit or other property of Owner. Tenant shall not permit, and represents that Pet will not cause any damage, discomfort, annoyance, nuisance or in any way inconvenience, or cause complaints from, any other Tenant.

4 Tenant acknowledges and agrees that Owner/Agent may, at any time and in Owner/Agent's sole and absolute discretion, revoke its consent by giving Tenant written thirty (30) day notice, if Owner/Agent receives complaints from neighbors or other residents about Pet, or if Owner/Agent, in Owner/Agent's sole discretion, determines that Pet has disturbed the rights, comfort, convenience, or safety of neighbors or other tenants. Tenant shall permanently remove Pet from Owner's property upon Owner/Agent's written notice that consent is revoked.

5. If any rule or provision of this Animal Agreement is violated, Owner/Agent shall have the right to demand removal of Pet from the community upon three (3) day written notice. Any refusal by Tenant to comply with such demand shall be deemed to be a material breach of the Lease or Rental Agreement, in which event Owner/Agent shall be entitled to all the rights and remedies set forth in the Lease or Rental Agreement for violations thereof, including but not limited to eviction, damages, and attorney's fees.

6. Tenant shall be strictly liable for the entire amount of any wrongful death, or injury to the person or property of others, caused by Pet, and Tenant shall indemnify Owner/Agent for all costs resulting from same, including but not limited to litigation costs and attorney's fees.

7. Tenant agrees that Pet will not be permitted outside Tenant's unit unless restrained by a leash, cage or other appropriate animal restraint. Tenant shall not tie Pet to any object outside the rental unit or premises. Use of the grounds or premises for sanitary purposes is prohibited and Tenant agrees to promptly clean up after Pet, if necessary. Pet shall be allowed or walked only in the exterior area(s) designated by the Owner/Agent. Tenant shall not permit Pet in swimming pool areas, laundry rooms, management offices, clubrooms, playgrounds, other recreation facilities, and other dwelling units.

_____   _____   _____   _____
Date   Owner/Manager   Date   Tenant

Figure 11-4: Animal Agreement.

You can't judge a book by its cover

I once had a resident manager who'd been in the rental management business for many years. She'd probably rented to literally hundreds of tenants and was consistently one of my best managers, with very high occupancy and rarely any uncollected rent. She used to tell me how, over the years, she followed all Fair Housing laws but began to feel as though she could "read" a person and had even developed a sort of sixth sense to anticipate which prospective tenants weren't likely to pass our thorough screening process.

One Saturday afternoon, a very well-dressed man in his 30s came in to see an apartment. He drove a fancy car and wore several pieces of expensive jewelry. He looked at a couple of apartments, and then said he'd take the larger unit at the back of the property because he preferred privacy. He said that he'd just arrived in town and had been staying at a nice hotel in the area, but he was anxious to get settled and wanted to know if he could move in the next day. The man was quite charming and very smooth. In fact, he was so charming that this seasoned resident manager didn't wait for the results of the tenant screening process. Instead, she accepted a personal check for all his move-in funds, even though this tactic was clearly against company policy. Unfortunately, his personal check bounced and it took more than two months to evict this "gentleman" from the rental unit. When we finally got possession of the unit, we found that this individual was quite a salesman — he'd installed more than a dozen phone lines in his apartment for his telemarketing operations.

Dogs, cats, birds, and fish aren't the only animal species people keep in their homes. With the broad variety of animals that tenants are known to keep (see the nearby sidebar, "Pythons and piglets and goats, oh my!" for more), I've broadened the rules from merely pets to animals in general. A good pet or animal policy clearly outlines exactly which animals are acceptable at your rental property. It may just be semantics, but you don't want to get to court and have your tenants argue that the large iguana that damaged your rental unit isn't subject to your rules because it's not their "pet."

Keep current photos of each animal living on your property in the individual files of their owners. This practice may seem ridiculous, but no matter how large your security deposit or how strict your rules, animals have the potential to cause significant damage. Determining the source of the problem can be difficult if you can't accurately identify the guilty animal.

After the initial move-in, tenants may be tempted to take advantage of your policy and bring in additional animals or pets. I've seen the goldfish in the small glass bowl succumb only to be replaced by a 200-gallon aquarium. Your tenant may decide that the small poodle you agreed to is lonely and needs the company of a Great Dane in your studio rental unit! Often tenants have very good and heartwarming stories about how they've ended up adding new animals to the mix, but you need to retain control over the numbers, types, and sizes of the animals on your property. One way to do so is to actually meet and photograph the animal so there's no doubt as to what you've approved. Also, remember that small puppies can grow into large dogs. Make sure your policies anticipate the animal at its *adult* size.

Collecting the money from your tenant

During your pre-move-in meeting, be sure to get the first month's rent and the security deposit. You need to collect this money *before* you give the tenant the keys to the rental unit. Payment may be in the form of cash, a cashier's check, or a money order. But don't accept a personal check, because you have no way of knowing whether it'll clear. Be sure to give your tenant a receipt for payment.

Although cash is legal tender, have a firm policy *against* accepting cash, and only accept cash for the move-in or the monthly rent payment when absolutely necessary. Regularly collecting cash for your rents can make you a target for crime. Tenants often move in on the weekends and in the evenings, so you don't want to have cash on you or at your home until you can get to the bank. Of course, if you have someone assist you in your rent collections, he's also at risk (not to mention the fact that cash is harder to keep track of, and your assistant may be tempted to skim off some of it for his own needs).

Tell your new tenant that your policy is to accept only a bank cashier's check or a money order upon move-in. (Most convenience stores offer money orders for a nominal cost and are open at all hours, so your tenant can easily carry the cash to the convenience store or a bank to get a money order.) Also, let him know whether your rent collection policy will allow him to pay his future monthly rent payments with a personal check.

Prior to handing over the keys to your new tenant and allowing him to take possession, you need to insist on having the cash in hand through *good funds* (as opposed to *insufficient funds,* where a person writes a check and doesn't have the money to cover it in his account). Most owners guarantee the receipt of good funds by requiring cash, a bank cashier's check, or a money order. But many rental property owners aren't aware that both bank cashier's checks and money orders can be stopped. Financial institutions and convenience stores allow the purchaser to obtain a stop payment because these financial instruments can be lost or stolen. However, bank cashier's checks and money orders are superior to personal checks because they do represent good funds and will, at the very least, not be returned to you because there's no money to cover them.

If, despite my strong advice, your tenant persuades you to accept a personal check, then at least don't give him access to the rental property until you've called and verified with his bank that the check will be honored. Your best bet is to physically take the check to the tenant's bank and cash it, or at least have it certified. If the bank certifies the check, it's guaranteeing that the tenant has sufficient funds available, and the bank will actually put a hold on the funds. Of course, cashing the check is the only sure way to collect your funds, because a devious tenant can always stop payment on even a certified personal check.

Inspecting the property with your tenant before move-in

The number one source of landlord-tenant disputes is the disposition of the tenant's security deposit. Many of these potential problems can be resolved with proper procedures before the tenant takes possession of the rental unit. But to do so, you need to walk through the property with your tenant before move-in and go over the following matters.

Having the tenant sign an inspection checklist

By using a Move-In/Move-Out Inspection Checklist, you can take care of many problems before the tenant moves in. This form is an excellent tool to protect you and your tenant when she moves out and wants the security deposit returned. In fact, the Move-In/Move-Out Inspection Checklist is just as important as your rental contract. The purpose of the inspection isn't to find all the items you or your maintenance person forgot to check, because you should've already looked carefully through the unit to ensure it met your high standards. The purpose of the move-in inspection is to clearly demonstrate to the tenant's satisfaction that the rental unit is in good condition except for any noted items.

When properly completed and signed, the inspection form clearly documents the condition of the rental property upon acceptance by and move-in of the tenant and serves as a baseline for the entire tenancy. If the tenant withholds rent or tries to break the lease by claiming the unit needs substantial repairs, you may need to be able to prove the condition of the rental unit upon move-in. When the tenant moves out, you're able to clearly note the items that were damaged or weren't left clean so that you can charge the maximum allowed under your state or local laws.

I include a complete version of this four-page inspection checklist on the CD. Feel free to download it and use it with your tenants. The first column is where you can note the condition of the unit before the tenant actually moves in. The last two columns are for use when the tenant moves out, and you inspect the unit with her again. Often, you don't immediately know the estimated cost of repair or replacement, so you can complete that portion of the checklist later and include a copy of it when you send your tenant her security deposit disposition form. (Chapter 15 has the scoop on how to figure out how much of the security deposit to return to a departing tenant.)

The Move-In/Move-Out Inspection Checklist is unique in that you use the form throughout the entire tenancy — upon initial move-in, during the tenancy (if any aspect of the rental unit is updated or repaired), and when the tenant finally vacates. Make sure you do the following when having a new tenant sign this form:

✔ **Physically walk through the rental unit with your new tenant and guide her through the inspection form** *together.* Let the tenant tell you the conditions she observes and make sure your wording of the noted conditions and comments accurately describes everything in detail.

If it's impossible for you to do this walk-through with your tenant, then you should complete the Move-In/Move-Out Inspection Checklist and ask that all adult occupants review and sign the form as soon as possible upon move-in. Inform the tenant you'll be glad to deliver her mailbox key after you have the approved form in hand. I never seem to get anything but bills and junk mail myself, but I've learned that the mailbox key is a very important and useful tool in motivating a tenant to promptly review and approve the inspection form. You can't refuse to give your tenant her mailbox key, but this suggestion is often effective.

✔ **Print legibly and be as detailed and specific as possible when noting the condition of each item.** Be sure to indicate which items are in new, excellent, or very good condition, as well as noting any items that are dirty, scratched, broken, or in poor condition. For example, rather than generally indicate that the oven is "broken," be specific and note that the "built-in timer doesn't work." This way your tenant understands the oven works, but she also knows to use a separate timer and knows she won't be held responsible for this specific item upon move-out. If the kitchen flooring is new, be sure to indicate that on the form. Many disputes can be resolved if the inspection checklist specifically notes the condition of each item. If you only comment on dirty or damaged items, a court may conclude that you either didn't inspect or forgot to record the condition of a component of the rental unit that you're now claiming was damaged by the tenant. You may think everyone knows and agrees that all items without any notation are in average or "okay" condition, but the tenant will likely tell the court that the item was at least somewhat dirty or damaged and that you shouldn't be able to collect for it.

When used properly, your Move-In/Move-Out Inspection Checklist not only proves the existence of damage in the rental unit but also pinpoints when the damage occurred. Don't fall for one of the oldest tenant ploys in the book. Tenants often try to avoid walking the rental unit with you upon move-in because they want to wait and be able to avoid charges for damage that occurs during their actual move-in. You must require your tenant to walk through the rental premises and agree that all items are in clean and undamaged condition *before* she starts moving in her boxes and furnishings.

Always note the conditions of the carpets and floor coverings, because this is one of the most common areas of dispute with tenants upon move-out. Although tenants shouldn't be charged for ordinary wear and tear, they should pay for the damage if they destroy the carpet. Indicate the age of the carpet and whether it's been professionally cleaned as part of your rental turnover process. When a tenant leaves after only six months and has destroyed the carpet, you can guarantee she'll remember the carpet as old, dirty, and threadbare. The tenant's selective memory won't recall that the carpet was actually brand-new, or at least in very good condition, and professionally cleaned upon her move-in!

If you discover any problems during your inspection walk-through, note them on the inspection form and take steps to have them corrected, unless the corrections aren't economically feasible. For example, you may have a hairline crack along the edge of the bathroom countertop. If you determine refinishing or replacing the countertop is too costly, just note the condition on the inspection form so that your tenant isn't erroneously charged upon move-out.

✔ **Be sure your Move-In/Move-Out Inspection Checklist reflects any repairs or improvements made after the initial walk-through inspection.** For example, if you and your tenant note on the form that the bathroom door doesn't lock properly, you should then have that item repaired, necessitating an update to the inspection form that your tenant must initial.

✔ **Be particularly careful to note any and all mildew, mold, pest, or rodent problems.** Doing so is important because these are health issues that must be addressed immediately before the tenant takes possession. There's been a trend toward tenant claims of an uninhabitable rental property or a unit that violates health and safety regulations. These claims often result in requests for rent reduction or even litigation. To prove you turned over the rental property in good condition, affirmatively indicate on the Move-In/Move-Out Inspection Checklist that no indication of any of these issues exists. If there are problems that persist after move-in despite your best efforts, then consult with the appropriate licensed professional to evaluate the sources of the conditions, the necessary responses, and remedial actions, plus advise the tenant of any potential health risk.

✔ **Be sure to give your tenant a copy of the completed and signed form for her records.** You should give your tenant copies of all documents, especially the inspection checklist, so that the tenant can review her own copy when she moves out if there are charges.

To avoid disputes over security deposits, take digital photos or record the rental unit's condition on video before the tenant moves in. In addition to your inspection form, you'll have some photos to help refresh the tenant's memory or show the court if the matter ends up there. If you use a camcorder to record the rental unit, be sure to get the tenant on video stating the date and time, if she's cooperative. If your tenant isn't present, bring a copy of that day's newspaper and include it in your recording. With all detailed photography, it's not always easy to understand exactly what the picture is showing unless specifically stated. So be sure to include a caption or descriptions with all still photos and provide a running detailed narrative with the recording.

Going over the nitty-gritty with your tenant

When your tenant moves in, you don't want to assume he knows everything about the property. Take a few extra minutes during your walk-through and make sure you remember the following:

- **Don't assume your tenant is familiar with the appliances and how they work.** Provide your tenant with the appliance manuals, or at least copies of the basic operating instructions. These manuals get lost over the years, but many manufacturers have manuals online, which can be downloaded easily and inexpensively.

- **If you have natural gas appliances or gas heat, instruct your tenant to contact the local utility company if he has any questions or concerns.** This step is particularly important if he detects the sulfur smell commonly associated with a gas leak or has any concerns or questions about proper operation of the appliances. The tenant should also contact the utility company or your maintenance person if he needs to relight a pilot light.

- **Tell your tenant where and how to shut off the utilities.** Include this step as part of your new tenant orientation. Utilities may need to be shut off due to severe weather, a water leak, electrical short, or fire on the property. If you have a serious storm or earthquake, your tenant needs to be able to immediately turn off the natural gas supply as well. Provide your tenant with an inexpensive special wrench, available from the natural gas utility company. Attach it to the gas meter with a simple cable so that your tenant or maintenance person can have it handy in case of an emergency.

Giving your tenant an informational letter prior to move-in

The key to success in managing rental properties is to develop an efficient system that reduces the time you spend managing your rentals. A good way to minimize your phone calls from tenants is to provide them with a tenant handbook or a *Tenant Information Letter* (see Figure 11-5; also on the CD), which outlines all your policies and procedures that are too detailed to include in your rental contract. You can also attach details on the proper operation and care of appliances, plus other important info your tenant needs to know about the rental unit.

The importance of changing locks between tenants

As the host of a live weekly radio show on real estate for more than 14 years, I'm often amazed at some of the stories I hear from callers. I'll never forget the call I received from a tenant in a small multi-unit rental property who was shocked to find out that another tenant had a key to his rental unit. Apparently, one of the tenants had loaned his key to a family member who got confused and inadvertently entered my caller's rental unit. When the caller confronted the property owner, the owner wasn't very concerned and didn't understand the tenant's concern. He stated that he always used the same locks so that he didn't have to carry around extra keys if he needed access to a rental unit in case of an emergency!

Customize the handbook or letter to present the *house rules,* a more simple term for policies and rules, you've implemented for each rental property. Although this information should be customized for each property, here're some of the basic items to include:

- ✔ Property manager name and contact number
- ✔ Procedures to follow in case of an emergency
- ✔ Rent collection information, including when rent is due, how payment is to be made, where to pay or mail rent, and how late fees and other charges are handled
- ✔ Requirements for ending the tenancy, including the notice requirement
- ✔ Procedures for the return of the security deposit
- ✔ Handling of new or departing roommates
- ✔ Proper procedure for requesting maintenance and repairs
- ✔ Lockout procedure and charges for lost keys
- ✔ Renter's insurance requirements
- ✔ Guest occupancy policy
- ✔ Annual interior unit inspection walk-through policy, if any
- ✔ Utility shut-off locations, including a separate diagram for the individual unit
- ✔ Trash collection and recycling program information
- ✔ Parking policies
- ✔ Property rules and policies
- ✔ Community association or homeowners' association rules and policies

Tenant Information Letter

Tenant Name(s) _____

Rental Unit Address _____

Dear _____,

We are very pleased that you have selected our property to be your home. We hope that you enjoy living here and would like to share some additional information that will explain what you can expect from us and what we will be asking from you:

1. Owner/Manager:

2. Rent Collection:

3. Notice to End Tenancy:

4. Security Deposits:

5. New or Departing Roommates:

6. Maintenance and Repair Requests:

7. Lockout Procedure/Lost keys:

8. Renters Insurance:

9. Guest Occupancy Policy:

10. Annual Safety Inspection:

11. Utility shut-off locations:

12. Trash collection or recycling programs:

13. Parking:

Please let us know if you have any questions.

Sincerely,

_____   _____
          Owner/Manager   Date

I have read and received a copy of this Move-in Letter.

_____   _____
            Tenant   Date

_____   _____
            Tenant   Date

Figure 11-5:
Tenant
Information
Letter.

Many tenants misplace this information when they need it most during the tenancy, so many professional rental owners and property managers are using the Internet to improve the efficiency of managing their properties. You can put the majority of this information online in an electronic tenant handbook that you can update as necessary.

Remember that having this information online may be efficient and handy, but it's not in lieu of giving your tenant actual physical copies of all items upon move-in. Any changes to the tenant handbook should also be given in writing to your tenants. Changes in legal terms or rules and policies must be provided in writing as required by law.

Distributing the keys to your tenant

Distributing the keys is a very serious issue that has significant liability for rental property owners and managers. A problem in key control can allow access to a tenant's rental unit, potentially leading to theft or crimes of serious bodily injury. Keys require careful handling and should be stored only in a locking metal key cabinet or safe.

As the property owner, you're responsible for ensuring that the rental property can be properly secured. Include an entry lock set and a sturdy deadbolt with at least a $^{13}/_{16}$-inch throw on all exterior entry doors. Provide peepholes on the main or primary exterior entry door as well.

Some states have laws specifically requiring rental property owners to provide window locks. Whether legally required or not, I recommend you provide locks for all windows that can be opened. Install window locks on upper-level windows as a safety device and as a way of minimizing the chance that young, unsupervised children may fall from an open window.

For the convenience of your tenants, have a single key that works all entry locks for their particular unit while also being able to operate common area or laundry room locks.

One of the least desirable aspects of managing rental property is handling tenant lockout calls. Tenants rarely seem to get locked out of their rental units during normal daylight hours, so you need to inform your new tenants about your lockout and lost key policies and charges. Set up a policy that acknowledges the difference between a lockout during reasonable business hours and nonworking hours. For example, you can charge the tenant $20 for a lockout Monday through Friday from 9 a.m. to 6 p.m. and $40 for a lockout at all other times.

Changing the locks between tenants is extremely important. Prior tenants may have retained copies of the keys and may return to steal or commit some other crime. You can purchase and install an entirely new lock, or you can have your maintenance person or a locksmith rekey the existing lock. If you have several rental units, it makes economic sense to substitute the existing lock set with a spare lock set. Keep several extra lock sets in inventory so that you can rotate locks between units upon turnover. Have your new tenant sign a statement indicating she's aware that the locks have been changed or rekeyed since the prior tenant vacated. Give her a copy of the locksmith receipt for her records.

The rental housing industry relies on locks, and until recently technology hasn't really changed. But, following the lead of the hospitality and lodging industries, rental property owners are beginning to see many more options that offer better security and key control for rental housing. The cost of many of these systems is still too high for the average rental property owner with just a few rental units, but this advancement is an important trend that will be beneficial for owners, property managers, and tenants down the road.

If you have a master key system for your rental properties, be extremely careful with it. Don't keep any extra copies or loan the master key to anyone whom you don't trust implicitly. Although locksmiths are required by law to have written authorization prior to duplicating a key marked "Do not duplicate," remember that an individual who wants a copy of your key to commit a crime isn't likely to be concerned about breaking the law by illegally copying the key.

Setting Up the Tenant File

You need to be able to immediately access important written records, and one way of doing that is to have an organized filing system to ensure you don't waste time searching aimlessly for a lost or misplaced document. The best way to accomplish this goal is to immediately set up a new tenant folder for each tenant at the time of his or her move-in.

Set up a file folder for each rental property with individual files for each tenant. Your tenant file should include the following:

- Rental application
- Rental application verification form
- Credit report
- Background information
- Holding deposit agreement and receipt, if applicable
- Signed rental contract
- Lead-based paint disclosure form
- Smoke detector agreement
- Any other addenda to the lease or rental agreement
- Move-In/Move-Out Inspection Checklist
- Photos or DVDs of the unit, taken at move-in

Turn to this file throughout the tenancy, adding to it all new documents such as rent increases, notices of entry, maintenance requests, and correspondence. Keep tenant files for four years after the tenant vacates.

Preparing a Welcome Package for Your New Tenant

Tenant satisfaction and retention are critical to success in rental management. One way to make a positive first impression is to provide your new tenant with a welcome package when he moves in. Welcome packages can be very elaborate, or just a few inexpensive but thoughtful items.

Give your new tenant a simple welcome package with a few useful items he needs. For example, a couple of bottles of spring water in the refrigerator, a bar of soap and a roll of paper towels in the kitchen, a few change of address forms, a pad of scratch paper and a pen by the phone, and a roll of toilet paper in the bathroom can be very handy in the first couple of days when your new tenant still has everything packed away in boxes. A discount coupon or a gift certificate for a free pizza is another great way to impress your new tenant.

Another simple idea that really impresses new tenants is offering one or two hours of free maintenance assistance when they first move in. Every new tenant needs to hang a few pictures, install a paper towel holder, or do some other minor maintenance work to make your rental unit feel like home, so why not give them a helping hand?

All your efforts to make a great first impression by offering some free maintenance can backfire if the tenant doesn't clearly understand the limitations of your offer or if the maintenance person is rude or doesn't do quality work. Provide your new tenant with a list of suggested items for your maintenance person and be sure to have your tenant sign a simple disclaimer form waiving his right to sue you or make a claim if your maintenance person damages his favorite picture while hanging it on the wall.

Chapter 12

Collecting and Increasing Rent

If location is the most important element in real estate investing, then collecting rent in full and on time is the most important element in managing your rental investment. But how can you make sure your tenants pay their rent on time every month? The reality is that most tenants don't have significant cash resources, and many live from paycheck to paycheck. So if a tenant's paycheck is delayed, her car breaks down, or she has an unexpected major expense, then her ability to pay the rent in full and on time is in jeopardy. And because the tenant's funds are so tightly budgeted, when she falls even one month behind on rent, catching up again is even more difficult. Fortunately, you can take steps to increase the likelihood that you'll get all your rent money, all the time.

You can begin laying the foundation for successful rent collection before your property is rented. The best preventive measures include targeting your advertising to responsible tenants and establishing a thorough and careful tenant screening and selection process.

Collecting the rent is a key part of property management, as is keeping your rent competitive with the market. Raising the rent to reflect trends in your area is a necessary part of managing rental properties. Many property owners hesitate to raise the rent for existing tenants, but trust me when I say that it can be done effectively, without risking the loss of your tenants.

In this chapter, I fill you in on what you can do to guarantee you're getting paid on time and that you're requesting a competitive rent.

Creating a Written Rent Collection Policy

The fundamentals of property management are very straightforward: You provide the tenants with a clean and comfortable place to live; they pay the rent, live quietly, and keep the rental unit clean. Problems and confusion can arise, however, if you and your tenant don't understand the rights and responsibilities that come with the landlord-tenant relationship.

The keys to success when it comes to rent collection are establishing policies and procedures and being firm with your enforcement of rent collection. Setting up a successful rent collection policy, putting it in writing, and giving it to your tenants in the tenant handbook or information letter is the best way to avoid confusion. Be sure to point out that each tenant is joint and severally responsible for the full payment of rent. *Joint and severally* is a legal term that means each of your tenants is responsible for paying the rent. So regardless of any agreement between co-occupants or roommates, each and every tenant can be legally required to pay the entire rent, not just his share. By mentioning this fact, you can be sure all tenants are informed. No single rent collection policy works for *all* rental property owners, but every policy should cover certain key issues, which I outline in the following sections.

When rent is due

I recommend that you require your tenants to pay the full monthly rent in advance, on or before the first of each month. This method is the most common, and many state laws require it unless the rental contract specifies otherwise.

Review your rent collection procedures with each adult occupant of your rental unit before accepting his or her rental application so that no one can misunderstand how important you consider the prompt payment of rent. Then make rent collection a featured topic of your pre-move-in orientation meeting with the tenants when they review and sign the rental contract.

Although rent is traditionally paid in full at one time, it's perfectly legal for you and your tenant to agree that the rent will be divided up and paid twice a month, every week, or in any other mutually agreed time frame. Try to avoid accepting more frequent payments, because your goal is efficiency, and handling the rent collection process as few times as possible each month is definitely more efficient.

You and your tenant can determine that the monthly rent is due on any mutually agreeable date during the month; rent doesn't have to be paid on the first of the month. This approach may make sense if your tenant receives income or financial assistance payments on certain dates. For example, you may have a tenant who receives an income check on the 10th of each month, so you set the monthly rent due date for the 15th of each month.

Be careful to document that any differences in rental collection terms are based on legitimate business decisions, or else your actions may be seen as favoring one tenant over another. Of course, you may have a tenant who formally requests an accommodation in payment terms under Fair Housing laws. In this case, seek advice from local landlord-tenant legal counsel.

In addition to Fair Housing concerns, think about the ramifications of accepting rent based on the tenant's scheduled receipt of income rather than your usual rent due date. By accommodating the tenant, you're tacitly acknowledging that he needs that payment in order to afford the rent. But one of the most fundamental tenets in rental housing management is to avoid tenants who can't afford the rent. If your tenant needs that income to pay your rent that month, you have no safety net if the tenant's check is lost in the mail, his car breaks down, or he's temporarily laid off from his job.

To avoid surprises and delinquent rent, you don't want your tenants to have their finances so tight that they need this month's income to pay this month's rent. Check out Chapter 10 for tips on effectively selecting tenants with enough financial cushions to pay this month's rent from cash already on hand.

Some owners make the rent payable each month on the date the tenant first moved in. For example, if the tenant moves in on the 25th of the month, then his rent is due on the 25th of each future month. This practice is legal and may be acceptable if you have only a few tenants and are willing to keep track of each due date. On the other hand, having all your rents due on the first of the month makes life simpler and avoids confusion, or the chance of making an error on legal notices for nonpayment of rent.

If your rent due date falls on a weekend day or a legal holiday, most states allow the tenant to pay by the next business day. This policy may not be mandatory in your state, but adopting it is a good idea.

Prorating rent

Life would be simpler if all your tenants moved in and out on the first of the month, but they don't. If your tenant's occupancy begins in the middle of the month, and your rent collection policy states that all rents are due on the first of each month, then you need to prorate the tenant's rent at move-in. Following are two basic ways to prorate the rent at the beginning of your new tenant's occupancy:

✔ **If your tenant moves in toward the end of a month, collect a full month's rent (for the next month), plus the rent due for the prorated portion of the current month.** For example, if your tenant takes occupancy on June 25, collect six days' rent for the period of June 25 to June 30, plus a full month's rent for the month of July, upon move-in. A new tenant is usually glad to oblige if just a few days are prorated.

✔ **If your tenant moves in early in a month, collect a full month's rent prior to move-in and then collect the balance due for the prorated rent on the first of the next month.** For example, if your tenant moves in on May 10, collect a full month's rent, before he takes occupancy that covers the period of May 10 through June 9. Then on June 1, collect the balance due for June 10 through June 30 (21 days' worth). By July 1, the tenant is on track to pay his full rent on the first of each month.

Unless otherwise agreed, rent is normally uniformly apportioned from day to day using a 30-day month. Divide your monthly rental rate by 30 to determine the daily rental rate, and multiply your answer by the actual number of days in the partial rental period. This formula applies to February as well.

Providing a grace period

Many rent collection policies allow for a *grace period* that provides tenants with a few extra days to make the monthly rent payment in full before incurring late charges. Most tenants incorrectly believe that if they pay rent within the grace period, their payment is legally on time. However, the rent is due on or before the rent due date. If paid later, it's considered delinquent from a legal perspective, regardless of the terms of the grace period.

Make sure that your rental contract and the tenant information letter are very clear about the fact that the rent is due on or before the first of the month and that it's technically late if paid during the grace period.

Grace periods are optional in most states and can be any number of days in length. However, a few states (including Connecticut, Delaware, Maine, Oregon, and Rhode Island) have mandatory grace periods or restrictions on serving a Notice to Pay Rent or Quit, so be sure to check your local and state laws. Unless restricted by law, I recommend that you set up your grace period to expire on the third of the month and allow an extra day or two if the third falls on a weekend or holiday.

In most states, you don't have to wait until the grace period expires to begin your collection efforts with tenants who show a pattern of being late. You can even serve legal notices demanding the rent payment. Your rental contract should contain a specific provision that you have the right to refuse payment after the expiration of your legal demand notice so that you aren't obligated to accept an offer of rent from the tenant and can move forward with eviction, if necessary.

Where rent is paid

You can collect your rent in several ways, but unless otherwise agreed, many states require that rent be collected at the premises. Although stopping by the unit allows you the opportunity to see your rental property, it isn't time-efficient unless you live on or very close to your property, especially if you have to make multiple trips. The benefits of in-person collection also depend on your tenants' expectations. Tenants in low-rent properties often expect the owner or property manager to come by and collect the rent in person, whereas renters at middle- to higher-rent properties tend to think you're too nosy if you personally come by for the rent.

If you'd rather not collect the rent in person, you can have your tenants pay in other ways. Just make sure you agree upon this information when each tenant signs the rental contract. Tenants can

- **Mail the rent to you.** For most rental property owners and tenants, the most popular way to remit the monthly rent payment is to have the tenants mail it. Because collecting rent by mail is only effective if your tenants pay on time, I strongly suggest you make doing so extremely simple for your tenants by providing them with stamped, preaddressed envelopes. Giving tenants several envelopes at once is efficient as long as the tenants don't lose them or use them to pay other bills.

  If you and your tenants agree that the monthly rent will be mailed, you may run into a major question: Is the rent considered paid when it's postmarked or when it's received? Check your local laws and have a clear, written agreement in your rent collection policy. Absent any legal requirements, I recommend that you consider the rent paid when the payment is postmarked. By mailing the payment on time, tenants are acting in good faith, and you don't want to unfairly penalize your tenants if the mail is delayed.

- **Bring the rent to your home or office.** Although this method may be very convenient for you, many tenants object to having to personally deliver their monthly rent. For this reason, asking tenants to deliver the rent to you in this way isn't conducive to getting it on time. Instead, this request places an additional burden on your tenant when your goal is to simplify the rent collection process for everyone involved.

Technology has made the issue of where rent is paid moot if your tenants are willing to make their monthly rent payments electronically (check out the "Digitizing the day-to-day: Electronic payments" section in this chapter).

How rent is paid

Your rental contract should clearly indicate how rent is to be paid: by personal check, cashier's check, money order, cash, or electronic payment. Regardless of its form, give your tenants a receipt for all money received.

Putting pen to paper: Checks

For many rental property owners, accepting checks (personal, cashier's, or money order) is routine. Most tenants have a personal checking account, and paying by check is easy for them. Check processing has also improved greatly with new federal regulations for the banking industry that allow checks to be scanned and converted to an electronic funds transfer. Check with your financial institution to see whether you can use this technology to simplify your rent collection, give you immediate use of the funds, and eliminate several trips to the bank.

Some rental property owners request post-dated checks in advance from their tenants with the idea that they'll already have the rent payment in hand, and the tenants just need to make the funds available to cover the check. I strongly advise against accepting post-dated checks. Often these checks aren't good, and many state laws consider a post-dated check a promissory note. You may be unable to file an eviction action for nonpayment of rent while the note is pending.

Payment by check is conditional. If the check isn't honored for any reason, it's as if the tenant never paid, and late charges and returned check charges should apply. Check scanning can give you immediate notice that funds aren't available, allowing you to contact the tenant and promptly begin collection efforts.

Never accept second-party checks, such as payroll or government checks. Instead, institute a policy that all rent payments made after the grace period must be in the form of a cashier's check or money order.

Busting out the big bucks: Cash

Although some tenants may want to pay rent with cash, avoid accepting it whenever possible. Turning down cash is always difficult, and your tenants may remind you that cash is legal tender. However, according to the U.S. Department of Treasury, you have the legal right to refuse cash because

- **Accepting cash can make you a target for robbery.** Even if you use a safe, you have an increased risk.

- **Accepting cash can add the risk of employee theft, if you have employees.** Plus, you're potentially putting your employees in danger.

> ✔ **Accepting cash attracts tenants who may be involved in illegal businesses that deal primarily in cash.** These tenants don't want to have their activities tracked and prefer rental properties where cash payments are allowed. Don't make your rental property more attractive to the criminally inclined.

Clearly state in your rental contract that cash isn't accepted under any circumstances. Don't accept even small amounts of cash for rental application fees or late charges. However, if you have a tenant who's facing eviction and offers full payment in cash, you may want to accept the funds because you may find the eviction court won't be inclined to allow you to terminate the tenancy.

Good accounting practices suggest that all your income and expenses be clearly documented. The IRS may consider auditing your rental housing if it learns of frequent cash transactions at your property.

Digitizing the day-to-day: Electronic payments

Technology is making the rent collection process much more efficient and timely. Rental owners and property managers can now benefit from their financial institution's relatively new ability to process hundreds of monthly rent payments in a matter of minutes. Due to improvements in software automation and *security encryption,* which prevent the theft of confidential information, electronic payments are actually more secure than the conventional check payment method.

Several companies now offer technology for the electronic transfer of funds in order to allow tenants to pay their rent. These companies provide you with computer software that enables you to download the details on all payments processed each month. You're automatically notified if a tenant doesn't have sufficient funds to cover the transfer so that you can enforce your regular rent collection policies. Check with your local IREM chapter or NAA affiliate for more info on these companies.

Most tenants are quite comfortable paying electronically rather than manually writing out and mailing a check each month. With electronic payments, a tenant simply fills out a form one time, and the preauthorized amount is deducted on a designated day (usually between the first and fifth of each month) from her bank account and is deposited directly into your account.

If you want to set up your tenants to pay electronically, refer to the Automated Clearing House (ACH) form on the CD. Consult with your financial institution for the necessary banking information to ensure payments are properly credited to your rental property account.

Managing multiple rent payments

When you have multiple tenants or roommates in one of your units, you'll probably receive several payments for portions of the total rent due. And you may not receive all the rent payments at the same time or for the proper amount. When you call the tenants, you may hear from one of the roommates that he paid his share, and you need to track down one of the other tenants. Remember that how your tenants choose to decide to divide the rent between them isn't your problem.

Accommodating your tenants and accepting multiple payments can cause administrative nightmares and lead roommates to erroneously believe that they're not responsible for the entire rent. Instead, have a firm policy of requiring one payment source (either check, money order, or electronic payment) for the entire month's rent.

This practice offers more than just administrative convenience. Legally, each roommate in your rental property is *joint and severally* liable for all rental contract obligations, meaning if one skips out, the others owe you the entire amount. If you allow roommates to pay separately, they may forget that they're each responsible for the entire rent.

Encourage your tenants to let the delinquent roommate know that although everyone else has paid a portion of the rent, they're all on the hook until the balance is paid. After all, your tenants are in a better position to track down their elusive roommate than you.

Dealing with Rent Collection Problems

You're a rental property owner, not a banker (unless, of course, that's your day job). So your tenants must always pay the entire rent due in good funds on or before the due date. But when that doesn't happen, you need to have policies in place for the most common problems you'll encounter in rent collection.

These rules outline the specific penalties enforced for tenants who bounce a check, don't have the funds to cover an electronic payment, fail to pay in full, or occasionally pay after the due date and (or grace period, if any). I cover some of these key issues in the following sections.

Apply your rent collection policies, including your late charges, partial payment, and dishonored payment rules consistently with all tenants. If you don't, you can be accused of discrimination by simply allowing some tenants to pay late or by accepting multiple payments from some roommates and not from others.

Collecting late rent

One of the most difficult challenges for a rental property owner is dealing with a tenant when the rent is late. You don't want to overreact and begin serving threatening legal rent demand notices, because doing so definitely creates tension and hostility if the tenant has a legitimate reason for the delay. Then again, late rent can be a very serious issue.

Communication is the key to keeping your response in line with the magnitude of the problem. Remain calm and businesslike, and focus on determining why the rent is late before taking any action. If you're having trouble collecting rent on time, consider these options:

- ✔ **Mail (or better yet — e-mail) your tenants monthly payment reminders or invoices.** Although electronic payments are the best approach, some owners find that a rent coupon book (just like a mortgage payment coupon book) can be helpful in improving their rental collections.

- ✔ **Call slow rent payers routinely.** When you call, remind these slow payers that the rent is due on or before the first of the month. You can also remind them that you expect your rent to be top priority among their various financial obligations.

    Landlords and property managers personally seeking payment of delinquent rent aren't subject to the regulations set by the Fair Debt Collection Practices Act, so you can call tenants at home *and* at their places of business. Although you may not want to bother your tenants at work, don't feel bad calling there as long as you're respectful and professional. You do have a right to know when to expect your rent.

    I don't recommend calling and reminding tenants indefinitely, because your time is too valuable to baby-sit them. If they consistently fail to pay the full rent on or before the due date, don't renew the contract; make sure to give a written notice to terminate the tenancy.

- ✔ **Go to the rental unit and speak directly with tenants.** Don't be shy, or paying the rent will quickly become a low priority for your tenants.

The most effective way to collect rents and determine whether you should exercise a little patience is to contact your tenants directly. Simply mailing a rent reminder or hanging a late notice on the front door can be effective with tenants who just need a reminder, but these tactics typically don't get the job done with tenants who are financially strapped and likely to respond only to direct personal contact.

When personally contacting tenants, your goal isn't to harass them but to remind them about rent payments, or to be solution-oriented and work out an agreement to get your rent. Whatever agreement you reach, make sure that it's in writing and signed by the tenants.

If you're having trouble locating a tenant, check with his neighbors or call the emergency contact listed on his rental application. Check to see whether the utility company has been told to cancel the utilities; maybe the tenant has skipped town without notifying you.

Charging late fees

Charging tenants late fees when they don't pay their rent on time is one of the most effective ways to encourage timely payments. Although many rental property owners have late charges, these charges are often enforced inconsistently, making them ineffective. Other rental property owners set very long grace periods or fees so high that the amounts are unenforceable if challenged in court. As a result, the fees are often waived.

Late charges are very controversial, and many state courts have ruled that excessive late fees aren't enforceable. More than a dozen states have laws specifically addressing restrictions on late charges, so be sure to check with your local National Apartment Association affiliate before establishing a late fee policy. Generally speaking, implementing and enforcing a late charge policy makes sense, as long as it's reasonable and relates to your actual out-of-pocket costs or expenses incurred by the late payment.

Don't allow tenants to form the impression that your late charge policy approves of late rent payments as long as the late charges are collected. Your late charge should be high enough to discourage habitual lateness, but not so high as to be unreasonable. Send written warnings to those tenants who regularly pay late (even if they pay the late charges) clearly indicating that their late payments are unacceptable and are a legal violation of the terms.

You can assess late charges in one of several ways:

- ✔ **Flat fee:** The most common late charge is a *flat fee,* which can be any set amount, due immediately after the grace period. Typical flat fees range from $20 to $50 and are usually set at 4 to 6 percent of the monthly rental rate. The problem with the flat fee late charge is that many tenants are only one to two days late, making the flat late charge unreasonable. Rental property owners in this situation often end up waiving the flat fee. If the matter ever goes to court, the tenant will usually challenge the fee, and the court may throw it out.

- ✔ **Percentage late fee:** A *percentage late fee* is calculated as a percentage of the periodic or monthly rent payment and ranges from as low as 4 percent to as high as 8 percent of the monthly rental rate. The customary late fee percentage for late rent payments is either 5 or 6 percent. Be aware that some states have legal limits on late charges expressed as a percentage of the rent.

✔ **Daily late fee:** If you use a *daily late fee,* you set a daily late charge with a reasonable cap or maximum fee. I've found that a late charge of $5 per day, with a maximum of $50 per day, works very well. A tenant who's only one day late is charged a nominal $5. A tenant who's eight days late pays a heftier $40. The purpose of the cap (which can also be expressed as a percentage of the rent, such as a maximum of 5 percent of the monthly rent) is to keep the late charge reasonable. By the time you get to the cap (at ten days late), you'll have already sent the proper legal rent demand notices.

The flat fee and the percentage late fee methods both fail to provide an incentive for the tenant to pay rent promptly. After the late charge has been incurred, the tenant often finds other financial obligations more important than your rent. Assessing a daily fee offers the incentive some tenants need to get their rent in sooner rather than later.

Waiving the late charge excuses late payment of rent and can send the wrong message to your tenants. If you routinely accept late payments and waive the late charges, you can't suddenly change your attitude and begin eviction proceedings the next time a tenant pays late. Instead, you need to provide a written notice that you're once again actively enforcing the strict rent collection terms of your rental contract. You also need to be consistent in applying your late charge policy to all tenants equally — or risk facing claims of discrimination.

If you receive a late payment by mail, always keep the envelope with the postmark in case the tenant wants to dispute the late charge.

Except where restricted by law, you need to evaluate your own increase in costs as a result of late rent payments in order to determine what a reasonable late charge should be for your property. Put this amount in writing and be prepared to explain your policy if challenged in court. Additional costs may include phone calls and in-person meetings with the tenant, the preparation and sending of warning letters and required legal rent demand notices, time and costs spent preparing delinquency lists, and additional accounting and bank deposits when the funds are received.

Handling returned rent payments

Dishonored rent checks or electronic payments can cause major problems for your rent collection efforts, so you need to charge tenants a fee when you're unable to collect good funds per your rent collection policy.

Early-payment rent discounts: Yes or no?

Some landlords have tried to get around the late charge problems by using early-payment rent discounts to entice their tenants to pay rent on time. These landlords set the rent in the rental contract slightly higher than the market rent and then offer tenants a reduced rent if it's paid in full and on time. For example, if a landlord really wants to have a $900 rent and a $75 late charge, he sets the contracted rent at $975 with a $75 discount if the tenant pays on or before the third of the month.

Although this tactic may be creative, the U.S. legal system has consistently determined that the actual rent is the discounted amount. The courts view that giving a large discount for an on-time payment is the same as charging an excessive late fee.

Don't play the early-payment rent discount game. If you're challenged, your case will be thrown out of court. At least two large class-action lawsuits specifically on this practice have occurred, and the landlords were creamed with major legal costs and severe financial penalties. This practice is a scam, and the courts have seen right through it. If you want more rent money, raise your rent amount. If you want tenants who pay on time, carefully screen your prospects. Establish a reasonable and fair late charge policy and apply it uniformly to all tenants.

Often, when you contact your tenant, she'll have some excuse for the returned item and tell you that her payment is now good. Check with your bank about its policy for handling dishonored electronic payments. For old-fashioned paper checks, I recommend that you go to the tenant's bank and cash the check immediately instead of depositing it again. Or you can get the check *certified*, which means the bank reserves the funds for payment when you deposit it in your bank. ***Note:*** Unless you receive good funds before the end of your grace period, your tenant is also responsible for late charges.

The best policy is to demand your tenant immediately replace a returned check with a cashier's check or money order. After a tenant's check is returned a second time, regardless of her excuse, require all future payments to be made only electronically, or with a cashier's check or money order (both of which are guaranteed to have sufficient funds). Tenants can still cancel their electronic payments or request a stop-payment on a cashier's check or money order, so be sure to process the transaction right away.

Like late charges, dishonored electronic payment and returned check charges should be reasonable. Try setting the fee at $15 to $25 per returned item, or slightly higher than the amount your bank charges you. Some states' laws allow you to charge interest and penalties on returned checks.

Dealing with partial rent payments

Occasionally, you'll encounter a tenant who isn't able to pay the full rent on time. This tenant may offer to pay a portion of the rent with a promise to catch up as the month proceeds. Your written rent collection policy shouldn't allow partial payments of rent, and deviating from this standard generally isn't a good idea.

In some instances, however, allowing for partial rent payments may make sense. If your tenant has an excellent rental payment history, and you can verify that this partial payment is a one-time situation, then you're probably safe in accepting a partial rent payment. Of course, you need to be careful and watch for the tenant who's delaying the inevitable and stalling you from pursuing your legal options.

If you do accept a partial payment, prepare the proper legal notice for non-payment of rent or draw up a written notice outlining the terms of your one-time acceptance of the partial rent payment, including late charges. Then present the tenant with the legal rent demand notice or written agreement when he gives you the partial payment. This way, you can be sure he understands your terms.

In most areas, the acceptance of a partial payment voids any prior legal notices for nonpayment of rent. If your tenant is causing trouble besides the delinquent rent, don't accept any partial payments, or you'll have to begin your eviction proceedings from scratch.

Always apply rental payments to the oldest outstanding past-due rent amount, even if the tenant tries to indicate the payment is for a different time period.

Serving legal notices

If you're having trouble collecting rent from one of your tenants, you may need to pursue legal action. In most states, you don't need to wait until the end of the grace period to serve a legal rent demand notice, but you should serve it personally whenever possible. The laws of each state do offer alternative means of achieving legal process service. Contact your local affiliate of the NAA for the process serving requirements in your area.

Legal notices for nonpayment of rent and similar breaches of the rental contract vary widely from state to state. The generic forms available from office supply stores may be ineffective or even invalid in your region. Contact your local NAA affiliate or the state or local National Association of Realtors member board in your area for current and legally correct forms.

Rewarding timely payments

Because timely rent collection can make or break your career as a rental property owner, you may want to offer your tenants incentives to pay on time. If you have several rental units, one good way to motivate your tenants to pay the rent is to offer a monthly prize drawing for everyone who pays rent in full by your due date. Of course, you need to carefully outline your rules in writing and make sure you don't violate any local or state laws.

The drawing should be simple and easy for your tenants to understand. Limit eligibility to tenants who are current with their rent and automatically enter tenants when you receive their full rent on or before the due date. Inform tenants of the time and place for the drawing and try to hold it in a common area at one of your rental properties. You can also give a second entry to tenants who pay early, but be sure your rules disqualify a winner whose rent payment is later returned for any reason.

The prize can be a gift certificate to a local store or restaurant. (Often the merchant is willing to discount or donate the prize if it gets some good publicity from your drawing.) You may even want to offer a rent discount off the next month's rent. Either way, consider sending out a written announcement congratulating your monthly drawing winner.

How to Handle Increasing the Rent

Increasing the rent is one of the most difficult challenges rental property owners face. If you need to raise the rent, you may be wondering how to go about doing so, worrying that tenants will leave or questioning how local rent control ordinances may impact your efforts. I help clear up these murky waters in the following sections.

Figuring out how to raise the rent

The best way to establish your rent increase is to regularly review and survey the rental market to determine the current market rental rate for *comparable rental properties* — ones that are of similar size and condition and that have the same features and amenities. Turn to Chapter 6 for more information on evaluating the competitive rental market and setting rents.

Unless you're in a rent controlled area, you have no limit on the amount or frequency with which you can increase the rent of a month-to-month or periodic tenant, with proper legal notice. If your tenant is on a lease, you need to hold off on raising rent until that lease expires. You can raise the rent as much and as often as your good business judgment and the competitive rental market will allow. But don't be too aggressive, or you'll lose your best tenants. Trying to get that last $25 per month can cost you a vacancy with significant turnover costs, plus the lost rent that's likely much more than $25 per month!

Many wise rental property owners intentionally keep their rents slightly below the maximum amount the competitive rental market will allow as part of a policy to retain the best tenants. Unless you're planning a major upgrade of your rental units with a new tenant profile and much higher rents across the board, tenant turnover is usually bad business.

Be careful when raising the rent so that you're not accused of giving retaliatory rent increases. An increase immediately after a tenant complains to the local Health Department or building code enforcement agency, or an increase that's much higher than what other tenants received, is likely to lead to problems. As always, your best defense is to have a sensible rent increase policy, keep good records, and be consistently fair and equitable with all your tenants.

Keeping your tenants (relatively) happy

Whether you're raising the rent for the first time in several years or raising it on a semiregular basis, most tenants naturally have a very negative reaction to a rent increase. So you need to do your homework and make sure that yours is reasonable and justified. When the rental market is tight, you should adjust your rent by small amounts with greater frequency rather than large amounts less often. Most tenants don't leave over a small rent increase.

Before increasing your rent, be sure to determine what improvements you're going to make in the common area of your rental property or, better yet, in the tenant's rental unit. I suggest setting a budget equivalent to three to six months of the rent increase and planning on making an immediate upgrade to the tenant's rental unit. Often just painting and cleaning or replacing the carpet helps your tenant accept the rent increase. Installing new plumbing or light fixtures is usually appreciated as well.

Although you're legally required to give only a 30-day notice in many cases, I recommend a minimum rental increase notice of 45 days. If the rent increase is significant (10 percent or more), a 60-day written notice is advisable. Some owners fear that giving their tenants notice also gives them plenty of time to find another rental. However, if you've set your increased rent properly, you want your tenants to have the opportunity to compare the new rental rate to the market conditions.

ON THE CD

Realizing how rent control may affect you

If you don't live in California, Maryland, New Jersey, New York, or the District of Columbia, then — good news! — you don't have to worry about rent control limiting your rental rates. But if you live in one of these regions, know that many of the larger cities and certain surrounding communities have rent control laws that regulate many aspects of the landlord-tenant relationship.

Although the local rent control ordinances differ by area, they all feature regulations that landlords must know, which may be broader than simply limiting the setting or adjusting of rental rates. These ordinances also invoke specific requirements that must be met prior to increasing the rent.

If you own rental property in a rent controlled city, you typically must register your rental property with the local rent control agency. Always have a current copy of the rent control ordinance on hand and be sure you have a good understanding of all the regulations or procedures you must follow. The services of a landlord-tenant legal expert are extremely important for all rental property owners, but especially so in jurisdictions with any form of rent control. See the CD for links to the Web sites of many rent controlled cities.

If possible, inform each tenant personally of the pending rent increase and be sure to follow up by legally serving a formal written notice of the increase and keeping a copy in each tenant's file. The letter doesn't have to be a literary work, but you may consider attaching any market information obtained from your market survey (see more about market surveys in Chapter 6) so that your tenants can see you've made an informed decision.

Chapter 13

Keeping the Good Tenants — and Your Sanity

In This Chapter

▶ Retaining your tenants by recognizing their desires and making sure they're fulfilled

▶ Knowing whether renewing a lease is the best option for you and your tenant

An occupied rental unit is the key to your success as a property manager. Yet this basic fact is something many rental property owners quickly forget. Advertising your vacancy, having a well-polished presentation, knowing all the latest sales closing techniques, implementing a thorough tenant screening program, and moving in your prized tenants with amazing efficiency are all key parts of your job. But the reality is that the day your tenant moves in is the day your most important job — keeping your good tenants satisfied and happy — begins.

You want your best tenants to stay and pay. If you offer a quality rental experience at a reasonable price, you'll have lower turnover than other rental properties. You can achieve this goal by treating tenants with the same personal attention and courtesy you demonstrated when you first spoke to them on the phone or gave them a tour of the vacancy.

Knowing what your customers want is the key to success in any business, and as a rental property owner, your tenants are your customers. In this chapter, I let you know what most tenants are looking for in a rental experience so that you can make sure you're meeting those needs. I also give you some tips on getting to the point where your tenants not only enjoy their experiences at your property but want to renew their leases.

Knowing What Tenants Want

If you're trying to raise your level of tenant satisfaction (and that should always be your goal), you need to determine what your tenants want and how to deliver that to them. This section looks at what your tenants are basically looking for.

Out of sight shouldn't be out of mind

In my early years as a property manager, my wife and I lived on-site at one of the properties I oversaw for a large firm. We lived across the shared stairwell landing from Beatrice — one of the kindest and quietest neighbors you could ever have. Beatrice was a widow who kept to herself and only ventured out a handful of times per week for church and bridge club. She always paid her rent early and never complained. So what's the problem?

Well, Beatrice didn't want to bother any of the neighbors, and she failed to ask for routine maintenance. So when she eventually vacated her apartment, our on-site management staff was quite surprised when they did their pre-move-out walk-through with her: Only one stove burner worked, and one of the two toilets hadn't worked in years. It took a crew of three handymen a full week to turn over her apartment. When the property's on-site manager asked Beatrice how she could live with so many problems in her apartment and reminded her that two full-time maintenance pros lived on-site, Beatrice's only comment was that she could see how busy everyone was, and she didn't want to bother anyone.

Checking in on tenants periodically — even the quiet ones — can be worth a fortune in time and money if you can discover issues early before they become expensive problems at move-out.

Timely and effective communication

A variety of issues concerns most tenants — and those issues are usually fairly obvious. Good tenants don't like loud or noisy neighbors, unkempt common areas, broken or unserviceable items in their units, or unsubstantiated rent increases. Fortunately, most of these problems can be solved if you have good communication and follow-through.

The one problem that tenants don't ignore is a landlord's apathy. If you seem uncaring or nonchalant about tenants' concerns, they'll get the message that you don't value their business. The perception of apathy is often created by the unwillingness or failure to communicate. If you give your tenants the impression that you only care about them when their rent's late, you're headed straight down that apathy path.

Keep your tenants informed. No one likes surprises, and tenants are no different. If the pest control company cancels its service call, let your tenants know right away. If the walk-through with your new lender has been changed to earlier, call or e-mail your tenants instead of arriving unexpectedly with a weak apology. Common courtesy goes a long way.

Quick responses to maintenance requests

One way to set your rental management apart from your competition is to handle tenant maintenance requests quickly and professionally. Providing prompt resolution to your tenants' problems keeps them happy.

If a new tenant notes any problems after moving in, don't view these complaints as negatives. Instead, think of them as opportunities to let your tenant know you care. By quickly and professionally addressing the problems, you actually improve your tenant relations. Successful rental owners don't have to be perfect; they just need to admit a problem exists, communicate openly and candidly, and take the steps to resolve the issue.

A very common complaint about rental owners is that they're unwilling to maintain, and especially upgrade, their rental units for current tenants. In my experience, this complaint's valid. Refusing to repaint, recarpet, or upgrade the appliances for a great tenant makes no sense. After all, if you don't do it for the great tenant you already have, and that tenant gets frustrated with your lack of effort and moves out, you have do the work anyway in order to be competitive in the rental market and attract a new, unproven tenant.

Rental property owners often also overlook punctuality when it comes to making repairs. Undoubtedly, you're a very busy person, so it's easy to lose sight of the fact that your tenants are busy, too. If you tell your tenants that you're going to call or meet them at a certain time, be there — or, at the very least, call and let them know you're running late. Require your property manager, maintenance personnel, or contractors to treat your tenants with the same level of respect as well.

Treating your tenants as important customers can be the best decision you ever make. When working with a tenant concern or complaint, try to ask yourself how you'd want to be treated. Treating your tenants in this manner makes your tenant relations much more pleasant, dramatically decreases your tenant turnover, and improves your net income — a win-win situation for all!

Consistent respect for their privacy

A vast majority of tenants hate rental owners who fail to respect their privacy. In most states, the property manager or owner can enter the premises only with advance written notice or a tenant's permission, except in the event of an emergency situation that's a threat to the property or a life-safety issue. Examples include pressurized water floods, fire or natural gas leaks, or any other imminent threat to life or limb. Always leave a note indicating that you had to enter the rental unit; include the date and time, as well as the reason.

The minimum required written notice of entry is 24 hours in most states. A few states require two days' notice, and many don't have any specific law at all. In these cases, 24 hours is generally considered reasonable notice. See the CD for more information about your state laws, if any, regarding required notification for entering a tenant's rental unit.

Your request for entry should only involve normal business hours. A few state laws offer specific day and time parameters, but many don't. Without the guidelines, some rental owners feel that as long as they give proper legal notice, they can enter the rental whenever they want. However, I recommend limiting your entry to Monday through Saturday from 9 a.m. to 6 p.m., unless the tenant requests or voluntarily agrees to a different time.

Legally, you may have to post a notice only a few days in advance of when you want to enter the rental unit, but that isn't enough notice to maintain a positive and mutually respectful relationship with your tenants. Even though you own the property, the last thing you want your tenants to feel is that their home isn't really theirs. If you don't respect your tenants' privacy in their own home, they'll be less likely to show respect for you or your rental property during or at the end of their tenancy.

Equal enforcement of house rules

A frequent source of tenant complaints is the rental property owner's failure to enforce reasonable *house rules,* the policies and regulations you set for your property (check out Chapter 11 for more on establishing house rules). In fact, good tenants actually want and appreciate fair and reasonable policies and rules. They know that they're going to be quiet and respectful of their neighbors, and they want to know that their neighbors must reciprocate. Establishing house rules for your rental properties and enforcing them fairly are all parts of the job of managing rental property.

Tenants talk to one another, and they quickly discover if you have different rules for different tenants. Inconsistent or selective rule enforcement has legal implications. For example, you may think that waiving a late fee for a tenant you've known for years but charging the late fee to a new tenant in similar circumstances is okay. After all, you've known the first tenant longer, and you're willing to forgive that oversight once in a while, right? Wrong. You can't have different interpretations of the rules, because the legal consequences you may face are severe.

Fair rental rates and increases

Rent increases are always unpopular, and if you don't handle them properly, they can easily lead to increased tension and tenant dissatisfaction. No one likes to pay more, but, of course, the good stuff in life isn't cheap. Most tenants don't mind paying a fair and competitive rent, as long as they're sure you're not gouging them with unnecessary rent hikes.

Although they may initially be upset with the increase, your tenants may be thinking to themselves that you can now finally address their peeling paint and missing window screens. If your rental property has these issues and you've just increased the rent, address those problems right away — if you want your tenants to be satisfied.

Increasing your price isn't a sin — after all, you're running a business. But common sense and prudence dictate that you explain to your tenants the reasons for the rent increase and what benefits are in it for them.

Recognizing the Ins and Outs of Renewing Leases

Tenants who renew their leases — thus locking in solid, long-term commitments — are a sign that you're doing a good job in your initial tenant screening and selection process, plus you're keeping your tenants satisfied and meeting their needs during the tenancy. Lease renewals are one of your most productive activities as a rental property manager. Of course, despite your best efforts, not all tenants are good candidates for lease renewal, but renewing a lease with a current tenant clearly has a benefit over a lease with a new tenant. After all, you have a track record with your current tenant; you know her rent payment history and whether she treats the property and her neighbors with respect. You can never be 100 percent sure of that kind of information when you're starting from scratch with someone new.

Plus, your tenant knows what to expect from you as a rental property owner. She knows your standards for maintaining the property, your interest in and response to her requests, your house rules (and whether they're fairly enforced), and the courtesy and respect you have for her privacy. Your tenant has a certain comfort level with you, and as long as you're willing to be competitive with your rental rate, it's in her best interests to stay.

Reducing your turnover

One of the most effective ways to be successful in the rental housing business is to retain those tenants who are your best customers. Reducing turnover not only keeps the rental income flowing in but also lowers your expenses. The tenant retention process really starts the moment the tenant moves in, and one fundamental step in that process is simply keeping track of when your leases are expiring.

Although renewing leases can reduce turnover and provide many benefits, renewing a lease in a strong rental market may not be in your best interest, because a lease prevents you from raising the rent or changing any terms. Plus, with a lease in place, evicting a problem tenant is much more difficult. Being contacted by your tenant to request a lease renewal may seem a blessing, but you need to be certain that he's treating your property properly and that the rental rate is competitive before signing a new long-term lease extension.

Understanding the costs of turnover

If the tenant moves out, you incur extensive turnover costs for maintenance, painting, and cleaning, plus you lose rent for every day the rental unit sits vacant. The greatest wear and tear to your rental units occurs during the moving process. So basically, if you can minimize the number of times you change tenants, then your property holds up better over time and doesn't incur as much cumulative damage that makes it look tired, even with routine repairs. For example, you can patch holes in drywall from furniture nicks, but the result's never quite like new unless you have an exceptional contractor.

In addition to maintenance and repair expenses, you also have advertising costs, as well as the time and effort involved in showing the rental unit and screening each applicant. And after all that, you still may not have a tenant who'll treat your rental property and the neighbors respectfully and be prompt with rent payments.

Following is a look at what the typical costs are for a turnover of a $1,500 per month rental home that takes six weeks to re-rent, plus marketing and rental unit preparation charges.

Costs	Dollar Amount
Lost rent	$2,250
Advertising and signage	$400
Maintenance and repair parts	$175
Maintenance labor	$450
Painting	$475
Cleaning	$250
Total turnover cost	$4,000

You may be able to legally deduct some of these costs from your tenant's deposit if he only lived in the property a short time, but this analysis doesn't include your time if you self-manage or the turnover fees from your property management company to cover its out-of-pocket expenses. Only you can put a value on your time, but the typical property management company charges from 50 percent to 100 percent of the monthly rent as a leasing fee.

Convincing tenants to re-sign

In order to avoid turnover, you need to get your tenant to re-sign his lease. Unless your lease contains an automatic renewal clause, it expires on the date specified. If you want your tenant to stay, don't be afraid to ask him to sign another lease effective when the current one expires. Contact your tenant at least 60 days prior to his lease expiration.

Keep the following in mind as you work to retain your good tenants and reduce turnover:

- ✔ **Plan your lease renewals so you don't have vacancies during those challenging times of year when rental traffic's slow.** Many rental owners and property managers blindly seek the 12-month lease renewal as if that's the only option. When you're reviewing your upcoming lease expirations for tenants whom you want to renew, why not try something different? Steer the new lease expiration date away from times when other leases are expiring and towards dates that are more favorable times for strong rental activity in your local market. For example, most rental markets are traditionally slow from mid-November until mid-January, so if you have a lease that's up in the second week of November, you want to offer your tenant a 16- or 18-month lease. The new lease then expires in the spring.

- ✔ **Provide exemplary customer service at all times.** Personally, I find that the customer service practices of certain retailers keep me coming back again and again. You can have that same customer service attitude just as easily. Anticipate your customers' needs and work to reinforce their positive image of your rental property and your ability to quickly respond to and competently address legitimate concerns that they raise.

- ✔ **Contact your strong tenants before their leases expire and discuss their satisfaction.** Doing so gives you a pretty good idea about which tenants are strong candidates for lease renewal. Remember, these quality tenants have the most leverage because they're so desirable. So if you want to impress a quality tenant with your proactive customer service, I suggest contacting him by phone two to three months before the current lease expires and briefly reviewing the service requests he has made to date to confirm whether he is satisfied with your response. Always ask whether you can do anything else for him. After he recovers from the shock that you're calling and genuinely have an interest in his needs, he'll tell you whether any problems exist so you can address them now rather than later. Most tenants are quite conservative in their requests.

Low turnover is financially rewarding, but you should resist the temptation to renew the lease of a tenant who doesn't pay rent on time or who creates other problems. If you're uncertain but cautiously optimistic that your tenant will pull through some temporary issues and be the great long-term tenant you want, don't offer a lease. Keep the tenant on month-to-month instead until he or she can demonstrate enough stability to warrant a new lease.

Listen and consider your tenants' requests

Throughout the 30 years that I've been a rental housing owner and manager, I've found many industry quirks that simply don't make any sense. One baffling mistake is the knee-jerk denial of a tenant request to make needed upgrades during the tenancy. One of the most common requests from tenants is to replace the carpeting. The standard rental owner's reaction is that his practice is to change carpeting only on tenant turnover. Why institute a blanket policy that upgrades can only be made between tenants when the goal is to keep the same tenants for many years? I recommend first evaluating whether the request is reasonable and whether the tenant created the poor condition of the current carpeting.

Clearly, you don't want to replace the carpet for a tenant whose pet just ruined it; that's a rational business reason to deny the request unless the tenant wants to pay for some or all the cost. But if your inspection reveals a true need to replace the carpet, then you need to make the proper business decision. If the current tenant vacates and the carpet has to be replaced in order to attract a new tenant, why not replace the carpet for your current good tenant? So often an upgrade or improvement request from the tenant is summarily denied by the rental owner or property manager without proper consideration. Rethink this standard practice and give your good tenants a reason to stay.

Offering incentives for tenants to stay

One of the main differences between rental property owners and managers who enjoy their rental housing experience and those former rental owners who tell horror stories is the ability to find and retain long-term, excellent tenants. If you can master the skill of attracting, screening, and holding on to your best tenants, you'll find that being a rental property owner and manager may even be enjoyable. Offering incentives to your tenants is an easy way to get them to stick around.

One successful technique I've used to keep properties in the positive-cash flow mode and to keep those good tenants happy is a Resident Appreciation Day. Call your tenants in advance and bring them some breakfast treats or juice and gourmet coffee to start their day.

You can show your appreciation in hundreds of inexpensive yet meaningful ways, and the incentives you offer are limited only by your imagination and your budget — just don't get carried away. Following are some additional ideas to help get those brain juices flowing:

- ✔ Coupons for free DVD rentals, pizza, or other food items
- ✔ Gift certificates to a popular local restaurant, the local mall, or a general merchandise store
- ✔ Movie theater passes

✔ Professional carpet cleaning or another type of pro cleaning service

✔ Two hours with your maintenance person for use at the renewing tenant's discretion (which can even involve moving furniture, hanging wall decorations, or anything else to make your rental unit the tenant's home)

Most good tenants like to have a landlord who demonstrates a sincere concern for them and is willing to invest the time and funds necessary to make sure they always have well-maintained rental property. So why not make a few upgrades to the rental unit a couple months before the tenant's lease expires? As a reminder that you care about the tenant's satisfaction, of course.

When you offer incentives to entice your tenants to stay, develop several choices for them that reflect the current and expected market conditions. If the rental market is weak, you need to be more generous than if you're in a tight rental market. Offer your tenants renewal incentives that improve your rental unit for future tenants — like mirrored closet doors, built-in water filter systems, security screen doors, ceiling fans, intrusion alarms, new kitchen countertops, new plumbing or lighting fixtures, or built-in microwave/stove hood units.

An excellent way to improve your rental property and allow your tenant to personalize her home at the same time is to give your tenant a list of comparably priced service items or unit upgrades and let the tenant choose which upgrade she wants. You can have your contractor paint a few accent walls (in a tenant-selected color from a palette you control) or install quality wall coverings. Or you can give your tenant a few options to choose from for new, upgraded window coverings. This way, you send the message that you value her input and strive to reward her business.

In a competitive rental market with increasing rents, most tenants who intend to stay are glad to renew their current leases or even sign new leases at higher but still reasonable rents. Perform a rental market survey before setting the rent for any extended-term lease renewals so that you know your rental rate is fair to both you and the tenants.

Renewal incentives are great if they make sense, but some creative, well-meaning ideas with frightening and unintended consequences are out there. For example, I once saw an incentive for "one free late rent payment" if a tenant renewed the lease. Is that really something you want to encourage? Another head-scratcher is the recommendation that you return the tenant's entire security deposit upon lease renewal if he or she has a history of prompt rent payment. My advice is never, never, never (did I mention never?) give back the security deposit until your tenant vacates the property! I can tell you hundreds of stories I've read about the problems of not having a security deposit to keep tenants honest and responsible. That small amount of money is your best insurance against damage to the rental unit, because even the best tenants are careless when they know you aren't holding any security deposit.

Following up with tenants after move-out

Sometimes good tenants leave, and that's out of your control. Just make sure you maintain a professional relationship with them, because you never know when they may refer you to a friend or family member.

One of the most common reasons a tenant leaves or doesn't renew a lease is the intent to purchase a home. Although homeownership is a very worthy goal, you may want to advise your tenant about other options. For example, if you want to entice him or her to stay, you may offer a lease option (see Chapter 21 for more info) or a long-term lease at a fixed amount that provides rent stability. A number of calculators are available on the Internet to help people determine whether they're better off renting or buying, given their overall financial situation. Letting your tenants know about their options — without discouraging them from buying if that's really best for them — makes sense.

Make sure departing tenants complete tenant exit surveys. This survey may not help you retain your moving tenants, but asking some basic questions about the reason for their move gives you valuable, candid feedback on what they liked and disliked so that you can make appropriate changes for the future.

Chapter 14

Dealing with Problem Tenants

In This Chapter

▶ Knowing how to handle typical tenant problems

▶ Checking out ways to avoid eviction

▶ Navigating your way through the eviction process

▶ Being prepared for situations beyond the norm

Although the proper tenant screening and selection techniques greatly improve your success in picking good tenants, they aren't a guarantee, which means that at some point in your rental property management tenure, you're sure to come across a problem tenant or two. Some tenants avoid paying rent, disturb the neighbors, damage property, or keep a growing collection of inoperative cars on the front lawns, and you need to take steps immediately to remove these tenants and replace them. But other tenants — like the one who pays his rent a few days late every single month, or the one who sneaks in an animal even though pets aren't allowed — are more subtle in the problems they present, and their behavior may not warrant eviction. This chapter gives you tips for handling some common tenant problems and lets you know about valuable alternatives to evictions. Plus, I prepare you for some situations you may encounter so that you know how to deal with them.

Recognizing and Responding to Common Tenant Problems

The level of response you have toward a problem tenant depends on how severe the problem is and how frequently it occurs. Some issues — including nonpayment of rent, additional occupants not on the rental contract, noise, and threats of violence or intimidation — are breaches of the rental contract and clearly call for serving a legal notice.

Documentation is critical whenever you have a problem with a tenant. Even minor problems are worth documenting, because over time, they may add up or increase in severity. If you find yourself needing to evict a tenant, you must have written proof of the entirety of the problem.

The next few sections highlight a few of the more common problems you may experience with your tenants and how you can handle them.

Late or nonpayment of rent

One of the toughest issues you'll encounter is how to deal with a tenant who consistently pays her rent late or, even worse, who doesn't pay her rent at all. In other respects, the tenant may not create any problems, but she just can't seem to get the rent in on time. You may have to serve a Notice of Nonpayment of Rent in order to get the tenant to pay — and even then, she may not include the late charge. In my experience, this nagging problem doesn't go away unless you put a stop to it.

When you're faced with a tenant who just can't seem to get her rent payment in on time, you have many factors to consider (such as whether the tenant is creating any other problems for you or your other residents). But the strength of the rental market is usually the most important issue. If it's a renter's market, and you know that finding another tenant to rent the property will be difficult, you may be willing to be more flexible.

Specific legal notices are available in most states to deal with the issue of nonpayment of rent, but you should document other violations of the rental contract in writing using a Lease or Rental Agreement Violation Letter, like the one in Figure 14-1 and on the accompanying CD.

Don't ignore the problem of a tenant who consistently pays late. Clearly inform her in writing that she has breached the rental contract — and be sure to do so each and every time she pays late. If you fail to enforce your late charges, the tenant can later argue that you've waived your rights to collect future late charges. Be sure to let the tenant know in writing that chronically late payments are grounds for eviction — even if you're not necessarily willing to go that route just yet. (Chapter 12 describes how to handle late payments and late charges.)

Lease or Rental Agreement Violation Letter

_____

Date

_____

Name

_____

Street address

_____

City/state/zip code

Dear _____,

This is a formal legal reminder that your lease or rental agreement does not allow:
_____
_____.

It has come to our attention, that recently or beginning _____ and continuing to the present, you have broken one or more terms of your tenancy by:
_____
_____
_____
_____

It is our sincere desire that you will enjoy living in your rental unit, as will all of your neighbors. To make sure this happens, we enforce the Policies and Rules and all terms and conditions of your Lease or Rental Agreement. So please immediately:
_____
_____
_____
_____

If you are unable to promptly resolve this matter, we will exercise our legal right to begin eviction proceedings.

Please feel free to contact us if you would like to discuss this issue.

Sincerely,

_____

Owner/Manager

Figure 14-1:
Lease or
Rental
Agreement
Violation
Letter.

Additional occupants

Tenants frequently abuse the guest policy by having additional occupants in their rental units for extended periods of time. But you may have trouble determining the difference between a temporary guest and a new live-in occupant. Talk to your tenant to find out what's going on if you suspect he has added an additional occupant. Be sure to get his story before jumping to conclusions. This practice is sound not only because it's considerate but also because you need to be careful to avoid claims of discrimination, particularly if the additional occupant is a child.

If you find that the tenant isn't complying with your guest policy, immediately send him a Lease or Rental Agreement Violation Letter indicating that he must have the additional occupant leave as soon as possible or the individual will be formally added to the rental contract as a tenant. (*Remember:* All new adult occupants must complete a rental application, go through the tenant screening process, and sign the rental contract if approved.) If the tenant fails to cooperate, you may need to take legal action.

A common guest policy in the rental housing industry is to allow the guest to stay in the rental unit for up to 14 consecutive days. But savvy tenants just ask their guest to leave for a day or two and then return. Although tough to enforce, I suggest modifying your guest policy to limit visits to a total of no more than 14 days in any six-month time frame. This policy should be uniformly enforced to the best of your ability to avoid allegations of discrimination.

You must be careful when determining whether an additional occupant is a rental contract or guest policy violation when the individual may qualify under Fair Housing law as a *caretaker,* which is a disability accommodation. Typically, a caretaker isn't on the rental contract and isn't responsible for rent payment and often can be a family member. He or she must, however, routinely perform assistance services and follow the community rules, except he or she is exempt from senior housing age restrictions. Seek the advice of legal counsel if you have any questions.

Inappropriate noise level

You usually hear about a noisy tenant from one of the tenant's neighbors. Let the complaining tenants know that they should always contact law enforcement and file an official complaint as soon as the noise level becomes a problem. Then they should let you know that they've done so.

Have a policy requiring all tenant complaints regarding neighbors, especially noise, to be in writing. Neighbors usually don't want to go to court to testify; they just want you to quickly solve the problem and allow them to keep their anonymity. But if the noisy tenant disputes the charges, the courts are usually reluctant to accept your unsubstantiated testimony. A report from law enforcement and a written complaint made simultaneously by a neighbor carry a lot of weight.

Unsupervised children

Under federal law, with the exception of the limited number of HUD-certified seniors housing properties, you must accept children at your rental property. Unfortunately, one of the toughest dilemmas you'll face is dealing with a tenant's unsupervised child on the grounds of your rental property. If you don't do anything and the child gets hurt, you may be sued for failing to take reasonable action. But if you don't handle the matter properly, the tenant may claim that you're discriminating against families with children. In this case, you need to be able to prove that you acted reasonably and consistently.

If you become aware of an unsupervised child at your rental property who's in a potentially dangerous situation, immediately take the child home to her parents. Take the child home again if the problem happens a second time and send a letter to your tenants warning them of the seriousness of the matter. If the written notice isn't effective, you can always call the police or social services while advising your tenants, in writing, that an eviction may be warranted.

If your tenants fail to properly supervise their children and the children damage your rental property, don't just talk to the children about the problem. Immediately contact the tenants and officially advise them of the issue, stressing the fact that property damage by tenants of any age is unacceptable. This kind of action is usually sufficient, but if the damage is severe or continues, notify the tenants in writing and bill them for the damage; warn them that any continued problems will result in eviction.

Exploring Alternatives to Eviction

Evictions are both expensive and emotionally draining. They can also be costly in terms of lost rent, legal fees, property damage, and turnover expenses. And they can earn a negative reputation for your rental property with good tenants in the area. So be sure to evaluate each situation carefully and only turn to eviction as a last resort.

When you're looking for an alternative to evicting a problem tenant, such as the solutions presented in the following sections, don't underestimate the importance of communicating with your tenant. Be sure to document any conversations you have or agreements you reach.

If the most likely outcome of an issue with a tenant is an expensive and time-consuming eviction, do your best to minimize or cut your losses. A court judgment against a tenant without any assets doesn't help your cash flow, but a nonpaying or bad tenant is much worse than no tenant at all. Your primary goal should be to regain possession of the rental unit and find a new tenant as quickly as possible.

Negotiating a voluntary move-out

You may be able to negotiate a voluntary move-out with your tenant, in which you forgive the unpaid rent if the tenant agrees to leave by a mutually agreed upon date. Another approach is to agree to refund the tenant's full security deposit immediately after he has vacated the property (as long as no significant damage has been done to it).

Although you may feel strongly that your tenant should keep up his end of the rental contract, you may come out ahead by avoiding legal action and not having to worry about him anymore. *Note:* If you agree on a voluntary move-out, don't count on a verbal agreement. Make sure you get it in writing.

Using mediation or arbitration services

If you aren't able to reach an agreement with your tenant about a voluntary move-out, consider taking your dispute to a neutral third-party mediation or arbitration service. *Mediation* is an informal opportunity for both parties to resolve their disputes with the assistance of a local mediation group at little or no cost. Often confused with mediation, *arbitration* is legally binding and enforceable, and can be a relatively quick and inexpensive alternative to litigation. Mediation typically involves only the parties to the dispute (you and your tenant), whereas arbitration often uses attorneys, witnesses, and experts. Many organizations offer both mediation and arbitration services, so if mediation doesn't resolve the issue, you can always try arbitration.

Taking your tenant to court

Rather than eviction, you may want to consider using the court system. Rental property owners in roughly 20 states can turn to small claims or municipal courts to resolve the issue of the rental unit's possession in an eviction. Courts with limited jurisdiction are often used to resolve landlord-tenant matters restricted to monetary demands. The jurisdictional limits for these courts range from $2,000 to $15,000, but the majority are $5,000 or less. Consult with your local court for its limits.

The popularity of court TV shows means almost everyone is generally familiar with the roles of the participants in and the procedures of small claims courts. Although this knowledge can make the participants more comfortable with the format, note that most small claims or municipal court proceedings aren't as entertaining as what you see on TV because matters are handled quickly and efficiently. If you plan to head to court with your tenant, don't be afraid to be overly prepared.

Giving 'Em the Boot: Evicting a Tenant

Some tenants just don't pay their rent; others violate the rules or are involved in criminal activities. In these situations, after you've explored your other options, you may have no other reasonable alternative but an eviction. The eviction process can be intimidating and costly, but keep in mind that allowing the tenant to stay only prolongs the problem.

The eviction process varies greatly from state to state, and many attorneys who specialize in representing rental property owners offer guidebooks that outline the specific legal steps for an eviction action in your area. Your local Institute of Real Estate Management (IREM) chapter or National Apartment Association (NAA) affiliate can provide attorney references, so see the CD for these groups' contact information. In the meantime, the following sections can provide you with a general overview of the eviction process.

Serving legal notices

In order to evict a tenant, you have to first terminate the tenancy by giving an appropriate legal Notice of Termination. Month-to-month tenancies generally can be terminated with written 30-day notices, whereas leases only expire at the end of their terms (unless they're renewed or contractually converted to month-to-month rental agreements).

Although the terminology varies from state to state, three basic types of legal notices are required, depending upon the circumstances:

- ✔ **Pay Rent or Quit notices:** These notices are given to tenants who haven't paid rent and require tenants to pay the rent or move out. Tenants are typically allowed from 3 to 10 days to pay in full, depending on the law in your state, but some jurisdictions allow up to 30 days.

- ✔ **Cure or Quit notices:** This paperwork is given to tenants who've violated one of the terms or conditions of the rental contract. It gives tenants a limited number of days (determined by state law) to cure the violation and vacate the premises, or be subject to an eviction action.

- ✔ **Notice to Quit or Unconditional Quit notices:** These documents are the most severe types of notices and require tenants to vacate the premises without the opportunity to cure any deficiency. Most states discourage the use of these notices unless tenants are conducting illegal activity, have repeatedly violated a significant term or condition of the rental contract, or have severely damaged the premises.

The following sections outline how the process works and what you need to do (and not do) to help the eviction process run as smoothly as possible.

Knowing what happens during the eviction process

If your tenant doesn't cure the violation or leave the rental property after receiving the appropriate legal notice, she isn't automatically evicted. Instead, you must begin a formal eviction action. The formal eviction process follows these steps:

1. **You file the required forms with your local court and arrange to have the tenant properly served with a summons and complaint.**

   The complaint is usually a preprinted form, and you can only seek unpaid rent and actual damages. Any attempt to demand late charges or other fees can cause your complaint to be denied.

    Serving a legal notice isn't simply a matter of mailing the notice or slipping it under the tenant's door. You must have an authorized person physically deliver the legal notice to the tenant face to face. Every state has specific rules and procedures as to what exactly constitutes *proper legal service,* including who can serve notices, the method of delivery, the specific parties who can be legally served, and the amount of time the tenant has to respond to the legal notice. Check with your local attorney for the requirements in your area.

2. **By law, a trial date is set, and your tenant has a certain number of days to file an answer to your summons and complaint.**

   Tenants usually either deny the allegations you've made in your eviction action or claim that they have an *affirmative defense* (a legal justification for their actions). The tenant may deny your allegations, for example, if she has a cancelled check showing that the rent was paid and your records are in error.

   Frequently, tenants know that they've materially breached their rental contracts and voluntarily leave the premises. Or sometimes tenants settle with you out of court.

    If your tenant settles informally, you must officially dismiss your court eviction action. Not only is dismissing your court eviction action under these circumstances the proper way to treat your tenants but it also preserves your reputation with the court. After all, courts have limited resources and don't respond well to parties who resolve their matter and fail to file a timely dismissal. Also, failing to dismiss an eviction action can result in a negative credit standing for your tenant.

3. **If your tenant doesn't file an answer in a timely manner, the eviction action proceeds to court without the tenant.**

   This scenario is known as an *uncontested eviction.* The court requires you to prove your case, but the tenant isn't there to respond to or deny your charges. Typically, you can easily prevail in this situation, as long as you have good documentation.

4. **If your tenant files an answer and appears at court, each party receives the opportunity to present its evidence before the court makes a ruling.**

   This scenario is known as a *contested eviction*. If you're prepared and professionally present the facts in a well-supported case, you can generally win. However, the courts can be very harsh if you've acted illegally or in a retaliatory or discriminatory manner toward the tenant.

   A tenant may be able to argue either that he's entitled to additional time to work out a payment plan for the unpaid rent or that he has a hardship that requires the court's leniency. Although not legally required in most states, courts have been known to allow a tenant an extension due to inclement weather, an appeal of the ruling, or the improvement of the tenant's health or other personal situation.

5. **If you win the eviction lawsuit, you must present the judgment to local law enforcement.**

   The local law enforcement gives the tenant one final notice before going to the rental unit and physically removing the tenant and her possessions. Arrange to have someone meet the law enforcement officers at the rental property at the designated time and have the locks changed after you receive legal possession of the unit.

Remembering some do's and don'ts during the eviction process

Although the eviction process is rather straightforward in most areas, you still want to ensure you don't do anything to jeopardize the proceedings. I can't guarantee that the process will run smoothly, but if you keep the following do's and don'ts in mind, you can alleviate many headaches:

- ✔ **Do use an attorney.** The filing and serving of eviction actions are governed by very precise and detailed rules. The smallest mistake can result in delays or even the loss of your case on technicalities, regardless of the fact that the tenant hasn't paid rent or has otherwise violated the rental contract.

- ✔ **Don't fail to properly respond to maintenance requests.** Even if you're in the middle of an eviction process with a tenant, you're *always* responsible for properly maintaining the premises. If someone gets hurt because of your failure to keep the rental property in good condition, you can be sued.

   Tenants and their attorneys are very sensitive to maintenance issues. Any failure to respond to a tenant's request for maintenance can be used as a defense in the eviction action.

✔ **Don't get too emotionally involved in an eviction process and make an irrational decision that can be construed as a self-help eviction.** A *self-help* or *constructive eviction* is a situation in which the owner takes illegal actions to effectively force the tenant to vacate the premises.

Veteran rental property owners love to tell stories about the good old days when they could just change the locks or shut off the electricity or water to encourage a tenant to immediately vacate the premises. But in today's reality, no states tolerate these aggressive tactics, regardless of how bad the tenant may be. In many states, even reducing or eliminating free services like cable television can create a serious problem; the court can consider this move an illegal self-help measure, and the tenant can sue for significant penalties.

Collecting judgments

When you win in court and your tenant owes you for unpaid rent, damages, or legal fees, you've received a *money judgment* against the tenant. But the judgment isn't worth much unless you're able to collect. If you know that the tenant has a job or other unencumbered assets, in most states you may be able to obtain a court order to garnish his salary or have local law enforcement seize his assets and sell them, with the net proceeds of the sale going to you.

The majority of problem tenants aren't easy to locate, so your best bet may be to hire a licensed collection agency to attempt to locate and collect your judgment from your tenant. These agencies are usually paid on a contingency basis and receive a portion of the collected amount, typically ranging from one-third to one-half of the amount. Sometimes they add any out-of-pocket or hard costs of collection to the amount they retain. Although you may want to make your own efforts to enforce the judgment, remember that collection agency success rates and fees are often tied to the age of the bad debt. So the sooner the judgment is submitted for collection, the easier it is for the agency to collect, lowering the fee you have to pay.

Your success in collecting judgments often depends on how hard you worked at the beginning and throughout the tenancy. The rental application typically contains very valuable information for a collection agency, including the tenant's Social Security number or Individual Taxpayer Identification Number, prior addresses, current and prior employment information, banking and credit card accounts, vehicle information, and emergency telephone numbers. If you require a tenant to complete this application and verify its accuracy, you have a great place to start hunting him down for collections.

Handling Unusual Tenant Situations

After a year or so as a rental property owner, you may begin to think you've seen it all, but new and interesting twists always arise to keep rental management challenging. Knowing how to handle these unusual — yet surprisingly common — situations, some of which I cover in the following sections, can make life much easier.

Bankruptcies

One last-ditch effort some tenants make when they're in financial trouble is to file bankruptcy. Traditionally, many rental owners suffer severe financial blows when tenants file bankruptcy during the eviction process because doing so institutes an *automatic stay,* which immediately stops any lawsuit involving an eviction action. The rental owner must then petition the federal bankruptcy court for permission to proceed with the eviction by requesting a motion for Relief from Automatic Stay, which can delay the eviction process for 30 to 90 days.

The Bankruptcy Abuse Prevention and Consumer Protection Act of 2005, however, gives rental property owners some relief. Under this act, you can proceed with your eviction if you already have a judgment for possession when the tenant files for bankruptcy. The law also provides that the court can lift the stay in 15 days if you can show that the tenant is using illegal controlled substances or is endangering the property.

As soon as you become aware of your tenant filing bankruptcy, you should immediately stop any collection or eviction efforts and contact a landlord tenant legal expert, because severe penalties exist for rental owners who violate the stay. Your legal counsel knows what steps to take in each situation and can file pleadings with the federal bankruptcy court requesting a motion for Relief from Automatic Stay in order to proceed with the eviction, if necessary.

Even if you routinely handle your own legal work, have an attorney handle all tenant bankruptcy matters. Bankruptcies are complicated, and you need good legal advice.

Illegal holdovers

Rental owners have a rough time when a tenant fails to vacate the rental property as mutually agreed in the rental contract. Unless you accept rent, tenants who continue to live at your property are referred to as *holdover tenants.* Many states require you to give holdover tenants a legal notice to vacate immediately; other states allow you to proceed directly with an eviction action.

If you accept rent, you've agreed to a continuation of the tenant's rental, generally on at least a month-to-month basis, unless state law indicates differently.

Broken rental contracts

Although you may occasionally be faced with a tenant who refuses to leave as agreed, plan to encounter a tenant who leaves before the expiration of her rental contract and doesn't want to pay the balance of her financial obligation to you. In this case, in practically all states, you don't have the right to demand that the tenant pay the rent due each month for the balance of the rental contract.

You should first attempt to confirm that the tenant has indeed given up her right of possession. Then take reasonable steps to mitigate or limit the ongoing rent and other charges to the departed tenant by preparing the rental unit for re-renting. In most states, you must make a reasonable effort to promptly re-rent the property, including the use of advertising or other standard rental marketing methods. If you don't make an effort, the tenant may be released from any further legal obligation to pay the balance of rent owed under the rental contract.

Handle the marketing of this rental unit just like any other unit. You don't need to lower the rent, lower your tenant selection standards, or give this rental priority over any other available rental unit. Of course, you can't be vindictive and attempt to make yourself rich either.

Tenants frequently dispute whether your efforts were reasonable in mitigating their financial obligations. If challenged in court, you need to be able to show that you maintained detailed records clearly indicating the actions you took to re-rent the property, including copies of all documents, and dates you took them. The tenant generally has the burden of proof, but courts are often sympathetic to tenants who may have hardships, so be prepared.

Tenants sometimes have legitimate reasons for breaking their rental contracts, and in these situations, they don't have any further obligations to you. These legitimate reasons are all subject to state and local laws, but they can include the following:

- Harassment of the tenant by the property owner
- Provision of an uninhabitable rental unit
- Violation of a significant rental contract condition

Some state laws allow the tenant to leave under certain specified circumstances, like job transfer, military transfer, or health reasons. Make sure you know the laws in your area. See Appendix B for state-by-state information on a landlord's duty to re-rent the rental unit.

Assignments or subleases

A tenant may approach you and request the right to assign or sublease his interest in the rental unit. If you allow an *assignment*, the new tenant takes over all aspects of the original tenant's rental contract, and you can take legal action directly against the new tenant. On the other hand, *subleases* are a relationship solely between your tenant and the new tenant. You can't directly sue the new tenant for unpaid rent or damage to the property; all you can do is go after the original tenant.

Tenants usually only request this right because they must suddenly relocate for personal or professional reasons. Typically, rental contracts prohibit subleases or assignments because you want to have a direct relationship with the occupant (meaning, you screen him and approve his application).

 Subleases needlessly complicate the landlord-tenant relationship and prevent you from directly taking legal action against the occupant of your premises. If the proposed occupant meets all your rental criteria, propose terminating the current rental contract and entering a new one with him.

Departing roommates

On occasion, you may receive a notice that a particular tenant or roommate will be leaving the rental property in the middle of a lease. The departing tenant usually requests a refund of a portion of the security deposit, even though not all the individuals on the rental contract are vacating the premises. You should retain the entire security deposit until all contracted occupants have vacated the property (see Chapter 15).

If one tenant chooses to vacate early, then the tenants need to resolve any security deposit issues themselves. For example, if a new roommate is moving in, that individual can inspect the premises and pay the departing tenant an agreed amount for her share of the security deposit. Or the remaining tenant can reach some other fair and equitable agreement with the departing tenant.

 If the rental contract is going to change, require the departing tenant to complete a Deposit Assignment and Release Agreement (available on the accompanying CD). This document releases you from liability.

Domestic problems

Couples (or any combination of two or more individuals) who rent the premises together and have domestic disputes provide a tough challenge for rental property owners. As with disputes between neighbors or roommates, you need to avoid getting involved. You lack the authority to side with one party or the other, so stay neutral, encourage the couple to resolve their problems themselves, and continue treating all parties fairly and equally.

Unfortunately, some disagreements between tenants involve domestic violence, and you may receive a request from one occupant to change the locks or remove one of the cotenants from the lease. Don't agree to any such changes, regardless of the strength of the tenant's argument, without first seeking legal advice and requiring a copy of a restraining order or other appropriate court order from the requesting tenant. Insist on a verifiable letter or agreement and consent of the other party as well. Be careful not to discriminate against the victim of domestic violence by evicting him or her, especially if the perpetrator is no longer in the rental unit and doesn't return to the property.

The Violence Against Women Act of 2005 prohibits public housing agencies and rental properties that accept Section 8 vouchers from denying an applicant because she has been a victim of domestic violence or stalking. Some states have passed legislation protecting women in similar situations, so check with local legal counsel if you run into one.

Tenant deaths

If you have reason to suspect the death of a tenant who lives alone, try calling the tenant or bang loudly on his door. Check with the neighbors, and call the tenant's place of employment, as well as the emergency contact number from the rental application. If you still aren't sure, exercise your right to inspect the rental unit in an emergency or contact the police or fire department.

When officials have confirmed the death and removed the body, you must immediately take reasonable steps to safeguard the deceased tenant's property, including denying access to the unit except for obtaining limited personal effects for a funeral. Secure the unit and allow access only to legally authorized persons or law enforcement. If you have any doubts about the authority or actions of the tenant's relatives or friends, contact your attorney for further advice.

At this time, you may also find yourself in the middle of a dispute as to who has access to the rental unit. Although you should be sympathetic to your tenant's grieving relatives, make sure you don't grant rental unit access to an unauthorized person, or you may be held liable if Aunt Margo's prized goldfish-shaped cookie cutter turns up missing.

Chapter 15

Moving Out the Tenants

In This Chapter

▶ Providing your tenant with the necessary paperwork and info to make move-out a breeze

▶ Understanding how to classify damage during the walk-through

▶ Dealing with security deposit disputes

▶ Knowing what to do when a tenant abandons your property

Although hanging on to your great tenants forever would be nice, the reality is that all tenants leave at some point. Your goal is to make the experience as straightforward and painless as possible by maintaining clear communication and having procedures in place. Don't just assume that your tenants are familiar with proper move-out procedures. Instead, have a proactive plan that involves your tenants in the process of preparing the rental unit for the next tenant.

Start preparing for your tenants' eventual move-out when they first move in. The Tenant Information Letter (covered in more detail in Chapter 11) provides tenants with the legal requirements of move-out, as well as your expectations for giving proper notice. The Move-In/Move-Out Inspection Checklist (also explained in Chapter 11) is completed upon move-in to establish the baseline condition of the rental unit. Use this same detailed checklist to evaluate the unit's condition on move-out and calculate the appropriate charges, if any.

This chapter covers the importance of having a written notice (the Move-Out Information Letter) and proper procedures in place for returning the security deposit. I also cover the definition of ordinary wear and tear and help you handle special move-out situations.

Requiring Written Notice of Your Tenant's Move-Out Plans

When giving notice that they plan to move, most tenants often call or verbally mention it when they see you — even though your rental contract most likely contains clauses that require written notice. (Many states have laws that specifically require a tenant's notice to be in writing, with the exact date she plans to move out.)

Some tenants put their notices in writing by sending you simple letters or e-mail. Often these written notices are only one or two sentences and can be ambiguous, leaving out critical information or important details. Although any type of written notice from a tenant is usually legal, a proper notice should provide much more information.

To be sure you're complying with the law in all regards, require your tenants to use a Tenant's Notice of Intent to Vacate Rental Unit Form (like the one shown in Figure 15-1; also available on the CD). This form contains important information, including the tenant's approval of your ability to enter the unit upon reasonable notice to show it to workers, contractors, and prospective tenants. Be sure to include all agreed-upon terms, including the following:

- ✔ How the notice must be given
- ✔ How long before entry is allowed
- ✔ The number of hours you may access the unit
- ✔ Whether you can access the rental unit in the tenant's absence

When you receive verbal or written notice, go ahead and honor the date of the notice, but also insist the tenant complete the Notice of Intent to Vacate Form, because doing so is simply good policy. If you don't have this info in writing, many misunderstandings can arise. You may not remember the move-out date and be caught off guard. Or you may schedule a new move-in only to find that the tenant won't be out until the following week. Surprises aren't good business!

Time is truly of the essence when it comes to an occupant's move-out. Several states have deadlines of only 14 or 15 days, and virtually *all* states require the security deposit accounting to be completed within three to four weeks.

Tenant's Notice of Intent to Vacate Rental Unit

Date _____

Owner/Manager _____

Street Address _____

City, State and Zip code _____

Dear _____,

This is to notify you that the undersigned tenant, _____
hereby give your written notice of intent to vacate the rental unit at _____
on _____.

I understand that my Lease or Rental Agreement requires a minimum of _____ day's notice before I move. This Tenant's Notice of Intent to Vacate Rental Unit actually provides _____ days notice. I understand that I am responsible for paying rent through, the earlier of: (1) the end of the current lease term; (2) the end of the required notice period per the Lease or Rental Agreement; or (3) until another tenant approved by the Owner/Agent has moved in or begun paying rent.

(Optional Information)
We are sorry to learn that you are leaving. We would appreciate a moment of your time to tell us the reason for your move.

_____ Moving to a larger rental unit _____ Moving to a smaller rental unit _____ Buying a home _____ Moving out of area
_____ Dissatisfied with rental unit or common area (explain) _____
_____ Dissatisfied with management (explain) _____
_____ Other (explain) _____
Is there anything we can do to encourage you to continue as our tenant? _____
_____
Other comments _____
_____

In accordance with our Lease or Rental Agreement, I agree to allow the Owner/Agent reasonable access with advance notice in order to show our rental unit to prospective renters or workmen and contractors.

Sincerely,

_____
Tenant

Figure 15-1:
Tenant's Notice of Intent to Vacate Rental Unit Form.

Often rental property owners and managers receive less than the legally required notice or no notice at all. So how do you determine the tenant's financial responsibility in such cases? Say the required notice is 30 days, and the tenant gives you a written notice on the 10th of the month that she plans to vacate at the end of the current month. The tenant must vacate as agreed, but she's responsible for the full rent through the required 30-day notice period. In such instances, you may have a legal obligation to re-rent the property; however, in situations where only a few days are remaining in the required notice period, most courts don't expect you to re-rent the unit.

Providing Your Tenant with a Move-Out Information Letter

Many tenants are afraid you're going to cheat them on their security deposit refund. After all, security deposit disputes are the number one issue in many small claims courts. Just as the Tenant Information Letter (covered in Chapter 11) helps to get the landlord-tenant relationship off to a good start, the Move-Out Information Letter can help end the relationship on a positive note.

The Move-Out Information Letter (see Figure 15-2; also available on the CD) thanks your tenants for making your rental unit their home and provides them with the procedures for preparing the rental unit for the final move-out inspection. It also informs them of your policies and method of returning their security deposit after any legal deductions.

Provide your tenant with a Move-Out Information Letter as soon as he gives his written notice to vacate. Although state law and your rental contract may contain information on the security deposit refund process, most tenants appreciate receiving this information so that they know what to expect without having to search for their rental contract while trying to pack.

The Move-Out Information Letter includes language that reminds tenants that their security deposit can't be applied to the last month's rent and is only to be used as a contingency against any damages to the rental unit, or for other lawful charges. If no portion of a tenant's deposit is called "last month's rent," you aren't legally obliged to apply it in this way. Unless your rental contract uses this wording, don't allow your tenants to try to apply their security deposit toward their final month's rent, or you may not have enough money on hand to cover any legally allowed charges.

If the vacating tenant is a good one, ask whether you can provide him with a letter of recommendation. A positive reference can be very helpful to tenants, whether they're moving to a new rental property or buying a home. This kind of offer is welcome and courteous — and one that most tenants have never received from prior landlords. If you offer to provide a letter of recommendation, tenants often work extra hard to make sure that the rental unit is clean and undamaged in order to thank you for your positive comments.

Move-Out Information Letter

Tenant Name(s) _____
Rental Unit Address _____

Dear _____.

We are pleased that you selected our property for your home and hope that you enjoyed living here. Although we are disappointed to lose you as a tenant, we wish you good luck in the future. We want your move-out to go smoothly and end our relationship on a positive note.

Moving time is always chaotic and you have many things on your mind, including getting the maximum amount of your security deposit back. Contrary to some rental property owners, we want to be able to return your security deposit promptly and in full. Your security deposit is $_____. Note that your security deposit shall not be applied to your last month's rent as the deposit is to ensure the fulfillment of lease conditions and is to be used only as a contingency against any damages to the rental unit.

This move-out letter describes how we expect your rental unit to be left and what our procedures are for returning your security deposit. Basically, we expect you to leave your rental unit in the same condition it was when you moved in, except for ordinary wear and tear that occurred during your tenancy. To refresh your memory, a copy of your signed Move-in/Move-out Inspection Checklist is attached reflecting the condition of the rental unit at the beginning of your tenancy. We will be using this same detailed checklist when we inspect your rental unit upon move-out and will deduct the cost of any necessary cleaning and the costs of repairs, not considered ordinary wear and tear, from your security deposit.

To maximize your chances of a full and prompt refund, we suggest that you go through the Move-In/Move-Out Inspection Checklist line by line and make sure that all items are clean and free from damage, except for ordinary wear and tear. All closets, cabinets, shelves, drawers, countertops, storage, refrigerator, and exterior areas should be completely free of items. Feel free to check off completed items on this copy of the Move-In/Move-Out Inspection Checklist, as we will use the original for your final inspection.

Some of our tenants prefer to let professionals complete these items. You can contact your own professional or, upon request, we will be glad to refer you to our service providers so that you can focus on other issues of your move. You will work directly with the service provider on costs and payment terms, knowing that you are working with someone who can prepare the unit for the walkthrough inspection. Call us if you would like contact information or for any questions as to the type of cleaning we expect.

Please be sure to remove all personal possessions, including furniture, clothes, household items, food, plants, cleaning supplies, and any bags of garbage or loose items that belong to you. Of course, please do not remove any appliances, fixtures, or other items installed or attached to your rental unit unless you have our prior written approval.

Please contact the appropriate companies and schedule the disconnection or transfer of your phone, cable, and utility services in your name. Also, cancel any newspaper subscriptions and provide the U.S. Postal Service with a change of address form.

Please contact us when all the conditions have been satisfied to arrange an inspection of your rental unit during daylight hours. To avoid being assessed a key replacement charge; please return all keys at the time you vacate.

You have listed _____ as the move-out date in your notice. Please be reminded that you will be assessed holdover rent of $_____ per day for each partial or full day after the above move-out date that you remain in the rental unit or have possession of the keys. If you need to extend your tenancy for any reason, you must contact us immediately. Please be prepared to provide your forwarding address where we may mail your security deposit.

It is our policy to return all security deposits either in person or at an address you provide within _____ after you move out and return all keys. If any deductions are made for past due rent or other unpaid charges, for damages beyond ordinary wear and tear, or for failure to properly clean, an itemized explanation will be included with the security deposit accounting.

If you have any questions, please contact us at _____.

Thank you again for making our property your home. We have enjoyed serving you, and we hope that you will recommend our rental properties to your friends, family, and colleagues. Please let us know if we can provide you with a recommendation letter. Good luck!

Sincerely,

_____
Owner/Manager

Figure 15-2:
Move-Out
Information
Letter.

Walking Through the Unit at Move-Out

After your tenant vacates your rental property, inspect it as soon as possible. Doing so allows you to determine any work that needs to be done to make the property ready for a new tenant, as well as assess any charges that should be deducted from the former tenant's security deposit.

A good way to motivate tenants to comply with your move-out procedures is to give them a simple reminder that they'll receive the full sum of their refundable security deposit if they leave the rental unit in clean condition, with no damage beyond ordinary wear and tear.

In order to ensure the walk-through runs smoothly, you need to understand the process and how to handle the security deposit if you uncover damages. The following sections can help.

Getting the 411 on the walk-through

The only way to determine the condition of some parts of the rental unit is to wait until it's vacant. So try to schedule the move-out inspection with your vacating tenant just *after* she removes all her furnishings and personal items, turns in all her keys, and either disconnects the utilities or converts them to your name as the property owner. Another plus for doing the inspection at this time is that you want to make sure the tenant doesn't do additional damage after the inspection while she's removing her possessions.

Unfortunately, you can't always arrange to do the inspection with your tenant at this time. If that's the case, conduct the move-out inspection as soon as possible and preferably with a witness present (or at least a digital camera). If you wait too long to inspect the unit and then discover damage, the tenant may claim that someone else must have caused the damage, and you may face an uphill battle in court.

I strongly recommend that you try to perform the final move-out inspection with the vacating tenant present, because doing so resolves many of the issues that can later become contentious enough to end in small claims court. If you live in a state that allows the tenant to be present when you're determining the proper security deposit deductions, consider doing that as well.

Tenants have been known to show up for the walk-through but deny that they know anything about the damaged items you find. Refer to your Move-In/Move-Out Inspection Checklist in these situations. If the item is clearly indicated on the checklist as being in good condition when the tenants moved in, their claim doesn't stand much of a chance. However, if the move-in remarks are blank or vague, you may have some problems justifying a deduction. ***Remember:*** As the rental housing professional, the courts hold you to a higher standard of recordkeeping and usually interpret your vague documents in the tenants' favor.

For California rental property owners

If you own rental property in California, you need to comply with special rules and procedures for vacating tenants. California landlords must provide their tenants with written notice that they're entitled to request and be present for an initial pre-move inspection. A vacating tenant can decline, but if he accepts, then the rental property owner or manager needs to provide him with feedback on what cleaning and repairs, if any, need to be addressed to receive his security deposit back in full.

Paying (or not paying!) the security deposit

Security deposit disputes are the number one problem in landlord-tenant relationships. Although the proper use of the Move-In/Move-Out Checklist eliminates many of these disputes, the definition of *ordinary wear and tear* is one of life's greatest mysteries (see the next section for help figuring it out).

Many owners see a tenant's security deposit as a source of additional income that's theirs for the taking. However, as a business practice, returning the security deposit in full is actually much better for the owner. You can minimize arguments with former tenants and avoid small claims courts by making only fair and reasonable deductions and providing the security deposit accounting and any refund within legally required time limits. Refer to Appendix B for info regarding each state's time limitations for providing former tenants with an accounting or return of the balance of their security deposit.

Although state laws vary, typically the only lawful deductions from a tenant's security deposit are for cleaning, damages beyond ordinary wear and tear, keys, and unpaid rent. Therefore, the actual out-of-pocket costs to renovate the rental unit for the next tenant are greater than the legally allowed deductions, because you must pay for all damage that falls within the scope of ordinary wear and tear. Be careful not to charge excessive deductions to try covering these expenses, or you may fight a losing battle in small claims court.

Encourage tenants to earn the full return of their security deposit. Some states allow for a nonrefundable security or cleaning deposit, and in those states, you can even offer the tenant the opportunity to receive some or all of the nonrefundable deposit. This situation can be a win-win — the tenant can use the money, and you can quickly clean and sanitize the unit to begin showing it to new prospective tenants. Typically, you can't charge the outgoing tenant for lost rent incurred while maintenance and cleaning are being done. So if you can quickly prepare the rental unit and get it back on the market, you're well ahead of the game.

Tenants often request the chance to do some more cleaning or make repairs if you indicate that deductions will be made from their security deposit. If you feel that they're capable of the work and can do it quickly, you may want to give them a second chance at cleaning or simple repairs, as is now legally required in California. However, be wary of tenant repairs that can cost you more to correct later or that create liability issues. When it comes to the majority of repairs, you're better off refusing tenants' requests to fix them themselves.

Defining ordinary wear and tear

Legally, you're entitled to charge your tenant for damages beyond ordinary wear and tear. But virtually all disputes over security deposits revolve around this elusive definition. It's your job to be able to tell the difference between ordinary wear and tear and more serious damage that you can legally deduct from your tenant's security deposit.

The standard definition of *ordinary wear and tear* in most states is deterioration or damage to the property expected to occur from normal usage. The problem then is what's considered to be *normal usage.* Judicial decisions vary from state to state and court to court. If you ask 100 small claims court judges or commissioners, you'll likely receive nearly 100 different interpretations of this definition.

The bottom line is that there are no hard and fast rules on what constitutes ordinary wear and tear and what the tenant can legally be charged. Table 15-1 gives you some ideas for comparison to help you determine what's ordinary wear and tear, and what goes beyond ordinary into damage you can charge for.

Table 15-1	Ordinary Wear and Tear versus Damage
Ordinary Wear and Tear (Landlord's Responsibility)	*Damage beyond Ordinary Wear and Tear (Tenant's Responsibility)*
Smudges on walls, near light switches	Crayon marks on walls or ceilings
Minor marks on walls or doors	Large marks on or holes in walls or doors
A few small tack or nail holes	Numerous nail holes that require patching and/or painting
Faded, peeling, or cracked paint	Completely dirty or scuffed painted walls
Carpet worn thin from normal use	Carpet stained by bleach or dye

Ordinary Wear and Tear (Landlord's Responsibility)	Damage beyond Ordinary Wear and Tear (Tenant's Responsibility)
Carpet with moderate dirt or spots	Carpet that has been ripped or has urine stains from pets
Carpet or curtains faded by the sun	Carpet or curtains with cigarette burns
Moderately dirty miniblinds	Bent or missing miniblinds
Doors sticking from humidity	Broken hinges or doorframes

Using a Security Deposit Itemization Form

After you've inspected the rental unit and determined the proper charges, you need to prepare the Security Deposit Itemization Form (available on the CD). Complete this form and give the vacating tenant a check for any balance due within your state's maximum time guidelines. Most states allow rental property owners 14 to 30 days to complete the accounting, but several states have no specific legal deadline. Either way, make sure you don't wait until the last minute, because the consequences in most states are severe, including forfeiting your rights to any deductions and punitive damages.

Send the security deposit accounting and refund, if any, as soon as you're sure of the final charges. Tenants need this money, and the longer they wait, the more impatient and upset they become — and the more likely they are to challenge your charges. Of course, you need to make sure your maintenance personnel have been through the entire rental unit carefully and found all tenant damage beyond ordinary wear and tear. In theory, you can always seek reimbursement for items discovered after you refund the security deposit, but your chances of collecting in this case are slim.

Some tenants want to personally pick up the security deposit as soon as possible, whereas others don't even tell you where they can be reached. Generally, you should mail the Security Deposit Itemization Form to the address provided by your tenant on his Notice of Intent to Vacate Form. If you don't have your vacating tenant's forwarding address, send the security deposit itemization to his last known address, which may be your own rental unit. Perhaps he's forwarding his mail to a new address; if not, the check will be returned to you.

If your Security Deposit Itemization Form and refund check are returned undeliverable, be sure to save the returned envelope in case the former tenant claims you never sent the legally required accounting. Many states have very severe penalties for improper deductions or failure to provide the security deposit accounting in a timely manner. Check with your state laws to determine the proper disposition of the tenant's uncashed security deposit refund check.

Be sure you're able to prove that you've met the legal requirements in terms of returning the security deposit in a timely manner. Otherwise the small claims courts may rule against you, because as a major player in the rental housing business, you're held to a higher standard of recordkeeping.

You can send the deposit accounting and check via certified mail (as required by some states) in order to prove the date you sent it. However, it's much more cost-effective to go to the post office and ask for a *certificate of mailing,* which records the date you sent the check (and doesn't require the recipient's signature for delivery).

Tenants, particularly roommates or married couples in the midst of a separation or divorce, may fight among themselves over the security deposit. Legally, the security deposit belongs equally to all tenants who signed the rental contract, unless otherwise agreed in writing. If you arbitrarily split the check between the tenants, you can find yourself liable to the other party.

If you have a court order or a written agreement or instructions signed by all the tenants, you should always handle the deposit as directed. If not, plan to follow these steps for paying out the security deposit in multi-tenant situations:

1. **Make your security deposit refund check payable jointly to all the adult tenants.**

2. **Prepare a mailing that includes the security deposit refund check for one of the tenants with a copy of the check to the others.**

   Leave it up to the tenants to handle the check's endorsement.

3. **Mail copies of your Security Deposit Itemization Form to each of the tenants at their respective forwarding addresses.**

Deducting from the security deposit

If you make deductions from the security deposit, be sure that your paperwork is accurate and detailed. Because property damage deductions are only for damages beyond ordinary wear and tear, you need to be sure that your description of the item explains why the damage exceeds that.

For example, if you merely indicate "Pet damage — $100" on the Security Deposit Itemization Form, you may be challenged. However, if you provide details like "Steam cleaned carpeting in living room to remove extensive pet urine stains — $100" and include your actual receipt, you greatly improve your chances of winning if the matter gets to court or, better yet, of not even being challenged in the first place.

Every rental property owner and manager can recall claims from former tenants protesting security deposit deductions because they "left the property cleaner" than it was when they moved in. Fortunately, the advent of digital photography is a real advantage, and I strongly encourage you to liberally use this technology to fully document your security deposit deductions.

Bust out that digital camera or video recorder and follow these guidelines when listing charges on your Security Deposit Itemization Form:

- **Indicate the specific item that's been damaged.** List all damaged flooring, window coverings, fixtures, appliances, or pieces of furniture separately.

- **Indicate the specific location of the damaged item.** Note the room and which wall, ceiling, or corner of the room the damaged item is located in. Use compass directions, if possible.

- **Note the type and extent of the damage.** Be sure to describe the damage in detail by using appropriate adjectives, like *filthy, substantial, excessive, minor, scratched, stained, soiled, ripped, cracked, broken, inoperative, missing, burned,* or *chipped.*

- **Note the type and extent of repair done.** Describe the repair by using words such as *spackle, patch, paint, steam clean, deodorize,* or *refinish.* Indicate if an item is so damaged that it has to be replaced and, if so, why. Indicating the item's age is helpful, especially if it was new when the tenant first occupied the rental unit, and its life span was supposed to exceed the length of the tenancy.

- **Indicate the cost of the repair or replacement.** List exactly how much you spent or plan to spend based on a third-party estimate. Include copies of receipts whenever possible.

You may not know the actual charges for certain items until after the work is completed and you receive the contractor's final invoice. Plus, damages often aren't discovered until the rental unit preparation work is underway. So during the walk-through, note that the item is damaged on the checklist and advise the tenant that you reserve the right to deduct the actual repair costs. When you know the actual charges, you can update the checklist and include a copy with your security deposit itemization.

If you won't know the final charges and deductions from the tenant's security deposit before your state's deadline for the accounting and/or return of the security deposit balance, then you should send the tenant a written itemized accounting of the charges you do know and indicate that you're waiting for additional information. Be sure to include an estimated time that you expect to have the final charges and then send the final accounting and any remaining funds as soon as possible.

Don't withhold the entire security deposit if you know the undetermined items are likely to be much less than the balance of the security deposit. In those instances, conservatively estimate the potential remaining charges and refund the balance of funds, along with your explanation letter, by the deadline. Most judges will consider this move a good faith effort and won't penalize you if the matter ultimately ends up in court.

Some rental property owners give all vacating tenants a *pricing chart* with a list of costs that will be charged for different services or damaged items. These owners believe pricing charts minimize disputes, because the charges are predetermined and are given to the tenants in advance. They argue that the tenants will see how expensive repairs are and will take care of some of the work on their own. This method has some logic, but it also poses potential problems because prices frequently change and most courts insist on actual charges, not estimates. Also, many items can't possibly have preset prices for repair, because different contractors may charge different amounts.

Rest assured that a tenant won't pay up if your actual charge turns out to be much higher than the preset charge indicated on your pricing chart. But if the tenant challenges your deductions, and your actual invoice shows you paid less than what you charged the tenant, you'd better have your checkbook ready.

Dealing with Special Situations

Although you may have worked very hard to make sure everything goes smoothly during your tenant's move-out, a few special situations inevitably arise. And the more you know as a rental property owner about how to handle these situations, the less likely they are to become significant problems.

Forking out the dough: When damage and unpaid rent exceed the security deposit

As a rental property owner, you're probably going to encounter a time when a tenant's security deposit isn't sufficient to cover the unpaid rent and the damage caused by the tenant. Unless legally prohibited, you should allocate the security deposit to first cover the damage and then cover the unpaid rent, because it makes sense to apply the security deposit to items that are more difficult to prove in court.

Say you're holding a $500 security deposit from a tenant when she vacates, owing $350 in delinquent rent. When you inspect her unit, however, you find $400 in damage beyond ordinary wear and tear. The total of the rent owed and the damages done is $750, but you have only $500 in the form of a security deposit. What should you do? First, apply the $500 security deposit to cover the full $400 in damage and allocate the remaining $100 toward the unpaid rent. You can then pursue the $250 delinquent rent balance with your rent collection ledgers and records as evidence to clearly prove this amount is owed.

Be sure to always record the actual costs for damages, even if you don't intend to pursue the tenant for the balance owed. This way you can prove your expenses in court if you ever need to.

In most states, even if your lawful deductions exceed the departing tenant's security deposit charges, you must provide the tenant with a full accounting of the damages. You must do so even if you file a small claims lawsuit for the balance due. So be sure to always follow the required procedures for the accounting of the security deposit.

Having your facts straight: When disputes arise about the security deposit

No matter how fair and reasonable you are with your security deposit deductions, sooner or later you're bound to have a former tenant challenge them. Even if your deductions were proper and you're sure that you're right, going to court over this matter may cost you more than the deduction amount in legal fees. Often, the actual disagreement is over a relatively small amount of money.

For example, you may have deducted $100 for painting touch up, but your former tenant may believe that the charge should be $50. So you're arguing over a mere $50 difference. Explore possible negotiations to resolve the matter before going to court. If you're sure that your charges were fair, always maintain that in your discussions with your former tenant, even if you want to see whether a settlement is a possibility.

If you charge your tenants for damage to the rental unit either during their tenancy or afterward by deducting from the security deposit, you need evidence to back up your claim in case a tenant disputes the damage. Digital photos or videotape of the damage can be effective tools to resolve disputes with tenants or prove your position in court. In fact, many courts now have video monitors that you can use to show the judge or jury your evidence. Just be sure you have possession of the unit or have given proper legal notice before entering it to videotape.

Reclaiming what's yours: When the rental is abandoned

Occasionally, tenants abandon your rental unit without notice. This discovery can be good news if you're taking legal action against the tenant, because you're sure to save lost rent days and may be able to reduce your legal costs.

Each state has its own definition of abandonment, so make sure you comply with all state legal requirements before trying to determine that the rental unit is abandoned. The best way to know for sure is to contact the tenant and have him give you a statement in writing relinquishing his rights to possession of the rental unit.

Have a policy in place stating that your tenants must inform you if they plan to be absent from the rental unit for more than one or two weeks. This policy can be helpful in determining whether a property is abandoned or its tenant is just on a long vacation.

Consider giving the tenant a legal notice in order to enter the rental unit if you suspect that the tenant has abandoned your property. You can serve this notice by mailing a copy to your tenant at the rental unit address and/or posting the notice on the front door as required by your state law. After you're inside the unit, look for additional evidence, including removed furniture, clothing, and toiletries; stale, spoiled, or missing food; and absent pets. You can also send your tenant a note or letter. If it's returned undeliverable or forwarded to a new address, then that can be an indication your tenant has abandoned the rental unit.

Dealing with abandoned personal property

One of a rental property owner's worst nightmares is discovering that a tenant has suddenly abandoned the rental unit and left all her furnishings and household items behind. More common, however, is finding that a tenant has moved out and returned the keys, but left behind a few items of personal property. Often these items are junk that even your favorite charity will refuse to accept.

When you first discover that your tenant appears to have left behind personal property, immediately try to locate the tenant and ask her to reclaim her property. Serve the appropriate legal notices as required by your state. (Note that state laws vary widely in terms of the standards for establishing that a tenant's personal property has been abandoned and your obligation in handling that property.)

If you're unable to locate the tenant, or the tenant refuses to claim the items, you need to have an impartial witness assist you in preparing a written and photographic inventory of the abandoned items. If possible, carefully move and consolidate the abandoned items into a secure storage area until you can proceed with the sale or disposal of the possessions per state law. If the personal property is extensive, hiring a third-party firm that specializes in such situations to prepare appraisals and conduct the sale or disposition is a good idea. Keep copies of all appraisals and photos for your records.

Several states allow the rental owner an automatic lien on the personal property to be used toward unpaid rent or storage costs. So after the expiration of legal notices, you can attempt to sell the items and generate funds to offset your associated expenses incurred, with any balance applied toward unpaid rent. Any excess funds beyond those items belong to the tenant.

In some states, selling or disposing of a tenant's abandoned property requires advance court approval. Be extremely careful to follow the specific legal requirements for your area before you sell, give away, or keep any of the tenant's abandoned personal property, because the penalties for breaking the law can be very stiff.

If you already have an eviction action underway, your legal counsel may suggest that you continue the legal process until you receive possession. This way you can minimize your potential liability in the event that the tenant shows up later and claims the right to the rental unit. Or if no eviction action is in progress, be sure to serve the required legal notice of belief of abandonment. When you've met your state requirements, you can take possession of the rental unit and begin your turnover work to put it back on the rental market.

Part IV
Techniques and Tools for Managing the Property

The 5th Wave   By Rich Tennant

"Don't worry, Mrs. Morse. As soon as the plumber's done patching the roof I'll have him call the electrician to finish wallpapering the dining room."

In this part . . .

A huge aspect of rental property management involves people other than your tenants — everyone from employees you hire to contractors you work with. And just as owning your own home involves a lot of maintenance work, the same holds true for owning rental property. Plus, as a landlord, you have to be aware of the safety and security of your property — and your tenants. In this part, I cover all these issues so that whether you're managing a painting contractor or thinking about a new security system for your property, you have the information you need.

Chapter 16

Working with Employees and Contractors

In This Chapter

▶ Knowing what to look for in an employee

▶ Dismissing an employee fairly

▶ Assembling a quality team of contractors and vendors

A s your rental property business grows, you'll find you *are* limited in how much you can handle yourself, and you may begin to consider hiring employees. But before you jump into being an employer, you need to fully understand the responsibilities, financial consequences, and increased liability associated with having employees. You also need to determine how much hiring an employee costs and then compare that amount to how much that employee is worth to you based on the time-consuming aspects of rental management that the employee can take off your plate.

Extensive legal requirements and responsibilities also come with being an employer. So you may find that using independent, self-employed contractors, or hiring companies with employees who can handle your maintenance and service needs, is easier and less risky. In fact, you may actually be better off financially paying the higher cost of an independent contractor or service company than employing your own on-site manager or maintenance person.

This chapter touches on the benefits and burdens of hiring employees to assist you in the management of your rental properties, plus the proper way to locate, hire, and supervise contractors. Property management is a time-consuming job, but you can lessen the burden a bit by hiring people.

Hiring Employees

If you own only a few rental units, you probably don't need any employees, because you can handle all your duties by yourself or with the help of contractors. However, when you begin acquiring a large number of rental properties, either many small rental properties in different locations or one or two larger apartment buildings, you probably need to hire an employee.

For most rental owners, that very first hire is an on-site manager. In some areas of the country, laws actually require rental property owners to have an on-site manager if a single location hosts a certain minimum number of rental units. For example, rental properties with 8 or more units in New York City or properties with 16 or more units in California require an on-site manager or responsible party.

On-site managers offer several advantages. They can handle many of the day-to-day problems, make sure the property is properly maintained, and notify you or your maintenance person if an emergency occurs. They can also assist in marketing the vacant rental units and resolving a budding conflict between tenants. However, on-site managers provide some disadvantages too, namely the added expense and the difficulty finding and retaining good qualified help. But don't let these challenges stand in your way if a manager is an asset in your particular situation.

If you do decide to hire employees, check out the following sections regarding the aspects of managing them.

Establishing job duties, work schedule, and compensation

Before you begin looking for a new employee, you need to determine what that employee's job duties, work schedule, and compensation are going to be. As you decide what those items are, put them in writing.

Most rental property owners don't create written job descriptions for their on-site managers and maintenance personnel, but this is a mistake you don't want to make. If you rely solely on verbal agreements, disputes are sure to occur — and they're usually resolved in the employee's favor.

Many local National Apartment Association (NAA) affiliates offer great on-site manager employment agreements written specifically to comply with federal and state employment laws. Use these forms to formally record your mutual agreement regarding duties, authority limits, compensation, hours, and rental unit credit, if applicable. Check state laws concerning limits on the rental credit. Also, take particular care to ensure that the employee has set hours and compensation that at least meet the federal or state minimum wage. Require any overtime to be approved in advance.

Have your employees fill out a timesheet every day and be sure to pay overtime or allow compensating time off within the same pay period, or within the limits of your state law. Failing to clearly define a contract, carefully document hours worked, and strictly enforce limits on extra hours can lead to exorbitant claims for back pay and overtime from a disgruntled employee in the future. The CD has a sample timesheet.

Screening employees

Because your employees will have close contact with your tenants, you want to make sure you screen the candidates. To do so, have each prospective employee complete an employment application that lists his education, experience, and references; plus, specifically have him authorize your right to investigate the provided information. If you're hiring an employee who'll live on-site, you should also require that she complete a separate rental application and rental contract.

The evaluation and selection of your on-site manager is one of your most critical tasks, and you should make every effort to be diligent and objective. As my good friend, rental industry educator Dorothy Gourley, has advised owners for many years, your on-site manager needs to be fair, firm, and friendly — not always an easy combination to find in one person. The ideal manager candidate combines honesty and integrity, perseverance, and good communication or people skills. He or she also has a good employment history, the ability to work with you, and a professional, stable demeanor that complements your tenant profile. Prior experience isn't necessary if you're willing to train or provide educational opportunities from the Institute of Real Estate Management (IREM) or the local NAA affiliate.

Begin by prescreening your prospective employees on the phone. Describe the job requirements, hours, and compensation. Then discuss the applicant's current employment status, review her qualifications and experience, and reconfirm her interest in the position with the proposed work schedule and compensation. If there seems to be mutual interest, schedule an in-person interview and a tour of the rental property.

The employment screening process is much more difficult than tenant screening due to the numerous state and federal laws protecting prospective employees. These laws make it difficult for the small rental owner to meet all the legal requirements of hiring. If you own just a few properties, you may want to consider using outside employment firms for locating and screening potential employees. Focus your pre-employment screening on education, job history, and personal references, plus a criminal background search and drug/alcohol screening.

Be sure to check with an employment law specialist before initiating a pre-employment screening policy to ensure your application procedures meet all legal requirements and to help you avoid federal law pitfalls. For example, a job applicant's credit history can be important if the employee will be handling money. Yet the federal Fair Credit Reporting Act (FCRA) covers employee background checks, and several mandatory disclosures are required. Also, the Americans with Disabilities Act (ADA) severely restricts an employer's ability to seek information about an applicant's medical history. The employee can volunteer information, but you can't ask questions concerning physical limitations, prior workers' compensation claims, lost time due to illness or injury, and prior drug and alcohol addictions. Be very careful; employers who violate the FCRA or ADA regulations suffer significant penalties.

Some small rental property owners find using employment agencies or employment-screening firms when hiring staff is actually easier and cheaper in the long run. You can no longer rely on a résumé, an interview, and a list of references when making hiring decisions. And due to the minimal day-to-day supervision in many positions, the rental housing industry and building maintenance trades have historically been relatively easy for individuals with poor work history, alcohol or substance abuse problems, and serious criminal convictions to find employment. But many managers and maintenance personnel are in a position of trust; they often assist in rent collection and have ready access to building equipment and supplies. When combined with their regular tenant contact and keys that provide access to the rental units, the liability for a rental owner who fails to properly screen employees or contractors is very high.

The ever-changing and more restrictive employment-screening regulations are creating a strong demand for employment-screening firms. I recommend using these firms, particularly those that specialize in the rental housing industry, whenever possible. The ability to gather criminal conviction information has improved since September 11, 2001, but it's not consistent in all locations. Check with employment-screening firms in your area for their recommendations, but you may need to specify that you want them to conduct a criminal background check in every county where your prospective employee lived, attended school, and worked. This type of check costs more up front, but it's a good investment that pays dividends and offers peace of mind in the long run.

Be wary of employment-screening firms that claim to be able to conduct a single national criminal database search. Not all states offer statewide searches, and the data is often inaccurate or dated in those states that do. Also, the statewide data typically only includes felony records, not serious misdemeanors, so the most thorough information must still be gathered on a county-by-county basis.

Knowing your responsibilities

Being an employer has very serious legal obligations and requirements. Besides being responsible for wages, employment taxes, and reporting, you're also accountable for properly supervising your on-site manager (or any employee) and can be held liable for his actions. So you want to make sure that your manager always abides by all Fair Housing laws, acts within the scope of his job description, stays within his level of authority, and has basic knowledge of the law.

The right on-site manager can make all the difference in the world. Make sure you're very competitive with your compensation. You should also use recognition rewards and financial incentives that acknowledge positive results, such as low turnover, minimal lost rent due to vacancy and bad debt, and efficient expense control. A competitive compensation package is a wise investment that allows you to hire and retain the best on-site manager.

Employees are typically paid based on a salary or hourly wages. The exact amount varies based on their responsibilities and work schedules, but you still need to meet the minimum wage requirements in your area. You can often contact other rental property owners or your local NAA affiliate to obtain information on the wages and benefits you need to offer to stay competitive.

Posting all the legalities

Federal law requires all employers — yes, even if you have just one employee — to post signs explaining employees' legal rights. This signage "must be posted in a prominent and conspicuous place in every establishment of the employer where it can readily be observed by employees and applicants for employment." Federal informational posters are required on the following topics:

✔ The Employee Polygraph Protection Act (EPPA)

✔ The Federal Labor Standards Act (FLSA)

✔ Job Safety and Health Protection

✔ The Uniformed Services Employment and Reemployment Rights Act (USERRA)

These federal posters should be visible based on certain conditions:

✔ **Equal Employment Opportunity Act:** Post this signage if you have 15 or more employees.

✔ **Family and Medical Leave Act:** Post this signage if you have more than 50 employees in a 75-mile radius.

Some of the mandatory posters are available at no charge online at www.dol.gov/elaws/asp/posters/posters.htm. Be sure to check whether your state has additional requirements or posters that supersede the federal law.

You're also responsible for your employee's tax withholdings, Social Security contributions, federal and/or state unemployment insurance, and workers' compensation insurance. Never agree to pay an employee in cash or in any manner that doesn't cover all the proper deductions for payroll burden, because you can be held responsible for paying all these sums (even the employee's share) if you're audited. Federal and state agencies are looking for abuse by businesses like the rental housing industry where cash compensation is prevalent, so you should always comply.

You must provide your employees with workers' compensation insurance that pays them and covers their medical expenses if they're injured or become ill as a result of their jobs. Employee safety must always be a top priority, but workers' compensation is a no-fault system that provides benefits regardless of your workplace's safety, or even if the employee's own negligence contributed to his injury or illness. Every state has workers' compensation laws; be sure to fully comply with them. In some states, this insurance coverage is available through a government agency, whereas private insurance companies also offer coverage in other areas.

Although some states may not require you to carry this coverage unless you have a minimum number of employees, I advise carrying workers' compensation insurance even if you don't have *any* employees. For example, any contractor you hire to perform work on your rental property should have his own workers' compensation insurance policy to cover all his employees. However, if someone gets hurt, and the contractor has limited or even no coverage, you can bet that his injured employee will come after you for compensation. Don't take chances; this insurance can often be added to your standard policy for a nominal cost.

Many rental owners prefer to have payroll handled by an accountant or a firm that specializes in this service. But you can also use an employee leasing company as the *employer of record,* an organization that's responsible for payroll, withholding taxes, workers' compensation, benefits, deductions, regulations, and reporting. You can pay the firm with a single check and let it deal with the paperwork. Check with your local IREM chapter or NAA affiliate for referrals.

Working with your manager

You have to walk a fine line between being an involved and caring rental owner and an overbearing micromanager who inhibits your on-site manager from properly running the property. Good managers treat the property as if it's their own and often make a major effort to keep the property in excellent condition to maximize your net income. Of course, many incompetent managers out there only do what they're literally forced to do. Stay out of the way of the good manager and terminate the bad or uncaring one.

Your on-site manager must have the tenants' respect in order to collect rents, deal with problems, and respond to maintenance service requests. As the rental owner or property manager, you should back up the on-site manager whenever possible. However, your on-site manager must earn respect from you and the tenants. Backing up a manager when she's wrong can create a much larger problem.

When dealing with tenant complaints about your on-site property manager, remain neutral and calmly investigate the facts before getting back to the tenant with a formal response. Never ignore a tenant's concerns, but always be sure to balance the need to investigate the complaint with well-reasoned trust of your employee.

Fortunately it doesn't happen often, but be very careful if you ever have any indication that your employees display abusive tendencies, make threats, or show any signs of violent or disruptive behavior. You aren't always liable if one of your employees threatens or harms someone. But workplace violence is a concern throughout the country, and rental housing employees are often in positions of authority, with access to personal information and rental units. Watch for any signs or indications of threats, illegal possession, or use of weapons. If you become aware of any of these signs, or if you find out about prior attacks or convictions for violent crimes, immediately contact your employment law specialist for advice on the proper response, which may include a written warning or the employee's immediate termination.

Sexual harassment claims by tenants against managers, other employees, contractors, or even other tenants are a growing concern for rental property owners. You need to have a clear, firm, written zero-tolerance policy against sexual harassment and promptly and fairly investigate any complaints. Cases of employee or contractor misconduct have been a problem for years. However, recent litigation against owners is making this matter even scarier in cases where one tenant accuses another tenant of sexual harassment and alleges that the owner or manager either condoned such actions or failed to take proper steps to address the concerns. This territory is dangerous, so don't jump to conclusions, because balancing the need for a prompt and accurate investigation against the rights of the accused individuals can be difficult. Immediately contact your attorney for advice when you're told about any sexual harassment allegations.

Firing an employee

In virtually all situations, you have the right to terminate an employee at any time, as long as you don't do so for an illegal reason like discrimination or retaliation. As with any employment situation, always document any concerns about job performance in writing and discuss them with the employee as soon as possible.

Independent contractor versus employee status

As a rental property owner, you may routinely receive assistance from workers who perform jobs like cleaning, painting, and landscaping. These workers are classified as either independent contractors or employees. You're responsible for the employment taxes of your employees, but independent contractors pay their own employment taxes. The advantage of classifying these workers as independent contractors is obvious. However, the IRS is actively investigating businesses that traditionally use independent contractors to be sure they're not classifying employees as independent contractors incorrectly.

The IRS has established very detailed, comprehensive requirements to qualify as an independent contractor. For example, workers must provide their own tools and equipment, offer services to the public at large, perform their services in such a manner that they have control over the process and the outcome, and be in a position to potentially incur a loss as a result of their work.

Most on-site managers, and possibly other maintenance workers, can't meet these stringent requirements. They're usually being paid a salary or an hourly wage, working under the guidance and control of the rental owner or property management firm, and following set hours and specific job responsibilities.

Check with your attorney or accountant, but my advice is to not even try to structure your relationship with your on-site manager as anything other than an employer-employee relationship. If the IRS or a state agency later determines that your independent contractor was really your employee, you'll be liable for back taxes, penalties, and interest. To make matters worse, you also must retroactively pay the employee's share of these employment taxes.

If you need to fire an employee, be prepared to show that the termination was for cause and was carefully documented. Reasons for terminating an employee include

- Dishonesty
- Failure to follow the written job description
- Participation in illegal or criminal activity
- Poor job performance
- Theft

Although the logistics of terminating your employees probably aren't on your mind when you hire them, you need to have clear written documentation about the process of parting company, particularly with on-site employees. Rental property owners often have legitimate concerns that a terminated on-site manager or other on-site employee may cause problems. Because they typically receive a rent discount, these ex-employees also take their time relocating unless you have a clear policy upfront.

Keep a written agreement clearly indicating that the rental unit is a condition of and incident to employment. Any rights to occupy a rental unit cease upon the employee's termination. Although some people advise giving on-site employees only 24 hours' notice to vacate, I believe that one week is reasonable to find a new place and make the move, particularly because these folks are now unemployed. You can always be flexible, but have a holdover rent clause in place that calls for rent at the rate of 125 percent of the current market rent as an incentive for former on-site staff to relocate quickly. Although the utilities and telephone service should be in the employee's name, if these items are included in his compensation for any reason, be sure you can require him to put them in his name immediately.

Building Your Contractor and Vendor Dream Team

Every rental property owner depends on contractors and vendors to assist with the proper management of the rental units. The real challenge for many rental property owners is finding the right people or companies for the job and ensuring that they're paying a competitive price for quality services or materials. Not to worry though. The following sections can assist you in assembling your team.

Whoever you hire, be sure to issue an IRS Form 1099, Statement of Miscellaneous Income, at the end of each calendar year to each independent contractor or vendor who isn't incorporated and was paid more than $600.

Recognizing what to look for

I'm going to let you in on a secret: Having a list of competent and reliable contractors, vendors, and suppliers who price their services and materials fairly is crucial to successfully maintaining your sanity as a rental property owner. You can count on these high-quality individuals and firms for any situation or need that arises at one of your rental properties. Unfortunately, finding them can be a real challenge, and you may be wondering where to turn. Locating and screening vendors is a constant process, because the best contractors often become so busy that they can't handle all the work, leaving you to find another contractor.

To locate the better contractors, check with other property owners or the product service council of your local NAA affiliate or IREM chapter. Be sure to obtain several references and call them before signing the dotted line. Look for a contractor or vendor with a proven track record, all required insurance, and a minimum of three to five years of experience.

After you find a contractor, start her on a relatively simple job and supervise her carefully so that you can see the quality of her work firsthand and avoid any billing surprises. If you own one or only a few rental units, you have too much at stake and can't afford any problems or delays.

You typically pay a major portion of your overall expenses to contractors and service providers, so spending these dollars wisely is important. Care must be taken to ensure that the contractors are honest, dependable, and competent.

Giving a contractor unlimited, unsupervised access to a rental unit can be dangerous, because you usually have very little, if any, personal background information on the contractor or her employees. Likewise, don't ever hire day laborers who congregate in front of your local home improvement or building supplier, because the savings are illusory and the risks are tremendous.

In addition to good work, dependable response, and competitive pricing, when you hire contractors, you must insist that they provide a copy of their certificates of insurance, including current and adequate workers' compensation and liability insurance coverage. Contact your state contractors licensing board to ensure that your vendor's license is current and that she has any required bonds. This information is often available online at each state's official Web site.

Avoiding common pitfalls

Remember one of my favorite sayings and understand that it clearly applies to the management of rental housing and contractors: "You get what you pay for." I've found that this statement is painfully true through my own experience and through the feedback I've received over the years from my nationally syndicated landlord-tenant advice columns *Rental Roundtable* and *Rental Forum*.

Many rental property owners are so concerned about keeping their expenses down that they get into trouble by selecting contractors based strictly on pricing. Pricing is important, and the profit margins in rental housing require diligent conservation of financial resources, but you don't want to skimp on hiring contractors and vendors.

To avoid any potential problems down the road, watch out for the following:

✔ **Bids that are much lower than others:** The bid may be fine, but be sure you're not asking for trouble by hiring an unlicensed, uninsured contractor who doesn't pay or properly insure his workers. The greatest challenge for professional contractors who play by all the rules is the number of fly-by-night rogue companies that pop up, undercut their bids, and either do shoddy work or don't even complete the job. Avoid a painful lesson and just trust me that the cost to have another contractor clean up an unqualified vendor's mess isn't worthwhile.

✔ **Contractors who don't have full-time employees:** Some firms hire day laborers who don't have the required job skills. If something goes wrong, you can count on being on the wrong end of a claim or lawsuit.

✔ **Products and services that either barely meet the minimum or far exceed what you need:** You want to find the right balance between going with products or services that meet the bare minimums but also hold up under typical rental conditions. Overspending with customized or indulgent upgrades is wasteful and doesn't justify the added expense.

One example is window coverings. I've seen some rental property owners use inferior window coverings that don't even fit the window properly and don't last through one average-length tenancy with normal use. On the other hand, I've seen rental units with custom wood shutters or luxurious drapes that clearly were a waste of money for a rental. You want to be competitive in your local rental market and attract the best tenants who appreciate and value the features and benefits of quality finishes. For most rental properties, a good balance is a quality vertical or miniblind product, although for some rental properties, a good quality drapery can be appropriate.

✔ **Service contracts with odd terms:** When hiring a contractor on a service contract, be careful to avoid some common unpleasant surprises. Some contractors or vendors propose multiyear contracts or ones with an automatic renewal clause. I strongly recommend avoiding any service contract that can't be cancelled with or without cause upon a written 30-day notice. Even if you must pay a penalty to prematurely terminate the contract, you always want this option.

Many rental property owners don't have legal backgrounds but find that they have to review and approve multipage contracts that contain a lot of legalese. Have your attorney review all contracts before signing them. Also, although vendors initially say otherwise, all terms of the service contract should be negotiable. Unless this contractor has a monopoly in your area, seriously consider another if the one you're talking with refuses to negotiate.

✔ **Quotes that aren't competitive or bidders who aren't using identical specifications:** Have the firm with the best reputation and qualifications set the scope, specifications, and proposed time schedule of the bid. Then you can let the other competitors bid using the same information, with the pricing deleted.

Good quality and service cost money. I include a very comprehensive example of a Request for Proposal for a major landscaping project on the CD. You can modify this document for any type of project at your rental property to ensure that you receive competitive quotes and that all the bidders are quoting on the same specs.

✔ **Unclear billing and/or payment expectations:** Payments should be made in *arrears,* or after the work is done, and should be due generally in 30 days; more prompt payments should coincide with the completion and your approval of the work. If you're contracting out a very large project, you may want to authorize progress payments, but always withhold at least a 10 percent retainer for your final walk-through upon completion.

✔ **Contractors who don't supervise their employees:** Make sure your contractors properly supervise their employees and require them to remove all debris from your property upon completion of the project. And hold them accountable if they do any damage.

✔ **Vendors who demand payment before the work is done:** Never pay for services in advance, unless the work requires some special order or customized product. Even then, pay only a small deposit. Unethical contractors have been known to demand large payments upfront and then suddenly file bankruptcy or leave town. Don't be a victim. Check with your state contractors licensing board for any dollar limits on advance payments required by contractors.

Chapter 17

Maintaining the Property

In This Chapter

▶ Setting up a maintenance plan for your rental property

▶ Knowing what types of maintenance problems you're likely to face

▶ Responding to your tenants' maintenance requests professionally

*M*aintenance — the work required to keep something in proper condition or upkeep — is just part of the territory when you own rental property. Although maintenance isn't anyone's favorite job, you can enhance your investment by making needed repairs promptly and maintaining the entire property in the best possible physical condition.

Although owning and operating rental property clearly requires ongoing physical maintenance, many rental owners aren't prepared for the work involved. If you have experience in maintenance and repairs, you may welcome the opportunity to do some of the work yourself. But maintenance requests don't always coordinate with your schedule. And many needed repairs require special tools, skills, and training that only a pro has. Whether you do the maintenance work yourself or hire and oversee a contractor or maintenance person, take the time to know enough about basic maintenance so that you can make sure whoever you hire is doing a good job.

Besides the benefits in marketing and keeping your property full, you're required by law to properly maintain and repair your rental property to meet all building, housing, health and safety, and habitability codes. In legalese, this is called the *implied warranty of habitability*. In plain English, it means that, from the day the tenant moves in until the day the tenant moves out, you must keep the rental property in a safe and habitable condition. Check your state and local laws or statutes for specific habitability requirements, as well as any limitations on access, that apply to your rental property.

In this chapter, I cover the reasons why a good maintenance plan is essential for all rental properties, the most common types of maintenance, and some sound procedures for handling rental property maintenance and saving money.

Recognizing the Importance of a Maintenance Plan

One of the most common reasons dissatisfied tenants leave a rental property is the rental owner's failure to respond to their basic requests for maintenance. But you can use this disappointment to your advantage when you show your well-maintained rental unit by informing your prospective tenants about your system for promptly addressing maintenance issues. If you have a solid maintenance plan in place, you'll consistently reel in higher rents and have much lower turnover.

A good maintenance plan includes regularly scheduled exterior property inspections. The frequency of these inspections varies depending on the location, type, age, and condition of your rental property, but they should be performed at least semiannually and again upon each tenant turnover. A customized property inspection checklist for each rental property is a good management tool. The CD contains a sample form from the Institute of Real Estate Management for inspecting the exterior of a small apartment building.

When you're working with a maintenance plan, you can control your expenses and keep them to a minimum. Why? Because you greatly reduce the need for emergency or extraordinary repairs (which always cost more) simply by having a plan. And you have the names of contractors and suppliers on hand so that you can have the proper repair done the first time (instead of having to fix a botched job).

Because long-term, satisfied tenants are the key to financial success in managing rental properties, you need to establish a responsive maintenance system that properly maintains the premises in order to avoid operating losses and potential legal problems. An ill-maintained property leads to higher tenant turnover and tenants of progressively lower caliber who're willing to accept the poor condition of the property. A tenant can also use the property's shoddy shape as a reason to call the local housing inspector, withhold rent, vacate in the middle of a lease, defend an eviction, or even sue under state laws or special slumlord statutes found in most urban areas.

Although not required, consider taking a proactive approach to maintenance. You can include a clause in your rental contract allowing you the right of access to the rental unit's interior to conduct an annual property inspection walk-through. Most tenants cooperate fully, but a few states prohibit you from entering just to inspect the unit without the tenant's advance permission. In these cases, or as an additional tool to improve your tenant relations, you can send your tenant a nonintrusive note and maintenance checklist that allows a quick response. Implementing this policy can protect you from claims of poor maintenance, allows for repairs when problems are small, and keeps your good tenants satisfied. However, this policy doesn't absolve the tenant from his ongoing responsibility to notify you immediately in writing of any concerns or needed repairs so you can respond promptly.

Your tenant has a responsibility to maintain the premises in a clean and sanitary manner and to properly use the premises in a usual and customary fashion. Always hold the tenant financially accountable for any damage caused to the property by his or her negligence or misuse.

Being Prepared for Maintenance Issues

Maintenance isn't just a matter of fixing a leaky faucet here and there — rental properties require several different types of maintenance, and you're sure to run into all of them at one time or another. Although every type of maintenance is critical, you need to respond to and handle each one in a unique way.

My first employer in property management taught me the saying, "To own is to maintain." It's something worth keeping in mind when you find yourself having to do maintenance work on your rental property. The following sections address how to prepare yourself for the plethora of maintenance issues you'll encounter.

Emergency maintenance

Part of being a rental property owner is being prepared for emergency maintenance requests at all hours of the day (or night!). Although your tenants should contact the appropriate authorities for life safety matters, expect to still receive your share of emergency maintenance requests.

When you receive a maintenance call from a tenant, first you need to determine whether the urgent maintenance request really is an emergency. *Emergency maintenance* is work that must be done immediately in order to prevent further property damage or minimize the chance of endangering people. The most common maintenance emergencies typically involve plumbing or electrical problems.

In a maintenance emergency, immediately advise the tenant of what steps to take to limit any further damage. For example, if a pressurized pipe is leaking, tell the tenant to shut off the water supply at the angle stop nearest the source or, better yet, at the water meter; this simple step can prevent further water damage. Instruct tenants not to use appliances or electrical systems that are malfunctioning until they've been inspected or repaired.

If a fire, flood, or gas leak emergency ever occurs at your rental property, or if a natural disaster hits the area, immediately shutting off the utilities may be imperative. Prepare charts and simple diagrams for each rental property indicating where to find all utility shutoff locations and the tools necessary to operate them — as well as instructions letting tenants know which situations warrant shutting the utilities off. Always include the emergency phone numbers for the utility companies so your tenants can immediately contact them. Tenants should only attempt to shut off the utilities on their own if the utility company isn't available and the situation warrants immediate action.

In many parts of the country, you may need to remind tenants that freezing outdoor temperatures can lead to water damage in unheated rental units. Tenants may want to turn off the heat when they go to work or when they're on vacation as a way to save money, but turning the heat off completely or setting the thermostat below 40 degrees Fahrenheit can lead to freezing and bursting pipes. Make heating the rental unit to a minimum of 40 degrees Fahrenheit a requirement in your rental contract and send out a newsletter or reminder letter when the seasonal weather begins.

Preventive maintenance

A sound preventive maintenance program can increase your cash flow and reduce the number of maintenance emergencies at your property. *Preventive maintenance* is the regularly scheduled inspection and maintenance performed to extend the operating life of a property's building systems. Although preventive maintenance requires your tenant's cooperation, it often includes annual maintenance surveys or inspections of the rental unit's interior.

One great example of preventive maintenance is regularly lubricating the motors and replacing the filters in heating and air conditioning systems. When performed annually on a service contract, this preventive maintenance is very inexpensive, and the lubricated motors and clean filters lessen the strain on the equipment so that it lasts longer and operates with greater energy efficiency.

Preventive maintenance can often address problems when the conditions are still minor, thus saving significantly over future emergency repairs or replacement. It also reduces the cost of maintenance labor, because maintenance personnel can work more efficiently by having all the necessary tools, parts, and supplies on hand. According to a study by the Institute of Real Estate Management (IREM), 80 percent of the cost of most maintenance repairs covers labor and only 20 percent covers the actual parts and supplies.

For even further savings, schedule preventive maintenance work during a contractor's slow season. For example, schedule your roof inspection and any water-proofing repairs during the dry season. This is the best time to conduct this type of work, because you can be flexible on the timing to obtain favorable pricing.

Be sure to give all tenants written notice before beginning maintenance work that requires any utility service to be discontinued. A temporary shutoff of utilities (particularly water) is often necessary in emergencies or while performing preventive maintenance and repairs at your rental property. Advising your tenants in advance can minimize their inconvenience — and any requests for rent credits. The courts generally allow reasonable utility shutoffs as long as you're diligent in making the necessary repairs in a timely manner.

Corrective maintenance

Although planning and performing preventive maintenance work is usually cheaper than fixing or replacing items, the reality is that if something breaks, it must be fixed or replaced in a timely manner, which is what *corrective maintenance* covers. Consequently, the most common tenant maintenance requests are for corrective maintenance. If you respond professionally and in a timely manner, you'll earn a reputation as a good rental property owner.

Even with the best preventive maintenance in place, corrective maintenance is a normal part of any maintenance program. Anything in a rental unit can, and eventually will, break or need attention with normal usage, including toilets and sinks that clog, roofs or windows that leak, doors that stick, and appliances that malfunction. The key to tenant satisfaction is often dependent upon whether you have a system for efficiently accepting and responding to tenant maintenance requests.

Although cellphones, pagers, or answering services or machines are still the best ways to communicate urgent maintenance requests, e-mail is becoming more popular with both owners and tenants for many nonemergency maintenance situations. E-mail works well for owners, who often prefer not being interrupted by a phone call at a potentially inconvenient time. It also works well for tenants, who appreciate being able to send the request at any time of the day or night instead of having to wait until normal business hours to reach you. Upon receiving the e-mail, you can reply with a confirmation or ask for more details. You can even forward the e-mail directly to the maintenance contractor who'll be handling the service request. Either way, be sure to get the tenant's permission to enter the rental unit to fix the problem.

Custodial maintenance

Custodial maintenance is the regular day-to-day upkeep of the rental property and the most frequently occurring type of maintenance. The curb appeal and physical appearance of your property and grounds depend on regular patrolling and cleaning. In single-family rentals, the tenant typically handles this duty, and the specific responsibilities should be included in your rental contract. In larger rental properties, an on-site manager should be responsible for daily inspection and cleaning of the property.

Keep a list of routine maintenance items, including washing windows; hosing down parking areas, driveways, and walkways; and doing other tasks that keep the interior and exterior of the rental property clean and presentable. Don't forget to keep the trash bin areas clean and free of litter as well.

The number one complaint of tenants, and the bane of all rental owners, is deferred maintenance. Not really a type of maintenance at all, *deferred maintenance* is the result of obvious needed repairs that aren't properly addressed in a timely manner. Common examples are peeling paint, broken screen doors, overgrown landscaping, and minor roof leaks in the garage. Although every property has some deferred maintenance, your goal as an owner is to keep it to a minimum.

Cosmetic maintenance

Properties with great visual appeal are easier to manage and generate higher returns on your investment. So if you're willing to spend money to improve and upgrade the unit's appearance both inside and out, you'll reap the rewards of *cosmetic maintenance*. Examples of this type of maintenance include replacing old countertops, installing new light fixtures, repainting, and installing new window coverings.

One of the most common complaints tenants make is that their landlord refuses to paint the interior of the rental property every few years. Except for local rent control ordinances or the mitigation of lead-based paint, no federal or state laws require you to repaint the rental unit after any certain period of time for strictly cosmetic reasons. Of course, repainting the rental unit to keep your tenant satisfied if he's willing to pay more rent may be a good idea.

Handling Rental Property Maintenance

Even though you may be assertive in properly maintaining your rental property through regular inspections and diligent interior maintenance upon tenant turnover, you'll always need to make repairs. To help you deal with this fact of property management life, the next few sections cover the important pointers you need to remember.

Reimbursing tenants if repairs aren't made in a timely manner

In most states, if you fail to properly maintain the rental property in a safe and habitable condition after the tenant gives proper notice of a defect, the tenant has the right to have the defect repaired and then deduct some or all the repair cost from the following month's rent.

If your state provides for the repair-and-deduct remedy, you need to fully understand the remedy's limitations and the rights and responsibilities of both you and your tenant. In most states, the tenant must follow a prescribed procedure to use the repair-and-deduct remedy, including providing proper notification to the rental owner and allowing her reasonable time to respond. Specific guidelines limit the types of defects covered, the number of times this remedy can be used, and the amount that can be deducted (either as a set dollar amount or as a set percentage of the monthly rent).

Your goal as a rental owner should be to promptly respond to legitimate complaints about the rental property and to make sure that all maintenance work is done properly at a reasonable cost. When the tenant resorts to the repair-and-deduct remedy, you can face unpleasant consequences. The tenant may attempt to make the repair himself or hire a contractor who isn't skilled. Even worse, the tenant may hire a contractor who's very skilled but quite expensive and then have the bill sent to you.

The bottom line? Always make repairs in a timely manner, and you won't have to face these problems to begin with.

Responding to tenant maintenance request

Your first knowledge of a maintenance problem or needed repair will likely be when your tenant contacts you. In many industries, the companies with the best reputations and customer loyalty are those that efficiently address complaints with a positive attitude. The rental property business is no different.

Typically, a service request comes to you via phone or e-mail. Although you need to be respectful of your tenant's time, you also need to ask questions to gather a detailed description of the necessary maintenance and the precise location of the problem. This information allows you to make an educated decision as to the urgency of the problem and who's the proper person to handle the work. It also gives you the chance to confirm that the proper tools, equipment, and parts are available at the first service call, if possible.

Make sure your tenants know they can't contact your maintenance person or contractor directly. A tenant may think he is doing you a favor by contacting the maintenance person directly and not hassling you with his problem. Or he may remember another problem when the maintenance person is in his rental unit working on something else. Either way, require all service requests to be routed through management. Then whenever a tenant contacts you with a maintenance problem, you can properly record all information in writing on a Tenant Maintenance Request form (see Figure 17-1), regardless of how insignificant the problem.

Maintenance Request Form

_____   Maintenance Request Number _____
Date

_____
Name

_____
Street Address   Unit number, if any

_____
City/State/Zip Code

_____   _____
Home Phone   Work or Alternate Phone

Service Requested (Describe very specifically):
_____
_____
_____
_____
_____

Best time to perform service (Day and time): _____

Authorization: Owner/Agent/Service personnel are authorized to enter rental unit if Tenant is not present unless specific instructions have been given in advance to the contrary.

_____
Signature of Tenant

If verbal approval received, given by: _____. Received by: _____

Report of action taken
____ Completed, by _____ (Upon completion, describe problem/work done/materials used)
_____
_____

____ Unable to complete on _____, because _____
____ Outside professional assistance required, because _____
____ Will return to complete on _____

Charge cost to Tenant: _____ Yes   _____ No   If Yes, Reason _____
_____

Comments: _____
_____
_____

Received: _____   _____
      Date   Owner/Agent

Figure 17-1: Tenant Maintenance Request form.

Having proof that the tenant gave permission for maintenance personnel to enter the rental unit is essential. This proof can be visual, either by signing the Tenant Maintenance Request form in person or by stating it in an e-mail, or verbal, by giving approval on the phone. If the tenant can't sign the request in person, make a specific note indicating the date and time and who gave permission to enter. If the tenant didn't specifically give permission for a maintenance person to enter the unit, serve a Notice of Intent to Enter Rental Unit (see Figure 17-2), as legally required in your area.

If you're relying on an outside firm to handle your tenant maintenance request, make sure all personnel who may be entering your tenant's unit are licensed and bonded. (Flip back to Chapter 16 for tips on finding good contractors.) If your maintenance staff is on your payroll, this requirement is unnecessary.

Notice of Intent to Enter Rental Unit

_____
Date

_____
Name

_____
Street Address

_____
City/State/Zip Code

This notice is to inform all persons in the above Premises that on the _____ day of _____,
20 __ , beginning approximately between the hour of _____ a.m./p.m. and until _____
a.m./p.m., the Owner, Owner's agent or Owner's employees or representatives, will enter the
Premises for the following reason:

_____ To perform or arrange for the following repairs or improvements:

_____
_____

_____ To show the premises to:

_____ a prospective tenant

_____ a prospective or actual purchaser or lender

_____ workers or contractors regarding the above repair or improvement

_____ Other:

_____
_____

Naturally, you are welcome to be present. Please notify us if you have any questions or if the date or time is inconvenient.

Sincerely,

_____
Owner/Manager

Figure 17-2:
Notice of
Intent to
Enter Rental
Unit.

Enter all tenant maintenance requests in a master maintenance log in chronological order. (See Chapter 20 for more on computer software programs and the CD for a maintenance log for manually tracking maintenance requests.) A good tenant maintenance tracking system does much more than just record the service request and the fact that the tenant granted permission to enter. It can provide proof that the repairs were made, record the parts and materials used for the job, and serve as the basis of a billing record if the tenant caused the damage and needs to be charged for the service call.

Copies of Tenant Maintenance Request forms should always be archived in the tenant file and in a separate permanent maintenance file for each rental unit. If the tenant complains to authorities or makes allegations of a breach of habitability, Tenant Maintenance Request forms provide a repair history you can use to document that tenant complaints were actually made by the tenant and then properly addressed.

Your maintenance personnel and contractors are key in giving your tenants a positive or negative impression, because they have direct contact with your tenants and are a reflection on you. Remind your maintenance pros that they're entering your tenants' homes and therefore must immediately identify themselves properly by using a photo I.D. They must always be appropriately dressed, well groomed, respectful, and courteous, and they should never smoke in a rental unit, unoccupied or not. Your contractors must be businesslike and stick to the facts while keeping tenants informed about the status of the service request. They should also always completely clean up after themselves. And last but most certainly not least, they must always treat all tenants professionally and equally, or you can wind up facing Fair Housing discrimination claims.

Although responding to tenant maintenance requests can lead to excellent tenant relations, some tenants may have excessive demands. The best way to handle these tenants is to remain calm and courteous and to address all legitimate health and safety items or maintenance repairs that preserve your investment. When tenant demands become unreasonable, politely explain that providing extra service calls or cosmetic upgrades may necessitate an increase in rent to cover your additional expenses.

Keeping tenants from doing repairs

In most states, you can legally delegate some of your maintenance and repair tasks to your tenants, often in exchange for a rent reduction. However, you remain responsible for ensuring that the rental unit is habitable. Your tenants may be qualified and capable of handling many routine repairs, but you should really retain control of even the minor maintenance problems.

Tracking the life span of your appliances

Rental property owners often overlook the fact that they have a major investment in the appliances in their rental properties. Next to the physical structure itself, the appliances are one some of the most expensive components of a rental property. So knowing the average life expectancy of each appliance, and some easy steps you can take to properly maintain and often extend its usefulness, makes a lot of sense.

The average life of an appliance in a rental property varies dramatically based on the quality of the appliance and how the tenants treat it. So be sure to explain the proper use and care of all appliances to your tenants when they move in.

Here're the life expectancies for some commonly used appliances:

✔ **Dishwasher:** Plastic tub dishwashers have a life expectancy of 10 to 12 years. Unfortunately, this time frame is shortened if hard water mineral deposits damage and clog the pump, the impeller, or the float switch. Older porcelain-coated steel dishwashers regularly rust out in five to eight years if you have hard water. More common now though is the need to replace rusted racks. Run a cycle with a lime or hard water deposit remover every few months for best performance. If you have a vacant rental unit, run the dishwasher every once in a while to prevent the motor and pump unit from freezing up or the seals and gaskets from drying out and becoming brittle.

✔ **Stove and oven:** These pieces have the longest life spans of any household appliance and can last 20 years or more, because most of their parts are modular. Replacing the thermostat, burners, controls, and knobs is relatively easy. Check the gasket around the oven door periodically and make sure that the exhaust fan is clean.

✔ **Refrigerator:** If properly serviced, a fridge can last 12 to 15 years. For longer life and maximum energy efficiency, brush or clean the condenser coils, usually located under the front bottom grill. You also want to make sure the defrost drain is clear. Check the fridge's gasket by closing the door on a dollar bill in several places. If the dollar bill moves when you gently tug on it, replace the gasket.

✔ **Water heater:** This equipment can last 10 to 12 years with regular maintenance to maximize its energy efficiency and life span. Drain it every three to six months to remove mineral deposits and sediment, which build up on the bottom and create a popping or crackling sound. Check the pressure relief valve and all water lines and connections, too. For energy efficiency, buy a water heater with a thick, insulating shell and wrap a thermal blanket around the water heater to keep heat trapped inside. Natural gas water heaters are generally much more cost efficient than electric ones.

All new appliances come with manufacturer warranties covering the cost of replacement or repairs if the appliances break down during the warranty period. Be sure to keep all appliance and equipment warranties, plus copies of all purchase receipts, in a readily accessible file for each rental property. Read the warranty before attempting a repair yourself, or you may inadvertently void your rights to have the manufacturer replace or repair the appliance or equipment for free. After the basic warranty expires, many manufacturers offer extended service contracts for an annual fee, but these contracts generally aren't worthwhile if you have good quality appliances and a reliable service technician at your disposal.

Shifting utility costs to tenants

Historically, utility providers installed one meter (a *master meter*) for an entire apartment complex, leaving the landlord responsible for all utility costs incurred at the property. In the last few decades, numerous states have mandated that gas and electric utilities directly meter individual apartment units. However, most water utilities allow the installation of a single master meter for an apartment building, regardless of the number of rental units. Because of this situation, an entire industry has evolved that's devoted to shifting utility costs from the landlord to the tenant. And guess what — the change is good for the environment too because it encourages energy conservation!

Landlords of multi-family rental properties may now choose to shift utility costs via submetering or allocation systems. *Submetering* involves the installation of individual utility meters, generally inside each residential unit, that record the unit's utility usage. Consumption in each unit is generally determined by a third party utility billing company via a radio frequency system, which avoids any issues related to gaining entry into the unit or hiring meter readers. The readings are then used to calculate utility bills based on the local provider's rates.

Allocation systems, commonly known as *Resident Utility Billing Systems* (RUBS), employ specific formulas to allocate utility costs to individual apartment units. Common RUBS formulas include the number of occupants per unit, the square footage of each unit, or a combination of both occupancy and square footage. Under an occupancy-based RUBS, a rental unit with four residents pays approximately twice as much for utilities as a unit with two occupants.

Is one method really better than the other? Well, some of the benefits of submetering systems include a higher rate of conservation than what RUBS encourages (national studies have claimed from 25 to nearly 40 percent) and increased revenues. Submetering also makes tenants far more likely to report maintenance issues like leaks and running toilets. Additionally, state and local governments have historically been more accepting of submetering programs than RUBS.

On the other hand, RUBS can be implemented without having to purchase and install submeters because it relies on a formula and not equipment to calculate the bill. The conservation savings aren't typically as great with RUBS because tenants don't have direct control over their actual individual use, but overall savings do exist.

With either method, a professional third party company calculates the monthly charges and sends a utility bill to each tenant. Then the company either collects the money for the landlord or directs the tenants to pay the manager with rent. In addition to providing a user-friendly billing program for you and your tenants, these third parties can assist you with lease language and help ensure your utility billing system is compliant with all necessary regulations.

Whether you choose to investigate submetering or RUBS now or down the road, note that several areas in the U.S. have either mandated submetering of water or have considered such legislation in the last few years. This trend is likely to continue with the emphasis on green technology and the desire to conserve both water and energy consumption.

Initially, allowing your tenants to handle certain minor repairs seems to offer significant savings in cost and aggravation. However, most tenants lack the proper skills, training, special tools, or motivation to do the job properly. They may be willing to ignore or live with a problem that can be resolved inexpensively. But that little problem may soon become a major problem — and a major expense — leaving you with the responsibility of paying for it.

Although your tenant can probably handle many of the typical plumbing problems, be sure to instruct him to call immediately if the plumbing backup results in any amount of sewage overflow, because this can be a significant health and safety risk. If plumbing clogs become common, they're likely the result of damaged pipes, roots in the waste line, or a blocked vent pipe. If this situation happens, immediately have a professional correct the problem at your expense.

Almost every rental property owner (especially if you have single-family rental homes) has a tenant propose to take care of the landscaping and the pool or spa. If your tenant is actually a professional landscaper or the owner of a pool service, then lucky you! If not, don't allow tenants to perform landscaping or pool/spa maintenance in exchange for lower rent. The landscaping at many rental properties can be worth tens of thousands of dollars — an investment that wilts to nothing if your tenant doesn't know how to properly care for it. Likewise, maintaining your pool or spa requires dealing with toxic chemicals that can lead to serious liability and costly repairs if they're not used by an experienced and qualified individual. Save yourself some hassle: Hire pros to service all aspects of your rental property and include their cost in your rent.

One of the main advantages of renting is that someone else is responsible for the maintenance and repair of the property. Most tenants are relieved to know that you appreciate the opportunity to properly maintain the rental property and that they don't have to do a thing except alert you to problems when they arise. Furthermore, note that tenants with disabilities may have the right to modify their living space at their own expense after obtaining your approval.

Purchasing parts and supplies

As a rental property owner, you may have an uncanny interest in wandering through your favorite hardware store looking for obscure parts or flipping through a huge catalog for the latest sale on garbage disposals. Don't underestimate the importance of having reliable vendors with competitive pricing, because the ongoing maintenance and repair of a rental property greatly exceed its original construction cost.

You can receive trade discounts from most rental housing industry vendors and suppliers just by setting up accounts in the name of your rental property or management business. These discounts usually apply to all purchases, but you can often find special volume or bulk discounts for commonly used items.

Don't fall into the trap of buying items in greater quantities than you can immediately use if the items don't have long shelf life, regardless of the great savings offered at the time. A common mistake rental property owners make is buying tons of the latest discontinued paint on sale, only to be stuck with bad paint when it comes time to touch up the rental unit upon tenant turnover and have to buy paint all over again. Use the same standard color on all rentals so that you can always find the color, buy in bulk, and do touchups as needed.

Another growing trend is purchasing parts and supplies online. Web sites offer a wide variety of items, from appliances and plumbing and electrical fixtures to tools and hardware parts. They make the purchasing process very easy and typically offer free delivery. If you own just a few rental units, however, you may find that the savings are nominal unless you purchase in high quantities.

Chapter 18

Keeping Safety and Security in Mind

In This Chapter

▶ Handling and preventing crime at and nearby your rental property

▶ Enacting safety measures to protect your tenants and your property

▶ Shielding against environmental hazards, including fire, mold, and carbon monoxide poisoning

As a rental property owner, you need to take an active role in implementing policies and security measures for the safety of your tenants and their guests. Your property may be located next-door to the local police station, but you still need to implement proper building security measures. Crime can strike anywhere, even in so-called good neighborhoods. And even if crime isn't a problem in your area, you may face potential safety challenges from Mother Nature. Take the lead in working with local experts to prepare for the most likely natural disasters that may occur in your locale, including severe storms, wildfires, floods, hurricanes, tornadoes, and earthquakes.

Whether you're trying to ward off criminals or you're looking for ways to keep your rental property and tenants protected from hazardous environmental issues, I give you the suggestions you need in this chapter.

Tackling Crime in and around Your Rental Property

Crime's a fact of life for everyone, rental property owner or not. But part of your responsibility as a rental owner is to make your property as safe as possible for your tenants and to alert them to their responsibilities as well. In the next few sections, I give you some tips for keeping crime to a minimum in your area and responding to it if and when it occurs.

Turning to crime prevention programs

Although you can't directly control the amount of crime in your rental property neighborhood, you can be proactive. The best way of doing so is to check with your local police department and neighborhood association to see what programs are available in your area. The following sections highlight two of the more common ones.

The Crime Free Multi-Housing Program

One of the best crime prevention programs for rental property owners is available through most local law enforcement departments. The Crime Free Multi-Housing Program (www.crime-free-association.org/multi-housing.htm) unites rental property owners, local law enforcement, and tenants in an effort to fight crime and raise the local standard of living. Law enforcement representatives train owners and managers in how to keep illegal activity out of their rental properties. This training is comprehensive and covers applicant screening techniques, proper preparation of rental contracts, warning signs of drug activity, crisis resolution, and ongoing management responsibilities. Tenants receive instruction on how to identify criminal and suspicious behaviors, and they're strongly encouraged to take responsibility to prevent crime from occurring.

After the training is complete and you demonstrate that you're screening prospective tenants, evicting problem ones, and using the Crime and Drug-Free Housing Addendum (see Figure 18-1; also available on the CD), your property can be certified as a Crime Free Multi-Housing Community. After certification, you can display signs at the entrances to your rental property to alert any prospective tenants that your property doesn't tolerate any criminal or drug-related activity.

A large number of local law enforcement departments are actively supporting this program in conjunction with a traditional neighborhood watch program, because the combination trains tenants to recognize crimes or suspicious activity and to report any to police. Law enforcement works one-on-one with owners, managers, and tenants by sharing information regarding criminal activities that have occurred in the community. Its goal is to help these rental communities become certified and improve the quality of life for all.

Burglary Prevention Council

A great resource for information is the Burglary Prevention Council, which offers a free brochure with advice and suggestions to help you evaluate your rental unit's current safety features, the most likely points of entry, factors that attract or discourage criminals, tips on implementing a cost-effective security program, and a vacation checklist. This information can also be useful for your home or office and is available online at www.burglaryprevention.org.

Crime and Drug-Free Housing Addendum

This document is an addendum and is part of the Lease or Rental Agreement, dated
_____

by and between _____ ,"Owner/Agent",

and _____ "Tenant",

for the premises located at: _____ .

In consideration of the execution or renewal of a lease of the Premises identified in the Lease or Rental Agreement, Management and Lessee agree as follows:

1.   Lessee, any member of Lessee's household, or a guest or other person under the Lessee's control shall not engage in criminal activity, including drug-related criminal activity, on or near said Premises. "Drug-related criminal activity" means the illegal manufacture, sale, distribution, use, or possession with intent to manufacture, sell, distribute, or use a controlled substance (as defined in section 102 of the Controlled Substance Act (21 U.S.C. 802)).

2.   Lessee, any member of Lessee's household, or a guest or other person under Lessee's control shall not engage in any act intended to facilitate criminal activity, including drug-related criminal activity, on or near said Premises.

3.   Lessee or members of the household will not permit the Premises to be used for, or to facilitate criminal activity, including drug-related criminal activity, regardless of whether the individual engaging in such activity is a member of the household or a guest.

4.   Lessee or members of the household will not engage in the manufacture, sale, or distribution of illegal drugs at any location, whether on or near said Premises or otherwise.

5.   Lessee, any member of Lessee's household, or a guest or other person under Lessee's control, shall not engage in acts of violence, including, but not limited to, the discharge firearms on or near said Premises.

6.   Violation of any of the above provisions shall be a material violation of the Lease or Rental Agreement and good cause for termination of tenancy. A single violation of any of the provisions of this addendum shall be deemed a serious violation and a material noncompliance with the Lease or Rental Agreement. It is understood and agreed that a single violation shall be good cause for termination of the Lease or Rental Agreement. Unless otherwise provided by law, proof of violation shall not require criminal conviction, but shall be by a preponderance of the evidence.

7.   In case of conflict between the provisions of this addendum and any other provisions of the Lease or Rental Agreement, the provisions of the addendum shall govern.

_____   _____   _____   _____
Date   Owner/Agent   Date   Tenant

                                                          _____   _____
                                                          Date   Tenant

Figure 18-1:
Crime and
Drug-Free
Housing
Addendum.

Paying attention to tenant questions and complaints about safety-related issues

When a tenant directly inquires about safety or security at your rental property, always provide an honest answer and inform him of any recent confirmed serious or violent criminal incidents. Of course, rental owners aren't routinely advised or aware of crime in the area, or often in their own rental property. You obviously can't disclose what you don't know, but you should refer prospective or current tenants to local law enforcement for more information.

Although describing your building's security devices can be an effective marketing technique, you must take care to avoid inadvertently increasing your liability. This problem arises when you represent or even imply that your rental property is safer and more secure than other properties. If you make these kinds of claims, your security had better live up to your statements. In reality, no rental property is immune from crime.

So why not just exclude the words *safe, secure, security,* or any variations thereof from your vocabulary? Don't use them in your advertising, phone conversations, or vacancy showings, because if your tenant ever becomes a crime victim, he'll certainly claim that your ads or comments gave him the expectation of security. Be honest with people, but be sure they understand that neither you nor the law enforcement officials can guarantee any level of safety for them, their family and guests, or their personal possessions or vehicles. When discussing any building features, speak generically without embellishment. For example, if you happen to have an alarm device in your rental unit, don't refer to it as a "security protection system" or imply that the tenant's safety is assured due to this or any other building feature.

Test any alarm and demonstrate the proper use of all security devices in the presence of your tenants. Then have them sign an acknowledgment. Remind your tenants in writing to test these devices, because they can fail or malfunction, and to call immediately for repairs or replacement.

Some rental property owners put disclaimers in their rental contracts that say the owner isn't responsible if a tenant suffers damage or an injury, regardless of the cause. Because they have this disclaimer in place, owners get careless and slow in responding to tenant complaints about lighting or malfunctioning window locks. But what these owners don't realize is that these disclaimers are almost certainly unenforceable. Many states have laws that invalidate these broad clauses, because they attempt to shift the owner's duty to properly maintain the premises in order to avoid responsibility for a tenant's injuries or damage. However, informing tenants of the following within your rental contract language is a good idea:

- ✔ You don't promise security of any kind.
- ✔ The tenants acknowledge that you don't and can't guarantee the safety or security of them or their guests.
- ✔ You don't guarantee the effectiveness or operability of security devices.
- ✔ The tenant should have renter's insurance.

See your local legal counsel for assistance preparing the proper documentation.

Responding to crimes when they occur

If a serious or violent crime occurs at your property, give your tenants written notification as soon as possible, along with any warnings or safety tips provided by law enforcement. Some rental owners are concerned that telling tenants about crime at the property or in the immediate area will lead to increased vacancies. Occasionally you may lose someone this way, but warning your tenants so they can be more conscious of safety and security issues is important and helps prevent other similar crimes from occurring.

No specific rules exist about what crimes should be reported to your tenants. But you should notify them of any crime concerning physical attack or bodily injury, and also of any attempted or actual rental unit break-ins, burglaries, or robberies. A random car break-in or minor isolated vandalism on the property usually doesn't rise to the level of notification unless the incident occurs repeatedly. You can use a letter or memo to inform tenants about criminal activity; owners of larger rental properties can use the community newsletter or tenant meeting as a forum for discussing the issue.

The dated, written notification should tell your tenants that a crime has occurred. Be sure to include any information, composite sketches, or safety tips provided by law enforcement. Don't use the victim's name or address unless that person has requested you do so or unless you have advance approval. Remind tenants to be careful regarding security and to call law enforcement immediately if they suspect a crime. Also, remind tenants that security is their responsibility. And be extremely careful that you, your on-site manager, or any other employees avoid making statements that can be used against you in any future legal action.

You have personal information on your tenants, including where they live and work, what cars they drive, and all their personal identification and financial information. Consequently, you have a tremendous responsibility to keep this information confidential. Institute a policy of not providing any information to anyone unless the tenant has specifically given you advance written authorization to do so. Securely lock all your property and tenant files in unlabeled file drawers to prevent intruders from rifling through these documents to target vulnerable tenants, such as elderly or single women. You may also want to consider eliminating tenant rosters, or at least limiting the information to only last names on controlled-access directories. Check with your mail carrier about putting the tenants' names only on the insides of the mailboxes.

Taking Necessary Security Precautions

One of the best ways to keep crime from occurring at your rental property is to make security a top priority. Although you can't guarantee to your tenants that your property's safe (you can see what I mean earlier in this chapter), you should do what you can to increase the likelihood that they won't encounter problems. In the following sections, I cover some security issues worth considering, not only for your property's safety but for your tenants' well-being, too.

Keys and access-control systems

Rental unit locks are useless as security devices when keys aren't effectively controlled. Some properties employ a master key system where one single key works on all locks. Although this method is convenient, I strongly advise against using it, because one lost key can require you to rekey an entire property. Instead, use a duplicate system with different keys for each lock.

All owner or manager keys should be kept in a locked metal key cabinet or key safe. They shouldn't be labeled with the tenants' addresses or unit numbers, but should be coded so that if they become lost or stolen, they can't be used easily. If a tenant reports a lost or missing key, change or rekey the lock instead of just giving her a duplicate key, unless she's sure the key is irretrievably lost. Charge the tenant a reasonable fee to cover your costs of getting a new key made. **Remember:** If you have contractors or suppliers working on-site, always arrange to have someone provide needed access instead of giving them a key.

Although you must always change or rekey all entry locks upon tenant turnover, some tenants want to change, rekey, or install additional locks during their tenancy. Doing so is fine as long as they give you a duplicate key so that you can enter the rental unit to resolve emergencies and make agreed-on repairs. If you find an added or changed lock, verbally explain your policy and request a copy of the key. If the tenant doesn't want to give you a copy of the new key, send a polite but firm letter informing her of your policy. Ultimately, you may need to consider eviction if you aren't able to obtain a copy of the key.

More sophisticated card key and other access-control systems are now available and are regularly used in the hospitality industry. When combined with full-perimeter fencing, these card systems can be effective in controlling access, as long as your tenants cooperate and don't let anyone follow them in. Unfortunately, these systems are generally not cost-effective except for larger rental properties. Always remember to invalidate any lost or stolen card keys.

I've personally installed smart card access-control systems with great success. *Smart cards* are the size of a credit card and contain a small microchip that provides a unique identification number that's almost impossible to forge. Smart card readers can be installed at all access control points on the property, such as vehicle and pedestrian gates, as well as common area facilities. Another great feature of smart cards is that, with the use of an ATM-type station, they can store monetary value and be used for laundry machines, tennis court lights, or any other amenity that you want to charge for or control.

In addition to keys and/or access-control systems, use standard rental unit security devices like deadbolts (preferably with minimum 1-inch throws) and locking passage sets. All wood entry doors should be solid core and have wide-angle peepholes or door viewers. Window locks and safety pins for all sliding glass doors, or even simple wood doweling for window tracks, are also extremely cost-effective yet valuable security devices. Make sure your tenant initials on her Move-In Checklist that all these security devices are operative and that she knows to contact you immediately if any locks or security devices are inoperative. Repair any broken locks or security devices immediately upon notification.

Make sure that any security devices you install are easy to operate and difficult to disable. A determined criminal can break in to any rental community, but you want to make yours a more difficult target. Also, avoid installing security devices that create an illusion of security, because they can actually lower tenants' guard and make them more vulnerable to crimes. For example, don't install phony security cameras or monitors in an attempt to deter criminal activity. Courts have routinely held that if such security measures are installed, the owner's required to employ the appropriate staff to oversee them. Never forget that you're in the rental housing business, not in the business of installing and monitoring security systems.

Lighting

Effective outdoor lighting has many benefits to dissuading crime. Proper lighting is an extremely cost-effective way to protect your property and your tenants. It can serve as a deterrent to vandalism while illuminating your building walkways and the common areas to help prevent injuries to tenants and guests. The right lighting plan can also beautify your building and improve your property's curb appeal. Just remember that lighting is only effective if it's operative, properly located, and has the right type of fixture and light bulb for the intended purpose.

When lighting your rental property, keep these tips in mind:

- **Replace any exterior lighting on clock timers with photocells that automatically detect darkness.** This step keeps your property well lit and eliminates the need to constantly adjust timers because the daylight hours vary with the seasons. Plus, photocells turn on the exterior lights on dark, stormy days. You can easily inspect and test your lights during the day by blocking the photocell sensors with tape to simulate darkness.

- **Establish a regular schedule for inspecting the common area exterior lighting and immediately repair broken fixtures and replace any burned-out bulbs.** The best time for inspecting and testing your lights is at night, when you can see that all fixtures are working properly and providing sufficient illumination in the correct locations. Proper lighting in parking lots is very important, because many tenants routinely use parking areas after dark. Be sure to ask your residents to notify you of any inoperative lighting and log your lighting inspections and repairs or bulb replacements in your maintenance records.

Security firms

Most small rental property owners don't need on-site security firms or random patrols of their property. However, if you own rental properties in areas where security firms are necessary, you can choose from two common types: standing guard or drive-through services. *Standing guard services* can be quite expensive, particularly if you use them full-time. A *drive-through and property lock-up service* that makes a predetermined number of random checks of the premises each evening (either by vehicle or on foot) and includes securing of common area facilities is a cheaper alternative.

If you need a security service, you may want to hire guard services part-time, with a schedule that constantly shifts the guards' days and hours. This way, you're balancing the high cost of security guards with a limited but random schedule to keep the criminal element deterred and guessing. Another option is having standing guards on some shifts interspersed with drive-throughs.

If you decide to hire a security firm, carefully interview and screen the company, including speaking to the actual guards who'll be assigned to your property. Always reserve the right to request a different guard and make sure he understands your expectations and behavior guidelines, including a strict policy against socializing with tenants.

Check the firm's references and inquire about the status of all required state and local licenses or permits, including a business license, security protection firm permits, or guard cards. Require a current certificate of insurance with general liability coverage of at least $3 million, with both you (the owner) and your rental property manager (if you have one) named as additional insureds. Request to be notified at least 30 days in advance of any lapse in coverage and require proof of workers' compensation and employer's liability insurance, plus auto liability insurance and a fidelity bond.

Your agreement should be in writing and should clearly indicate that the security firm is an independent contractor. The agreement should also feature a short termination notice requirement, because service from security firms can deteriorate very quickly.

Avoid armed guards unless absolutely necessary for your area. If a security firm indicates that armed guards are required at your location, immediately contact local law enforcement for confirmation of that opinion. And think seriously about whether you even want to own this type of property.

Law enforcement officers in some areas are allowed to offer their off-duty services to patrol your property, and some are even allowed to take their law enforcement vehicles home at night. This off-duty presence can be a powerful deterrent to the criminally inclined; however, you need to be extremely careful in establishing any such arrangement. Even if you offer a rent discount, you should use your standard rental contract with an addendum that clearly indicates the officer is an independent contractor and outlines the general services provided and the exact financial terms. Make sure you have insurance coverage that covers the use of off-duty law enforcement and consult with your legal counsel to draft the documents. See Chapter 16 for more info on working with independent contractors.

Addressing Environmental Issues

Although crime is usually the first safety concern that comes to rental property owners' minds, important tenant safety topics also include those I outline in the following sections.

Fire safety

Fire safety is a critical issue for rental owners. Every year, several thousand Americans die in fires and more than 100,000 are injured. Fires can spread quickly and fully engulf an entire room, rental unit, or home in a matter of minutes. Fire also produces poisonous gases and smoke that are disorienting and deadly.

Work with your local fire department to develop an evacuation plan for your property, including written notification to authorities of any rental units occupied by tenants with children or tenants with physical or mental challenges who may require assistance in an emergency.

Fire inspections are conducted regularly in most areas; when your property's inspected, you receive written notification of any deficiencies. These noted items must be addressed immediately, and you must contact the appropriate officials in writing to acknowledge that the items have been corrected and to request a new inspection. Be sure to obtain written confirmation that all items have been satisfactorily corrected.

In some areas, rental owners are required by law to provide fire extinguishers and to properly inspect and service or recharge them upon tenant turnover. A multipurpose dry chemical fire extinguisher can be a valuable and effective tool to quickly extinguish a small fire. If not required by law, evaluate your potential liability in the event the fire extinguisher is defective, used improperly, or unsuitably maintained by your tenant. If she gets hurt because the fire extinguisher you provided wasn't working properly when she needed it, you can be held liable. Fortunately, local fire departments are often willing to offer your tenants instruction on the proper use of extinguishers.

Fires are always serious, but the most dangerous ones are those that start while the tenants are asleep. That's one of the reasons virtually all states require rental owners to install smoke detectors in all rental units. Even if not legally required in your area, I strongly recommend installing smoke detectors in all rental unit hallways and near, or preferably just inside, all sleeping areas, in compliance with applicable local building or fire codes and the alarm manufacturer's specifications.

Always inspect and test the smoke detector according to the manufacturer's instructions upon tenant turnover. If a fire hurts a tenant because the smoke detector wasn't working properly when she moved in, you can be sued for responsibility. So be sure to keep written records of your inspection and testing of the smoke detector and have your tenant initial her rental contract or Smoke Detector Agreement (check out Chapter 11 for more on this document) indicating that the smoke detector was tested in her presence and that she can perform her own tests.

Also, be sure to immediately address all tenant requests for smoke detector inspections and repairs. Note such a request in your maintenance log, along with the date that the smoke detector was repaired or replaced. If the tenant is present, have her sign to acknowledge that the smoke detector now works properly. Smoke detector complaints are always a top priority requiring immediate attention, so keep new smoke detectors on hand for this reason.

Carbon monoxide

Carbon monoxide, a colorless, odorless, and poisonous gas produced when fuel burns incompletely, can build up in a rental unit in mere hours. If the leak occurs when the tenants are asleep, they can easily lose consciousness, suffer a serious injury, or die before noticing anything's wrong.

The following items can all emit carbon monoxide:

- Fireplaces
- Gas or kerosene space heaters
- Gas water heaters
- Natural gas and oil furnaces
- Wood-burning stoves

When these items are working properly, carbon monoxide is safely vented to the chimney or another venting system. If they aren't vented properly, then carbon monoxide can build up within a rental unit.

Naturally, carbon monoxide poisoning is a particular concern for rental owners with properties in cold weather areas of the country where tenants rely on some of these items to heat their rental units. Carbon monoxide detectors are only legally required in certain areas; however, I strongly advise installing one if your rental unit has a fireplace or uses carbon monoxide-producing heating appliances. Even if you don't, when in the rental unit upon request, have your on-site manager and maintenance personnel look out for any tenant misuse of a portable gas or kerosene heater, because these devices are a major cause of carbon monoxide poisoning and death.

All heating systems should be checked for basic operation prior to tenant move-in, but, during the tenancy, your tenant needs to be proactive to safeguard her own health and safety. If your tenant alerts you to a concern about the system operating properly during the tenancy, you may want to have a pro from your oil or natural gas supplier inspect all heating systems. If your supplier doesn't offer this service, you can hire a professional heating appliance repair company. If you have fireplaces, you need to hire a chimney cleaning company to periodically inspect your chimney, chimney connections, and insulation for cracks, blockages, or leaks. Have the recommended work done as soon as possible and quickly respond to any tenant complaints about possible carbon monoxide poisoning.

Electromagnetic fields

Electromagnetic fields (EMF) are controversial environmental hazards with varying scientific opinions regarding their potential danger to humans. Electric power lines, wiring, and appliances all create some level of EMF. Although the forces created by these sources are minimal when compared to the normal electrical activity found within the human body, scientists can't agree definitively as to whether EMF exposure can or does increase a person's chance of developing certain types of cancer, particularly childhood leukemia.

This potential problem is well beyond your control, but you should be aware of this issue in case you receive a tenant complaint. Because you can't insist that the electric utility remove its power lines and transmitters, the only viable solution for a tenant with legitimate concerns about EMF is to move. Evaluate the legitimacy of your tenant's concerns to determine whether it's in your mutual best interest to release him from his lease.

Mother Nature's wrath

Every region in the U.S. experiences its own set of challenges from Mother Nature, so make sure that you and your tenants are prepared for whatever natural disaster may be possible at your rental property. Every state and many local jurisdictions have emergency preparedness offices that can provide information and tips to help you and your tenants take the appropriate steps now, before an emergency happens. You can find these offices' contact info in the front of your local telephone directory.

The Federal Emergency Management Agency (FEMA) has many great resources available online to identify and assess your risk for hazards that can potentially impact you. Its Web site (www.fema.gov) even has a Hazard Information and Awareness section that allows you to see exactly what natural disasters or hazards have occurred historically in your area.

In many parts of the country, snow and ice accumulation can create dangerous conditions. Many states or local municipalities have laws requiring owners to remove snow and ice from walkways or driveways, whereas others don't. Either way, in most states, you aren't responsible if a tenant slips and falls on natural accumulations of snow and ice.

The EPA and mold: What you can do

EPA guidelines emphasize that the key to mold prevention is moisture control and that drying water-damaged areas within 24 to 48 hours is important. They advise that although eliminating all mold and mold spores from an indoor environment is impractical, you can clean up mold with detergent and both determine and eliminate the source of the moisture. If you don't remove the moisture source, your mold problem will reoccur.

Although the Internet is full of Web sites promoting air testing, the EPA indicates that testing for mold is generally unnecessary if visible mold growth is present. You should proceed with mold cleanup and remediation per the appropriate EPA guidelines or the advice of a qualified professional. The EPA does advise that surface sampling using analytical methods recommended by the American Industrial Hygiene Association (AIHA), the American Conference

of Governmental Industrial Hygienists (ACGIH), or other professional organizations may be useful after mold removal to determine whether an area has been adequately cleaned.

The EPA provides a cleanup and mold prevention guide for various materials and classifies mold contamination in different categories based on the surface area of the affected space. The EPA recommends different responses for areas of 10 feet or less (approximately 3 feet by 3 feet), areas of 30 to 100 square feet, and areas greater than 100 contiguous square feet. A professional should be consulted for mold contamination greater than 100 contiguous square feet.

For more info about mold, check out the EPA's Web site at www.epa.gov/mold/moldresources.html. I especially recommend you click the Ten Things You Should Know about Mold section for valuable help.

Mold

Mold is the common term for a variety of types of fungi commonly found in the natural environment. Mold is everywhere, and its effect on health has become an increasing concern for rental property owners and managers.

According to the Environmental Protection Agency (EPA), mold has the potential to cause health problems for some persons who have asthma or are allergic to certain types of mold. For these individuals, contact with specific molds can cause allergic responses such as sneezing, runny nose, red eyes, and skin rash. But mold can also irritate the eyes, skin, nose, throat, and lungs of nonallergic folk. Symptoms other than these reactions aren't commonly reported as a result of mold inhalation.

You should inspect your rental unit for mold carefully before the tenant moves in and minimize the possibility of mold by quickly identifying and remedying the source of any moisture. But note that mold can develop under normal living conditions, particularly in high-moisture rooms like kitchens and baths. Chapter 11 discusses the specific paperwork you need your tenants to sign concerning mold.

If despite their best efforts, your tenants suspect any issues of elevated moisture or smell, or see any mildew or mold, they should notify you immediately. You in turn must take claims of visible mold seriously, possibly by arranging for a maintenance person or contractor to investigate. Follow the EPA guidelines regarding mold removal (available at www.epa.gov/mold) and consult with experts if the problem is severe and persistent. In such cases, use qualified professionals and carefully document all communication to minimize the prospect of being sued by your tenants.

If you want more information about mold and how to minimize or get rid of it, I suggest you check out the following resources:

- ✔ **Guidelines on Assessment and Remediation of Fungi in Indoor Environments:** This document, published by New York City's Department of Health and Mental Hygiene, is widely considered to be the first comprehensive document to establish best practices for mold assessment and remediation. It can be found online at www.nyc.gov/html/doh/html/epi/moldrpt1.shtml.

- ✔ **A Brief Guide to Mold, Moisture, and Your Home:** This publication, produced by the Environmental Protection Agency (EPA), is an excellent resource for both rental property owners and tenants. It's available at no charge from the EPA at www.epa.gov/mold/publications.html.

Part V
Money, Money, Money!

The 5th Wave   By Rich Tennant

"In going over your figures, you calculated your rental property has depreciated 9 percent over the year. However, by trying to do your own taxes, we've calculated your brain has depreciated by nearly 72 percent."

In this part . . .

Keeping track of your money is important no matter what business you're in, but it's especially important in property management. In this part, I make two not-so-fun issues you have to deal with as a rental property owner — insurance and taxes — easy to understand. I also give you some great tips for keeping records and managing your finances.

Finally, if you're looking to increase your cash flow (and who isn't?) — and after you have a little landlording experience under your belt — you may want to try your hand at some more unusual endeavors. Here, I present you with some options so you can figure out whether they're right for you and then use them to your advantage with few worries.

Chapter 19

Two Necessities of Property Management: Insurance and Taxes

· ·

In This Chapter

▶ Insuring yourself against loss and liability

▶ Wading through the tax laws

· ·

As a rental property owner, two of the major financial responsibilities you must deal with are insurance and taxes. Getting into the game knowing the rules ahead of time is the best way to play, and in this chapter, I let you know just what to expect.

Cover Me, I'm Going In: Making Sure You Have the Insurance You Need

Some insurance companies want to sell you coverage against any possible danger or loss in the world. And a sharp insurance agent is a master at describing all sorts of horrible problems that can befall your rental property. If you want to make sure you're covered at a reasonable cost, you need to sift through the sales pitch and decide which type of coverage is right for you. *Remember:* Your goal is to pay only for coverage for events and losses that are most likely to occur at your property. Buying hurricane insurance in Minnesota may not make a ton of sense, but purchasing the right insurance coverage is worth a lot.

You also need to be concerned about lawsuits and having the proper insurance coverage to defend yourself and protect your assets. According to a recent national study by Liability Consultants, Inc., a national consulting firm for security issues, apartment complexes were sued more than any other type of business entity with allegations regarding inadequate premises security (see Figure 19-1).

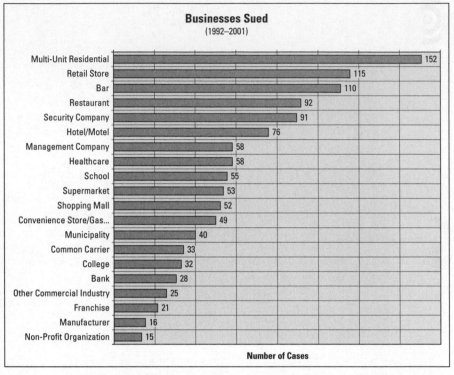

Businesses Sued
(1992–2001)

Business	Number of Cases
Multi-Unit Residential	152
Retail Store	115
Bar	110
Restaurant	92
Security Company	91
Hotel/Motel	76
Management Company	58
Healthcare	58
School	55
Supermarket	53
Shopping Mall	52
Convenience Store/Gas...	49
Municipality	40
Common Carrier	33
College	32
Bank	28
Other Commercial Industry	25
Franchise	21
Manufacturer	16
Non-Profit Organization	15

Figure 19-1: Apartment complexes are sued more often than most people realize. Be aware of your risks and protect yourself against them.

© Liability Consultants, Inc.

As intimidating as these statistics may be, you'll most likely be okay if you have sound ownership and management policies, combined with an insurance coverage program customized for your specific needs. The following sections can help you determine what those needs are.

Telling the difference among the types of insurance coverage you can get

One of the first steps in getting the right insurance is understanding the different types of insurance available to you. The proper insurance coverage can protect you from losses caused by many perils, including fire, storms, burglary, and vandalism. A comprehensive policy also includes *liability insurance,* which covers injuries or losses suffered by others as the result of defective conditions on the property. Liability insurance also covers the legal costs of defending personal injury lawsuits; because legal defense costs are commonly much greater than the ultimate award of damages, if any, liability insurance is a valuable feature.

The coverage you can get as a rental property owner varies from insurance company to insurance company, so do the following when selecting one:

- ✔ **Interview and choose a qualified insurance broker or agent who understands your unique needs.** The insurance professional can then provide you with information on the kinds of coverage worth considering.

- ✔ **Look at the company's ratings and its reputation for quickly and fairly handling and paying claims.** Although several rating firms exist, the most widely known is A.M. Best Company. It uses an *A* through *F* rating scale, just like in grade school. The top companies have an *A,* or preferably an *A+* or *A++* rating (as high as the scale goes). You can visit A.M. Best online at www.ambest.com and search for ratings on insurance companies you're considering.

Insurance professionals are either independent brokers or exclusive agents who just write policies for one company. Talk with an insurance broker and a couple of company agents to ensure you're receiving the insurance coverage you need at the best value. Keep in mind that the lowest premium often isn't the best policy for your needs. Ask a lot of questions and insist on evidence that the insurance company has provided coverage with a *written binder,* a document issued by an agent to the insured prior to the formal issuance of the insurance policy, as soon as you have coverage. Your best proof of coverage is a formal certificate of insurance.

Basic, broad form, and special form coverage

Most insurance companies offer basic coverage packages that insure your rental property against loss from fire, lightning, explosion, windstorm or hail, smoke, aircraft or vehicles, riot or civil commotion, vandalism, sprinkler leakage, and even volcanic action. This coverage often doesn't include protection against claims alleging property damage or personal injury from mold, or protection for certain contents, such as boilers, equipment, and machinery, unless specifically added as an endorsement. Fair Housing discrimination claims aren't typically covered either, but recently, coverage has become available.

A second type of insurance is *broad form coverage,* in which you get the entire basic package, plus protection against losses due to glass breakage, falling objects, weight of snow or ice, water damage associated with plumbing, and collapse from certain specific causes.

The broadest coverage available is *special form,* which covers your property against all losses, except those losses specifically excluded from the policy. This coverage offers the highest level of protection but is typically more expensive. Many insurance companies, however, offer competitive insurance packages specially designed to meet the needs of rental owners, so remember to shop around.

If you own multiple rental units, you may receive discounts (and better coverage!) if you have a single insurance policy that covers all locations. For example, if you currently own three properties, each with a $1 million policy, you can get a single policy with a $3 million limit at a more competitive cost. Doing so provides up to $3 million in coverage for each property. You can also benefit if you have an *aggregate deductible,* which is the portion of your loss that you essentially self-insure, because the losses at any of your three properties can be used toward meeting the aggregate deductible. Extremely competitive rates on group package policies are also sometimes available for the clients of professional property management firms.

Supplemental coverage

Flood, hurricane, and earthquake insurance are examples of coverage available for a separate cost. This coverage can be critical in the event of a natural disaster. However, these policies often are very expensive with extremely high deductibles, making them uneconomical for the average small rental property owner. Get quotes nonetheless and see whether it's something you think you can afford.

Seriously consider replacement cost coverage. An insurance company can pay owners for losses in two ways: *actual cash value* pays the cost of replacing property after subtracting for physical depreciation; *replacement cost* pays the cost of replacing the property without subtracting for physical depreciation. The standard policies most insurance companies offer provide for actual cash value coverage only; you must specifically have an endorsement and pay extra for replacement cost coverage.

If you decide to rent out your personal residence, immediately contact your insurance agent and have your homeowner's policy converted to a landlord's policy. A landlord's policy contains special coverage riders that aren't in the typical homeowner's policy. Due to the increased liability risk for rental properties, your current insurance company may not even offer this coverage, whereas certain insurance companies specialize in this business. Either way, make sure you possess proper landlord's coverage for your rental property, or you may face the possibility of having your claim denied.

Umbrella coverage

Umbrella coverage can be a very cost-effective way to dramatically increase your liability exposure and is designed to supplement your other policies. Your primary policy may have liability limits of $500,000, but an umbrella policy can provide an additional $1 or $2 million in vital coverage at a reasonable cost. Depending on the value of your property and the assets you're seeking to protect, buying an umbrella liability policy with higher limits makes sense.

Purchase your umbrella policy from the same company that handles your underlying liability insurance. Otherwise you may find yourself dealing with conflicting strategies on how best to defend you in litigation.

Other insurance coverage

A variety of other insurance coverage options make sense for certain rental property owners. For example, a policy that includes *loss-of-rents coverage* provides income if your property is uninhabitable due to fire or another calamity and allows you to continue making your mortgage and other payments. The following nonstandard options are available:

- **Nonowned auto liability coverage:** If you plan to have any maintenance or management employees assisting you with your rental activities, consider buying this type of coverage. It protects you from liability for accidents and injuries caused by your employees while working and using their own vehicles.

- **Fidelity bond:** This type provides reimbursement if a dishonest employee steals your rents. An *endorsement for money and securities* can protect you from losses occasioned by the dishonest acts of nonemployees.

- **Building ordinance:** This type protects you in the event your rental property is partially or fully destroyed. It covers the costs of demolition and cleanup, plus the increased costs to rebuild if the property needs to meet new or stricter building code requirements.

Don't assume that all potential losses are covered by your insurance. Your best defense against losses is to properly manage your rentals and assertively eliminate, transfer, or control the inherent risks of owning and managing rental property.

Determining the right deductible

A *deductible* is the amount of money you must pay out-of-pocket before your insurance coverage kicks in. Deductibles generally range from $250 to $500, or sometimes $1,000. The higher the deductible, the lower your insurance premium.

Evaluate the possibility of having a higher deductible and using your savings to purchase other important coverage. Contact your insurance agent for quotes on the potential premium reduction based on each level of deductible. To score a lower insurance premium, you must be willing and able to absorb the amount of a much higher deductible. And because you always want to minimize the number of claims, remember that you're unlikely to submit any

Paying attention to coinsurance clauses

Some insurance companies have *coinsurance clauses* that require rental property owners to carry a minimum amount of coverage. If you carry less than the minimum amount, the insurance company imposes a coinsurance penalty that comes out of your recovery. *Coinsurance penalties* reduce the payment on the loss by the same percentage of the insurance shortfall.

If you carry only $1 million in coverage when you should have $2 million, you're only carrying 50 percent of the minimum required insured value. If the building suffers a loss, the insurance company will only pay 50 percent of that loss.

claim for an amount that's just higher than your deductible. For example, if you decide you can increase your deductible from $500 to $2,500, you're realistically agreeing that you aren't going to submit any claim for less than $3,000 to $4,000, because making a claim for a small amount beyond the deductible doesn't make sense. Always contact your insurance agent to discuss any potential claims, because not all claims negatively impact your future coverage or premium charges.

Letting your tenants know about renter's insurance

Renter's insurance is something your tenants obtain and pay for themselves; it covers losses to a tenant's personal property as a result of fire, theft, water damage, and so on. Tenants often think they don't need renter's insurance because they posses few valuables, but renter's insurance covers much more than just their personal possessions. It also provides protection against claims made by injured guests or visitors. The insurance offers supplemental living expenses if the rental unit becomes uninhabitable due to fire or smoke damage. And it protects the tenant in the event that he or she causes damage to another tenant's property.

Although the number of tenants with renter's insurance has increased significantly in the last decade, a recent Insurance Research Council study shows that 96 percent of homeowners have a homeowner's insurance policy, but only 43 percent of renters have a renter's insurance policy.

Renter's insurance is no laughing matter

The importance of renter's insurance was reinforced to me early in my management career when a bad fire occurred at one of the properties I managed. Apparently, a new tenant was getting help from *six-pack movers* — friends who assist with a move in exchange for a six-pack of their favorite beverage. The fire started when one of the new tenant's friends negligently placed a box of paper goods right on top of the gas-stove pilot light.

Luckily, no one was seriously injured, but 12 of 16 rental units in the building were completely destroyed. None of the tenants had renter's insurance, and even the innocent neighbors lost everything they owned. Although legally you can point to the fact that each and every one of the tenants had initialed the rental contract clause indicating they should have renter's insurance, facing tenants who'd just lost everything because they didn't get around to buying renter's insurance was still difficult.

As a rental property owner, you benefit from renter's insurance, because it covers any claims in the event that the tenants start a fire or flood. Their premiums go up instead of yours. So to protect your property, be sure to place a clause in your rental contract that clearly points out the requirement that every tenant must have a renter's insurance policy. Depending on the policy limits, renter's policies typically cost from $150 to $300 per year, with deductible amounts of $250 or $500. As with car insurance, the insurance company only pays for losses over and above the deductible amount.

A Renter's Insurance Addendum is a document that informs renters about insurance coverage so that they can protect against loss and helps prevent misunderstanding about the owner's and tenant's insurance coverage. It also allows you the option of requiring the tenant to obtain renter's insurance. See the Forms/CAA Forms folder on the CD.

Handling potential claims

Immediately document all facts when an incident occurs on your rental property, particularly if it involves injury. Use an Incident Report form (like the one shown in Figure 19-2; also available on the CD) to record all the facts. Be sure to immediately get in touch with your insurance company or your insurance agent. Follow up with a written letter to ensure your contact was notified and has the information on file.

Incident Report

Date _____ Time _____ Name of Reporting Person _____
Date of Incident _____ Time of Incident _____ Property _____
Specific Location of Incident _____

Type of Incident: Accident ____ Crime ____ Fire ____ Police ____ Paramedic ____
Mechanical ____ Theft ____ Flood ____ Other _____

Details of what happened: _____
_____
_____
_____

Details of injury/damages: _____
_____
_____
_____

Names, addresses, phone numbers of people involved: _____
_____
_____

Names, addresses, phone numbers of witnesses: _____
_____
_____

Specific conditions at time of incident: _____
_____
_____
_____

Name of insurance company _____ Policy number _____
Name, address and phone number of insurance agent: _____
_____
Date and time insurance company notified _____ By phone ___ By mail ___

Request from/permission granted by insurance company to document incident: Yes or No
If yes, how: Photos ____ Video ____ Audio ____ Written statements _____

Date and time police/paramedic notified: _____
Time of police/paramedic arrival: _____ Report number _____

Follow-up required/taken: _____
_____

Figure 19-2:
Incident
Report form.

The Tax Man Cometh: Knowing Which Taxes You're Responsible for Paying

Taxation laws regarding investment real estate are unique and far more complex than those regarding homeownership. If you're just starting out in property management and you're confused by tax laws, you're not alone. Because tax laws can work for or against real estate investors, you need to have a general understanding of the basic concepts. The following sections can help you paint a clearer picture of some tax-related issues you're likely to face.

Tax laws change frequently, so be sure to check with your tax advisor before taking any action. Use a certified public accountant (CPA) or tax specialist to prepare your tax returns if you own investment real estate.

Making sense of income taxes

To get a firm grasp on paying Uncle Sam, you first need to understand all about income taxes. Taxpayers generally have two types of income:

✓ **Ordinary income:** This type includes wages, bonuses and commissions, rents, dividends, and interest, and is taxed at various rates, up to 39.6 percent.

✓ **Capital gains:** You generate this type of income when you sell possessions, including real estate and stock, for a profit. Capital gains are classified as

• **Short-term:** Short-term gains (12 months or less) are taxed at the same rate as ordinary income.

• **Long-term:** Long-term gains are taxed at lower rates than ordinary income, with a maximum of 15 percent.

The taxable income you receive from your rental property is subject to taxation as ordinary income. The positive cash flow is determined by deducting all operating expenses, including

✓ Advertising costs

✓ Capital improvement expenses

✓ Damages

✓ Debt service interest

✓ Depreciation from rental income

✓ Insurance

✓ Interest paid on mortgage debt

✓ Maintenance and repair costs

✓ Management fees

✓ Payroll

✓ Property taxes

✓ Theft

✓ Utilities

You don't have to pay taxes on security deposits received until they become income. When received, the security deposits are a liability that must be paid back to the tenants at a later time. However, after a tenant vacates and you withhold a portion of the security deposit, it may become classified as income. Essentially, the security deposit isn't taxable as long as you have an expense for the same amount as the deduction. For example, if you deduct $300 from a tenant's security deposit in order to paint, and if you actually hire a painter for $300, then you don't owe any taxes on that $300 you retained. But if you deduct $300 and then do the work yourself for $100, you owe taxes on the $200 difference, which is classified as income.

Understanding passive and active activity

Rental property owners often start out with their real estate activities serving as a second income. They typically generate the majority of their income from professions and sources totally unrelated to real estate. The taxation rules that apply to these part-time real estate investors are different than the ones that apply to real estate pros. Unless you qualify as a real estate professional, the IRS classifies all real estate activities as *passive* and limits your ability to claim real estate loss deductions.

The IRS has defined a *real estate professional* as a person who performs at least 50 percent of his or her services in businesses related to real estate, or spends at least 750 hours per year in these endeavors. These individuals are considered *active investors* and are allowed to claim all their real estate loss deductions in the year incurred. All others are considered *passive investors,* and they're subject to limitations on the real estate losses they can deduct. However, if you're a passive investor, you may still be able to use rental property losses to shelter ordinary income if you're actively involved in the management of your rental property.

According to the IRS, you're *actively involved* if you oversee or approve the setting of rent, approval of tenants, and decisions about capital improvements. This allowance doesn't mean, however, that you can't hire a property management company to handle the day-to-day activities while you oversee its efforts.

If you meet the IRS standard of being actively involved, you can take a rental property loss deduction up to $25,000 against other income in the current tax year, as long as your adjusted gross income doesn't exceed $100,000. If it does, you'll be denied 50 cents of the loss allowance for every dollar over $100,000, which means the entire $25,000 loss allowance disappears at an adjusted gross income of $150,000. Any losses disallowed in one year can be saved and applied to reduce rental or other passive income in future years. If the losses can't be used in this manner, you can use them when you sell your property to effectively reduce the taxable gain. Thus, the losses ultimately benefit you.

Taking advantage of depreciation

Depreciation is one expense that allows you to shelter positive cash flow from taxation. *Depreciation* is an accounting concept that allows you the right to claim as a deduction a certain portion of the value of a rental property just because you own it, with no relationship to whether it's actually wearing out or losing value. Depreciation lowers your income taxes in the current year by essentially providing a governmental, interest-free loan until the property sells.

Before 1993, depreciation could be accelerated in the early years of rental property ownership, but under current tax laws, recently acquired rental properties can only use straight-line depreciation. *Straight-line depreciation* reduces the value of the rental property by set equal amounts each year over its established economic life. The period of time during which depreciation is taken is called the *recovery period.* Currently, the IRS mandates that residential rental property has a recovery period of 27.5 years, and owners are required to use straight-line depreciation and deduct a depreciation loss of $\frac{1}{27.5}$, or about 3.64 percent each year. Depreciation is prorated for the first or last year of ownership.

Depreciation is only allowed for the value of the buildings; land isn't depreciable. Often, you can use the property tax assessor's allocation between the value of your buildings and land to determine the appropriate basis for calculating depreciation.

Using tax-deferred exchanges to your benefit

A *tax-deferred exchange* is an important tool if you're looking to increase the size of your real estate holdings. You can defer taxation of capital gains by effectively exchanging one property for another. Therefore, you can keep exchanging upward in value, adding to your assets without ever having to pay any capital gains tax.

Section 1031 of the Internal Revenue Code allows exchanges, sometimes called *Starker exchanges,* which permit the postponement of capital gains tax payment when another property of like kind is purchased within a specified time period. The tax is deferred, not eliminated. For real estate purposes, the IRS defines *like-kind property* as any property held for business, trade, or investment purposes. This broad definition allows real estate investors to use a Section 1031 exchange to defer taxes when they sell an apartment building and buy raw land, or vice versa. Check out www.irs.gov for the basic rules for the Section 1031 exchange.

The IRS also allows a reverse Section 1031 exchange. This regulation permits a real estate investor to purchase a new investment property first, before following the 1031 guidelines to close on the sale property within the 180-day limitation while deferring any capital gains taxes.

Grasping (and appealing) property taxes

Local municipal and governmental agencies generally receive a major portion of their operating funds by taxing real estate within their jurisdictions. Typically, property taxes are an *ad valorem* tax (based on the property's value). In certain areas of the country, improvement districts have been established with special assessments in addition to the property tax obligations. These taxes are usually flat fees or amounts based on square footage, as opposed to the property's value.

Naturally, problems can arise in determining the value to place on a property. Real estate is valued, or *assessed,* for real estate taxation purposes by governmental tax assessors or appraisers. These public employees are responsible for determining a market value for each property in a jurisdiction. The *market value* of a property is the price the property would most likely sell for in a competitive market.

The building and land are appraised separately, and most states have laws that require the property to be periodically reassessed or revalued. A tax or mill rate is then applied to the assessed value to determine the actual tax billed to the property owner. The higher the assessed value of your property, the higher your property tax bill. Property taxes are typically due in two semiannual installments, and unpaid taxes or special assessments become liens on the property. A *lien* is a claim or attachment against property as security for payment of an obligation.

You may feel helpless against the property tax bureaucracy in your area, but remember that tax assessors have been known to make clerical errors or fail to take all pertinent factors into account when placing a value on your rental property. If you feel that your property assessment's too high, contact your local tax assessor. The assessor may be willing to make an adjustment if you can back up your opinion with careful research and a good presentation. Or you may need to make a formal property tax protest. Tax protests are often first heard within the tax assessor's office or a local board of appeal. If a dispute still exists, appeals may be taken to court in many states.

Contact your local assessor and inquire about a reassessment if real estate values decline in your area. A lower assessment leads to a direct reduction in your property tax bill and a corresponding increase in your cash flow.

Many municipalities have implemented business license or rental unit taxes for rental property owners. Sometimes these resources are used to finance code enforcement or mandatory inspections of some or all rental properties. But these special taxes may just generate revenue for the general fund. Contact your local government to ensure you're meeting all its specific requirements. The licensing or rental taxes are high enough, but the fines and penalties can be extreme.

Chapter 20

Financial Management and Recordkeeping

In This Chapter

▶ Setting up a filing system to keep track of your paperwork

▶ Hanging on to the records you need for the right amount of time

▶ Taking advantage of computer software to help you with your accounting

*I*f you ask several rental property owners what their least favorite part of the job is, you're probably going to hear "paperwork" more than any other response. Most owners don't mind the hands-on aspects of managing their properties, like cleaning or painting the rental unit; many of them even enjoy that. And meeting rental prospects and showing the property is fun compared to recording rents, sending out late notices, and writing checks to pay the bills. But the financial management aspects of accounting for all the funds you receive and expend are critical elements of running your rental housing venture. In this chapter, I show you how to get a handle on good financial record keeping.

Organizing Your Files

If you have an aversion to keeping track of documents, then managing your own rental properties may not be for you. If you own rental property, you need to prepare many important written records and keep them ready for prompt retrieval. Every rental property owner must be organized, which includes having a basic filing system with separate records for each rental property.

Scanning and storing documents electronically is easier today than ever, so you may opt to keep many of these files and copies of all important documents on your computer. If you're not computer savvy or you own only a few rental units, a manual system works just fine. If you own a few more rental units, your filing system can be a simple accordion filing box with dividers, available at any office supply store. If you outgrow the accordion filing box, moving up to a filing cabinet (preferably one that's lockable) makes sense.

From the moment you take your first steps toward purchasing an investment property, begin storing your paperwork in a property ownership file. Keep all the important documents of this transaction together, including

- ✔ Purchase offers and contracts
- ✔ Closing statement
- ✔ Appraisals
- ✔ Loan documents
- ✔ Insurance policies
- ✔ Due diligence inspection and pest control reports
- ✔ Correspondence
- ✔ Photocopy of your deed (store the original in a fireproof safe or safety deposit box)

To help you keep track of everything you need, I suggest you use separate file folders on the following topics for each rental property:

- ✔ **Tenant information:** Create a tenant file for each rental unit that contains all the important documents for each specific tenant, including the rental application, rental contract, and all other legal notices, tenant maintenance requests, and correspondence. Always keep the original and provide the tenant with a photocopy.

- ✔ **Income and expense categories:** Set up a file section for each of your rental properties with separate folders for income items, as well as a separate folder for each of the property expense categories. Keep copies of all receipts in the expense folders so that you can easily locate the information you need when tax time rolls around.

- ✔ **Maintenance:** Keep a master maintenance file for housing records and receipts from all maintenance and capital improvements at each rental unit. Doing so gives you a history of the physical condition of each rental unit throughout your ownership.

- ✔ **Tenant complaints and maintenance requests:** Store this info all in one place to provide a valuable paper trail if a dispute ever arises regarding your conduct as an owner in properly maintaining the premises. Failing to have good records can very well result in a court dispute that's your word against your tenant's — and your odds aren't as good under such circumstances.

✔ **Insurance:** Hang on to a copy of the insurance policy for each property. Make sure you ask each tenant to give you a copy of her renter's insurance. Furthermore, keep a master insurance file that contains current policies for all types of insurance coverage on all your rental properties. This file should also have a calendar in which you can track the expiration or renewal dates for each policy and ensure that you've requested competitive bids well in advance of the policy expiration date. Keeping accurate records of any incident reports or claims against your insurance coverage is also critical.

When a tenant vacates, attach a copy of his Security Deposit Itemization Form and bind the entire tenant file together. Transfer it to a separate file for all former tenants, filed alphabetically by rental property. You should always retain these records as required by your state real estate commission or other legal authority, which generally means saving them for three or four years.

Maintaining Property Records

Maintaining complete and accurate records of all transactions is extremely important in the world of property management. Courts typically take the stance that tenants are merely consumers, so the burden is primarily on the owner to provide any documents outlining the relationship or understanding between the parties. If the owner can't provide the required records, the tenant almost always prevails.

But you also want to keep proper records because you have to report your income and expenses for each rental property on the IRS Schedule E Form to determine whether you have a profit. The IRS requires rental property owners to substantiate all income and expenses by maintaining proper records, including detailed receipts of all transactions. Don't put yourself in a situation where you can't support the accuracy of your tax returns.

Document your profits in income journals and keep all bank deposit slips. Rental property expenses, even if you write business checks, must be accompanied by written receipts that fully document the expenditures. The IRS may not accept a check as proof of a deductible property expense unless you have a detailed receipt as well.

If you own or manage multiple rental properties, you can develop and assign a one- or two-character code for each property and mark each receipt accordingly. (Indicate the unit number, if appropriate.) When you have info for multiple properties on a single receipt, make photocopies and store the receipts in the respective properties' folders. This way, you can provide evidence of the expense for each property instead of having to wade through all your folders looking for the info you need.

If you're using your vehicle for your rental property activities, be sure to keep a detailed, written log of all your mileage. Your mileage is a deductible business expense, as long as it's directly related to your rental property and you have accurate documentation. This simple log should indicate the date, destination, purpose, and total number of miles traveled. You may be surprised at the number of miles you travel each year in your rental activities; the deductible expense can be substantial.

Keep all records pertaining to your rental property for a minimum of three to five years. (The time period usually depends on the legal requirements of the state regulatory commission or department of real estate where you live and/or own property.) Personally, I suggest keeping documents at least a full year past the minimum requirement. For taxation purposes, most certified public accountants advise keeping records regarding the purchase and capital improvements made during your ownership for as long as you own the property, plus another six years in case the IRS wants to review your tax return.

Certain rental property records, such as those concerning injuries to minors, should be maintained forever. There's no *statute of limitation* (the law restricting the time frame during which a specific legal action can be taken) for injuries to minors. For example, if a young child is hurt on your property, the statute of limitations doesn't begin until that child has reached 18 years of age. In these cases, the tenancy records and maintenance records can be subpoenaed and become critical for defending your actions of 20 years ago.

Taking Care of Business: Accounting

The IRS doesn't require you to keep a separate checking account for each rental property you own, but you do need to keep your rental property activities separate from your personal transactions.

If you own or manage just a few rentals, you may consider tracking your tenants' rent payments in your head, but don't rely on your memory. Always track each rental payment in writing. If your tenant pays by check, you can let the cancelled check serve as the tenant's receipt. However, the best policy is to provide a receipt whenever possible, regardless of the payment method. See the CD for an example of a tenant receipt. *Note:* Make sure you record "all other income" you may receive from your rental property, including dollars from laundry, vending, parking, or furniture rental, just to name a few.

Be sure you accurately record the payment of a tenant's security deposit. These funds are typically not considered income; instead, they're a future liability that's owed back to the tenant if she honors the terms of the rental contract. The security deposit may become income at a later date, if you apply any portion of it to cover delinquent rent, cleaning, repairs, or other charges.

Although rental property accounting is fairly straightforward, you may not have the time or inclination to do it. If you aren't prepared to handle your own accounting and recordkeeping, hire an accountant or a property management company to handle it for you. Some property management firms are willing to perform solely rental property accounting services, for a fee. However, if you want to try your own hand at rental property accounting, the following sections can help you with the basics.

Creating a budget and managing your cash flow

Every rental property needs a budget. A *budget* is a detailed estimate of the future income and expenses of a property for a certain time period, usually one year. A budget allows you to anticipate and track the expected income and expenses for your rental property. Many rental owners neglect to allocate and hold back enough money for projected expenses, so when it comes time to make a repair, for example, they don't have the money set aside to cover it. But if you set up a budget, you're better able to anticipate your expenses.

Although the budget for a single-family home or rental condo is fairly simple, a proper budget for a newly acquired multi-unit apartment building can require some careful planning. That planning includes a thorough review of past expenses and the property's current condition. Trends in expenses, like utilities, can also be important when estimating the future cash flow of a rental property, so don't overlook them.

Many owners rely on cash flow from their rental properties not only to cover their expenses but also to supplement their personal income. Particularly if you're a small rental property owner, you need to have a built-in reserve fund set aside before you start taking out any rental income funds for personal reasons. Maintain a reserve balance large enough to pay your mortgage, cover the full security deposit refund, and all the basic property expenses for *at least* one month, without relying on any rental income.

Set aside money for anticipated major capital improvements in a bank account. For instance, you may own a rental property that will need a new roof in the next five years. Rather than seeing your cash flow wiped out for several months when it comes time to pay for that roof, you can begin setting aside small amounts of money into a capital reserve account over several years. This is the same way homeowners' or community associations reserve funds for major capital items.

Don't forget to allocate and reserve funds to cover semiannual and annual expenses, such as property taxes and potential income tax due on your rental property net income.

Doing your accounting manually

Most rental property owners begin their real estate investing with a single rental home or condo. Although more and more people are using computer programs to do their accounting, the math's extremely simple at this level. So if you choose to do your accounting manually with pencil and paper in a simple spiral notebook or on an accountant's columnar pad, that's okay. But as you expand your real estate empire, you need to look for better and more efficient systems geared to the specific needs of rental property accounting.

The classic manual accounting system for rental property is the pegboard that allows for a *one-write system,* in which each transaction is entered once using stacked, carbonized documents. A single entry records information needed for a consecutively numbered rental receipt, the tenant's individual ledger card, a bank deposit ticket, and the daily journal that provides a master record of all transactions. This popular rental accounting system is still used by some rental property owners and managers and is available from Peachtree Business Products (800-241-4623 or www.pbp1.com).

Using computers for financial management

Unless you really enjoy manual accounting, I strongly recommend you use your computer and specialized property management software to simplify one of the most mundane yet essential tasks for rental property owners and managers.

It wasn't that long ago that an attempt to use your computer to properly handle the accounting for rental properties required the use of a spreadsheet program customized to track different rental units, along with a general accounting software program. As is often the case when you're dealing with two different software systems, obtaining needed results could be extremely difficult, and you could spend a lot of time wishing you'd stuck with manual accounting.

A number of today's property management software companies feature everything you need in a single, seamless package. Wading through the myriad of choices to make a decision can be difficult unless you really know what you're seeking in specific features. The next two sections help demystify the software selection process.

Evaluating and comparing software solutions

With so many property management software packages being offered, knowing some of the different choices and options available to you is important.

The software programs you need typically offer the following:

- ✔ Complete accounting (general ledger, accounts receivable, accounts payable with check writing, budgeting, and financial reporting)
- ✔ Tenant and lease management, including many standard rental management forms
- ✔ Tenant service requests, maintenance scheduling, and reminder notes
- ✔ Additional services like electronic payments, tenant screening, payroll, and utility billing

Many property management accounting packages are available for a nominal investment, but as always, you get what you pay for. Many of the less expensive systems may work in the short run, but if something goes wrong, you may be left stranded without technical support or help. If a software firm has only a few systems in place, you're in for a much higher risk of program errors or incorrect results. The software may not even be updated or supported years down the road. Your financial investment, and all the timesaving and other significant benefits of computerized accounting, may be lost if the software package isn't backed by a solid company.

Another advantage to using most computerized rental property accounting software packages is the ability to have your mortgage and bill payments deducted electronically. Or you can work with these software packages to pay your bills online. If your tenants pay their rent electronically as well, you can decrease the time you spend handling rent collection and accounting.

You can also customize the financial reporting offered by software programs to meet your needs. Monthly reports often contain income and expense information compared to the monthly budget, as well as year-to-date numbers. Figure 20-1 shows an example of a very basic monthly financial statement for a single-family rental home.

When you use a management company, you typically receive several important accounting reports within a couple of weeks after the end of each accounting month. If you review these reports regularly, they can provide you with a good understanding of your rental investments and give you the opportunity to inquire about or suggest operational changes. But if you manage your own property and do your own accounting, you need to actually review and analyze the financial reports in the same manner as if you'd entrusted your investment to a property manager. You may think you know everything you need to know about your rental property, and setting aside those monthly reports until tax time may seem harmless, but they're great tools to improve your management results if you use them properly.

437 Grand View Street (gvs) **Income Statement** For The Period Ending May 2008 Books = Cash	Month to Date	%	Year to Date	%
Rental Income				
Rent	2,250.00	100.00	11,250.00	100.00
Net Rental Income	2,250.00	100.00	11,250.00	100.00
Other Income				
Effectove Gross Income	2,250.00	100.00	11,250.00	100.00
Operating Expenses				
Payroll				
Administrative Expense				
HOA Dues	125.00	5.56	625.00	5.56
Total Administrative	125.00	5.56	625.00	5.56
Utilities				
Water and Sewer	94.87	4.22	405.77	3.61
Total Utilities	94.87	4.22	405.77	3.61
Repairs and Maintenance				
General Repairs	114.22	5.08	126.83	1.13
Total Repairs and Maintenance	114.22	5.08	126.83	1.13
Management Fees				
Management Fees	180.00	8.00	900.00	8.00
Total Management Fees	180.00	8.00	900.00	8.00
Total Operating Expense	514.09	22.85	2,057.60	18.29
Total Operating Income	1,735.91	77.15	9,192.40	81.71
Net Income Before Interest	1,735.91	77.15	9,192.40	81.71
Mortgage Expense				
Mortgage	1,043.50	46.38	5,217.50	46.38
Total Mortgage Payments	1,043.50	46.38	5,217.50	46.38
Net Profit	692.41	30.77	3,975.90	35.33
Total Net	692.41	30.77	3,975.90	35.33
Net After Depreciation	692.41	30.77	3,975.90	35.33

Figure 20-1: A monthly financial statement for a single-family rental home.

Identifying some of the better programs

Each of the many program types available has its own strengths and weaknesses. Following are a few programs that I highly recommend:

- ✔ *Quicken Rental Property Manager (RPM):* This entry-level program is from Intuit, the company that dominates the tax preparation and basic accounting software market. Unfortunately, it's essentially just a rent- and expense-tracking tool, not a comprehensive, integrated accounting software package like the next three that I recommend.

  The main benefit to *Quicken RPM* is that you can print out income and expense information for your tax accountant, or you can easily export data if you use the companion *Quicken TurboTax* software.

  One major drawback (which may be addressed in future releases) is that *Quicken RPM* doesn't integrate with Quicken personal financial software or *QuickBooks*. Also, it doesn't have useful features like check register or online rent receipts/bill pay. You may want to start with *Quicken RPM*, but only if you're looking for a basic program at a very affordable price (under $100) that can keep you organized and better prepared at tax time.

RentRight: If you want a more-advanced, fully integrated, built-in accounting package and own fewer than 50 rental units, I recommend you use *RentRight.* This software package, from Domin-8 Enterprise Solutions, has many features of the more robust *TenantPro* (featured next) but at an affordable price range that starts at $250. Visit www.rentright.com for more details.

Tenant Pro: I recommend using *Tenant Pro,* an advanced, comprehensive, Windows-based rental accounting software package offered by Domin-8 Enterprise Solutions, if you own between 50 and 500 rental units. It combines a property management database and a complete accounting system with general ledger, accounts receivable, and accounts payable modules, eliminating the need to enter data twice. This is powerful yet easy to use property management software that tracks information on owners, properties, units, tenants, and vendors.

The additional features — which are available for purchase and deal with tenant background screening, electronic rent collection and credit card payments, maintenance request tracking, payroll, online payments, and rental insurance — offer an advantage. Another great feature available is the module for utility metering and billing that simplifies charging tenants for their individual utility usage.

Tenant Pro is available in different versions depending on the number of units you own or manage, and pricing ranges from $595 to 2,195. This program is perfectly suited for rental owners with both residential and commercial properties. *Tenant Pro* is also an excellent choice for small property management companies, particularly due to a new feature that exports tenant payments to the general ledger in Intuit's popular *QuickBooks* program.

Its reporting capabilities are impressive with more than 120 customizable financial and property management reports. You can generate reports in *Microsoft Excel* or export them to an alternate electronic format for e-mailing to clients or posting on an internal Web site. *Tenant Pro* is also integrated with *Microsoft Word* and includes more than 45 property management letters and agreements. When you outgrow your current module, you can upgrade to the next level by paying the difference in price rather than losing your initial investment. *Tenant Pro* is an excellent accounting package for rental owners who want to have the benefits of efficient accounting and recordkeeping. Go to www.tenantpro.com for more information and to download a free demo.

✔ **Yardi Systems Property Management Solutions:** For rental property owners or property management companies with portfolios of at least 500 or more rental units, I recommend the *Yardi Voyager* asset and property management software suite. My property management company uses this industry-leading, browser-based software, and I've been very impressed with its ability to provide real-time daily and weekly reporting needed to effectively manage properties. *Yardi Voyager* also offers detailed monthly financial reports, which allow my company to provide a greater level of service to clients and outperform the competition.

For smaller property owners and managers, Yardi also offers a fully integrated, Windows-based product, *Yardi Genesis,* with much of the same functionality of *Voyager,* but with less sophisticated reporting capabilities and more limited accessibility. *Yardi Voyager* is accessible anywhere via the Internet, whereas *Yardi Genesis* is accessible only through a local network. Both of these software solutions include all the basic features of prospect and tenant management, fully integrated accounts receivable and accounts payable, general ledger, and cash management. As a bonus, they also allow ready access to information, elimination of duplicate entries, and spontaneous delivery of reporting.

Yardi has annual service fees, which range from $1,700 to $5,000 per year for *Yardi Genesis* and $17,000 to $100,000 per year for *Yardi Voyager,* depending on the number of users, modules, and hosting options. Yardi's also a leader in the Application Service Provider (ASP) arena, where it hosts and maintains your database on redundant servers and performs all IT functions, including automatic software upgrades. This offering can save any size organization tremendous costs on both staffing and hardware, and it's becoming an increasingly popular option. Although the initial ASP users are typically larger real estate owners and property managers, increasing numbers of owners and managers with small to medium rental property portfolios are implementing this technology for competitive and cost-saving reasons.

When evaluating different software packages, gather as much info as possible. Be sure to talk to actual product users, preferably people in your area with comparable rental properties and similar accounting needs. Determine what features a program offers, how easy it is to operate, its computer hardware requirements, the availability and cost of technical support, and the strength and reputation of the company backing the product. Obtain a demo or trial version of the software that you can use before you buy, just to make sure it's truly what you want.

Chapter 21

Finding New Ways to Increase Your Cash Flow: Only for the Daring

....

In This Chapter

▶ Getting creative with ways to increase your non-rent revenue

▶ Taking advantage of lease options as a way to increase your income

▶ Making the most of governmental program benefits

▶ Finding niche markets to bump up your cash flow

....

The goal of owning and managing rental housing is to maximize your *net operating income,* which means the more money you bring in and the lower your expenses while properly maintaining your property, the higher your actual income. Achieving that goal is easier said than done, because you have to be willing to look outside the box. So in this chapter, I offer you some new ideas about revenue opportunities that have nothing to do with rent.

As a rental property owner, you need to be aware that the government can assist you and your tenants if their limitations and requirements are met and you're interested in participating in certain federal programs. So I explore the ins and outs of government programs that can subsidize your tenants' rent or allow you to rehabilitate your property. I also look at niche opportunities to expand your target market to tenants who traditionally don't have as many rental options. Catering to these folks can lead to long-term, stable tenancies and reduced turnover.

Considering Non-Rent Revenue

Savvy rental property owners are always looking for additional ways to increase their building's buildings' incomes. And you can do this regardless of whether you have a rental home or condo, a small apartment property, or a large multi-family apartment building. Every property is different, so you need to evaluate what services or features you can put to work for you. The best way to do this is by looking at your property from the perspective of your current and prospective tenants.

Although rental property owners should always focus on ways to maximize rent, if you have a single-family home or condo rental, then you're more restricted on some of these options, such as charging for parking and storage, which are almost always included in the base rent in your case. If you own a multi-family rental property, you may be able to take advantage of other opportunities to generate income.

Non-rent revenue is income from sources other than basic rent, like income from laundry machines, storage, parking, Internet access, and vending machines. Just as important, these services can give your rental property the competitive advantage to attract and retain tenants long-term.

You can charge your tenants for the non-rent services and amenities in this section separately from the rent, or you can bundle them together as rent. The method you choose may depend on what's common practice in your area.

Earning some cash with the wash: Laundry machines

Providing your tenants with laundry equipment is one of the best ways to increase your non-rent revenue. But your ability to meet this need probably depends on the size of your rental property.

If you own a single-family rental home, including a washer and dryer can allow you to charge an extra $50 to $75 in monthly rent. The plumbing and connections are probably already installed (or if they aren't, they can be added easily). But unless you want to see all your potential profits go down the drain, make sure your tenants pay for the utilities, including the water and sewer charges, through a process called *submetering*. Check out Chapter 17 for more on submetering.

Rental property owners with 2 to 12 rental units have the toughest time offering laundry equipment, because they often lack appropriate locations. If washers and dryers can't be installed directly in the rental units, look for a place to build a common area laundry facility. You may be able to convert a garage or build an enclosure in a carport space, but be sure the location is safe and secure. Always use a licensed and bonded general contractor and get the proper permits.

Larger rental properties are ideally suited for common area laundry facilities with coin-operated or coinless smart card washers and dryers. Typically, one washer and dryer for every eight to ten rental units is sufficient, but check first with other owners in your area to see what they're offering. If you purchase your own equipment, you'll have an initial cash investment and the burden of ongoing equipment maintenance, but you'll have added to your net income. You can also negotiate competitive contracts with laundry service contractors who install, maintain, and collect the revenue from the machines. They often pay upfront bonuses, plus send you a monthly check for your share of the gross proceeds to cover your utility costs and generate a profit. Some laundry service companies are willing to lease or sell you laundry equipment with a service contract. You then handle your own collections.

Stowing some dough: Storage

If your rental property doesn't have proper storage, you may be faced with the challenge of tenants who regularly leave items on their patios, balconies, or yards. If that's the case, your property can begin to look unsightly in very little time. Instead of getting upset with your tenants, keep in mind that they don't have much choice. New rental units are becoming smaller and smaller, and they often don't include adequate storage. At the same time, many renters are acquiring more and more possessions, and their need for storage is increasing.

If you're creative, you can turn this lemon into lemonade. Consider adding secure, weatherproof, lockable storage units. Ideally, your storage units should be at ground level, be at least 5-x-5-feet square with a height of 6 feet or more, have a heavy-duty locking mechanism, and be constructed out of solid material so that no one can see the contents. The money spent in obtaining quality storage units is a great investment, because the price per square foot of storage in many urban rental markets rivals or even exceeds the cost of the rental unit itself. Plus, if you offer storage facilities with your rental unit, you'll have a competitive advantage that helps you keep your property occupied and allows you to charge a higher rent.

Selling your space: Parking

You may have a rental property where parking is abundant, but at many properties, parking is a real problem. A good solution — like the carports and garages in high demand in many areas of the country — can be an excellent source of additional revenue. Look around and you may be surprised to see what the going rates for parking are at other properties in your area.

If your rental property doesn't have extra parking, check to see whether you can add a parking area. Parking is very important to many tenants who gladly pay for the convenience of a reserved space. Even if you have limited parking, consider charging separately for rent and parking. Some tenants may not have vehicles, so instead of including a fee in their rent for a parking space they won't use, you can keep their rent lower while generating additional income by renting parking spaces to tenants who need them.

If you charge for parking, be sure to implement detailed parking rules and have reserved parking stickers or permits. You also want to put up proper signage in keeping with local code that allows you the ability to enforce your parking regulations through fines or towing.

Converting the World Wide Web to cash: Internet access

Almost everyone has a computer, and Internet access is a must for virtually all rental properties. The days of dial-up connections are gone, and the demand for access to high-speed broadband Internet is rising. Currently, owners of small rental properties in urban areas can usually only offer their tenants Internet access through a local cable television, traditional phone, or Internet Service Provider (ISP) company. But some owners of larger rental properties have been able to negotiate master contracts with ISPs that provide revenue to the landlord when tenants sign up for service with the ISP.

High-speed Internet technology is improving all the time, and the costs to provide this service are dropping. Currently, these four basic types of high-speed Internet connections are available:

- ✔ Cable Internet
- ✔ Digital subscriber lines (DSL)
- ✔ Satellite Internet
- ✔ Wireless Internet Service Providers (WISP)

Check with service providers in your area; certain technologies are better suited and more cost-effective for certain properties and locations.

Cashing in on the ol' dining room set: Furnished rentals

The majority of rental properties are offered unfurnished, because most tenants already have their own furnishings. In urban areas, short-term renters may need furnished units, but this group is a specific market that's usually addressed by one or more major apartment owners or hospitality companies. However, in some suburban or rural areas, you can find a demand for furnished rental units for short- or long-term rentals.

Your target market and specific location often have a bearing on whether you want to consider offering your rental units partially or fully furnished. Furnishing your rental is a major investment, but if your rental property is adjacent to a major employer who regularly relocates employees into the area, you can often generate significantly higher rents for a furnished rental unit.

Consider using a company that specializes in this market (such as CORT, www.cort.com) if you're looking to competitively offer furnished rental units. This type of company can supply all the furnishings, housewares, and accessories, plus provide corporate relocation referral services that can assist you in locating tenants for your rental property. High demand for furnished single-family homes or condos can be common in urban areas with major corporations, so be sure to do some research and see whether offering your property as a corporate rental is a good opportunity for you.

Putting Lease Options to Work for You

Offering short-term lease options is another way to generate additional cash. A *lease option agreement* generally consists of a standard lease, plus a separate contract that gives the tenant the right to purchase the property at either a later fixed date or within a mutually agreed time frame. Lease option agreements typically require an upfront payment and/or monthly payments to secure the purchase option, which is often credited toward the down payment or the purchase price.

Although every lease option is unique, here's an example of how a deal may be structured for a rental home with a current market rent of $1,000 per month and a current market value of $120,000. Real estate forecasts indicate that appreciation will be 4 percent, or approximately $5,000, in the next 12 months. The tenant signs a 12-month standard lease and agrees to pay $1,200 per month, with $1,000 as rent and $200 as a nonrefundable option fee that will be applied to the down payment. At the same time, you and the tenant enter into a lease option agreement that offers the tenant the right to buy the rental property within 12 months of the lease for an amount of $125,000. This amount is the mutually agreed-upon estimated fair market value of the rental property by the end of the option period.

In this situation, you receive an additional cash flow of $200 per month, and the tenant treats the property with care, because he may very well be the new owner soon. If the tenant exercises the option, he receives a credit toward the down payment of $200 per month for each month he paid the option fee. On the other hand — because you used your standard lease form and guaranteed the lease option documents were drafted properly — you still have the right to evict the tenant for nonpayment of rent or any other material lease default.

In most instances, the tenant isn't able to exercise the purchase option because he doesn't have the money required for the down payment and his share of the closing costs. In the meantime, you're increasing your monthly rental income by $200 and have a good tenant. Of course, at the end of the option, the tenant is well aware that he has paid an additional $2,400 in rent that would've been applied to the down payment or purchase price if he had exercised his purchase option. Depending on the circumstances, you can either renegotiate an extension of the purchase option with the tenant or negotiate a new lease without the purchase option.

Lease options are a strategy to consider as a way to increase cash flow from your rental under the right circumstances. They can work very well, or they can be a complete disaster if you don't have the right agreement in place. Both you and the tenant must have a thorough understanding of the unique benefits and challenges of lease options for them to benefit you both. Table 21-1 lists some pros and cons of lease options for your consideration.

Table 21-1	Pros and Cons of Lease Options
Pros	*Cons*
The lease-option tenant is usually better financially qualified.	The lease-option tenant may not be willing or able to buy the rental property at the end of the lease.
The lease-option tenant pays a nonrefundable option fee upfront or with his rent that's applicable to the down payment or purchase price.	Lease options have tax ramifications and can trigger due-on-sale clauses in your financing or a reassessment of your property under certain circumstances.
Strong demand for lease options exists; the tenant typically stays longer and often treats the property better.	The agreed option purchase price may be much lower than actual fair market value of rental property if the property appreciates significantly during the option period.
A lease-option tenant may be willing to pay a top-dollar option price.	The lease-option tenant may not exercise the option and instead insist on the return of the extra rent paid, or demand a renegotiation of the option terms.
You continue to receive the tax benefits of owning rental property.	A lease-option tenant who doesn't exercise the option after paying a large nonrefundable fee may get even by damaging your rental property.

The availability of lease options often fluctuates with the strength of the rental market. When you're having difficulty finding qualified tenants, a lease option may make good sense. If you have an abundance of qualified tenants, however, a lease option offers you fewer advantages.

Avoid long-term lease options of more than two years, because real estate appreciation can be very unpredictable. Don't provide a set option purchase price for any longer than one or two years or else be sure to include a clause that the purchase price will increase by an amount equal to the increase in the average median home price in your area. Consider setting the option purchase price slightly *higher* than the current market rent in your area to account for potential significant appreciation in the property's value.

If you do decide to go with this option, hire a real estate attorney with extensive experience in lease options to review your lease option contract in advance. Lease options can have very serious business and ethical problems if they aren't drafted properly. An improperly structured lease option can be considered a sale and can trigger the due-on-sale clause with your lender, causing you to lose the tax benefits of depreciation and deductible expenses. Your property may be reassessed for property taxes, you may be liable for failure to comply with seller disclosure laws, or you may be prevented from evicting the tenant, even if he has defaulted on the lease. Keep the nonrefundable option fee reasonable so that if the value of the property declines or your tenant doesn't exercise his option for any reason, you can feel comfortable that you've treated the tenant fairly. Or you may want to renegotiate or consider offering an extension.

Taking Advantage of Government Programs

Housing is generally the largest single expense for many families, and the U.S. is facing a very severe affordable housing crisis. According to the federal government's definition, housing is "affordable" as long as the rent and utility costs don't exceed 30 percent of household income. But people who receive Supplemental Security Income (SSI) or who work in low-wage jobs often have trouble finding affordable housing.

Demand for new rental units is high in most areas of the country, yet construction of new rental housing is at all-time lows. When the demand for rental housing exceeds the supply, a shortage of available rental units occurs, which leads to increased rents. In this situation, many tenants are forced to pay a very large share of their incomes in rent.

With such a shortage of decent, affordable rental units, low-income tenants have a very difficult time finding rental housing. To make matters worse, many rental property owners have a firm policy of not accepting rental applicants who rely upon subsidies to assist with their rent payments. Rental property owners' most common complaints about subsidy programs are that the rent limitations are too low, program administrators fail to cooperate, and some rental property inspectors are unreasonable in their required repairs and extensive paperwork.

In the following sections, I review some of the benefits and concerns of rent subsidy programs for rental property owners. If you're not sure whether participating in rent subsidy programs is for you, read on.

The scoop on rental subsidy programs

A *rental subsidy* is a payment of some or all the rent by a governmental or nonprofit agency for the use and occupancy of a rental unit for qualified individuals. These individuals may receive subsidies as a result of insufficient income, disability, relocation assistance, or other similar programs. All aspects of the tenancy relationship with participants in rent subsidy programs are usually the same as with any other tenants.

Many types of rental subsidy programs are offered by local housing agencies, religious organizations, and charitable groups. The majority of the local rent subsidy programs only offer short-term assistance, whereas Section 8 — a federal Department of Housing and Urban Development (HUD) program — offers rent subsidies on an ongoing basis.

Be careful with local rental subsidy programs that only offer short-term financial assistance to your tenant. Some programs provide payment of the security deposit and assist with a few months' rent. But you need to be sure that the tenant meets your tenant screening criteria, including possession of sufficient income to meet the full rent and utility costs on an indefinite basis, so that when the short-term assistance runs out, the tenant can still pay you.

Some rental subsidy programs have their limitations. But the need is significant, and many lower-income families and other needy tenants receive important assistance from them. Rental subsidy programs are targeted in their approach and allow you to retain control over tenant selection and all other aspects of the rental relationship.

The lowdown on Section 8

The Section 8 program was established in 1974 by HUD as the federal government's major program for assisting very-low-income families, the elderly, and the disabled in renting decent, safe, and sanitary housing in the private market.

Section 8 is the largest rental subsidy program, with more than 2 million tenants participating, and is offered and administered through the 2,500 state, regional, and local public housing authorities (PHAs) throughout the country.

Section 8 helps twice as many families as the next largest nationwide housing program, public housing. It's available to qualified low-income tenants and requires each tenant to pay a percentage of his or her monthly income toward rent, with the balance paid by the local PHA. You can find complete details of the Section 8 program online at `www.hud.gov/offices/pih/ programs/hcv/forms/guidebook.cfm`. In the meantime, the next few sections give you an overview on what you need to know about Section 8.

Understanding how Section 8 works

The Section 8 program has two goals:

- To allow low-income households more choice in housing
- To reduce the concentration of low-income households living in particular neighborhoods

A wide variety of residential rental housing qualifies for Section 8 certification, including single-family homes, condos, duplexes, apartments, and mobile homes. HUD requirements state that the rental unit must comply with HUD occupancy standards guidelines, which generally allow two occupants for every bedroom.

HUD allows you to establish your own occupancy standards for your property, which can be higher or lower than the federal standards as long as they're based on legitimate business reasons or are required to protect your tenants' health and safety. Of course, you must abide by any more stringent state or local restrictions.

Section 8's Housing Choice Voucher Program provides tenant-based rental subsidies or vouchers that can be used to rent privately owned rental housing chosen by the tenant. Tenants with household incomes that are less than the published PHA maximum annual income by family size for a local area are eligible for Section 8 assistance. The overall income caps for families admitted to the voucher program are usually set between 50 percent and 80 percent of the local median income.

After qualifying, tenants receive Section 8 vouchers or certificates and have up to 60 days to locate rental units. In certain tight rental markets, tenants have up to 120 days to find suitable rental units. The local PHA makes inspections to ensure that the rental unit meets the HUD Minimum Housing Quality Standards at the beginning of the tenancy, upon annual renewal, and upon request if the tenant believes the condition of the rental unit is unacceptable.

The PHA pays the rental subsidy directly to the rental property on behalf of the program participant. Under this program, the tenant must pay whichever amount is greater — the PHA minimum rent (usually $25 to $50) or the Total

Tenant Payment (TTP), which is based on either 30 percent of a tenant's monthly adjusted income or 10 percent of a tenant's monthly gross income. Usually the calculation — based on 30 percent of the adjusted monthly income — is the basis for setting the minimum tenant portion of the rent. If the tenant selects a unit with rent higher than the PHA limits, the program also provides for a maximum initial rental burden limit so that the tenant's share of the rent doesn't exceed 40 percent of his monthly adjusted household income.

The Section 8 rental subsidy is based on the HUD Fair Market Rent, available from local PHAs. At least annually, the PHA surveys the local rental housing market and determines the median rents and utility allowance for each rental unit type based on the number of bedrooms. The amount of rent that owners can charge is limited to amounts set by the local PHA that don't exceed a maximum of the HUD Fair Market Rent level for the particular county. Section 8 tenants may choose rental units with higher rents than the PHA maximums and then pay the difference, or they may choose lower cost rental units and keep the difference for themselves.

In some areas of the country, the maximum allowable rents are reasonable. But in a lot of areas, the maximum rents set by the local PHA rule out many of the local rental units because they are too low. In these locations, Section 8 participants and rental property owners are effectively unable to work together to achieve decent affordable housing. The PHAs have been allowed to adjust the maximum Section 8 rents up to 10 percent higher than the HUD Fair Market Rent to be consistent with actual rents in the area and allow tenants more alternatives.

The maximum rents vary based on whether the owner or the tenants pay the utilities. In general, you're better off having the tenants pay their own utilities, because the HUD utility allowances are typically insufficient, and owner-paid utilities don't encourage your tenants to conserve energy.

Knowing what to do if you rent to Section 8 tenants

If you take part in Section 8, you're required to enter into a one-year lease with a participating tenant using a standardized, HUD-approved lease form or a combination of your lease with a HUD addendum. You're locked into the one-year lease agreement except for nonpayment of rent or another serious breach. You must also sign a contract known as a Housing Assistance Payments (HAP) contract with the local public housing authority authorizing the payment of rent, which can be deposited directly into your bank account.

Use your own standard rental application, rental contract, and all other forms and procedures. Attach the PHA lease and HAP contract to your paperwork. If your Section 8 tenant doesn't pay her share of the rent, or you have another problem, immediately notify your contact person at the local PHA. Although the PHA is limited in what it can do, it *can* be helpful in resolving issues.

The greatest benefit to rental owners is that the local PHA pays the majority of the tenant's monthly rent like clockwork, and the tenant's portion is low enough that she usually doesn't have any problem meeting this financial obligation. Also, if the tenant fails to pay her portion of the rent, you have the right to evict her and apply the security deposit to any unpaid rent or rental unit damage. Some PHAs may have formal or informal requirements to contact them to resolve any issues before beginning an eviction action.

Process a Section 8 tenant's move-out just like any other tenant, but be sure to notify the local PHA. The availability of Section 8 assistance is limited, with long waiting lists. This fact can be very helpful in motivating your tenants to be responsible, because the termination of their leases for nonpayment or other breaches often results in a loss of their rental assistance.

For most rental property owners, participating in the Section 8 program is very easy. Contact the PHA in your city or county for more info or to be sure your rental rates are within their maximum guidelines. If they are, your local PHA will refer eligible applicants to you and prepare the necessary documents should you decide to rent to an eligible applicant. Make sure you obtain a copy of the Section 8 rules and procedures from HUD before determining whether the Section 8 rental program will work for you.

You can't charge higher rent for a Section 8 rental unit than you would if you were renting the same unit to a private, unassisted tenant. Make sure you regularly conduct market surveys of rents for comparable properties in your area so that you know your rents are reasonable.

Understanding the pros and cons of Section 8

The Section 8 rental subsidy program can be a great resource for rental property owners in certain areas of the country. The key is to ensure that the PHA-determined maximum rental rates for your area are competitive and the PHA's inspection requirements are reasonable. If these criteria are sound, then Section 8 can provide you with additional rental prospects. Screen the tenants carefully and work with the local PHA representative to avoid problems.

Participating in Section 8 may provide you with stable, long-term tenants at market rents, where the majority of the rent is paid by a government agency, and the tenants are highly motivated to pay their share of the rent and abide by your rules and guidelines. But weighing the pros and cons is still worthwhile.

Here are some advantages to participating in the Section 8 program:

- ✔ You encounter less competition, because many rental property owners refuse to participate.
- ✔ A portion of the rent is guaranteed by the local PHA and backed by the federal government.

✔ You retain full control over the screening and selection process, with the PHA providing the names and addresses of the current and one prior landlord for verification and reference checking.

✔ You may collect a full security deposit up to the maximum allowed under state and local laws, plus rent may be adjusted annually, subject to PHA maximum rents for comparable rental units in the area.

✔ You gain a stable tenant profile with competitive rents and property that's inspected regularly.

And here are some disadvantages to participating in the Section 8 program:

✔ Additional paperwork leads to a delay in initial occupancy.

✔ The first payment is delayed, and you may have difficulty stopping payment when the tenant leaves.

✔ You must meet HUD Minimum Housing Quality Standards through regular inspections by your local PHA and make all required repairs.

✔ Rents and utility costs can't exceed HUD's Fair Market Rent determination.

The 4-1-1 on rehabilitation loans

A large percentage of rental housing in the U.S. is old and in need of renovation and modernization. According to National Multi Housing Council tabulations from the 2005 U.S. Census Bureau's American Housing Survey, less than 15 percent of the apartments in the country have been built since 1990. Clearly, great opportunities exist for rental property owners to renovate rental units.

With the difficulty in providing new low-income rental housing, HUD encourages the rehabilitation of existing rental units through state and local governmental agencies, including the HOME program; community development block grants; and rural housing programs. Most programs are administrated by local PHAs. They allow owners of qualified rental units to obtain improvement grants or borrow money to upgrade and rehabilitate their rental housing properties. The grants cover weatherproofing and other health and safety issues, and the low- or even no-interest loans allow owners to make capital improvements.

As with most governmental programs, you can expect to fill out numerous forms and wait for processing, inspections, and approvals when you apply for a rehabilitation loan. However, besides offering below-market interest rates, these loans are often *assumable,* which means a purchaser is allowed to take over the below-market interest rate loan as part of her financing upon acquisition.

Some programs offer owners of larger rental properties rehabilitation funds if they provide housing for specific targeted groups. For example, people with physical and mental disabilities find it difficult to locate private and affordable rental housing, so if you rent to them, you may qualify for rehabilitation funds.

Demand for special housing for the aging population, as well as for people struggling with HIV/AIDS and substance abuse, is growing. Due to the lack of new rental housing construction, the federal government is developing programs to encourage the renovation and conversion of existing rental units, particularly single-family houses, targeted for these particular groups.

Contact your local PHA or visit the HUD Web site at www.hud.gov for more information on funding programs and qualification standards.

Working in Niche Markets

Sometimes thinking outside the box and looking for angles, like niche rental markets, that other rental property owners overlook or aren't willing to pursue makes sense. You may own property in a soft rental market, or you may just want to find a market niche where your rental units can outperform others.

The following sections explore several of the niche rental markets — ranging from students and senior citizens to nonsmokers and tenants with pets — that you can use to your benefit. These niche markets may or may not be right for you. But be sure to at least consider whether you can dip into one or more of them and increase your cash flow in the process.

Taking another look at your pet policy

In today's rental market, one of the most effective strategies to keep your rental units occupied with stable, paying tenants is to allow pets. Although many owners immediately reject this idea, the reality is that rental options are extremely limited for pet owners — meaning that if you're one of the few landlords who accept pets, you immediately increase the demand for your rental unit.

Allowing pets under certain conditions can result in much higher rental income and fewer vacancies. Accepting pets can be successful if you

✔ **Have a rental property that's suitable for pets:** Some rental properties are particularly well suited for tenants with pets. An older rental property or one with certain features such as a fenced yard, hard-surface flooring (as opposed to carpeting), and vertical blinds (as opposed to curtains) is a good candidate for tenants with pets.

✔ **Verify through references and an interview that your tenant is a responsible pet owner:** Be sure to confirm all references and ask specific questions about the pet. Conducting an actual interview with the pet to determine its demeanor is a good idea. Be sure to properly complete the pet or animal agreement addendum to your rental contract and have the tenant agree to your terms. Restrict any animal with dangerous or potentially dangerous tendencies, and take a photo of the pet for your tenant file.

✔ **Implement and enforce stringent pet policies and rules:** For your pet policy to run smoothly, you need detailed rules, including a limit on the number of animals allowed. You also need to have clear policies about pet and tenant behavior. For example, you want to forbid tenants from flushing cat litter down the toilet (otherwise you'll end up with clogged pipes). Put limits on what you consider to be an acceptable pet; think about making exotic animals off-limits.

✔ **Require an extra deposit for tenants with pets:** Because so few rental properties accept pet owners, those that do are able to charge higher rental rates and collect much larger security deposits. Most responsible pet owners don't balk at a reasonable monthly rental rate premium or an increased security deposit of several hundred dollars. Avoid using the labels *pet rent* or *pet deposit;* instead, try to keep the language generic. A *pet deposit* can limit your use of those funds to damage you can prove was caused by the pet. Your goal is to ensure that the rental rate and larger security deposit provide adequate compensation and protection against any or *all* damage to the rental unit that results in increased cleaning or repair costs.

The Humane Society of the United States is among the many pet advocacy and rescue organizations becoming increasingly involved in addressing the issue of pets in rental housing. The Humane Society offers advice and tips for both tenants and rental owners at its Web site, www.rentwithpets.org.

Even "no pet" properties must accommodate renters who have companion or service animals if they're prescribed by a medical doctor under the Americans with Disabilities Act (ADA). For more on this topic, flip to Chapter 10.

Renting to students

A large number of rental properties are located near colleges and universities; yours may be one of them. But many rental property owners have the same strong feelings against renting to students as they do about accepting pets. The major problem, however, is that (except for the ADA exemption) you can legally have a "no pet" policy, but you can't unlawfully discriminate against students if they meet your tenant screening criteria.

The National Multi Housing Council has researched the nationwide student housing market and published some excellent reports that point out that many of the 75 million *Echo Boomers,* people born between 1976 and 1994, will be entering college in the next decade. The Council has studied 64 college towns across the country and found that the demand for off-campus, privately owned student housing is very high.

One of the most common problems with renting to students is the fact that students have special needs regarding the lengths of their leases. Many schools are in session for only four or five months in the fall and spring and two or three months in the summer. If you only offer a 12-month lease, you may end up with student tenants who default on their leases and leave right after the end of the semester.

If your rental properties attract prospective student tenants, be sure to adopt policies and leases that allow you to take advantage of this large target market while minimizing its downside. One strategy is to offer 3-month and 9-month leases at a premium rental rate rather than the 12-month leases available at competitive rental properties. Students attending the fall and spring sessions will be delighted with the 9-month term, and summer students will go for the 3-month term.

The other primary concern with renting to students is their behavior. Combat this risk by implementing strict policies and rules concerning noise and, ideally, having an on-site manager to enforce them. Be sure to consistently require a larger security deposit and/or cosigner or guarantor of the lease at properties where you rent to students. Also, you should insist on receiving the full rent each month in a single check (as explained in Chapter 14).

Catering to senior citizens

The need for rental housing for active seniors is increasing as America's rapidly expanding population of older adults chooses to maintain and prolong its independent living status. The U.S. Census Bureau estimates that the number of seniors (age 65 or older) will swell from the present 40 million to a projected 86 million by the year 2050. As a result, many rental property owners are finding the demand for senior housing a great investment opportunity.

Senior rental housing is no longer required to offer "significant facilities and services" designed for the elderly, but it must show that one person who's 55 years of age or older lives in at least 80 percent of the occupied rental units. Federal law also requires that rental property owners follow policies and procedures that demonstrate intent to provide housing for persons age 55 or older. This requirement typically means that a sign must be posted outside, and all literature provided to the public must include a statement indicating that housing for older persons is available.

Before designating your multi-family rental property as housing for older persons, be sure to check with an attorney about discrimination laws in your area. (Note, however, that qualified seniors rental properties can exclude families with children without violating the Fair Housing Act.) Many state and local Fair Housing laws may still be modeled after the former federal Fair Housing law requiring owners to provide "significant facilities and services."

Seniors are typically excellent long-term tenants; however, do some advance research to determine whether your multi-family rental property is ideally suited for seniors. Evaluate your rental units to consider their proximity to local transportation, shopping, medical facilities, special senior centers or activities, and places of worship.

If your rental property has services and facilities for seniors, prepare to attract a senior target market. Be sure to advise local agencies catering to seniors about the availability of your rental units.

Designating your rental units smoke-free

One of the most controversial issues in rental housing management today concerns the ability of a rental property owner to restrict the use of the rental unit to nonsmoking status. The growing trend in the United States is to restrict smoking in almost all public areas; the elimination of smoking on airplanes is even becoming widely accepted internationally. Although the hotel industry has successfully implemented policies offering both smoking and nonsmoking rooms for years, rental property owners are just beginning to address this issue.

I've found that a strong demand exists for rental properties and rental units where smoking is partially or completely restricted. One frequent complaint I receive from tenants who write in to my *Rental Roundtable* newspaper column is about secondhand smoke from a neighbor. Unfortunately, in some rental properties, tobacco smoke can drift from one rental unit directly into another. The smoke can enter from hallways, stairs, balconies, and patios, usually through windows and doors, but sometimes also from the building's common ventilation system.

Although you can prohibit the behavior or act of smoking in rental units or on the premises, you can't refuse to rent to someone just because that person is a smoker. Not renting to a smoker is a form of discrimination and a violation of Fair Housing laws.

The majority of Americans are nonsmokers. Smoking is considered a controllable behavior, not a disease, so people who smoke aren't categorized as a protected class under federal and state Fair Housing or antidiscrimination laws. Although tenants who smoke need places to live, so do nonsmoking tenants who want to avoid drifting secondhand smoke.

However, currently no federal or state laws prohibit you from adopting a policy that requires all or part of a building to be smoke-free, including individual rental units. Because the rights of individuals who smoke and those opposed to secondhand smoke are constantly changing, be sure to check local and state laws in your area before deciding to implement a smoke-free rental program.

Following are some good business reasons to consider offering smoke-free rental units:

- ✔ Lack of damage from cigarette burns
- ✔ No need to thoroughly clean carpets, drapes, and other surfaces or completely repaint the unit just to remove a permeating smoke smell
- ✔ Potential for reduced insurance premiums

Some groups promote the concept of rental properties that don't allow smoking on the premises. For example, in southern California, the Smokefree Apartment House Registry (www.smokefreeapartments.org) offers a free listing service to rental property owners with total or partial smoke-free policies. I believe that this concept will be very popular throughout many areas of the country in the next few years.

Although you can simply put a "no smoking allowed" clause in your rental contract, I recommend surveying your current tenants before doing so. You may find that prohibiting smoking in common areas, rental units, balconies, and patios is a popular idea — or you may meet with more resistance than anticipated. Knowing where your tenants stand on this issue should be an important part of your decision.

As with any major policy change, be sure to implement a conversion to a smoke-free rental property upon tenant turnover or only after giving proper legal notice to current tenants. If you want to implement a smoke-free policy at a larger rental property, start by prohibiting smoking in all common areas, such as the rental office, laundry room, and recreational facilities. Then you can expand the smoke-free policy to individual rental units if the program is positively received by your tenants.

Part VI
The Part of Tens

The 5th Wave By Rich Tennant

"I could rent you this one. It's got a pool in the backyard. Then I got a six bedroom with a fountain out front, but nothing right now with a moat."

In this part . . .

This wouldn't be a *For Dummies* book without the Part of Tens. Here you can find short bursts of information on everything from why you should buy rental property in the first place to how to rent a vacancy. So if you're looking for a lot of information, but you don't have much time, you've come to the right part.

And if you want a little more info to whet your appetite, I include a bonus Part of Tens chapter on the CD covering ten common mistakes landlords make and how you can avoid them.

Chapter 22

Ten Reasons to Become a Rental Property Owner

*O*wning rental property isn't for everyone. So if you're just starting to think about investing in real estate through rental property, check out these ten great reasons to take the plunge. Of course, I believe so strongly in real estate investing that I wrote *Real Estate Investing For Dummies* with Eric Tyson (Wiley).

You Can Diversify Your Investments

Buying rental property helps vary your investments. Owning your own home is a first step toward diversification, but owning rental real estate is a prudent strategy to protect your assets from volatility in certain areas of the economy. Unlike owning your own home, owning a rental property that someone *else* calls home is an investment because you don't have to live there.

You Don't Need Much Money to Start

A lack of money is often cited as the number one factor that keeps people from investing in real estate. But you can typically purchase real estate for a down payment of 20 percent or less, with the balance provided by others. Real estate loans are readily available at very competitive terms throughout the U.S. Some sellers are willing to assist the buyer by financing a portion of the purchase price. Plus, if you're a first-time homebuyer, you may qualify for up to 100 percent financing. So basically, you can take advantage of a first-time homebuyer program, build up equity in your home, and then refinance it to generate additional capital, which you can use as the down payment to buy rental property.

It Can Be a Second Income

If you have any doubts about real estate's role in making many of the world's great fortunes, just look at the annual *Forbes 400* list that catalogs the richest people around the world.

The majority of residential rental real estate in the U.S. is owned by working middle-class individuals of all backgrounds and ages who sought viable opportunities to augment their current incomes or careers. Real estate investing can truly begin as a part-time job and supply a second income.

You Gain Tax Advantages

The federal tax code has many unique advantages for real estate. Property owners can benefit from expense deductions, depreciation write-offs, tax-deferred exchanges, and favorable capital gains tax rates. Owning and operating rental property is a business, and the tax laws allow deductions against your rental income for the cost of payroll, property management, advertising, maintenance and repairs, utilities, insurance, and property taxes.

Your rental property can be depreciated, giving you another tax break. Current federal tax laws allow you to depreciate your residential income property improvements over a 271/2year life span. The depreciation loss can reduce your taxable income or give you a taxable loss on the property, even if you have a positive cash flow. After depleting your depreciation on income-producing real estate, you can take advantage of IRS code 1031 (also known as a tax-deferred *Starker Exchange*) to postpone taxation on any gain by rolling over your equity into a new and often larger rental property.

Be sure you understand the basic concepts of real estate taxation issues, but rely on a tax specialist, accountant, or attorney for advice on details, procedures, and tax laws. Tax codes change from year to year, so discuss your personal tax situation with your accountant or tax preparer.

Real Estate Holds Its Value

Real estate is one of the most popular investments available, because income-producing rental properties have held their value through many economic cycles over the decades. Throughout history, the tangible nature of real estate has been extremely important to both people and the economy.

Real estate is cyclical. Many businesses have their ups and downs, and real estate is no exception. However, real estate usually rebounds and grows in value after a slump. Historically, many solid real estate investments have depreciated for a period of time but then grown again in value. Real estate appreciates because its quantity is limited. Over the long run, real estate is an established performer and offers a solid foundation for your financial future.

You Get Leverage

Real estate *leverage* is the use of mortgage financing to purchase an investment property with only a small cash outlay, with the expectation that appreciation and inflation will create a disproportionately high return on the original cash investment upon sale. The key to successfully using leverage is having a mortgage interest rate *lower* than the return on your real estate investment. Here's an oversimplified example: A buyer purchases a $150,000 rental home for $30,000 cash down and a $120,000 loan at a 7 percent interest rate. If the property appreciates and sells in three years for a net of $180,000, the owner will have earned $30,000, or 100 percent return on his money. This is called *positive leverage*. Conversely, high interest rates and flat real estate values with no increases in cash flow result in *negative leverage*, and undercapitalized investors may lose their properties.

It Beats Inflation

Inflation is the loss of buying power as prices rise. Most investments, such as money market accounts, bonds, stocks, and mutual funds, have trouble keeping up with the inflation rate. Thus, investors in these assets often find that they lose purchasing power over time. Real estate, however, is a formidable tool in the battle against inflation. When rental property is purchased with fixed-rate financing, the property's price and financing cost are set. Other operating costs, such as property taxes and utilities, are bound to increase, but rental property owners typically can increase the amount of rent charged to offset these heightened costs. Of course, temporary softness or downturns in the rental market may delay rent increases in the short run, but historically, real estate cash flows have been able to maintain an owner's purchasing power in the long run.

You Can Shelter Your Income

Currently, the taxation laws affecting real estate offer tax advantages to individuals actively involved in managing their rental properties. If you're an active investor and don't exceed the adjusted gross income limits, you may be able to qualify for substantial deductions for rental property losses to reduce your taxable earned income from other sources, a process known as *sheltering other income*. Using a property management firm doesn't preclude you from taking advantage of these tax write-offs as long as you're involved in setting the rents and policies for your rental property.

Qualified real estate professionals are allowed to claim all real estate loss deductions in the year incurred; however, the requirements to achieve the status of a real estate professional are strict, so you should consult your tax advisor.

You Get a Positive Cash Flow

Rental property owners know that the right investment property will generate sufficient rental income to cover the property's mortgage and operating expenses. And after the tax advantages of depreciation, real estate generally provides positive cash flow. This pattern may not always hold true in the first few years of ownership, but positive cash flow is a real benefit for many investors. Of course, after the mortgage has been paid, the positive cash flow can be very significant.

It Can Help You Retire

Real estate investment is one of the best methods to fulfill the dream of retiring wealthy. This worthy goal requires a diversified investment strategy with assets that are purchasable with leverage, generate cash flow, appreciate consistently over time, and maintain their purchasing power in an inflationary environment. Like most investments, the earlier you begin your real estate investment career, the better your results. Buying and holding the right rental properties for 20 to 30 years is an ideal way to hedge inflation, take advantage of unique tax benefits, and build wealth for retirement.

Chapter 23

Ten Ways to Rent Your Vacancy

In This Chapter

▶ Staying ahead of the competition

▶ Keeping the interests of your prospective tenants in mind

Every day that a rental unit sits vacant is a loss of revenue you can never fully recover, regardless of whether you eventually secure a higher rent. Here, I give you ten specific tips to help you rent your vacancy right away.

Maintain Curb Appeal

Your rental prospect makes his first impression when he drives up. If your property doesn't look clean and attractive on the outside, the prospect often doesn't wait to see the inside! Your chances of leasing your rental unit at a competitive market rent to a stable and financially solid rental prospect are about nil when your property doesn't have good curb appeal. You can't always dramatically improve the architectural look of your rental property, but you can usually control the appearance of its grounds.

Familiarity is the enemy of rental property owners; when you're familiar with your property, you may have trouble looking at it with an independent and critical eye. Drive up to your property and continually ask yourself what looks tacky or poorly maintained. You may really have to focus, but you'll find several items that need immediate attention. Take care of them now.

Keep the Unit in Rent-Ready Condition

Although you may eventually find a tenant willing to accept your rental unit before it's in rent-ready condition, you can almost guarantee that the unit will be returned to you in even worse condition when that tenant vacates. Naturally, the tenant will argue if you try to take any deductions from her security deposit, and the courts will probably side with her because the unit wasn't clean originally. Spare yourself this agony and make having a rent-ready unit that's clean and defect-free your goal.

Distinguish your rental unit from the others out there by keeping up its professionally maintained, clean, bright, and airy appearance — this noticeable difference will appeal to the best rental prospects.

Establish a Competitive Rent

If you don't have vacancies on a regular basis, and you're in a rental market where rents are fluctuating, setting the rental rate at the right amount can be a real challenge. Be sure to do your homework and carefully review the local rental market for rental properties that are truly comparable. If you set your rent too low, you'll have multiple qualified applicants and can select the best one, but you won't maximize your rental income. If the rent is too high, you'll suffer lost rental income. The key is to set your rent at or slightly below the market rent for your area.

Offer Prospects a Rate Guarantee

They may feel comfortable with your current rent, but virtually all rental prospects are concerned about your ability to unilaterally raise their rent, unless you offer a lease. Of course, a long-term lease isn't in your best interest, because you can't increase rent and may have trouble evicting a problem tenant.

If you know that you don't intend to raise your new tenant's rent in the near future, offer him a rental rate guarantee for a set period of time. This move allays his fears of being hit with an unreasonable rent increase soon after moving in. It also helps you avoid getting locked into a long-term lease that may one day lead to expensive and aggravating court action.

Stay Ahead of the Technology Curve

Every day, access to technology becomes more important, so prewiring your rental property or offering wireless high-speed Internet access can be a great way to distinguish your property from the competition. The four basic types of high-speed Internet connections (cable, digital subscriber lines [DSL], fixed wireless, and satellite) have their own advantages, but some types may not be available in your area.

Owners of larger rental properties typically find that the Internet service provider (ISP) covers installation costs and offers to share in the revenues. Single-family or small rental property owners may have more trouble getting service in many areas, but may be able to get free installation with a tenant commitment to subscribe to the service for a minimum time period.

Offer Referral Fees

Often your current tenants or your rental property neighbors can be the best sources for finding your next tenant. They may work with, go to school with, or participate in activities with someone who's looking for a new rental. So let them know that you have an upcoming vacancy and that you want to reward them for taking the time to refer a rental prospect to you. Referral fees can be an extremely cost-effective source of qualified renters. Another benefit is that most people don't personally refer a potential tenant whom they don't respect and trust. Referral fees thus allow tenants to make some money and have a hand in picking their own neighbors!

Accept Pets

Rental property owners who don't accept pets eliminate nearly 50 percent of the country's potential renters, according to the Humane Society of the United States. With the requirement to accept certain pets for tenants qualified under the Americans with Disabilities Act (see Chapter 10), many owners already find their ability to enforce "no pet" policies diminished.

So if you can't beat 'em, why not join 'em? If you establish sound pet policies, collect a larger security deposit, and meet both the tenant and the pet, you'll often find that you have an excellent, stable tenant for many years to come. For safety and insurance reasons, avoid dangerous animals or breeds of dogs, such as pit bulls.

Offer Move-In Gifts or Upgrades

The word *free* is one of my favorite words — and one of the most powerful sales tools ever! If you want to rent your vacancy today, seriously consider offering your prospect a move-in gift or an upgrade to the rental unit. Every day your rental unit sits vacant, you're losing money you never see again, so you may as well sweeten the pot!

You have a choice: You can offer a move-in gift that immediately belongs to the tenant, or you can offer an upgrade to the rental unit that stays when she leaves. For example, countertop microwave ovens make great move-in gifts, whereas a built-in microwave range hood or ceiling fan is an excellent unit upgrade. If you're planning to replace the carpet, consider giving your incoming tenant the option to choose among her favorite neutral carpet colors.

Contact Corporate Relocation Services

Many areas of the U.S. have a high demand for rental units for corporate employees relocating to the area. In particular, corporate relocation services have an extremely difficult time finding rental properties for families of executives requiring single-family homes with yards and plenty of storage. These services are often willing to pay significantly above-market rents for rental units or homes on short-term leases of 6 to 12 months. From your perspective, the additional turnover can be worth it if the rent's enough. From the services' perspective, your rent is much cheaper than placing their clients in extended-stay lodging.

Some corporate relocation pros will want to lease your property for multiple years with the provision that they can move in different occupants. Make sure you have very firm house rules, set a reasonable limit on the frequency of tenant turnover, and require a detailed inspection upon each move.

Accept Section 8

The Housing and Urban Development Section 8 program (see Chapter 21) is administered by 3,000 local public housing authorities located throughout the country. Some of those agencies aren't easy to work with; some have maximum allowable rents that are well below market value. If these factors aren't a problem in your area, you may find some tangible benefits in participating in the Section 8 program in that

- Your vacancy doesn't last long due to the severe shortage of rental units available for Section 8 tenants in many areas.
- The government typically pays the majority of the rent promptly each month, so you at least have that guarantee.

Appendix A

On the CD

*T*he accompanying CD is a valuable tool that makes *Property Management Kit For Dummies,* 2nd Edition, a resource you'll use again and again, because it has everything you need to answer all your questions and make your life as a property manager much easier. This appendix gives you all the information you need to navigate the CD.

System Requirements

Make sure your computer meets the minimum system requirements shown in the following list. If your computer doesn't match up to most of these requirements, you may have problems using the software and files on the CD. For the latest and greatest information, please refer to the ReadMe file located at the root of the CD-ROM.

- ✔ A PC running *Microsoft Windows 98, Windows 2000, Windows NT4* (with SP4 or later), *Windows Me, Windows XP,* or *Windows Vista*
- ✔ A Macintosh running *Apple OS X* or later
- ✔ A CD-ROM drive
- ✔ *Microsoft Office* software for either Windows or Mac

If you need more information on the basics, check out these books published by Wiley Publishing, Inc.:

- ✔ *PCs For Dummies,* 11th Edition, by Dan Gookin
- ✔ *Macs For Dummies,* 9th Edition, by Edward C. Baig

- *iMac For Dummies,* 5th Edition, by Mark L. Chambers
- *Windows 98 For Dummies* by Andy Rathbone
- *Windows 2000 Professional For Dummies* by Andy Rathbone and Sharon Crawford
- *Windows XP For Dummies,* 2nd Edition, by Andy Rathbone
- *Windows Vista For Dummies* by Andy Rathbone
- *Microsoft Windows Me For Dummies,* Millennium Edition, by Andy Rathbone

Using the CD

To install the items from the CD to your hard drive, follow these steps:

1. **Insert the CD into your computer's CD-ROM drive.**

   The license agreement appears.

   Note to Windows users: The interface won't launch if you have autorun disabled. In that case, click Start ➪ Run. (For *Windows Vista,* choose Start ➪ All Programs ➪ Accessories ➪ Run.) In the dialog box that appears, type D:\Start.exe. (Replace D with the proper letter if your CD drive uses a different letter. If you don't know the letter, see how your CD drive is listed under My Computer.) Click OK.

   Note to Mac users: The CD icon appears on your desktop. Double-click the icon to open the CD and double-click the Start icon.

2. **Read through the license agreement and click the Accept button if you want to use the CD.**

   The CD interface appears. The interface allows you to install the programs and run the demos with just a click of a button (or two).

Software

The files on the CD are in *Adobe PDF, Microsoft Word,* and *Microsoft Excel* formats. In case you don't have *Adobe Reader, Microsoft Word,* or *Microsoft Excel* on your computer, I've added the following to the CD so that you can access everything I've included:

- **Adobe Reader:** *Adobe Reader* is a freeware application for viewing files in the Adobe Portable Document format.

- **OpenOffice.org:** *OpenOffice.org* is a free, multi-platform office productivity suite. It's similar to *Microsoft Office* or *Lotus SmartSuite,* but *OpenOffice.org* is absolutely free. It includes word processing, spreadsheet, presentation, and drawing applications that allow you to create professional documents, newsletters, reports, and presentations. *OpenOffice.org* supports most file formats of other office software, so you should be able to edit and view any files created with other office solutions.

What You'll Find on the CD

The CD includes all the great forms you see in this book, plus a whole lot extra — like more than 60 additional forms you need to effectively manage rental properties. Many of these forms are ones I either use in my company or created for this book. The CD also has more than 60 forms from the Institute of Real Estate Management (IREM).

Landlord-tenant laws vary from state to state. Although I encourage you to use these forms at your properties, be sure to first have them reviewed by a landlord-tenant legal expert in your area before using them.

You should also check out the great information I've included about IREM and the National Apartment Association (NAA). Both organizations have graciously provided the latest materials on their professional designations and educational courses.

The following sections provide a summary of the forms and other valuable legal info and resources you can find on the CD. If you need help accessing the items on the CD, then see the instructions in the preceding section.

Forms

All the forms in this book, as well as the more than 60 additional forms I developed to make your job as a property manager much easier, are on the accompanying CD. When managing multiple rental properties, you realize the importance of being organized and having systems to handle different situations. Following is a breakdown of the categories of forms I've included to help you tackle any and every property management scenario, from the mundane to the challenging:

- **Accounting:** Here I include forms and spreadsheets to help you with keeping track of financial records.

- **Association material:** Because so many rental units are located within homeowners' or community associations, the CD contains forms to help you notify the association that you're renting your unit. It also features a form that advises your tenant that he or she must comply with the association's governing documents and rules and warns your tenant that he or she is responsible for assessed charges or fines for violations.

- ✔ **Forms referenced in the book:** In most chapters I reference forms that are helpful, including everything from an Animal Agreement to the Deposit Assignment and Release Agreement. Most of the forms I reference in the book are in this folder.

- ✔ **IREM forms:** IREM has generously permitted me to share more than 60 forms from its residential form database, including a basic property management agreement.

- ✔ **Leasing:** Use these forms, including the residential referral form and market survey to help you at different stages of the leasing process.

- ✔ **Other helpful forms:** This assortment of miscellaneous forms can help you at different stages of managing your property.

- ✔ **Rental contract material:** The CD includes both a month-to-month rental agreement and the great lease form from this book that you can customize to comply with your local landlord-tenant laws as well as several other important forms.

- ✔ **Rent collection material:** I highly recommend setting up as many of your tenants as possible to pay their monthly rent electronically, so the CD contains a Tenant ACH Debit form that you submit to your financial institution after your tenant completes it. Other rent collection–related items I've included are courtesy rent reminders, a receipt for rent and other charges, and a notice of cash payments for three months for tenants whose checks are returned.

- ✔ **Vendor or employee material:** Keeping your rental property looking sharp requires capital improvements from time to time, so the CD contains a very detailed example of a Request for Proposal. This particular form deals specifically with landscaping, but it can be modified to fit the appropriate scope of work for any major projects at your rental property when you want to have multiple contractors provide bids for the same work.

Legal information

Throughout this book, you see references to the importance of verifying state, and sometimes even local, landlord-tenant laws. On the CD (and in Appendix B), I share the Web links and specific code sections for the most common landlord-tenant laws. These regulations are constantly in flux, so making sure you have the latest information is essential. Routinely confirm that you fully understand and are complying with the pertinent landlord-tenant law that applies to your specific situation.

On the CD in the Legal Information folder (and in Appendix B), I share several tables that summarize some of the most important and commonly used landlord-tenant legal information, including

- ✔ Rent Control Laws by State
- ✔ States That Allow a Tenant to Repair and Deduct
- ✔ States That Allow a Tenant to Withhold Rent if Landlord Fails to Provide Essential Services or Habitable Premises
- ✔ Notice to Terminate a Month-to-Month Tenancy by State
- ✔ Landlord's Duty to Re-rent the Rental Unit
- ✔ Time Permitted for Tenant to Pay Rent after Nonpayment Notice Served
- ✔ States That Allow a Landlord to Use Unconditional Quit Notice without Permitting Tenant to Pay Past-Due Rent or Cure a Lease Violation
- ✔ Security Deposit Requirements
- ✔ Security Deposit Limits by State
- ✔ Deadline to Account for or Itemize Charges and Return of Balance of Deposit (If Any) by State
- ✔ Required Notice to Tenants for Landlord Access to Rental Unit in Nonemergency Situations by State

The CD also features required addendums for residential tenancies in California, Florida, and Chicago.

Bonus Part of Tens chapter

This fun chapter covers ten of the biggest mistakes landlords commonly make and what you can to do to avoid them. Reading this chapter can save you plenty of headaches and money.

Educational opportunities and professional designations

I emphasize the importance of education and urge you to consider gaining additional knowledge of the best practices in residential rental housing throughout this book. I also encourage you to get involved with your local rental groups and seek out professional designations.

Both IREM and NAA have local affiliates you can contact to attend their educational courses and regular meetings. They can also be extremely valuable resources on current and pending landlord-tenant laws, forms, legal referrals, tenant screening, and up-to-date market conditions. They're also your best source for local vendors, suppliers, and contractors that specifically cater to the residential rental housing market; many of these firms offer discounts to members of the local IREM chapter or NAA affiliate.

IREM has 80 chapters located in most major metropolitan areas in the U.S and is expanding internationally as well. Go to www.irem.org and search for your local chapter to find out about its regular meetings, seminars, and educational courses. IREM holds two major national meetings each year, which attract members from all parts of the country. One meeting is typically held in Washington, D.C., and the other meeting is held in varying locations.

The NAA has nearly 200 local affiliates, and many are quite active with monthly meetings and educational offerings, including seminars and workshops on new developments and legal updates. Some local NAA affiliates have annual education and trade shows. The CD contains a contact database for all the local NAA affiliates.

Both organizations provide a range of professional designations, which I highly recommend you look into. Specific information on each of these IREM and NAA designations is included on the CD, but here's a quick overview:

- ✔ **IREM designations:** IREM is the premier professional real estate management organization and is affiliated with the National Association of Realtors (NAR). IREM offers designations for individuals who combine a prescribed curriculum of coursework, experience, and ethics to attain the prestigious Certified Property Manager (CPM) designation or the Accredited Residential Manager (ARM) designation.

If you're just starting out as a rental property owner or manager, I suggest you consider the entry-level ARM designation, which is geared strictly toward managers of residential property. After you have the ARM, you can consider the more advanced CPM designation, which is for managers of all types of properties — including residential, commercial, retail, and industrial.

IREM also offers the Accredited Management Organization (AMO) designation for property management companies. This designation requires additional educational and minimum experience requirements, plus references, strict ethics, and minimum insurance coverage standards. The premier property management firms hold this designation.

✔ **NAA designations:** The NAA is the premier national residential rental housing industry trade association that offers several national designations, including the following:

- Certified Apartment Maintenance Technician (CAMT) and Certified Apartment Maintenance Technician II (CAMT II)

- Certified Apartment Manager (CAM)

- Certified Apartment Property Supervisor (CAPS)

- National Apartment Leasing Professional (NALP)

Resources

Although this book has a lot of great information, there's much more you need to know as a rental property owner and manager, so I've developed a comprehensive resource database with details on

✔ **Professional and trade organizations:** These groups are each actively involved with a different segment of the residential rental housing market, from development and management to affordable and public housing. In addition to providing contact information for the IREM and the NAA, the CD tells you how to get in touch with the National Multi-Housing Council (NMHC), National Association of Home Builders (NAHB), National Association of Residential Property Managers (NARPM), National Leased Housing Association (NLHA), National Affordable Housing Management Association (NAHMA), Urban Land Institute (ULI), and the National Council of State Housing Agencies (NCSHA).

✔ **Governmental agencies:** Important agencies to know include the Department of Housing and Urban Development (HUD) and the Environmental Protection Agency (EPA).

✔ **Media and newsletters:** Media regarding rental real estate can be very informative. That's why I provide details on the CD regarding Inman News Features; Mr. Landlord; *Multi-Housing News; Professional Apartment*

Management, Fair Housing Coach, and other publications from Vendome Group, LLC; "Rental Forum" and "Rental Roundtable" columns by Robert Griswold; and The Tenants Legal Center of San Diego.

✔ **Rental housing industry vendors/suppliers:** The list of national firms catering to the rental industry that I share on the CD is a great resource to research products and services you need for your rental property, or to simply find out more about what's available. Contact information and Web sites are included.

Troubleshooting

I tried my best to compile programs that work on most computers with the minimum system requirements. Alas, your computer may differ, and some programs may not work properly for some reason.

The two most likely problems are that you don't have enough memory (RAM) for the programs you want to use or you have other programs running that are affecting the installation or running of a program from the CD. If you get an error message, such as `Not enough memory` or `Setup cannot continue`, try one or more of the following suggestions and then try using the software again:

✔ **Turn off any antivirus software running on your computer.** Installation programs sometimes mimic virus activity and may make your computer incorrectly believe that it's being infected by a virus.

✔ **Close all running programs.** The more programs you have running, the less memory is available to other programs. Installation programs typically update files and programs; if you keep other programs running, installation may not work properly.

✔ **Have your local computer store add more RAM to your computer.** This is, admittedly, a drastic and somewhat expensive step. However, adding more memory can really help the speed of your computer and allow more programs to run at the same time.

If you have trouble with the CD-ROM, please call the Wiley Product Technical Support phone number at 800-762-2974. Outside the United States, call 1-317-572-3994. You can also contact Wiley Product Technical Support at `support.wiley.com`. John Wiley & Sons provides technical support only for installation and other general quality-control items. For technical support on the applications themselves, consult the programs' vendors or authors. To place additional orders or to request information about other Wiley products, please call 877-762-2974.

Appendix B

State Statutes for Landlord-Tenant Laws

• •

*T*he management of real estate requires knowledge about landlord-tenant laws, so this appendix (and the CD) includes what you need to know about the laws of your state. I provide tables with summarized info about many of the key landlord-tenant laws, along with a comprehensive list of additional landlord-tenant legal information for each state and the District of Columbia.

The following states have adopted the Uniform Residential Landlord and Tenant Act: Alabama, Alaska, Arizona, Florida, Hawaii, Iowa, Kansas, Kentucky, Montana, Nebraska, New Mexico, Oregon, Rhode Island, South Carolina, Tennessee, and Virginia. All other states have written their own laws.

The following list shows the main Landlord-Tenant Statutes for all 50 states, plus the District of Columbia. Landlord-tenant laws are constantly being revised, so be sure to use the links provided for each state or city to guarantee you have the latest information. Note that several major cities have rent control or other landlord-tenant laws that are different than state law. This information is for general background only; you should always consult with a landlord-tenant legal expert for specific issues. *Note:* For additional state-specific Web sites, check out the file on the CD.

Check with your local National Apartment Association (NAA) affiliate and Institute of Real Estate Management (IREM) chapter for info about recent or upcoming changes in landlord-tenant laws that impact you and your tenants.

Landlord-Tenant Statutes by State

Alabama

Web site: www.legislature.state.al.us/CodeofAlabama/1975/coatoc.htm
AL Code: Title 35 §35-9-101 to §35-9-603
Rent issues: §35-9A-161
Security deposit: §35-9A-201
Nonpayment of rent: §35-9A-421(a), §35-9A-421(d)
Breach of lease: §35-9A-105
Withholding of rent: §35-9A-407
Repair and deduct: §35-9A-407
Access by landlord: §35-9A-303
Retaliation by landlord: §35-9A-427, §35-9A-501
Abandoned property: §35-9A-423(d)

Alaska

Web site: www.legis.state.ak.us/folhome.htm
AK Statute: Title 34/Chapter 3 §34.03.010 to §34.03.380
Rent issues: §34.03.020(c)
Security deposit: §34.03.070
Nonpayment of rent: §09.45.105, §34.03.220
Breach of lease: §09.45.090, §09.50.210, §34.03.220
Withholding of rent: §34.03.190
Repair and deduct: §34.03.180
Access by landlord: §34.03.140, .300 (a) & (b)
Retaliation by landlord: §34.03.310(a), §34.03.360
Abandoned property: §34.03.260

Arizona

Web site: www.azleg.state.az.us/ArizonaRevisedStatutes.asp
AZ Revised Statute: Title 33/Chapter 3 (§33-301 to §33-381), Title 33/Chapter 10 (§33-1301 to §33-1381), Title 12/Chapter 8 (§12-1171 to §12-1183)
Rent issues: §33-1314(B), (C)
Security deposit: §33-1321
Nonpayment of rent: §33-1368(B)
Breach of lease: §33-1368(A)
Withholding of rent: §33-1365
Repair and deduct: §33-1363, §1364
Access by landlord: §33-1343
Retaliation by landlord: §33-1381
Abandoned property: §33-1370

Arkansas

Web site: 170.94.58.9/data/ar_code.asp
AR Code: Title 18, Chapter 16 (§18-16-101 to §18-16-306); Title 20, Chapter 27 (§20-27-601 to §20-27-608)
Rent issues:
Security deposit: §18-16-301 to §18-16-306
Nonpayment of rent: §18-16-101, §18-60-304
Breach of lease:
Withholding of rent:
Repair and deduct:
Access by landlord:
Retaliation by landlord: §20-27-608 (lead hazards)
Abandoned property: §18-16-108

California

Web site: www.leginfo.ca.gov/calaw.html
CA Civil Code: Division 3/Part 4/Title 5/Chapters 1-7 (§1925-1954, §1961-1962.7)
Rent issues: §1942, §1947, §1962; Orozco v. Casimiro, 212 Cal. App. 4th Supp. 7 (2004)
Security deposit: §1940.5 (g), §1950.5
Nonpayment of rent: §1161(2), §1162
Breach of lease: §1161(3)
Withholding of rent: Green v. Sup. Ct: 10 Cal. 3d 616 (1974)

Repair and deduct: Civ. Code §1942
Access by landlord: §1954
Retaliation by landlord: §1942.5
Abandoned property: §1965, §1980 to §1991

Colorado

Web site: www.michie.com/colorado/lpext.dll?f=templates&fn=main-h.htm&cp=
CO Revised Statute: (§38-12-101 to §38-12-104, §38-12-301 to §38-12-302, §13-40-101 to §13-40-123)
Rent issues:
Security deposit: §38-12-102 to §38-12-104
Nonpayment of rent: §13-40-104
Breach of lease: §13-40-104(1) (d.5), (e)
Withholding of rent:
Repair and deduct: Shanahan v. Collins, 539 P.2d 1261 (Colo. 1975)
Access by landlord:
Retaliation by landlord: W.W.G. Corp. v. Hughes, 960 P. 2d 720 (1998)
Abandoned property: §13-40-122, §38-20-116

Connecticut

Web site: www.cga.ct.gov/asp/menu/Statutes.asp
CT General Statute: Title 47a/ Chapter 830 (§47a-1 to §47a-74)
Rent issues: §47a-3a, §47a-15a, §47a-4a(8)
Security deposit: §47a-21, §47a-22a
Nonpayment of rent: §47a-15a, §47-23
Breach of lease: §47a-15
Withholding of rent: §47a-14a, §47a-14h
Repair and deduct: §47a-13
Access by landlord: §47a-16 to §47a-16a
Retaliation by landlord: §47a-20, §47a-33
Abandoned property: §47a-11b, §47a-42

Delaware

Web site: michie.lexisnexis.com/delaware/lpext.dll?f=templates&fn=main-h.htm&cp (Click the Delaware Code folder in the left panel.)
DE Code: Title 25/Part III/Chapters 53 and 55 (§5101 to §5907)
Rent issues: §5501(b), (d)
Security deposit: §5514
Nonpayment of rent: §5501(d), §5502
Breach of lease: §5513(a)
Withholding of rent: §5308(b)(3)
Repair and deduct: §5307
Access by landlord: §5509, §5510
Retaliation by landlord: §5516
Abandoned property: §5507, §5715

District of Columbia

Web site: government.westlaw.com/linkedslice/default.asp?rs=gvt1.0&vr=2.0&sp=dcc-1000
D.C. Code: §42-3201 to §42-3610; D.C. Municipal Regulations, title 14, § 300 to §311
Rent issues:
Security deposit: §42-3502.17; Mun. Regs. Title 14 §308 to §311
Nonpayment of rent: §42-3505.01
Breach of lease: §42-3505.01
Withholding of rent: Javins v. First Nat'l Realty: 428 F.2d 1071 (DC circ. 1970)
Repair and deduct: §6-751.10 (fire alarms only)
Access by landlord:
Retaliation by landlord: §42-3505.02
Abandoned property:

Florida

Web site: www.leg.state.fl.us/statutes/index.cfm?Mode=ViewStatutes&Submenu=1
FL Statute: Title VI, Chapter 83, Part II, §83.40 to §83.682; Title XL, Chapter 715

Rent issues: §83.46(1)
Security deposit: §83.49
Nonpayment of rent: §83.56(3)
Breach of lease: §83.56
Withholding of rent: §83.60
Repair and deduct:
Access by landlord: §83.53
Retaliation by landlord: §83.64
Abandoned property: §715.104 to §715.111

Georgia

Web site: www.lexis-nexis.com/hottopics/gacode/default.asp
GA Code: §44-7-1 to §44-7-82
Rent issues: §44-7-1 to §44-7-16
Security deposit: §44-7-30 to §44-7-36
Nonpayment of rent: §44-7-50 to §44-7-52
Breach of lease: LL can terminate with Unconditional Quit Notice
Withholding of rent: §44-7-54
Repair and deduct:
Access by landlord:
Retaliation by landlord:
Abandoned property:

Hawaii

Web site: www.capitol.hawaii.gov/site1/docs/docs.asp?press1=docs
HI Revised Statute: §521-1 to §521-78
Rent issues: §521-21(b)
Security deposit: §521-44
Nonpayment of rent: §521-68(a), (b)
Breach of lease: §521-51, 521-69 to §521-72
Withholding of rent: §521-78
Repair and deduct: §521-64
Access by landlord: §521-53, §521-70(b), §521-73
Retaliation by landlord: §521-74
Abandoned property: §521-56

Idaho

Web site: www3.state.id.us/idstat/TOC/idstTOC.html

ID Code: Title 6, §6-201 to §6-324; Title 55, §55-201 to §55-313
Rent issues: §6-301 to §6-324
Security deposit: §6-321
Nonpayment of rent: §6-303(2)
Breach of lease: §6-303
Withholding of rent:
Repair and deduct:
Access by landlord:
Retaliation by landlord: §55-2015; Wright v. Brandy, 126 Idaho 671, 889 P.2d 105 (Ct. App. 1995)
Abandoned property: §6-311C

Illinois

Web site: www.ilga.gov/legislation/ilcs/ilcs.asp
IL Compiled Statute: Chap. 735 §5/9-201 to §321; Ch. 765 para. §705/0.01 to §742/30
Rent issues:
Security deposit: Ch. 765 para. §710, §715
Nonpayment of rent: Ch. 735 para. §5/9-209
Breach of lease: LL can terminate with Unconditional Quit Notice
Withholding of rent: Ch. 765 para. §735/2 to §735/2.2
Repair and deduct: Ch. 765 §742/5
Access by landlord:
Retaliation by landlord: Ch. 765 para. §720/1
Abandoned property: Ch. 735, §5/9-318

Indiana

Web site: www.ai.org/legislative/ic/code/
IN Code: §32-31-1-1 to §32-31-8-6
Rent issues: Watson v. Penn, 108 Ind. 21, 8 NE 636 (1886)
Security deposit: §32-31-3-9 to §32-31-3-19
Nonpayment of rent: §32-31-1-6
Breach of lease: LL can terminate with Unconditional Quit Notice
Withholding of rent:

Repair and deduct:
Access by landlord:
Retaliation by landlord:
Abandoned property: §32-31-4-1 to 32-31-4-5, §32-31-5-5

Iowa

Web site: www2.legis.state.ia.us/IACODE/Current/
IA Code: Title XIV, §562A.1-.37 and §535.2
Rent issues: §562A.9(3), §535.2(7)
Security deposit: §562A.12
Nonpayment of rent: §562A.27(2)
Breach of lease: §562A.27(1), .27A
Withholding of rent: §562A.24
Repair and deduct: §562A.23
Access by landlord: §562A.19, §562.28, §562.29
Retaliation by landlord: §562A.36
Abandoned property:

Kansas

Web site: www.kslegislature.org/legsrv-statutes/index.do
KS Statute: §58-2501 to 58-2573
Rent issues: §58-2545(c)
Security deposit: §58-2550
Nonpayment of rent: §58-2507, §58-2508, §58-2564(b)
Breach of lease: §58-2559, §58-2564
Withholding of rent: §58-2561
Repair and deduct:
Access by landlord: §58-2557, §58-2565
Retaliation by landlord: §58-2572
Abandoned property: §58-2565

Kentucky

Web site: www.lrc.state.ky.us/statrev/frontpg.htm
KY Revised Statute: Chapter 383, §383.010 to §383.715
Rent issues: §383.565
Security deposit: §383.580
Nonpayment of rent: §383.660(2)
Breach of lease: §383.660(1)

Withholding of rent: §383.645
Repair and deduct: §383.635, §383.640
Access by landlord: §383.615, §383.665, §383.670
Retaliation by landlord: §383.705
Abandoned property:

Louisiana

Web site: www.legis.state.la.us/lss/toc.htm
LA Revised Statute: §9:3201 to §9:3261; Civil Code §2668 to §2729
Rent issues:
Security deposit: §9:3251 to §9:3254
Nonpayment of rent: CCP §4701, §9:3259
Breach of lease: CCP §4701
Withholding of rent:
Repair and deduct: Civil Code §2694
Access by landlord: Civil Code §2693
Retaliation by landlord:
Abandoned property: Donnell v. Gray, 34 So. 2d 648 (1948)

Maine

Web site: janus.state.me.us/legis/statutes/
ME Revised Statute: Title 14 §6001 to §6046
Rent issues: §6028
Security deposit: §6031 to §6038
Nonpayment of rent: §6002
Breach of lease: LL can terminate with Unconditional Quit Notice
Withholding of rent: §6021
Repair and deduct: §6026
Access by landlord: §6025
Retaliation by landlord: §6001
Abandoned property: §6005, §6013(3), (4)

Maryland

Web site: mgasearch.state.md.us/verity.asp
MD Code: §8-101 to §8-604
Rent issues: §8-208(d)(3)

Security deposit: §8-203
Nonpayment of rent: §8-401
Breach of lease: §8-402.1
Withholding of rent: §8-118, §8-211, §8-211.1
Repair and deduct:
Access by landlord:
Retaliation by landlord: §8-206, §8-208.1, §8-208.2
Abandoned property:

Massachusetts

Web site: www.mass.gov/legis/laws/mgl/
MA General Laws: Chapter 186 §1-22, Chapter 239
Rent issues: Ch. 186 §11, §15B(1)(c); Ch. 239 §8A
Security deposit: Ch. 186 §15B
Nonpayment of rent: Ch. 186 §11, §11A, §12
Breach of lease: LL can terminate with Unconditional Quit Notice
Withholding of rent: Ch. 239 §8A
Repair and deduct: Ch. 186 §14
Access by landlord: Ch. 186 §15B1(a)
Retaliation by landlord: Ch. 239 §2A, Ch. 186 §18
Abandoned property:

Michigan

Web site: www.legislature.mi.gov/
MI Compiled Laws: §554.131 to §554.201, §554.601-§554.641
Rent issues: Hilsendegen v. Scheich, 21 N.W. 2d 894 (1885)
Security deposit: §554.602 to §554.616
Nonpayment of rent: §554.134(2)
Breach of lease: §600.5714(c)
Withholding of rent: §125.530
Repair and deduct: Rome v. Walker, 198 N.W. 2d 458 (1972); §554.139
Access by landlord:
Retaliation by landlord: §600.5720
Abandoned property:

Minnesota

Web site: www.leg.state.mn.us/leg/statutes.asp
MN Statute: §504B.001 to .471; §609.5317
Rent issues:
Security deposit: §504B.178
Nonpayment of rent: §504B.135, §504B.291
Breach of lease: §504B.281, §504B.285
Withholding of rent: §504B.441
Repair and deduct: §504B.385
Access by landlord: §504B.211
Retaliation by landlord: §504B.285, §504B.441
Abandoned property: §504B.271

Mississippi

Web site: michie.lexisnexis.com/mississippi/lpext.dll?f=templates&fn=main-h.htm&cp (Click the Mississippi Code of 1972 folder in the left panel.)
MS Code: Title 89, §89-7-1 to §89-7-125, §89-8-1 to §89-8-27
Rent issues:
Security deposit: §89-8-21
Nonpayment of rent: §89-7-27, §89-7-45
Breach of lease: §89-8-13
Withholding of rent:
Repair and deduct: §89-8-15
Access by landlord:
Retaliation by landlord: §89-8-17
Abandoned property:

Missouri

Web site: www.moga.mo.gov/statutesearch/
MO Revised Statute: Chapter 441, §441.005-§441.880; Chapter 535, §535.010-§535.300
Rent issues: §535.060
Security deposit: §535.300
Nonpayment of rent: §535.010
Breach of lease: LL can terminate

with Unconditional Quit Notice
Withholding of rent: §441.570,
§441.580
Repair and deduct: §441.234
Access by landlord:
Retaliation by landlord:
Abandoned property: §441.065

Montana

Web site: data.opi.state.mt.
us/bills/mca_toc/index.htm
MT Code: §70-24-101 to §70-26-110
Rent issues: §70-24-201(2)(b)(c)
Security deposit: §70-25-201 to
§70-24-206
Nonpayment of rent: §70-24-422(2)
Breach of lease: §70-24-422
Withholding of rent: §70-24-421
Repair and deduct: §70-24-406 to
§70-24-408
Access by landlord: §70-24-312
Retaliation by landlord: §70-24-431
Abandoned property: §70-24-430

Nebraska

Web site: uniweb.legislature.
ne.gov/QS/laws.html
NE Revised Statute: §76-1401 to
§76-1449, §69-2301 to §69-2314
Rent Issues: §76-1414(3)
Security deposit: §76-1416
Nonpayment of rent: §76-1431(2)
Breach of lease: §76-1431
Withholding of rent: §76-1428
Repair and deduct: §76-1427
Access by landlord: §76-1423,
§76-1438
Retaliation by landlord: §76-14,
§76-1439
Abandoned property: §69-2301 to
§69-2314

Nevada

Web site: www.leg.state.nv.us/
law1.cfm
NV Revised Statute: §118A.010 to
§118A.530, §40.215 to §40.425

Rent issues: §118A.200(2)(g), (3)(c);
§118A.210
Security deposit: §118A.240,
§118A.250
Nonpayment of rent: §40.2512
Breach of lease: §40.2516
Withholding of rent: §118A.490
Repair and deduct: §118A.360,
§118A.380
Access by landlord: §118A.330
Retaliation by landlord: §118A.510
Abandoned property: §118A.450,
§118A.460

New Hampshire

Web site: gencourt.state.nh.
us/rsa/html/indexes/default.
html
NH Revised Statute: §540:1 to
§540:29 to 540-A:1 to §540-A:8,
§540-B:1 to §540 B:10
Rent issues:
Security deposit: §540-A:5 to
§540-A:8, §540-B:10
Nonpayment of rent: §540:2, §540:3,
§540:9, §540:9-a
Breach of lease: LL can terminate
with Unconditional Quit Notice
Withholding of rent: §540:13-d
Repair and deduct:
Access by landlord: §540-A:3
Retaliation by landlord: §540:13-a,
§540:13-b
Abandoned property: §540-A:3(VII)

New Jersey

Web site: lis.njleg.state.nj.
us/cgi-bin/om_isapi.dll?clie
ntID=159554&depth=2&expandhe
adings=off&headingswithhits=
on&infobase=statutes.
nfo&softpage=TOC_Frame_Pg42
NJ Statute: §46:8-1 to §46:8-50
Rent issues: §2A-42-6.1
Security deposit: §46:8-19 to §46:8-26
Nonpayment of rent: §2A:18-53,
§2A:18-61.1, §2A.18-61.2, §2A:42-9
Breach of lease: §2A:18-53(c),

§2A:18-61.1(e)(1)
Withholding of rent: §2A:42-85 to §2A:42-92
Repair and deduct: Marini v. Ireland, 265 A.2d 526 (1970)
Access by landlord:
Retaliation by landlord: §2A:42-10.10, §2A:42-10.12
Abandoned property: §2A:18-72 to 2A:18-82

New Mexico

Web site: www.conwaygreene. com/nmsu/lpext. dll?f=templates&fn=main-h. htm&2.0
NM Statute: §47-8-1 to §47-8-52
Rent issues: §47-8-15
Security deposit: §47-8-18
Nonpayment of rent: §47-8-33
Breach of lease: §47-8-33
Withholding of rent: §47-8-30
Repair and deduct: §47-8-29
Access by landlord: §47-8-24
Retaliation by landlord: §47-8-39
Abandoned property: §47-8-34.1

New York

Web site: public.leginfo. state.ny.us/menugetf. cgi?COMMONQUERY=LAWS
NY Gen. Obligation Law (GOB), Article 7, §7-101 to -109; Real Property Laws (RPP), Article 7, §220-238; Real Property Acts §701-853; Multi-Dwelling Laws (MDW), Articles 1-11; Multiple Residence (MRE), Articles 1-9
Rent issues:
Security deposit: GOB §7-101 to §7-109
Nonpayment of rent: RPA §711(2)
Breach of lease: RPA §711(3), § 711(6)
Withholding of rent: MRE §305-A, RPP 235-B
Repair and deduct: MRE §305-C, RPP 235-A

Access by landlord:
Retaliation by landlord: RPP 223-B
Abandoned property:

North Carolina

Web site: www.ncleg.net/ gascripts/Statutes/ Statutes.asp
NC General Statute: Chapter 42, §42-1 to §42-14.3; §42-25.6 to §42-76
Rent issues: §42-46
Security deposit: §42-50 to §42-56
Nonpayment of rent: §42-3
Breach of lease: LL can terminate with Unconditional Quit Notice if lease permits
Withholding of rent: §42-44
Repair and deduct:
Access by landlord:
Retaliation by landlord: §42-37.1 to §42-37.3
Abandoned property: §42-25.9, §42-36.2

North Dakota

Web site: www.legis.nd.gov/ information/statutes/cent-code.html
ND Century Code: §33-06-01 to §33-06-04, §47-16-01 to §47-16-41
Rent issues: §47-16-07
Security deposit: §47-16-07.1, §47-16-07.2
Nonpayment of rent: §33-06-01
Breach of lease: LL can terminate with Unconditional Quit Notice if term is material
Withholding of rent:
Repair and deduct: §47-16-13
Access by landlord: §47-16-07.3
Retaliation by landlord:
Abandoned property: §47-16-30.1

Ohio

Web site: codes.ohio.gov/orc
OH Revised Code: §5321.01 to §5321.19

Rent issues:
Security deposit: §5321.16
Nonpayment of rent:
Breach of lease: §5321.11
Withholding of rent: §5321.07
Repair and deduct:
Access by landlord: §5321.04(A)(8), §5321.05(B)
Retaliation by landlord: §5321.02
Abandoned property:

Oklahoma

Web site: oklegal.onenet.net/
statutes.basic.html
OK Statute: Title 41 §101 to §136
Rent issues: §109, §132
Security deposit: §115
Nonpayment of rent: §131
Breach of lease: §132
Withholding of rent: §121
Repair and deduct: §121
Access by landlord: §128
Retaliation by landlord:
Abandoned property: §130

Oregon

Web site: www.leg.state.or.
us/ors/
OR Revised Statute: §90.100 to §90.875, §91.010 to §91.225, §105.165
Rent issues: OR §90.240(6)(a), §90.260
Security deposit: §90.300 to §90.302
Nonpayment of rent: §90.400(2)
Breach of lease: §90.400(1), §90.405
Withholding of rent: §90.370
Repair and deduct: §90.360, §90.365
Access by landlord: §90.322
Retaliation by landlord: §90.385
Abandoned property: §90.425, §105.165

Pennsylvania

Web site: www.pacode.com/
PA Consolidated Statute: Title 68 §250.101 to §250-.510-B, §399.1 to §399.18

Rent issues:
Security deposit: §250.511a to §250.512
Nonpayment of rent: §250.501(b)
Breach of lease: §250.501, §250.505a
Withholding of rent: §250.206, §1700-1
Repair and deduct: Pugh v. Holmes, 405 A.2d 897 (1979)
Access by landlord:
Retaliation by landlord: §250.205, §399.11
Abandoned property:

Rhode Island

Web site: www.rilin.state.ri.
us/Statutes/Statutes.html
RI General Law: §34-18-1 to §34-18-57
Rent issues: §34-18-15(c), §34-18-35
Security deposit: §34-18-19
Nonpayment of rent: §34-18-35, §34-18-51
Breach of lease: §34-18-36
Withholding of rent: §34-18-32
Repair and deduct: §34-18-30, §34-18-31
Access by landlord: §34-18-26
Retaliation by landlord: §34-18-46
Abandoned property:

South Carolina

Web site: www.scstatehouse.
net/code/statmast.htm
SC Code: §27-37-10, §27-40-10 to §27-40-940
Rent issues: §27-40-310(c)
Security deposit: §27-40-410
Nonpayment of rent: §27-40-710
Breach of lease: §27-40-710, §27-37-10(B)
Withholding of rent: §27-40-640, §27-40-790
Repair and deduct: §27-40-630, §27-40-640, §27-40-790
Access by landlord: §27-40-530
Retaliation by landlord: §27-40-910
Abandoned property: §27-40-730

South Dakota

Web site: legis.state.sd.us/statutes/index.aspx

SD Codified Laws: §21-16-1 to 21-16-12, §43-32-1 to §43-32-30

Rent issues: §43-32-12

Security deposit: §43-32-6.1, §43-32-24

Nonpayment of rent: §21-16-2

Breach of lease: §21-16-2

Withholding of rent: §43-32-9

Repair and deduct: §43-32-9

Access by landlord:

Retaliation by landlord: §43-32-27, §43-32-28

Abandoned property: §43-32-25, §43-32-26

Tennessee

Web site: michie.lexisnexis.com/tennessee/lpext.dll?f=templates&fn=main-h.htm&cp (Click the Tennessee Code folder in the left panel.)

TN Code: Title 66, §66-28-101 to §66-28-521

Rent issues: §66-28-201(c), (d)

Security deposit: §66-28-301

Nonpayment of rent: §66-28-505

Breach of lease: §66-28-401, §66-28-505(d)

Withholding of rent: §68-111-104

Repair and deduct: §66-28-502

Access by landlord: §66-28-403, §66-28-507

Retaliation by landlord: §66-28-514, §68-111-105

Abandoned property: §66-28-405

Texas

Web site: tlo2.tlc.state.tx.us/statutes/statutes.html

TX Property Code: Title 8, §91.001 to §92.355

Rent issues:

Security deposit: §92.101 to §92.109

Nonpayment of rent: §24.005

Breach of lease:

Withholding of rent:

Repair and deduct: §92.056, §92.0561

Access by landlord:

Retaliation by landlord: §92.331

Abandoned property:

Utah

Web site: www.le.state.ut.us/~code/code.htm

UT Code: Title 57, §57-17-1 to §57-17-5, §57-20-1, §57-21-1 to §57-21-14, §57-22-1 to §57-22-6, §78-36-12

Rent issues:

Security deposit: §57-17-1 to §57-21-5

Nonpayment of rent: §78-36-3(c)

Breach of lease: §78-36-3

Withholding of rent:

Repair and deduct:

Access by landlord: §57-22-5(2)(c)

Retaliation by landlord: Bldg. Monitoring Sys. v. Paxton, 905 P.2d 1215 (Utah 1995)

Abandoned property: §78-36-12.6

Vermont

Web site: www.leg.state.vt.us/statutes/statutes2.htm

VT Statute: Title 9, Chapter 137 §4451 to §4469

Rent issues: §4455

Security deposit: §4461

Nonpayment of rent: §4467(a)

Breach of lease: LL can terminate with Unconditional Quit Notice

Withholding of rent: §4458

Repair and deduct: §4459

Access by landlord: §4460

Retaliation by landlord: §4465

Abandoned property: §4462

Virginia

Web site: leg1.state.va.us/000/src.htm
VA Code: Title 55, §55-217 to §55-248.40
Rent issues: §55-248-7(c)
Security deposit: §55-248.15:1
Nonpayment of rent: §55-225, 55-243, §55-248.31
Breach of lease: §55-248.31
Withholding of rent: §55-248.25, §55-248.25:1, §55-248.27
Repair and deduct: §55-248.32
Access by landlord: §55-248.18, §55-248.38
Retaliation by landlord: §55-248.39
Abandoned property: §55-248.38:1, §55-248.38:2

Washington

Web site: apps.leg.wa.gov/rcw/
WA Revised Code: Title 59, §59.04.010 to §59.04.900, §59.18.010 to §59.18.911
Rent issues:
Security deposit: §59.18.260 to §59-18.285
Nonpayment of rent: §59.12.030(3)
Breach of lease: §59.12.030(4)
Withholding of rent: §59.18.110, §59.18.115
Repair and deduct: §59.18.100
Access by landlord: §59.18.150
Retaliation by landlord: §59.18.240, §59.18.250
Abandoned property: §59.18.310

West Virginia

Web site: www.legis.state.wv.us/WVCODE/masterfrm3Banner.cfm
WV Code: §37-6-1 to §37-6-30, 55-3A-1
Rent issues:
Security deposit:
Nonpayment of rent: §55-3A-1
Breach of lease: §55-3A-1
Withholding of rent:
Repair and deduct: Chewrant v. Bee, 28 S.E. 751 (1978)
Access by landlord:
Retaliation by landlord: Imperial Colliery Co. v. Fout, 373 S.E. 2d 489 (1998)
Abandoned property:

Wisconsin

Web site: www.legis.state.wi.us/rsb/stats.html
WI Statute: Chapter 704, §704.01 to §704.50; Administrative Code ATCP §134.01 to §134.10
Rent issues:
Security deposit: Code ATCP §134.06
Nonpayment of rent: §704.17
Breach of lease: §704.17
Withholding of rent: §704.07(4)
Repair and deduct:
Access by landlord: §704.05(2)
Retaliation by landlord: §704.45, ATCP §134.09(5)
Abandoned property: §704.05(5)

Wyoming

Web site: legisweb.state.wy.us/titles/statutes.htm
WY Statute: §34-2-128 to §34-2-129, §1-21-1201 to §1-21-1211
Rent issues:
Security deposit: §1-21-1208, §1-21-1209
Nonpayment of rent: §1-21-1201 to §1-21-1203
Breach of lease: §1-21-1205
Withholding of rent: §1-21-1206
Repair and deduct:
Access by landlord:
Retaliation by landlord:
Abandoned property: §1-21-1210

Scenario-Specific Laws by State

States with Rent Control

California	Maryland	New York
District of Columbia	New Jersey	

States that Preempt Rent Control

Alabama	Idaho	Massachusetts	North Carolina	Texas
Arizona	Illinois	Michigan	North Dakota	Utah
Arkansas	Indiana	Minnesota	Oklahoma	Vermont
Colorado	Iowa	Mississippi	Oregon	Virginia
Connecticut	Kansas	Missouri	South Carolina	Washington
Florida	Kentucky	New Hampshire	South Dakota	Wisconsin
Georgia	Louisiana	New Mexico	Tennessee	Wyoming

Note: States not listed in the previous two tables don't have rent control and/or preemption.

States that Allow a Tenant to Repair and Deduct

Alaska	Illinois	Minnesota	New York	South Dakota
Arizona	Iowa	Mississippi	North Dakota	Tennessee
California	Kentucky	Missouri	Oklahoma	Texas
Connecticut	Louisiana	Montana	Oregon	Vermont
Delaware	Maine	Nebraska	Pennsylvania	Washington
District of Columbia*	Massachusetts	Nevada	Rhode Island	West Virginia
Hawaii	Michigan	New Jersey	South Carolina	

* Fire alarm installation only.

States that Allow Tenant to Withhold Rent if Landlord Fails to Provide Essential Services or Habitable Premises

Alaska	Illinois	Minnesota	New York	South Dakota
Arizona	Iowa	Missouri	North Carolina	Tennessee

California	Kansas	Montana	Ohio	Vermont
Connecticut	Kentucky	Nebraska	Oklahoma	Virginia
Delaware	Maine	Nevada	Oregon	Washington
District of Columbia	Maryland	New Hampshire	Pennsylvania	Wisconsin
Florida	Massachusetts	New Jersey	Rhode Island	Wyoming
Hawaii	Michigan	New Mexico	South Carolina	

Notice to Terminate a Month-to-Month Tenancy by State

State	Notice from Tenant to Landlord	Notice from Landlord to Tenant	Statute
Alabama	10 days	10 days	§35-9-3, §35-9-5
Alaska	30 days	30 days	§34.03.290(b)
Arizona	30 days	30 days	§33-1375
Arkansas	10 days	10 days	§18-16-101
California	30 days	30 days (60 days in some locations)	§1946, 827a
Colorado	10 days	10 days	§13-40-107
Connecticut	N/A	N/A	N/A
Delaware	60 days	60 days	§5106, §5107
District of Columbia	30 days	30 days	§42-3202
Florida	15 days	15 days	§83.57
Georgia	30 days	60 days	§44-7-6, §44-7-7
Hawaii	28 days	45 days	§521-71, §521-21(d)
Idaho	1 month	1 month	§55-208, §55-307
Illinois	30 days	30 days	§5/9-207
Indiana	1 month	1 month	§32-31-1-1, §32-31-5-4
Iowa	30 days	30 days	§562A.34, §562A.13(5)
Kansas	30 days	30 days	§58-2570
Kentucky	30 days	30 days	§383.695
Louisiana	10 days	10 days	§2728

(continued)

Notice to Terminate a Month-to-Month Tenancy by State *(continued)*

State	Notice from Tenant to Landlord	Notice from Landlord to Tenant	Statute
Maine	30 days	30 days	§6002,§6015
Maryland	1 month	1 month	§8-402(b)(3)&(4)
Massachusetts	Longer interval between payments or 30 days	Longer interval between payments or 30 days	§186,§12
Michigan	Interval between payments	Interval between payments	§554.134
Minnesota	Interval between payments	Interval between payments	§504B.135
Mississippi	30 days	30 days	§89-8-19
Missouri	1 month	1 month	§441.060
Montana	30 days	30 days	§70-24-441, §70-26-109
Nebraska	30 days	30 days	§76-1437
Nevada	30 days	30 days	§40.251, §118A.300
New Hampshire	30 days	30 days	§540:2, §540:3
New Jersey	N/A	N/A	N/A
New Mexico	30 days	30 days	§47-8-37, §47-8-15(F)
New York	1 month	1 month	§232-B
North Carolina	7 days	7 days	§42-14
North Dakota	30 days	30 days	§47-16-15, §47-16-07
Ohio	30 days	30 days	§5321.17
Oklahoma	30 days	30 days	§111
Oregon	30 days	30 days	§91.070, §90.427
Pennsylvania	N/A	N/A	N/A
Rhode Island	30 days	30 days	§34-18-16.1, §34-18-37
South Carolina	30 days	30 days	§27-40-770
South Dakota	1 month	1 month	§43-32-13, §43-8-8

State	Notice from Tenant to Landlord	Notice from Landlord to Tenant	Statute
Tennessee	30 days	30 days	§66-28-512
Texas	1 month	1 month	§91.001
Utah	N/A	15 days	§78-36-3
Vermont	1 rental period	30 days	§4467, §4456(d)
Virginia	30 days	30 days	§55-248.37, §55-248.7
Washington	20 days	20 days	§59.18200, §59.18.140
West Virginia	1 month	1 month	§37-6-5
Wisconsin	28 days	28 days	§704.19
Wyoming	N/A	N/A	N/A

Landlord's Duty to Rerent the Rental Unit

States Where Landlord Must Mitigate or Minimize Potential Loss of Rent if Tenant Vacates Early

Alabama	Hawaii	Kentucky	New Jersey	Oregon	Virginia
Alaska	Idaho	Maine	New Mexico	Rhode Island	Washington
Arizona	Illinois	Maryland	North Carolina	South Carolina	Wisconsin
California	Indiana	Montana	North Dakota	Tennessee	Wyoming
Connecticut	Iowa	Nebraska	Ohio	Texas	
Delaware	Kansas	Nevada	Oklahoma	Utah	

States Where Landlord Isn't Required to Rerent Unit

Arkansas	District of Columbia	Georgia	Minnesota	Missouri	Vermont
Colorado	Florida	Massachusetts	Mississippi	Pennsylvania	

NOTE: States not listed above don't have a statute or court case addressing a landlord's duty to mitigate loss of income when a tenant vacates early.

Time Permitted for Tenant to Pay Rent after Nonpayment Notice Served

State	Time Allotment	Statute
Alabama	7 days Landlord can terminate with Unconditional Quit Notice on 14 days' notice	§35-9A-421
Alaska	7 days	§09.45.090, §34.03.220
Arizona	5 days	§33-1368
Arkansas	Landlord may terminate with Unconditional Quit Notice	§18-60-304, §18-16-101
California	3 days	§1161(2)
Colorado	3 days	§13-40-104(1)(d)
Connecticut	9 days Landlord can't serve Unconditional Quit Notice unless rent is 9 or more days late	§47a-23, §47a-15a
Delaware	5 days	§5501(d), §5502
District of Columbia	30 days	§42-3505.01
Florida	3 days	§83.56(3)
Georgia	Landlord can file for eviction immediately if rent not paid; tenant has 7 days to pay	§44-7-50, §44-7-52
Hawaii	5 days	§521-68
Idaho	3 days	§6-303(2)
Illinois	5 days	§5/9-209
Indiana	10 days	§32-31-1-6
Louisiana	Landlord can terminate with Unconditional Quit Notice	§4701A
Maine	7 days (after rent is 7 days late)	§6002
Maryland	5 days	§8-401
Massachusetts	14 days or per lease; immediate for holdover tenants	§186, §11 to §12
Michigan	7 days	§554.134(2)
Minnesota	14 days	§504B.135

State	Time Allotment	Statute
Mississippi	3 days	§89-7-27, §89-7-45
Missouri	Landlord can terminate with Unconditional Quit Notice	§535.010
Montana	3 days	§70-24-422(2)
Nebraska	3 days	§76-1431(2)
Nevada	5 days	§40.2512
New Hampshire	7 days	40:2, §540:3, §540:9
New Jersey	30 days	§2A:18-53, §2A:18-61.1, §2A:18-61.2, §2A:42-9
New Mexico	3 days	§47-8-33(D)
New York	3 days	§711(2)
North Carolina	10 days	§42-3
North Dakota	Landlord can file eviction when rent is 3 days late; can terminate with Unconditional Quit Notice	§33-06-01
Ohio	Landlord can terminate with Unconditional Quit Notice	N/A
Oklahoma	5 days	§131
Oregon	72 hours (after rent is 8 days late); 144 hours (after rent is 5 days late)	§90.400(2)(b)
Pennsylvania	10 days	§250.501(b)
Rhode Island	5 days (after rent is 15 days late)	§34-18-35
South Carolina	5 days (or less, per rental contract)	§27-40-710(B), §27-37-10(B)
Utah	3 days	§78-36-3(c)
Vermont	14 days	§4467(a)
Virginia	5 days	§55-225, §55-243, §55-248.31

(continued)

Time Permitted for Tenant to Pay Rent after Nonpayment Notice Served *(continued)*

State	Time Allotment	Statute
Washington	3 days	§59.12.030(3)
West Virginia	Landlord can file for eviction immediately without giving notice or opportunity to cure	§55-3A-1
Wisconsin	5 days (month-to-month); 30 days (lease greater than 1 year)	§704.17
Wyoming	3 days (if rent is 3 days or more late); can also terminate with Unconditional Quit Notice	§1-21-1002 to §1-21-1003

States that Allow Landlord to Use Unconditional Quit Notice without Permitting Tenant to Pay Past-Due Rent or Cure a Lease Violation

Alabama	Illinois	Maine	New Hampshire	Ohio	Texas
Arkansas	Indiana	Minnesota	North Carolina	Pennsylvania	West Virginia
Georgia	Louisiana	Missouri	North Dakota	South Dakota	Wyoming

Security Deposit Requirements

States Requiring Security Deposits Held in Separate Account

Alaska	Florida[a]	Maine	New Hampshire	North Dakota	Washington
Connecticut	Georgia[a/b]	Maryland	New Jersey	Oklahoma	
Delaware	Iowa	Massachusetts	New York	Pennsylvania	
District of Columbia	Kentucky	Michigan	North Carolina	Tennessee[c]	
Connecticut	Illinois[e]	Massachusetts	New Jersey[g]	North Dakota	Virginia

District of Columbia	Iowa[f]	Minnesota	New Mexico	Ohio
Florida[d]	Maryland	New Hampshire	New York[h]	Pennsylvania

a Landlord can post bond in lieu of separate security deposit account.
b Only applies to legal entities, not natural persons who own rental units.
c Not required to disclose location in all cities.
d Not required, but conditions apply if interest paid on security deposits.
e Only if landlord owns 25 or more rental units.
f Landlord can keep interest earned on security deposit during first five years of tenancy.
g Not applicable if landlord owns fewer than ten units.
h Not required if building contains five or fewer rental units.

Security Deposit Limits by State

State	Limit
Alabama	1 month's rent (not including pet deposit, alterations, or increased risk)
Alaska	2 months' rent (if rent is up to $2,000 per month)
Arizona	1½ months' rent (unless tenant voluntarily agrees to higher deposit)
Arkansas	2 months' rent
California	2 months' rent (unfurnished); 3 months' rent (furnished); add ½ month's rent for waterbed
Colorado	N/A
Connecticut	2 months' rent (1 month's rent if tenant is age 62 or older)
Delaware	1 month's rent (1 year or longer lease); no limit (month-to-month); pet deposit up to 1 month's rent
District of Columbia	1 month's rent
Florida	N/A
Georgia	N/A
Hawaii	1 month's rent
Idaho	N/A
Illinois	N/A
Indiana	N/A
Iowa	2 months rent

(continued)

Security Deposit Limits by State *(continued)*

State	Limit
Kansas	1 month's rent (unfurnished); 1½ months' rent (furnished); pet deposit up to ½ month's rent
Kentucky	N/A
Louisiana	N/A
Maine	2 months' rent
Maryland	2 months' rent
Massachusetts	1 month's rent
Michigan	1½ months' rent
Minnesota	N/A
Mississippi	N/A
Missouri	2 months' rent
Montana	N/A
Nebraska	1 month's rent (no pets); 1¼ months' rent (pet)
Nevada	3 months' rent
New Hampshire	Greater of 1 month's rent or $100; no limit if landlord and tenant share facilities
New Jersey	1½ months' rent
New Mexico	1 month's rent (agreement less than 1 year); no limit for lease greater than 1 year
New York	N/A
North Carolina	1½ months' rent for month-to-month; 2 months' rent if lease
North Dakota	1 month's rent; greater of 2 months' rent or $2,500 if tenant has pet
Ohio	N/A
Oklahoma	N/A
Oregon	N/A
Pennsylvania	2 months' rent (1st year of tenancy), 1 month's rent thereafter
Rhode Island	1 month's Rent
South Carolina	N/A
South Dakota	1 month's rent (can be higher if mutually agreed where special conditions pose a danger to premises' maintenance)
Tennessee	N/A
Texas	N/A
Utah	N/A
Vermont	N/A

Virginia	2 months' rent
Washington	N/A
West Virginia	N/A
Wisconsin	N/A
Wyoming	N/A

Deadline to Account for or Itemize Charges and Return of Deposit Balance (If Any) by State

State	*Deadline*
Alabama	35 days
Alaska	14 days with proper notice; 30 days without proper notice
Arizona	14 days
Arkansas	30 days
California	3 weeks
Colorado	1 month or lease may state up to 60 days; 72 hours under certain dangerous conditions
Connecticut	Later of 15 days from receiving tenant's forwarding address or 30 days
Delaware	20 days
District of Columbia	45 days
Florida	15 to 60 days, depending whether tenant disputes itemized deductions
Georgia	1 month
Hawaii	14 days
Idaho	21 days; up to 30 days if mutually agreed
Illinois	30 to 45 days, depending whether tenant disputes itemized deductions
Indiana	45 days
Iowa	30 days
Kansas	30 days
Kentucky	30 to 60 days, depending whether tenant disputes itemized deductions
Louisiana	1 month
Maine	21 days; 30 days with written rental contract

(continued)

Deadline to Account for or Itemize Charges and Return of Deposit Balance (If Any) by State *(continued)*

State	Deadline
Maryland	30 to 45 days based on whether tenant was evicted or abandoned the rental unit
Massachusetts	30 days
Michigan	30 days
Minnesota	30 days after vacating and providing forwarding address; 5 days if building is condemned
Mississippi	45 days
Missouri	30 days
Montana	30 days; 10 days if no deductions
Nebraska	14 days
Nevada	30 days
New Hampshire	30 days
New Jersey	30 days; 5 days if tenant vacates due to fire, flood, condemnation, or evacuation
New Mexico	30 days
New York	Reasonable time frame
North Carolina	30 days
North Dakota	30 days
Ohio	30 days
Oklahoma	30 days
Oregon	31 days
Pennsylvania	30 days
Rhode Island	20 days
South Carolina	30 days
South Dakota	Two weeks to return entire deposit or portion and supply reasons for withholding; 45 days if tenant requests itemized accounting
Tennessee	No deadline to return deposit, bu 10 days to itemize
Texas	30 days
Utah	Later of 15 days from receiving tenant's forwarding address or 30 days
Vermont	14 days
Virginia	45 days
Washington	14 days
West Virginia	N/A
Wisconsin	21 days
Wyoming	Later of 15 days from receiving tenant's forwarding address or 30 days; 60 days if rental unit's damaged

Index

Wiley Publishing, Inc.
End-User License Agreement

READ THIS. You should carefully read these terms and conditions before opening the software packet(s) included with this book "Book". This is a license agreement "Agreement" between you and Wiley Publishing, Inc. "WPI". By opening the accompanying software packet(s), you acknowledge that you have read and accept the following terms and conditions. If you do not agree and do not want to be bound by such terms and conditions, promptly return the Book and the unopened software packet(s) to the place you obtained them for a full refund.

1. **License Grant.** WPI grants to you (either an individual or entity) a nonexclusive license to use one copy of the enclosed software program(s) (collectively, the "Software") solely for your own personal or business purposes on a single computer (whether a standard computer or a workstation component of a multi-user network). The Software is in use on a computer when it is loaded into temporary memory (RAM) or installed into permanent memory (hard disk, CD-ROM, or other storage device). WPI reserves all rights not expressly granted herein.

2. **Ownership.** WPI is the owner of all right, title, and interest, including copyright, in and to the compilation of the Software recorded on the physical packet included with this Book "Software Media". Copyright to the individual programs recorded on the Software Media is owned by the author or other authorized copyright owner of each program. Ownership of the Software and all proprietary rights relating thereto remain with WPI and its licensers.

3. **Restrictions on Use and Transfer.**

   (a) You may only (i) make one copy of the Software for backup or archival purposes, or (ii) transfer the Software to a single hard disk, provided that you keep the original for backup or archival purposes. You may not (i) rent or lease the Software, (ii) copy or reproduce the Software through a LAN or other network system or through any computer subscriber system or bulletin-board system, or (iii) modify, adapt, or create derivative works based on the Software.

   (b) You may not reverse engineer, decompile, or disassemble the Software. You may transfer the Software and user documentation on a permanent basis, provided that the transferee agrees to accept the terms and conditions of this Agreement and you retain no copies. If the Software is an update or has been updated, any transfer must include the most recent update and all prior versions.

4. **Restrictions on Use of Individual Programs.** You must follow the individual requirements and restrictions detailed for each individual program in the "About the CD" appendix of this Book or on the Software Media. These limitations are also contained in the individual license agreements recorded on the Software Media. These limitations may include a requirement that after using the program for a specified period of time, the user must pay a registration fee or discontinue use. By opening the Software packet(s), you agree to abide by the licenses and restrictions for these individual programs that are detailed in the "About the CD" appendix and/or on the Software Media. None of the material on this Software Media or listed in this Book may ever be redistributed, in original or modified form, for commercial purposes.

5. **Limited Warranty.**

   (a) WPI warrants that the Software and Software Media are free from defects in materials and workmanship under normal use for a period of sixty (60) days from the date of purchase of this Book. If WPI receives notification within the warranty period of defects in materials or workmanship, WPI will replace the defective Software Media.

(b) WPI AND THE AUTHOR(S) OF THE BOOK DISCLAIM ALL OTHER WARRANTIES, EXPRESS OR IMPLIED, INCLUDING WITHOUT LIMITATION IMPLIED WARRANTIES OF MERCHANTABILITY AND FITNESS FOR A PARTICULAR PURPOSE, WITH RESPECT TO THE SOFTWARE, THE PROGRAMS, THE SOURCE CODE CONTAINED THEREIN, AND/OR THE TECHNIQUES DESCRIBED IN THIS BOOK. WPI DOES NOT WARRANT THAT THE FUNCTIONS CONTAINED IN THE SOFTWARE WILL MEET YOUR REQUIREMENTS OR THAT THE OPERATION OF THE SOFTWARE WILL BE ERROR FREE.

(c) This limited warranty gives you specific legal rights, and you may have other rights that vary from jurisdiction to jurisdiction.

6. Remedies.

(a) WPI's entire liability and your exclusive remedy for defects in materials and workmanship shall be limited to replacement of the Software Media, which may be returned to WPI with a copy of your receipt at the following address: Software Media Fulfillment Department, Attn.: *Property Management Kit For Dummies, 2nd Edition*, Wiley Publishing, Inc., 10475 Crosspoint Blvd., Indianapolis, IN 46256, or call 1-877-762-2974. Please allow four to six weeks for delivery. This Limited Warranty is void if failure of the Software Media has resulted from accident, abuse, or misapplication. Any replacement Software Media will be warranted for the remainder of the original warranty period or thirty (30) days, whichever is longer.

(b) In no event shall WPI or the author be liable for any damages whatsoever (including without limitation damages for loss of business profits, business interruption, loss of business information, or any other pecuniary loss) arising from the use of or inability to use the Book or the Software, even if WPI has been advised of the possibility of such damages.

(c) Because some jurisdictions do not allow the exclusion or limitation of liability for consequential or incidental damages, the above limitation or exclusion may not apply to you.

7. U.S. Government Restricted Rights. Use, duplication, or disclosure of the Software for or on behalf of the United States of America, its agencies and/or instrumentalities "U.S. Government" is subject to restrictions as stated in paragraph (c)(1)(ii) of the Rights in Technical Data and Computer Software clause of DFARS 252.227-7013, or subparagraphs (c) (1) and (2) of the Commercial Computer Software - Restricted Rights clause at FAR 52.227-19, and in similar clauses in the NASA FAR supplement, as applicable.

8. General. This Agreement constitutes the entire understanding of the parties and revokes and supersedes all prior agreements, oral or written, between them and may not be modified or amended except in a writing signed by both parties hereto that specifically refers to this Agreement. This Agreement shall take precedence over any other documents that may be in conflict herewith. If any one or more provisions contained in this Agreement are held by any court or tribunal to be invalid, illegal, or otherwise unenforceable, each and every other provision shall remain in full force and effect.

BUSINESS, CAREERS & PERSONAL FINANCE

Accounting For Dummies, 4th Edition*
978-0-470-24600-9

Bookkeeping Workbook For Dummies†
978-0-470-16983-4

Commodities For Dummies
978-0-470-04928-0

Doing Business in China For Dummies
978-0-470-04929-7

E-Mail Marketing For Dummies
978-0-470-19087-6

Job Interviews For Dummies, 3rd Edition*†
978-0-470-17748-8

Personal Finance Workbook For Dummies*†
978-0-470-09933-9

Real Estate License Exams For Dummies
978-0-7645-7623-2

Six Sigma For Dummies
978-0-7645-6798-8

Small Business Kit For Dummies, 2nd Edition*†
978-0-7645-5984-6

Telephone Sales For Dummies
978-0-470-16836-3

BUSINESS PRODUCTIVITY & MICROSOFT OFFICE

Access 2007 For Dummies
978-0-470-03649-5

Excel 2007 For Dummies
978-0-470-03737-9

Office 2007 For Dummies
978-0-470-00923-9

Outlook 2007 For Dummies
978-0-470-03830-7

PowerPoint 2007 For Dummies
978-0-470-04059-1

Project 2007 For Dummies
978-0-470-03651-8

QuickBooks 2008 For Dummies
978-0-470-18470-7

Quicken 2008 For Dummies
978-0-470-17473-9

Salesforce.com For Dummies, 2nd Edition
978-0-470-04893-1

Word 2007 For Dummies
978-0-470-03658-7

EDUCATION, HISTORY, REFERENCE & TEST PREPARATION

African American History For Dummies
978-0-7645-5469-8

Algebra For Dummies
978-0-7645-5325-7

Algebra Workbook For Dummies
978-0-7645-8467-1

Art History For Dummies
978-0-470-09910-0

ASVAB For Dummies, 2nd Edition
978-0-470-10671-6

British Military History For Dummies
978-0-470-03213-8

Calculus For Dummies
978-0-7645-2498-1

Canadian History For Dummies, 2nd Edition
978-0-470-83656-9

Geometry Workbook For Dummies
978-0-471-79940-5

The SAT I For Dummies, 6th Edition
978-0-7645-7193-0

Series 7 Exam For Dummies
978-0-470-09932-2

World History For Dummies
978-0-7645-5242-7

FOOD, GARDEN, HOBBIES & HOME

Bridge For Dummies, 2nd Edition
978-0-471-92426-5

Coin Collecting For Dummies, 2nd Edition
978-0-470-22275-1

Cooking Basics For Dummies, 3rd Edition
978-0-7645-7206-7

Drawing For Dummies
978-0-7645-5476-6

Etiquette For Dummies, 2nd Edition
978-0-470-10672-3

Gardening Basics For Dummies*†
978-0-470-03749-2

Knitting Patterns For Dummies
978-0-470-04556-5

Living Gluten-Free For Dummies†
978-0-471-77383-2

Painting Do-It-Yourself For Dummies
978-0-470-17533-0

HEALTH, SELF HELP, PARENTING & PETS

Anger Management For Dummies
978-0-470-03715-7

Anxiety & Depression Workbook For Dummies
978-0-7645-9793-0

Dieting For Dummies, 2nd Edition
978-0-7645-4149-0

Dog Training For Dummies, 2nd Edition
978-0-7645-8418-3

Horseback Riding For Dummies
978-0-470-09719-9

Infertility For Dummies†
978-0-470-11518-3

Meditation For Dummies with CD-ROM, 2nd Edition
978-0-471-77774-8

Post-Traumatic Stress Disorder For Dummies
978-0-470-04922-8

Puppies For Dummies, 2nd Edition
978-0-470-03717-1

Thyroid For Dummies, 2nd Edition†
978-0-471-78755-6

Type 1 Diabetes For Dummies*†
978-0-470-17811-9

*** Separate Canadian edition also available**
† Separate U.K. edition also available

Available wherever books are sold. For more information or to order direct: U.S. customers visit www.dummies.com or call 1-877-762-2974.
U.K. customers visit www.wileyeurope.com or call (0)1243 843291. Canadian customers visit www.wiley.ca or call 1-800-567-4797.

INTERNET & DIGITAL MEDIA

AdWords For Dummies
978-0-470-15252-2

Blogging For Dummies, 2nd Edition
978-0-470-23017-6

Digital Photography All-in-One Desk Reference For Dummies, 3rd Edition
978-0-470-03743-0

Digital Photography For Dummies, 5th Edition
978-0-7645-9802-9

Digital SLR Cameras & Photography For Dummies, 2nd Edition
978-0-470-14927-0

eBay Business All-in-One Desk Reference For Dummies
978-0-7645-8438-1

eBay For Dummies, 5th Edition*
978-0-470-04529-9

eBay Listings That Sell For Dummies
978-0-471-78912-3

Facebook For Dummies
978-0-470-26273-3

The Internet For Dummies, 11th Edition
978-0-470-12174-0

Investing Online For Dummies, 5th Edition
978-0-7645-8456-5

iPod & iTunes For Dummies, 5th Edition
978-0-470-17474-6

MySpace For Dummies
978-0-470-09529-4

Podcasting For Dummies
978-0-471-74898-4

Search Engine Optimization For Dummies, 2nd Edition
978-0-471-97998-2

Second Life For Dummies
978-0-470-18025-9

Starting an eBay Business For Dummies, 3rd Edition†
978-0-470-14924-9

GRAPHICS, DESIGN & WEB DEVELOPMENT

Adobe Creative Suite 3 Design Premium All-in-One Desk Reference For Dummies
978-0-470-11724-8

Adobe Web Suite CS3 All-in-One Desk Reference For Dummies
978-0-470-12099-6

AutoCAD 2008 For Dummies
978-0-470-11650-0

Building a Web Site For Dummies, 3rd Edition
978-0-470-14928-7

Creating Web Pages All-in-One Desk Reference For Dummies, 3rd Edition
978-0-470-09629-1

Creating Web Pages For Dummies, 8th Edition
978-0-470-08030-6

Dreamweaver CS3 For Dummies
978-0-470-11490-2

Flash CS3 For Dummies
978-0-470-12100-9

Google SketchUp For Dummies
978-0-470-13744-4

InDesign CS3 For Dummies
978-0-470-11865-8

Photoshop CS3 All-in-One Desk Reference For Dummies
978-0-470-11195-6

Photoshop CS3 For Dummies
978-0-470-11193-2

Photoshop Elements 5 For Dummies
978-0-470-09810-3

SolidWorks For Dummies
978-0-7645-9555-4

Visio 2007 For Dummies
978-0-470-08983-5

Web Design For Dummies, 2nd Edition
978-0-471-78117-2

Web Sites Do-It-Yourself For Dummies
978-0-470-16903-2

Web Stores Do-It-Yourself For Dummies
978-0-470-17443-2

LANGUAGES, RELIGION & SPIRITUALITY

Arabic For Dummies
978-0-471-77270-5

Chinese For Dummies, Audio Set
978-0-470-12766-7

French For Dummies
978-0-7645-5193-2

German For Dummies
978-0-7645-5195-6

Hebrew For Dummies
978-0-7645-5489-6

Ingles Para Dummies
978-0-7645-5427-8

Italian For Dummies, Audio Set
978-0-470-09586-7

Italian Verbs For Dummies
978-0-471-77389-4

Japanese For Dummies
978-0-7645-5429-2

Latin For Dummies
978-0-7645-5431-5

Portuguese For Dummies
978-0-471-78738-9

Russian For Dummies
978-0-471-78001-4

Spanish Phrases For Dummies
978-0-7645-7204-3

Spanish For Dummies
978-0-7645-5194-9

Spanish For Dummies, Audio Set
978-0-470-09585-0

The Bible For Dummies
978-0-7645-5296-0

Catholicism For Dummies
978-0-7645-5391-2

The Historical Jesus For Dummies
978-0-470-16785-4

Islam For Dummies
978-0-7645-5503-9

Spirituality For Dummies, 2nd Edition
978-0-470-19142-2

NETWORKING AND PROGRAMMING

ASP.NET 3.5 For Dummies
978-0-470-19592-5

C# 2008 For Dummies
978-0-470-19109-5

Hacking For Dummies, 2nd Edition
978-0-470-05235-8

Home Networking For Dummies, 4th Edition
978-0-470-11806-1

Java For Dummies, 4th Edition
978-0-470-08716-9

Microsoft® SQL Server™ 2008 All-in-One Desk Reference For Dummies
978-0-470-17954-3

Networking All-in-One Desk Reference For Dummies, 2nd Edition
978-0-7645-9939-2

Networking For Dummies, 8th Edition
978-0-470-05620-2

SharePoint 2007 For Dummies
978-0-470-09941-4

Wireless Home Networking For Dummies, 2nd Edition
978-0-471-74940-0